D1569692

William Paterson

William Paterson
Lawyer and Statesman
1745–1806

JOHN E. O'CONNOR

Rutgers University Press
New Brunswick, New Jersey

LIBRARY OF CONGRESS CATALOGING IN PUBLICATION DATA

O'Connor, John E
William Paterson, lawyer and statesman, 1745–1806.

Includes bibliographical references and index.
1. Paterson, William, 1745–1806. 2. New Jersey—
Politics and government—Revolution, 1775–1783.
3. United States—Politics and government—1783–1809.
4. Legislators—United States—Biography. 5. United
States. Congress. Senate—Biography. 6. New Jersey—
Governors—Biography. 7. Judges—United States—
Biography. I. Title.
E302.6.P3027   973.4'092'4 [B]   79–15966
ISBN 0–8135–0880–0

For Mary, Annie, and William

Contents

	Preface	**ix**
	Chronology	**xi**
	Author's Note	xv
	Introduction	1
I	*FORMATIVE YEARS*	*5*
1	The Education of a Revolutionary	7
2	The Country Lawyer	21
II	*THE CONSERVATIVE DILEMMA AND THE AMERICAN REVOLUTION*	*45*
3	The Ideological Origins of the Revolution in New Jersey	48
4	The Decision to Revolt	68
5	Prosecuting the Revolution	88
III	*INVENTING A NATION*	*113*
6	Hard Money and the Dangers of Democracy	115
7	The Federal Convention, the New Jersey Plan, and the Politics of Nation Making	131
8	Federalism and the Senate	163
IV	*SERVING THE PUBLIC TRUST*	*181*
9	Paterson the Governor	183
10	The Reformer of the Laws	202

11 Parties, Politics, and the Crisis of 1798   223
12 The Nation and the Court   250

    Conclusion   280

    Abbreviations   286

    Notes   287

    Bibliographical Note   338

    Index   343

Preface

The characters of some historical figures are readily apparent in the documents they have left behind, diaries and letters containing their innermost thoughts about themselves, their families, and the world in which they lived. It has taken some extensive searching and a little reading between the lines, however, to get at the personality of William Paterson. Scholars have believed there to be a scarcity of manuscript sources in his case, and consequently no one has tried since the early 1930s to recount the details of his life or fully to assess his contributions to the nation's founding.

Some clues to Paterson's character began to appear early in my research— clues revealing a somewhat insecure young man striving for acceptance in a higher social rank, a compulsive worker slaving to maintain stability and order in New Jersey's legal system during the Revolution, a clever and effective politician maintaining a hard-line position among the most experienced and most capable American leaders at the Philadelphia convention, a passionately conservative Supreme Court justice striking out against those he saw as proponents of a dangerous radical philosophy, and, finally, a statesman rising above the partisanship of many of his colleagues to compromise ideology for the well-being of the infant republic. The effort of tracking down and documenting these clues, of trying to reconcile the sometimes paradoxical elements in Paterson's character, and of searching contemporary sources for deeper insights into the context of his actions and decisions, has consumed the greatest part of my research energies over the past eight years.

During that time I have accumulated numerous intellectual debts. E. James Ferguson of the City University of New York nurtured along my Ph.D. dissertation and then continued to offer his valuable assistance as it ultimately grew into this book. I am pleased to count him as a constructive critic and a friend. John Murrin of Princeton University, Dennis P. Ryan of the Papers of William Livingston, and Leonard B. Rosenberg of William Paterson College read the entire manuscript and made many helpful suggestions. When I found myself embroiled in early American legal history, a specialized field for which I had no formal training, Milton M. Klein of the University of Tennessee, Richard E. Ellis of SUNY Buffalo, and Herbert A. Johnson of the University of South Carolina offered invaluable assistance, especially on those chapters dealing with legal reform and Paterson's career on the federal bench. Others who freely offered counsel and encouragement at several stages during the research and writing include Richard P. McCormick and Seth Scheiner of Rutgers University, Carl E. Prince of New York University, and Larry R. Gerlach of the University of Utah. For whatever clarity and style readers may find in this work I am indebted to two friends: Robert Lynch a colleague at New Jersey Institute of Technology, and Peter C. Rollins of Oklahoma State University. As someone who will never forget being told by a graduate professor that his prose read like a telephone directory, I especially appreciate their efforts.

I would like to thank the editors of the *American Journal of Legal History* and *New Jersey History* for permission to incorporate into Chapters 3 and 10 articles that appeared in these publications. I also want to thank the many librarians and archivists who have been so willing to help. The special few who must be mentioned by name are Donald A. Sinclair of the Alexander Library at Rutgers University, Richard C. Morris and Don C. Schemer of the New Jersey Historical Society, William C. Wright of the New Jersey State Archives, and Charles F. Cummings of the Newark Public Library.

For their assistance in financing some of the research and typing expenses, I thank the New Jersey Historical Commission and the New Jersey Institute of Technology. Special appreciation is due to the Alumni Association and other campus organizations of William Paterson College, whose special grant to Rutgers University Press helped defray costs of publication. Finally, I must thank my family for the financial and emotional support that they freely offered. The one debt I can never fully repay is to my wife and children, who (though not without complaining) did without husband and father for months at a time as I visited libraries and closeted myself with a typewriter. As a first installment, I dedicate this book to them.

Chronology

1745   Born in the town of Antrim in what is now Northern Ireland.

1747   Emigrates to America with his family.

1750   Family settles in Princeton, New Jersey.

1757   Enters the Latin Grammar School founded at Princeton by Aaron Burr.

1759   Enters the College of New Jersey.

1763   B.A., College of New Jersey.
Apprenticed to Richard Stockton to study law.

1766   M.A., College of New Jersey.

1767   Co-founder of Cliosophic Society at Princeton.

1769   Admitted to New Jersey Bar.
Relocates to establish his first practice in New Bromley, Hunterdon County, New Jersey.
Appointed to position of surrogate by Royal Governor William Franklin.

1769   Speaks out in defense of lawyers.

1770   Criticizes doctors in controversy over smallpox inoculation.

1772   Moves to Raritan, Somerset County, New Jersey.

ca. 1774   Prepares "Address on the Rise and Decline of Nations."

1775   Selected as delegate to the First Provincial Congress of New Jersey; later chosen secretary of the congress.
Declines election to Second Provincial Congress, but after the first session serves again as secretary.

1776   Selected as delegate to Third Provincial Congress and continues to serve as secretary.
Votes to delay adoption of New Jersey constitution of 1776.

Appointed first attorney general of the State of New Jersey and
takes firm stand against Loyalists.

Elected to Legislative Council (serves until 1777).

1777   Works with Governor Livingston to establish Council of Safety.

1778   Selected to sit in Continental Congress and declines.

1781   Selected again for seat in Continental Congress and again
declines.

1783   Resigns as attorney general to devote full time to the practice of
law.

1785   Opposes paper money legislation and loosening of laws respecting
debtors.

1786   Supports requisition of the Confederation Congress.

1787   Selected to lead delegation to the federal convention in Philadelphia; successfully struggles for equal representation of states
in the United States Senate.

1788   Elected to serve in the first Senate of the United States.

1789   Selected for membership in the American Philosophical Society.

Attends first session of Senate and helps to frame the Judiciary
Act of 1789.

1790   Attends second session of Senate where he supports Hamilton's
plans for funding and assumption and is first labeled a
Federalist.

1791   Elected to succeed William Livingston as governor of New
Jersey.

Co-founder and first president of the New Brunswick Bridge
Company.

1792   Signs charter for the Society for Establishing Useful Manufactures, which names their site for him (now the city of
Paterson).

Begins revision and reform of the legal code and court practice
of New Jersey, later extended to include extensive penal reform; task completed in 1799 with publication of the *Laws
of New Jersey.*

1793   Begins first of several series of newspaper essays on state and
national issues.

Appointed associate justice of the United States Supreme Court
by George Washington.

1795   Presides over the trial of Whiskey Rebels in Pennsylvania.

In case of *Van Horne's Lessee* v. *Dorrance,* Paterson clearly
paves the way for judicial review of acts of congress eight
years before *Marbury* v. *Madison.*

Declines Washington's offers of the positions of secretary of state and attorney general of the United States.

Supports the Jay Treaty against popular opposition.

1798   Presides in the controversial case in which Representative Matthew Lyon of Vermont is convicted for sedition.

1800   Supports John Adams in election of 1800.

1801   Many senators favor his appointment as chief justice over the younger John Marshall, but Paterson discourages their efforts to change the president's mind.

1802   Opposes repeal of the Judiciary Act of 1801, but declines to follow the lead of Samuel Chase and create a constitutional confrontation between the Congress and the Court.

His daughter marries Steven Van Rensselaer and moves to his manor house on the Hudson.

1803   In case of *Stuart* v. *Laird,* Paterson closes the controversy over the Judiciary Act of 1801.

Participates in decision in case of *Marbury* v. *Madison.*

Steps down as Princeton trustee and president of New Brunswick Bridge Company.

1805   Honored with degrees of Doctor of Laws from College of New Jersey and Dartmouth.

1806   Honored with degree of Doctor of Laws from Harvard.

Presides over case of William Smith and Samuel Ogden, issuing subpoenas against several members of Jefferson's cabinet.

Dies at Albany (September 9, 1806) at the home of his daughter and is interred there.

Author's Note

Rather than attempting to modernize the spelling, capitalization, and punctuation of Paterson's words and those of his contemporaries and thus risk losing the flavor of the originals, I have left quotations as they appear in my sources. As the constant disruption of the narrative with the use of *sic* would only be annoying, I have allowed divergent spellings to stand. The reader should remember that the spelling of the period was totally eccentric.

It should also be noted that certain manuscript sources referred to in this volume were not dated by Paterson. This is especially true of many of his college essays and those newspaper essays for which the printed copies have been lost. In almost every case, careful analysis of internal evidence has yielded sufficient information to fix them in time. As a rule, the notes have not been encumbered with explanations of this process, but in a few cases, where questions remain about the dating of such documents, I have used the notes to explain the problems I encountered and the answers I preferred. Paterson did not usually title his college or newspaper essays. For the reader's convenience, I have supplied many of the titles used in the notes myself.

Introduction

"We are building a great empire," William Paterson wrote to his wife in 1791, "the prospect widens and brightens as we proceed and to every enlarged mind must give the largest pleasure." At the time, Paterson was representing New Jersey in the first Senate of the United States. Although, measured from the date that independence was declared, the American empire was only fifteen years old, its short history had already brought great changes to Paterson's life. His devotion to public service had in turn left its mark on the new nation. In fact, the Senate in which he sat owed its existence to the persistent Jerseyman who had fought so tenaciously for the interests of the small states in the federal convention of 1787. His term in the Senate, as it turned out, led him to the governor's chair and then to the Supreme Court, where he remained for the rest of his life.

Paterson's life reflected the profound changes that took place in American politics and society in the last third of the eighteenth century. He had not been born to status and power. His father was a moderately successful storekeeper who had been able to afford a college education for his son. At college, Paterson made a conscious effort to assume the style and manner of the elite and to cultivate influential friends and acquaintances who could help him later in life. During the American Revolution, his years of legal study and social climbing finally bore fruit, and the success that followed was more than he had ever hoped for. Paterson's personal life and legal career provide a clear example of the unexpected ways in which the turbulent events of the revolutionary era could influence the lives of individuals.

On another level, Paterson's experience is interesting because his complex system of ideological beliefs and values, in some ways central to the revolutionary cause, seems in other ways almost to contradict it. His story

1

cannot be told without confronting these apparent paradoxes in his personality. Paterson's political career seems to have been dominated by a series of transformations: from a critic of aristocratic power and privilege to an opponent of the unchecked popular will, from a states' rights particularist to a committed nationalist, from a champion for the independence of the judiciary to a politically prejudiced judge, and, finally, from an outspoken foe of the Jeffersonian Republicans to one who acquiesced in their rise to power in 1800. When Paterson's moral and political philosophy is understood, however, his reversals of opinion can be seen primarily as shifts in emphasis that reflect the realities of America's changing situation. Although personal ambition played an undeniable part in shaping his political decisions, Paterson also adhered to a complex pattern of ideas based largely on his education, his legal experience, and his moral beliefs. He was almost slavish in the consistency with which he held to his philosophy, even later in life when his self-righteous and, in some ways, elitist political ideas had become quite unpopular.

Paterson was an effective and loyal lieutenant in the movement for independence and in the political struggles that followed. His high hopes for the future of America were tempered by his skepticism about the nation's ability to overcome the problems met in establishing a durable republic. A realist rather than an idealist, Paterson was always willing to compromise his political ideals in the interest of stability and order. A skilled lawyer and debater, he was more adept at organizing and implementing other people's ideas than he was at creating new ones, and he brought these talents to the service of the young republic. His accomplishments were recognized by his contemporaries and still earn him mention in almost every general history, but until now no historian has successfully assessed his overall contribution. This book is an attempt to fill that void.

It has proven impossible for me to treat every aspect of Paterson's very busy life in full detail. Some of this difficulty is due to a paucity of evidence concerning long stretches of his personal and family life. Partially it has been a matter of choice. I have not concerned myself with a detailed analysis of his study for the bar or his practice as an attorney. Some of this work has already been done, and I have relied on the conclusions reached by Richard Haskett in his statistical analysis of Paterson's case load in several New Jersey jurisdictions in the 1770s and 1780s. The collection of William Paterson papers very recently acquired by William Paterson College in Wayne, New Jersey, includes hundreds of items relevant to Paterson's career at the bar. From them a skilled legal historian should be able to reconstruct an even fuller picture of the ways in which his practice developed. An example of another area that remains to be fully studied is the operation of the federal circuit courts during the period Paterson sat on the bench. Although this book does suggest some hypothetical conclusions based on Paterson's experience, a broader analysis must be undertaken elsewhere by a specialist in the field.

In evaluating Paterson I have endeavored to strike a balance between his personal life and legal career, which were clearly devoted to self-aggrandizement, and his public life, which was marked by considerable and selfless contributions to the emerging nation. Throughout this study I have tried to do justice to both the public and private interests that motivated Paterson's career. Unlike those giants of the American Revolution—Washington, Franklin, and Jefferson—no curtain of mythic virtue enshrouds William Paterson. Readers should therefore be prepared to see him both as an influential force in the success of the Revolution and the decisions of the early national period and as a man willing to take personal advantage of the opportunities afforded by those events. Far from lessening his significance, such human qualities make him all the more interesting. They deepen the insights to be drawn from an understanding of his life and his personal perspective on the dramatic events in which he took part.

PART I

FORMATIVE YEARS

Historians who have grappled with the problem of deciding how much influence education may have had in the shaping of America's revolutionary leaders will have particular interest in William Paterson's experience at Princeton. Paterson's family background was far less distinguished than that of many of his classmates at the College of New Jersey. Rather than being satisfied that his father could afford to give him an education, Paterson was determined to win higher social rank as well as a diploma. Unlike many others from finer families, Paterson was fully aware that his education was to be his only ticket to social respectability. The hundreds of pages of notes and essays that remain from his college years are clear testimony that he studied his lessons well. In these essays and disputations can be found the germs of the political ideology that would bring him to support the American Revolution. By devoting himself to the maxims of conduct he recorded in his college commonplace book, Paterson hoped to bridge the social gap between himself and his well-born fellow students.

But success, especially for the son of a Princeton storekeeper, was as much a matter of whom he knew as how much he knew. Thus, Paterson cultivated friends among his classmates and modeled his personal behavior after the accepted gentlemanly manners of the day. When he spoke out on public issues, he chose those that served his personal reputation as well as his desire for social recognition. Examples are to be found in his defense of lawyers and his petition to the consistory of the Dutch Reformed Church of Raritan. The high moral tone he assumed on many issues was practically a guarantee against criticism: Who would openly oppose virtue or defend vice and corruption? Young Paterson might join his friends in poking fun at the sanctimoniousness of some of his former tutors or the superstitions of simple people who believed in witchcraft and omens. But he had a deep and abiding respect for authority (tutors included) and he might sometimes agree with the conclusions reached by superstitious old women, though his reasons were more rationally conceived.

Paterson's puritanical moralizing and his posturing as a gentleman were based on his aristocratic view of society. The ideology he had adopted in a conscious effort to propel himself into a higher social stratum eventually became a part of him. Because he was not born to it, he was never totally comfortable with it, and his limited self-confidence caused him to be stiff and formal in his contacts with people. But he held onto the essentially conservative framework of political and social ideas he learned at Princeton for the duration of his life.

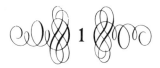

The Education of a Revolutionary

William Paterson was born in Ireland in 1745, the first son of Richard Paterson, who was described as a tin plate worker. The family sailed from Londonderry in 1747 and, after an uneventful passage, arrived at Newcastle on the Delaware.[1] During the first few years, as he moved his family from place to place in New Jersey, New York, and Connecticut, Richard Paterson apparently tried to reestablish himself in the tin plate business. (There were two brothers, also named Paterson, who had come to the area around Norwich, Connecticut, only a few years earlier and had begun to sell household utensils that they fabricated from sheets of imported English tin.[2]) But any thought Richard Paterson might have given to such an endeavor was set aside in 1750, when he settled his family in the little village of Princeton, New Jersey, and opened a general store. His father's decision doomed young William to many hours of boring chores around the store, but it also assured the family of at least a respectable place in the small community. Here, with his parents, his sister Frances, and two brothers Thomas and Edward, who were born in Princeton, William Paterson spent most of his childhood years.[3]

Business was good, and what the Patersons may have lacked in social prominence was soon compensated for by material comfort. A contemporary account described their house as

built of stone, two stories high, 53 feet in length and 30 in breadth;
there are on the first floor five rooms, with a fire place in every room,
one of which was formed for a store . . . ; the second floor contains six rooms with fire places in three of them.[4]

There was also a "commodious cellar" and a garret in which the Paterson
boys must have found special hiding places to squirrel away their secret
treasures. Before long the family fortune had grown to include several
other parcels of real estate and three slaves. For more than twenty years,
all through young William's formative years, the family lived very com-
fortably on the income from the store.[5]

The source of his earliest education is not recorded, but apparently
William's desire for learning was excited by the relocation of the College
of New Jersey from Newark to Princeton. The trustees' decision was
made in 1752, and by 1754 construction had begun on Nassau Hall. Laid
out in the traditional Georgian style, at the time of its completion in 1756,
it was the largest building in all of English North America. The vision
of this fine edifice rising over the little village had to influence young Paterson—it was located across the road, just one hundred yards from his
door. Nassau became the home for dozens of students who, following
the style of Old World scholars, paraded around the grounds in academic
caps and gowns.[6]

As close neighbors, the Patersons naturally became familiar with the
people from the college. From time to time, most of the students, the
tutors, and even the college presidents (there were four in the first ten
years) did business with the family.[7] Presumably, the alert young boy
doing errands around the neighborhood was noticed, and the father was
encouraged to look out more carefully for his son's education. But,
whether he needed prodding or not, William was thirsty to learn and
ultimately wanted to join the young men who studied in the imposing
building across the way.

The College of New Jersey (now Princeton University), which came
to play such an influential role in Paterson's life, had been founded in
1746 as an expression of the New Light fervor of the Great Awakening
in the middle colonies. From the beginning, it had devoted itself to the
preparation of new generations of leaders for both the spiritual and
temporal worlds.[8] As an underclassman, Paterson listened to President
Samuel Davies instruct the graduates of 1760.

Whatever, I say, be your Place, permit me my dear Youth to inculcate upon you this important instruction, IMBIBE AND CHER-

ISH A PUBLICK SPIRIT. Serve your Generation. Live not for yourselves, but the Publick. Be the Servants of the Church; the Servants of your Country; the Servants of all. Extend the Arms of Your Benevolence to embrace your Friends, your Neighbors, your Country, your Nation, the whole Race of Mankind, even your Enemies.[9]

Like those who had come before him (John Dickinson, the first chosen, who died after only four and one-half months in office; Aaron Burr, 1747–1757; and Jonathan Edwards, who succumbed to a bad reaction to a smallpox inoculation after serving only three months), Davies's reputation added to the prestige of the college. But, again like the others, his experience as an evangelical minister had not diminished his respect for learning or his concern for the well-being of the secular world.

The dual role of the college—to train social and political leaders as well as clergymen—was expressed in the curriculum. Students were required to study mathematics and science along with the classics and theology. This tendency to merge other disciplines with religion was not unusual. America's best-known revivalists, Jonathan Edwards and George Whitfield, had both recognized the value of such secular studies, providing, of course, that theology remained supreme. As Douglas Sloan has recently explained, "divinity—evangelical divinity—would not supplant the regular disciplines, such as natural philosophy and political philosophy, but it would determine goals and ensure that such subjects be used in the service of society."[10] This frame of mind was reinforced as the precepts of the Scottish Enlightenment were institutionalized at Princeton by John Witherspoon, who became president of the college in 1768.[11]

The students at the college enjoyed considerable intellectual freedom, as much a luxury then as it is now. The trustees claimed that care was being taken "to cherish a spirit of liberty, and free enquiry; and not only to permit, but even to encourage their right of private judgment."[12] Within the bounds of the religious and social values of the eighteenth century, the students were being taught to think for themselves. As Witherspoon explained, learning was not only to promote virtue and happiness, but also to prepare men to employ their lives "to the benefit of society in offices of power and trust."[13]

Because young men had to prove an ability to translate Greek and Latin before they could even qualify for admission, Paterson began his studies at the preparatory school, established by Aaron Burr.[14] After demonstrating his fluency in the classical languages, Paterson was accepted as a student at the college in 1759. The next four years were to have a great effect on him.

Even today, there is a wealth of manuscript evidence on Paterson's college years. There are dozens of his essays and orations written during his years as an undergraduate and thereafter as he lived on in Princeton and participated in the affairs of the college and especially in the Cliosophic Society, which he helped to found.[15] His commonplace book, dated 1763 and containing almost 300 pages, indicates the basic interests that Paterson acquired during his college years. It is heavily weighted toward literature and history. There are several essays on literary criticism and on the art of writing prose and poetry. His own prolific verse mostly celebrated the ladies around town, though he also wrote about weddings and other social events. The commonplace book includes extensive quotations from English literature, especially Shakespeare, Milton, Swift, and Pope. It refers to Kames's *Elements of Criticism,* Collier's *View of the English Stage,* and Montesquieu's *The Persian Letters.* Other favorites were *The Spectator, The Tatler,* the *Gentleman's Magazine,* and even *The Young Ladies' Magazine.*[16] His cardinal rule in composition was simplicity, and he even related this to his preferred pattern of life. "As simplicity of language constitutes the best style so simplicity of behavior constitutes good breeding," he explained. "The true gentleman is easy, without affectation, grand, without haughtiness, cheerful, without levity, and humble, without meanness."[17] Appreciation of good literature required a certain type of personality, too. For Paterson, "candor and liberal sentiments" were the main hallmarks of a literary critic.[18]

His papers and notebooks indicate that he gave particular attention to learning the marks of the gentleman and trying to make his own personality and appearance fit the mold. He carefully catalogued maxims of manners and style in music, dance, and dress. And, whenever he had the chance, he commented disparagingly about the absence of grace and good judgment in many of the people around him. At one point, for example, he was driven to distraction by Princeton undergraduates who wore "night gowns" in public.

> Gowns seem as essential to Nassau-students as black coats and grey wigs to divines. . . . How often do we behold a shameless collegiate of a sound, unthinking face, his hair frizzled and powdered to the tip of the mode, amble along, with now and then a hitch in his gait, in a party-coloured night-gown; or undress?[19]

"Hardly anything," he maintained, "is more difficult to attain than a graceful and easy deportment."[20] And he bemoaned the fact that "crowds of sinical coxcombs, and solemn fops" greatly abounded at "every place of public resort."[21]

In addition to being models of style and grace, Paterson felt that gentlemen also had social responsibilities. A true gentleman had to preserve the better nature of humanity. For example, "if you have debtors, let not your lenity get the better of your prudence; nor your care for your own interest make you forget humanity. A Prison is not for the unfortunate; but the knavish." Attention was also given to the proper behavior toward inferiors. They were to be treated "with Generosity and humanity, but by no means with Familiarity, on one hand, or Insolence on the other."[22] Apparently Paterson learned these lessons well. Formality and conventionality would always be the distinguishing characteristics of his social personality.

Along with his informal study of manners, Paterson concentrated his academic attention on history and moral philosophy. History was looked on as both a prestigious and a practical study. It had long been a major topic of study in the colonial colleges, and, in the intellectual climate of the eighteenth century, it was becoming even more important. Inventories of academic and private libraries and lists of material published in the colonial years indicate its wide popularity. Summing up an analysis of these sources, H. Trevor Colburn reported that "history was the main field of interest. If law is associated with history—and the colonists so regarded it—history emerges as the largest single category."[23] The study of the classics was also intimately related to history. The history of ancient Greece and Rome and the lives and characters of the main classical protagonists were favorite topics of colonial scholarship.[24]

During the Enlightenment, history came to be seen as the foundation for a new science of politics based on human nature. During these years, history began to replace theology as the study that offered the greatest insight into the human condition.[25] Describing the attention colonial leaders paid to history, one recent author explains that

> however imprecise, confused and eclectic the colonists' gleanings from history and quotations from philosophers may seem to us, they represented to eighteenth-century Americans the experience and wisdom of the Western World.[26]

Paterson considered history to be among the most important of his studies. He spent considerable time reading and thinking about it and applied its lessons widely in making judgments on all kinds of questions. In his commonplace book, agreeing with Cicero's "Requisites for the Historian," he noted that historians should make the effort to write well. He also recorded Voltaire's opinion that the historian should concern himself with moral judgments as well as narration of the facts. In phrases characteristic of the sententiousness of this neoclassical age, Paterson concluded that

> truth should be the object of the historian's enquiry: discernment should guide his research; judgment warrant his conclusions; candor direct his reflections; and eloquence of stile adorn his composition.[27]

History, Paterson thought, was necessary to an understanding of society. "It is not the true intent of history, so much to load the memory of the reader with a copious collection of public records, as it is to elevate his thoughts and enrich his understanding." He took notice of Montesquieu's opinion that "to understand rightly what a nation is, one should previously learn what it has been," and he believed that there were specific lessons to be learned from the past.

> How noble and useful a study is that of History, which at one View presents the Rise, Fortunes, & Catastrophes of the most eminent persons; and at the same Time that it records the good or bad actions of past ages, instructs the present to imitate the first, and avoid the last.[28]

It is evident that his vision of the past was partly responsible for his political decisions of the 1770s.

He read extensively in ancient history and outlined the characters of Julius Caesar, Antony, and Cicero. Although he was able to read original texts in Greek or Latin, it is likely that he studied the same translations and popularized histories as other colonial scholars. Charles Rollin's popular treatments of ancient history were, for example, repeatedly referred to in Paterson's commonplace book.[29] "Caesar," Paterson concluded, "resembles Cataline in many respects, but he had better abilities and was more successful." Of Antony, Paterson wrote that he "was of his own nature neither wicked nor cruel; though he committed some excesses through hurry of passion. . . . He was a very debauched man in a very debauched age." In contrast, his utmost respect was reserved for Cicero, who toward the end of the Roman Republic, "seemed to have lost one half of his existence when he saw the liberties of his country subverted." And on that most important quality of the public servant, virtue, Paterson wrote that

Pompey had only the outward shew of virtue; Caesar frequently
neglected even to preserve the appearance of it; Cato carried it to
excess; but Cicero was possessed of real virtue, together with vast
abilities, and very shining accomplishments.[30]

Aspects of modern history also earned an important place in Paterson's
commonplace book. The characters of Martin Luther, Charles XII of
Sweden, Louis XIV, and Marshall Turenne were analyzed, and Voltaire's
Universal History was quoted again and again. He reduced to his own
words the conclusions of both Rapin's and Smollett's histories of England
and incorporated them into a fifty-page sketch of British history. He went
to the trouble of pointing out where the various authorities voiced different
opinions (on the number of Britons killed in the Norman invasion, for
example). Summarizing and trying to deduce the most significant lessons
from the British past, he described the objectives of the various factions
in the Puritan revolution. One "more violent party," that "carefully
concealed their designs" at first, "extended their views to utter extirpation
of hierarchy and monarchical government."[31] The problem of violent
factionalism developing from successful revolution was one that Paterson
would face again later in his career.[32]

It is evident from Paterson's commonplace book that many of his later
arguments in politics and law were based on the background in history
acquired during his student days. The determining factors in his decision
to support a revolution for American independence were the measure of
corruption in the system and the possibilities for establishing a society of
virtue.

The study of moral philosophy, which was required for all Princeton
students, was related to history. To the people of that time, morality was
the measure of society as well as the measure of a man, and history seemed
to prove their point. This view was in part a reflection of the fact that
men continued to view society in organic terms. Each state had its infancy,
its manhood, and its period of decline. In a state where high moral standards were maintained, a strong and vigorous future life seemed assured.
But where vice and corruption were widespread, the depths of decline and
dissolution were thought to be close at hand.[33] Paterson's commonplace
book and college essays were heavily laden with comments on both individual and social morality. At several points, he noted the relationship
of individual morality to the institution of the law and, in very significant
arguments, pointed to the state of the morals of a nation as a sign of the
society's rise or decline.

For the New Side tutors under whom Paterson studied (to use the term established for eighteenth-century evangelical Presbyterianism in the middle colonies), the word "corruption" might immediately raise thoughts of those Old Side or rationalist clergymen who were thought to have compromised away the orthodox Calvinism of their fathers and allowed a diminution in the spiritual intensity of religious life. The Great Awakening represented a popular movement to return to these first principles and made such theological controversies a regular concern of many Princeton students, particularly those headed for ministerial careers. The doctrinal breach was healed (at least superficially) by a reunion of the Old Side and New Side factions in 1757, but the decline in orthodoxy that had made the Great Awakening necessary in the first place, was bound to continue once the rush of evangelical fervor was past. There were those who encouraged the growth of scepticism by openly challenging the strict Calvinistic doctrines on predestination and an emotional conversion experience. Under the direction of their stern tutors, some students at the college became embroiled in such theological debate. The lack of interest of others reflected the general secularization of society.[34]

Except for a few notes in his commonplace book and a prayer copied from a contemporary text, Paterson's college papers show little concern for formal theology. Most of his ideas relating to religion and morality were expressed in the terms of moral philosophy which, while no less theoretical than the details of doctrinal dispute, seemed to apply more readily to the secular society around him.[35] For Paterson, there was an inextricable bond between individual morality and social virtue. After reading Mason's *Self Knowledge,* Paterson noted that "he that is unable to govern himself, can never be fit to govern others, for he hath not the true Spirit of Government; because he wants the art of self government." At another point, he explained how all the political theory he had learned was of less importance than moral values because, without virtue, the best principles of government could be ill applied. He learned from the example of other cultures, too: "What the Chinese seem to understand best, and to have most improved, is Morality and the Laws. The respect which children bear their parents is the foundation of Chinese government."[36]

Civil law and moral virtue were seen as complementary forces that should work together toward the creation of a virtuous society. Where one was silent, the other could fill the void. "A good conscience is never lawless in [even] the worst regulated state, and will provide more laws for itself, which the neglect of the legislators hath forgotten to supply." Legal documents such as "Contracts and evidences, and seals and Oaths, were devised to tie fools, and knaves, and cowards: Honor and Conscience are the more firm and sacred ties of gentlemen."[37] In a society where civil law and moral virtue were operating together in the proper way, gentle-men of conscience and good breeding would fill the offices of public trust, and, from there, would oversee the enforcement of the civil law over the rest of society. "Among uncivilized nations," Paterson wrote, "the passions do in general exceed all rational bounds." But where educated gentlemen were sincerely concerned with the well-being of society, the situation could be very different.

> Happy it is, that, in polished society, the passions, by early discipline, are so moderated, as to be made subservient to the most important purposes. In this respect seminaries of learning are of the utmost advantage, and attended with the most happy effects.[38]

Besides studying these academic subjects, Paterson believed that he and his fellow students at the college were learning to curb their personal passions and govern themselves. As a result, he presumed that they would be better able to govern a society that included many individuals who would need their passions curbed by government and laws. As long as the savage instincts of men were controlled and corruption avoided, it mattered little whether individual virtue or fear of the state was responsible.

If passions somehow got too wild for government to control or if, be-cause of weakness, corruption, or factionalism, government became unable to curb them, the fate of the nation would be in question. He credited Solon with the insight that "a good government cannot subsist without rewards and Punishments; because impunity emboldens guilt; and virtue, when neglected and undistinguished, frequently becomes languished and declines."[39] If rewards began to be given for no good reason or men guilty of transgressions appeared to escape punishment, the people of the nation would lose respect for the law and authority of the government. They might even turn away from the injunctions to moral virtue built into the society. The result would not only be a decline in the morals of many of the individuals in the society but an even more lamentable decline in the cohesive force that holds great and virtuous nations together.[40]

At first these ideas were only theoretical. The countryside of rural New Jersey presented no serious threat of moral corruption or social decline. But soon the calmness and simplicity of Princeton life would begin to change, reflecting the developing problems of the British Empire.

Paterson remained in Princeton after his graduation in 1763 to take a master's degree and to study law under Richard Stockton, and in familiar surroundings he began to perceive the imperial struggle in the context of his social theories. As a sophomore he had attended graduation exercises that featured an oration on "The Military Glory of Great Britain." The text of the speech was soon published in pamphlet form, along with plans for a pageant and five pages of music proclaiming the glories of Amherst and Wolfe.[41] But unqualified praise for the British was gone by 1765. In the midst of the Stamp Act crisis, the class appeared for the first time dressed in cloth of American manufacture.[42] When Paterson was granted a master's degree and chose patriotism as the theme for his graduation speech in 1766, we can only assume that his remarks about the British were not as complimentary as they might have been a few years before.[43]

Before long, Paterson was tying together the intellectual threads of his Princeton experience and applying them to the troubles of the world around him. The lessons of history and his concern for moral rectitude were at the heart of his ideas. But the catalyst that helped him to draw together his own philosophy of society was his passion for proper manners and sturdy personal character. During his days at Princeton and there-after, in his essays, orations, and even in his correspondence, he carried on what became practically a personal crusade against what he called "the effeminacy and dissoluteness of modern manners."[44] Using the "manly and rough-hewn virtues" of the past for a model, Paterson criticized the moral degeneracy and love of luxury common to men of his own day. Even the traditionally "rugged and intrepid" British Navy, whose virtues were for "so long famous in story," appeared "softened down" by "the effeminacy of modern times." This was a "sad and evident symptom of degeneracy." Without offering any specific examples, Paterson reasoned that, "if luxury has wormed herself even into the breast of seamen, what dreadful havoc must she have made among others?"

> Fashion indeed seems to be the idol universally adored. By fashion we rise and by fashion we go to bed; we sleep by fashion, we eat by fashion, and in short by fashion regulate every movement of our lives. By fashion some go to hell, and more surprising still by fashion some expect to go to heaven.[45]

The inroads made by luxury and fashion into the character of a nation, of which the wearing of night-gowns by Nassau students was one indication, were unquestionable signs of weakness and corruption. Paterson believed that, where luxury led, venality and licentiousness would soon follow. He was beginning to note the luxurious tastes of British society, and before long he would blame the problems of empire on Britain's moral decline.[46] Later he would explain in detail how these same ideas led him to support the American Revolution.[47]

In his *History of the American Revolution,* David Ramsay explained that without the influence of the colonial colleges the "unequal contest" with Britain might have turned out differently. "These lights of this New World" were significant in creating the informed leadership necessary to maintain colonial unity during the long war. As he put it,

> it is a well-known fact, that persons unfriendly to the Revolution, were always more numerous in those parts of the United States, which had either never been illuminated, or but faintly warmed by the rays of science. The uninformed and the misinformed, constituted a great portion of those Americans, who preferred the leading strings of the parent state, those encroaching on their liberties, to a government of their own countrymen and fellow citizens.[48]

The education that Paterson received at Princeton helped to prepare him for the role he would play in the leadership of America's struggle for independence, but there were exceptions to the rule. Patrick Henry is one example of a revolutionary leader who did not attend a college, and others such as John Adams and Thomas Jefferson did some of their most serious reading and studying after finishing their college studies. But from the very beginnings of American settlement, especially in New England, there had been a large pool of college-educated talent from which to draw prospective colonial leaders. In the eighteenth century, the proliferation of institutions of higher learning in other areas of the colonies expanded this leadership potential further; and in an environment where there was a constant challenge to prepare men for practical pursuits, there remained a respect and awe for those educated in the classics.[49] Indeed, the respect that was shown to men with this background often consisted in the mass of the population deferring to their better judgment in matters concerning the government of society.[50]

Still, there are serious difficulties in establishing specific causal connections between the colonial colleges and the coming of the Revolution. The patriotic protests of the 1760s and 1770s were reflected in the attire worn at commencements, in the topics chosen for debate, and in a half-dozen little tea parties played out at the various colleges throughout the colonies, but historians have been unable to identify any solid connections between these revolutionary protests and the nature of student life or intellectual interests. Student protests seem to have been basically a reflection of the rest of society. What, if anything, it has been asked, did their "student-ness" have to do with their willingness to support the anti-British cause?[51]

While it has been difficult if not impossible to establish the precise intellectual influence that a formal college education might have had on the developing personalities of many colonial leaders, we can draw some conclusions about Paterson. The influence of a formal pattern of learning depended in large measure on the capacities of the individual student, the attitude he assumed toward his studies, and factors such as family background, economic interest, and social status. Paterson's personality and frame of mind seem to have made him especially susceptible to the intellectual atmosphere of the college. For one thing, Princeton was home to Paterson. When students came from cosmopolitan Philadelphia or the sophisticated plantation society of the Old Dominion to study in the Jersey countryside, they must have taken the dogmatic pronouncements of their tutors with a healthy skepticism bred through wider experience. But Paterson had spent his boyhood in the shadow of Nassau Hall. He must have dreamed of the opportunity that a Nassau education could provide to the son of a storekeeper, and once he was a student there he seemed to absorb uncritically everything that the place had to offer. Later he might look back with humor at the resoluteness and pomposity of some of his tutors, but by that time he had learned to be rather pretentious himself.[52] Some sipped at the cup of stolid Presbyterianism that accompanied the more rationalistic elements of the Princeton curriculum, but Paterson drained it to the bottom. The result was to add a religious urgency to his political and social ideas and an almost insufferable tone of puritanical moralizing to the way he presented them.[53]

Even though, as the eighteenth century wore on, more Princeton graduates chose the law or some other secular profession over a career in the ministry,[54] religion remained a pervasive force in the college curriculum. There is no evidence that Paterson ever formally accepted the Calvinist doctrine of predestination or went through the emotional conversion experience required for full New Side church membership. What is clear is that the beliefs of many of his classmates and tutors influenced his thinking. The millenarian impulse in American protestantism antedated the Great Awakening and was shared even by many Old Side believers, but in the years prior to the Revolution evangelical preachers appeared particularly active in extending their proscriptions on the moral law to the entire society, rather than applying it only to the individual regenerate soul. Jonathan Edwards spoke the thoughts of many eighteenth-century protestants when he proclaimed a coming millennium in the New World. God, convinced of the moral virtue and spiritual awakening of the people, would introduce a new era of beauty and harmony into American society—the challenge was to convince the Almighty that virtue was the basic governing principle of American institutions.[55] While the government of a virtuous society had to be strong enough to curb men's malevolent instincts, it was possible for such a strictly governed state to suffer from a lack of true moral direction and to be victimized by the elements of corruption and moral decay. It became a religious as well as a political ideal to establish a system that would encourage virtue in society as well as protect the state from the selfish desires of degenerate leaders. In this context, a revolution might be justified as part of a religious movement to purify a corrupt society and create a virtuous one.[56]

But the same religious ardor that might lead men into revolt also warned them that the unstable political system likely to persist through any revolutionary period would leave society unprotected from the immoral tendencies of licentious people. Here in sum was the position Paterson would take when America was set adrift in the mid-1770s. He might reluctantly agree to the necessity of revolutionary political change to establish a republic of virtue, but he did so with great hesitation bred by fear of the unpredictable social forces that revolution might set free. Ironically, these were the same forces that later elevated him to social prominence. By the time Paterson left college, he had expressed the basic elements of a world view based on historical experience, moral philosophy, and the influence of Princeton's New Side Calvinism. The positions he took and the arguments he phrased during the Revolution, in the crisis of the Confederation, and even in the political battles of the 1790s can almost all be found in embryonic form in his college notes and essays.

His years at Princeton also provided him with some of the skills necessary for political and social leadership. Public speaking was one particularly important talent that the college took pains to engender in its students. Their Latin pronunciation was a matter for serious critical judgment at the annual commencement exercises.[57] For a man who would never put aside the study of politics and law, efficient study habits were also necessary. Important too were the marks of gentlemanly deportment that he so assiduously made a part of his own lifestyle. Paterson's acquired manners may have given him more the countenance of a country squire than some of his cosmopolitan classmates who set off for Philadelphia to seek their fortunes, but in the rural countryside of New Jersey the squire might be more respected than his sophisticated counterpart from the city.[58]

Paterson emerged from the college with all the marks required of one of those "better" men that colonial voters seemed ready to defer to when it came to governing their society. To be sure, he still needed some seasoning, and special training in the law would serve to make him even more respectable. What he had learned from Tacitus and Voltaire about the hallmarks of a good society would be reinforced in his study of Blackstone and Coke. Combined with his religious fervor for averting moral decline and encouraging the development of a virtuous society, these lessons would help him to perceive a pattern in the rush of events in the years to come and would incline him toward the revolutionary cause. Unlike those classmates who chose vocations in the New Side Presbyterian ministry, Paterson undertook to serve society in the more secular role of an attorney. But he took on these responsibilities with the same solemn resolution that Princeton instilled in its politically minded ministry.[59]

"The man of honor," Paterson had written in one of his college essays, "holds a regular course throughout life, is the same in prosperity and adversity, acts his part with propriety, and is neither ashamed nor afraid of discharging his duty."[60] Paterson's concept of his duty brought him wealth and fame as he actively supported the American Revolution and later rose to high political and judicial office. As high as he rose, even to the Philadelphia convention, he would carry with him the lessons of history and the ingenuous Puritan moralism learned from his Princeton tutors.

Before we carry on with the discussion of his early career, it is important to note that the observations made here about the influence of Paterson's education on his ideas and actions after 1776 have been made with the benefit of considerable hindsight. At the time of his graduation, Paterson could not have imagined himself rising to the position of an influential statesman or an eminent jurist. He was, after all, the son of a Princeton shopkeeper who (since his family had settled there when he was five years of age) had never traveled further than Philadelphia. He had studied side-by-side with some young men who were clearly destined for impressive careers, but he could not consider himself one of them. His preoccupation with morals, manners, and the responsibilities of public service was no less significant to him. But the most he hoped for was the opportunity to devote himself to the legal and political guidance of a town such as the one he grew up in. If, after a lifetime of attention to the service of such a community, he achieved some degree of the respectability and deference enjoyed by Richard Stockton—who next to the current college president was the most notable person in Princeton—the young Paterson would have been satisfied. At this point in his life he could not have dreamed that he would rise much higher.

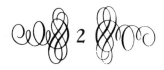

The Country Lawyer

As a young man with an enviable education, influential friends, and good prospects for the future, William Paterson thirsted for success. He still needed professional training, like most of his college classmates. But Paterson also seemed to lack the self-assurance necessary to open up avenues for his own advancement. At first, this presented no great problems. He could remain in Princeton for the next few years studying law and living under his father's roof while he also earned a master's degree and continued his participation in college activities. But, by the time he was admitted to the bar in 1769 and set out to begin his career, the forces that would unleash the American Revolution had begun to take shape. Petitions, protests, and violent demonstrations were marking the development of a revolutionary mentality. In the confusion, nearby cities such as New York and Philadelphia were providing opportunities for young men of ability. In spite of this, Paterson turned his attention toward rural Hunterdon and later Somerset counties, where he spent the next seven years trying to earn a meager living as a country lawyer.

Paterson had shown considerable talent as a student, but as a young lawyer it was by no means clear how far his abilities would take him. It was evident to him that professional success was largely a matter of personal contacts and associations, and at Princeton there were plenty of influential connections to be made. Among his college friends were Luther Martin and Oliver Ellsworth, who would later sit with Paterson in the Philadelphia convention; Aaron Burr (son of the former Princeton president), who would later study law under Paterson; and Henry Lee, who was to receive military glory as "Lighthorse Harry" during the Revolution. James Madison kept an account at the Paterson store.[1] Other Princetonians who achieved eminence in the law were Tapping Reeve of Connecticut; John Dickinson Sergeant, attorney general of Pennsylvania during the Revolution; and Jacob Rush, brother of Dr. Benjamin Rush, the famous physician of Philadelphia.[2]

In a college composition, Paterson defined friendship as "a great intimacy between two persons equally as well as strongly inclined to promote each other's interest or happiness." He bemoaned the natural tendency toward "inveterate selfishness" that influenced many personal relationships and suggested that true friendship could not exist unless it led to virtuous affection and benevolence. A vicious self-interest, on the other hand, might "prove ruinous to society, or the general good." In spite of these noble sentiments, one cannot help but conclude that Paterson was equally aware of the benefits that well-placed friends might bring him in his future career. He observed that

> it may in general be said that, in all our pursuits, whether of a virtuous or of a vicious kind, we are extremely prone to count those our friends, who are the most active in conducting us to the imaginary good we so ardently wish for, and so eagerly strive to attain.[3]

Although Paterson's family was well-off financially, it enjoyed no conspicuous mark of social respect. The contacts he was able to make for himself would therefore be especially important to him. Paterson thus endeavored to keep in touch with his Princeton friends after they had graduated and moved on to begin their careers. Josiah Stoddard had opened a school in the Jersey countryside, and Theodore Romeyn had become a minister in Ulster, New York. Paterson corresponded with Luther Martin and promised to canvass the rich farmers of his neighborhood to see if they would advance Martin the money he needed to purchase a parcel of land. He also tried to convince Reverend John Woodhull, a recent graduate and fellow member of the Well Meaning Society, to reconsider the invitation of a nearby congregation to become their minister. As Paterson prepared to move from his home in 1769, he wrote to Robert Ogden, Jr., who had been a fellow law clerk, seeking to establish a "mutual intercourse by means of letters." In his letter Paterson confessed: "You may laugh perhaps, but I do assure you, it pains me to leave a place in which I have spent the most happy hours of my life, and formed so many valuable connections."[4]

Paterson made several such attempts to begin a polite "epistolary correspondence" with college friends, most of whom came from families wealthier and more widely respected than his own.[5] The infrequency of the responses suggests that some of his well-bred comrades at school did not take the priggish grocer's son as seriously as he took himself. This could not have buoyed his self-confidence. The only friend who did keep in regular contact was John MacPherson, who had graduated in 1766 and had taken up the study of law as an apprentice to John Dickinson in Philadelphia. The letters between the two young men provide some interesting insights into Paterson's personality. Their relationship was affectionate and mutually promotional—the only type of friendship that Paterson defined as true and sincere. They continually questioned each other about their health and happiness, and Paterson pestered his friend to make his letters longer, more frequent, and more punctual: "He knows I love him, he knows I am pleased to hear of his good fortune, he knows I am delighted to correspond with him, why then is he so remiss in answering my last letter?" They tried to arrange meetings, even for a few hours, to renew their friendship in person. Paterson invited MacPherson to stay under his father's roof when he came to Princeton at commencement time, and when things were slow in the law office he almost begged his friend to come to spend some time with him in their old college surroundings.[6]

As both young men endured their apprenticeships, they commiserated with one another on the dreadful boredom of studying law. "To be a complete lawyer, is to be versed in the feudal system," wrote Paterson, "and to say the truth, I am not very fond of being entangled in the cobwebs of antiquity." He was driven to distraction, he said, by the dullness of unbroken hours in "the clutches of that pedantic, rambling, helter-skelter Master Coke," whose works were "breathed through" with "eternal egotism and dictatorial pomp."[7] From time to time they took advantage of their correspondence to quiz each other on legal study questions. They compared notes on their friends' careers and marriage plans. One Princeton classmate had given up the study of law to become a "stage-player," and another, Alex McCasland, had been forced to marry. MacPherson explained how their friend had "made free" with

Doctor Alison's younger daughter, which produced effects which might have been expected from Mr. McCasland's known virility.

The girl cried; the father stamped; his father raved; and to pacify all, Alex married his pre-enjoy'd darling. Lord save me from all such matches! For I so detest a whore, that I would not marry one of my own making.[8]

One of Paterson's letters described his unfortunate experiences on a trip from Philadelphia. In June 1767, Paterson traveled there with his sister and father and paid a visit to MacPherson. When he returned to Princeton, Paterson wrote his friend to describe the journey home: "I never had such an unfortunate jaunt in my life."[9] According to Paterson, the grooms of the stable and the unwholesome pump water of Philadelphia had made his horse sick. The half-dead creature had to be led to Bristol, and Paterson was forced to join his father and sister in their chair. At Bristol, he had hired another animal and traveled on, leaving his own horse to recuperate. Once home in Princeton, he stabled the hired horse for the night and arranged for a boy to pick it up at 3:00 A.M., return it to Bristol, and bring Paterson's own mount back before the heat of the day. But, as if there had not already been enough trouble, when the boy arrived at the stable before dawn the horse had disappeared. Awakened with the news, Paterson was driven to absolute frustration when he realized that he would have to sit and write advertisements to be posted in the neighborhood announcing the horse's disappearance. "I redoubled my ejaculations, and from the bottom of my heart wished hostlers, horses, pumps, and thieves, etc. the Devil's arse a-peak." Before the unbearably boring job of copying advertisements was complete, however, the horse was found grazing in a nearby field. In the end Paterson blamed the affair on "some negroes," who he supposed, "had the impudence to take him [the horse] on one of their nocturnal frolics." His tension and frustration, he said, might only have been eased by the apprehension of the thief and "the pleasure of seeing the rascal severely trounced."[10] The perpetrator seems never to have been identified.

Beyond reporting his personal frustrations, Paterson could share with MacPherson his philosophy of life. "Mankind are weak and feeble enough by nature," Paterson observed, "without the additional weights of luxury and intemperance." Yet wherever he looked, Paterson saw men "lend helping hands to their own undoing, and hasten the period of their lives by excessive voluptuousness." But while he criticized "the aspiring hopes of the proud and ambitious," he could still mention, in a friendly way, his own desire to retain contact with young men of rising fortunes. He asked to be remembered to Jacob Rush, at that time a law clerk with MacPherson, who Paterson thought would reach a high station. "I desire to keep on amicable terms at least with that gentleman, for you know he is to be the speaker of the Hon. House of Commons." Paterson wasn't far off the mark; Rush eventually became chief justice of Pennsylvania.[11]

While Paterson, in the intellectual atmosphere of Princeton, was, as he expressed it, "contemplating the vanity of riches . . . with the gravity of a philosopher," MacPherson was enjoying cosmopolitan Philadelphia.[12] MacPherson's letters described trips to the theater and the sermons that George Whitfield gave while he was in town: "He is not the man he was, but still has some very grand strokes."[13] The young men discussed the political events of the day in their letters, although MacPherson suspected that Paterson got most of his news from the newspapers. At one point Paterson wrote that he wished those who chose to wage their political battles in the newspapers had "slept in peace" instead. But before long MacPherson was himself involved in the protests, personally transcribing copies of *The Farmers Letters* for John Dickinson.[14]

In the spring and early summer of 1770, Philadelphia was alive with rumors and public outcry over Parliament's failure to repeal the Townshend duties in their entirety. The colonists had been organizing protests against these British revenue measures since they were passed in 1767. Finally in March 1770, most of the duties were rescinded. However, in late April, news reached America that the tax on tea had been retained. The radicals sought to maintain the policy of nonimportation agreed to by merchants in all the colonial ports until Parliament knuckled under completely.[15] At first the news from England was hopeful. MacPherson wrote on May 23, 1770, that three London ships had arrived in ballast (carrying only a few nonprohibited articles) and brought news that "the people in England are now desperate and are determined to strike." Philadelphians, according to MacPherson, were "very apprehensive of a civil war, for the King has formed two camps and laughed at the London Remonstrance." But at the same time word came that "the slaves [meaning the merchants] of Rhode Island . . . [had] dissolved their committee, and agreed to import."[16]

Within a few weeks, MacPherson was reporting that he had attended a meeting in Philadelphia that had passed resolves attacking the merchants of New York for resuming business with the British. "The New Yorkers have acted like scrubs," he wrote, "and deserve to be *tarred and feathered,* and it behooves every American to disclaim any connexion with them." Even the students at Princeton had reacted violently to the news from New York, proclaiming that the merchants were "betrayers of their country." Paterson was in New Bromley, thirty miles from Princeton at the time, and must have heard reports of the protest. Nevertheless his answers to MacPherson's letters were strangely quiet about these ex-traordinary events.[17]

Unlike many of his acquaintances who were able to broaden their out-look on the world by going abroad, Paterson's opportunities for travel were limited. His family could not have afforded more than an occasional journey to Philadelphia, and such excursions were probably partly devoted to business. When MacPherson made plans to travel to England in 1770 and proposed that his friend come along, Paterson found it impossible: "A few years hence I may go there, but I fear I cannot at present." As he lived on in the quiet countryside, Paterson longed to be in London, too. The letters he wrote to MacPherson describing his "fancies" about it suggest that Paterson unconsciously thirsted for some of the same aristo-cratic luxuries he decried as immoral and corrupt.

> Sometimes I fancy you figuring away in the beau-monde, frequenting playhouses, operas and balls, a professed admirer of every fashionable amusement; now sauntering along the Mall, or taking a turn at St. James, not so much for the sake of the walk, as to view the well-dressed Belles and beaux, and the strange medley of mortals that are to be met with in such places; sometimes a virtuoso, and arrant connoisseur in shells, in musty medals, and in Egyptian mummies; sometimes I follow you to your chamber, view you revolving on some obstruse point of law, or poring over the pages of Littleton and Coke; now a politician deep in the mysteries of state, adjusting the balance of Europe and betting on war or peace, on the life or death of Princes. Sometimes,—but there is no end to the vagaries of fancy.[18]

On another occasion he mused, "were I in England, I would collect anecdotes of persons eminent for station, learning, and genius. Hardly anything is sought after more here, or renders a person more agreeable in conversation."[19]

While these letters do not tell us much about Paterson's political ideas, they offer an interesting insight into his personality. Catapulted by his college experience from the chores of his father's store into the polite life of respectable society, he strove to retain all the social ties he could. Although his family's finances made extensive travel impossible, he could revel vicariously in his friend's experiences abroad. Despite all the time he spent in the countryside, Paterson was not unsophisticated, nor incapable of comprehending the world more than a few miles from his home. He felt trapped in his rural solitude and yearned for more intellectual stimulation, but still he seemed to shrink from the decision to leave his out-of-the-way neighborhood. He must have enjoyed the respect and deference of most people he met in rural Jersey, while in the city competition for status would have been far more acute.

His self-assurance seems to have failed again when it came to sexual relationships. Ladies were often on his mind, but there is no evidence that they were ever to be found in his chamber, or even on his arm. He chattered incessantly about the intellectual and physical charms of women, yet in one letter to MacPherson Paterson admitted that, "my ladies are quixotical, are purely imaginary, and have no more reality than the dreams of a Poet, or the schemes of a Projector."[20] He may have feared that his slight build was unappealing or that his financial dependence on his father's business made thoughts of a wife premature. But, whatever the reason, the closest he got to contemplating marriage in the fourteen years after his graduation from college was the gossiping he indulged in about the weddings of his classmates and friends.

If his personal problems in these years (the psychological depression brought on by long study, the foibles of young ladies, the unreliability of stable boys, or the frustration of having to write advertisements) seem somehow less significant than the plight of farmers who were suffering economic hardship or the slaves who may have sought diversion in "nocturnal frolics"—they do tell us something about Paterson's view of the world. In one letter to MacPherson, he went on at length about the benefits of being well bred and well born. The letter indicates that he was a little sorry that he could not claim a more significant lineage but "gloried at being a Scotchman" as a substitute for the "true blue" status that his immediate ancestry could not provide.[21]

MacPherson was probably Paterson's closest friend, but their intimacies had to be shared over the distance between Princeton and Philadelphia. Closer to home were his fellow students and alumni at the college, and even after he accepted a master's degree in 1766, he remained very active in the intellectual clubs that were a feature of eighteenth-century college life. In 1765, two rival student organizations were formed at the college—the Plain Dealing Society and the Well Meaning Club. Paterson was a founder of the latter. Their purpose was to provide a friendly atmosphere for the practice of rhetorical skills. They were certainly significant in helping Paterson develop his ideas and his ability to express them convincingly. But, according to accounts, the competition between the groups ran high, and the college trustees soon began to doubt the wisdom of allowing such fraternities to exist.[22]

Although he was no longer studying at the college, it is not surprising that Paterson was one of the guiding lights of the Well Meaning Club and regularly participated in their meetings. Aside from his law books and informal conversation, the societies offered nearly the only intellectual stimulation that was available in the neighborhood, and they also provided an obvious opportunity for Paterson to maintain acquaintance with the sons of elite families who continued to be drawn to Princeton from all over the colonies. Moreover, it must have been comfortable for him to associate with younger undergraduates who, regardless of their more prestigious backgrounds, could not help but respect Paterson's academic degrees and, later, his status as an attorney. It was Paterson who engineered a solution to the trustees' proposition to close the clubs, by helping to convince the members of both fraternities to join together to ward off their common foe. Later, when the union of the two groups proved unsatisfactory, he participated in the founding of the Cliosophic Society, one of the two new societies that took the place of the original clubs. The name of the society was adopted from the title of Paterson's 1763 graduation speech, a "Cliosophic Oration" or "oration in praise of wisdom."[23] Eventually the authorities withdrew their objections as both students and alumni fought to retain the fraternities. The other new club boldly called itself the American Whig Society in recognition of the recently published letters of William Livingston, newly appointed as a trustee.

The names enlisted in the Well Meaning Club for its first year indicate that Paterson found himself in very good company. In addition to Ellsworth, Martin, Reeve, and Sergeant, there was Jonathan Edwards, the son of the great revivalist, who was destined to become a minister himself and serve as president of Union College, and Robert Ogden, who would study law by Paterson's side in the office of Richard Stockton. In the first years after it was transformed into the Cliosophic Society, the years during which Paterson was most active, the club included Aaron Ogden, who later became governor of New Jersey; Samuel Spring, hero of the Revolution and a long-time religious leader of Newburyport, Massachusetts; Frederick Frelinghuysen, member of one of the state's most influential families, destined for a career in Congress; and Andrew Kirkpatrick, who would later study law under Paterson and rise to become chief justice of the New Jersey Supreme Court. It is interesting that most of these men tended to become Federalists later on, while the famous early leaders of the American Whig Society—Hugh Henry Brackenridge, Philip Freneau, and James Madison—became Republicans in the decade after 1790.[24] There is no discernable explanation for this pattern, nor for the geographic distribution that drew most students from south and west of Princeton to the American Whig Society and those from north and east to Clio. Such factors do suggest the type of people with whom Paterson felt familiar and at ease, although friendships were not limited by the bounds of membership. MacPherson, after all, was a Plain Dealer. Moreover, there is no evidence that either of the two clubs was any more radical than the other in support of the American Revolution; members of both groups distinguished themselves in the struggle for independence.

Though it would have been difficult, if not impossible, to keep matters of consuming public interest out of the affairs of these societies, politics was not their reason for being. Rather, the societies served as extensions of the formal curriculum where students could help train each other to improve their skills in thinking, writing, and speaking.[25] The themes that Paterson discussed were characteristic of the literary affectations of the day. Once he prepared a three-part humorous skit on the importance of a graceful literary style.[26] In 1772 he wrote and read before the society a poem that praised the charms of Betsy Stockton, "The Belle of Princeton," and criticized the students and tutors at the college who aspired to become her suitors. Paterson took the opportunity to poke fun at the very proper Samuel Stanhope Smith who would eventually become president of the college but was then a tutor there and a member of the other club.

> Tutor Smith, so wondrous civil
> Compound odd of Saint & Devil.
> This Smith a parson too, alas!
> He more resembles for an ass.[27]

When more philosophical or politically oriented questions concerned the club, Paterson's contributions reflected his moralistic political and social philosophy. Paterson applied his theories more pointedly as the problems of the Empire became more acute. In an "Oration on the Degeneracy of the Times," he warned that England was in serious decline because of the insidious character of luxury and political corruption. "Turn over the political pamphlets of the day," he suggested,

> and you will immediately see that selfishness, venality and licentiousness characterise the present Era and denote the Declension of Britain. . . . Dissention among the great, and furious commotions among the populace bode ill to a country burdened with heavy taxes, and ready to sink under an enormous national debt. Inconsistency, want of principle, and the most turbulent ambition in men of eminent stations lead to disgrace, distraction and inevitable ruin.[28]

Even in an oration "On Musick," presented before the Cliosophic Society in January 1773, Paterson showed the same concern for the moral degeneration of society. The lecture credited music with the power to render men humane, benevolent, and happy. Quoting Polybius, Paterson noted the importance the Greeks gave to the musical arts and contrasted the solemn inspiration of the ancients with the "unmeaning Warblers of the present day, who deal out the insipid Sing-song of Italian Operas." It was possible for music "to provoke irregular desires, and to excite a love of pleasures and voluptuousness," and this could prove dangerous to the nation as a whole.

> Light music of the looser sort ministers to luxury, and ought there-fore never to be tolerated in a well-regulated state. Musick of the latter kind taints the morals and vitiates the manners; it excites a love of pleasure, sinks into weakness, and melts into luxurious effeminacy [and] softness. Musick, when thus applied, is attended with unhappy effects; it lulls only to enfeeble, and soothes only to unnerve; it, Circe-like turns men into brutes.[29]

Paterson was convinced that contemporary men were indeed becoming brutes and that society in general was in decline. In countries where moral corruption had gone too far, radical—even revolutionary—steps might have to be taken to preserve the society and make it virtuous again.

Paterson often returned to speak before the Cliosophic Society, even later in life when he himself was a trustee of the college. He encouraged the students to exercise their talents as public speakers and sought to maintain a healthy competition between the sons of Clio and their rival society. Once when he addressed his society on the anniversary of its founding, Paterson was transported by memories of the fraternal brotherhood he had enjoyed: "Friendship like this smooths the current of the passions, makes them glide gently as the flow of a summersea, and fragrant as the breeze that fans the bosom of spring."[30] The fragrance Paterson hoped to find among his friends was the sweet smell of success. The Cliosophic Society was an important influence on Paterson. It encouraged him to refine and reinforce his ideas on politics and society and provided a convenient opportunity to meet more young men from the better families.

At least as influential in shaping his political views was Paterson's decision to become a lawyer. The American legal profession provided many recruits to the cause of revolution. Lawyers proliferated in America and, despite their occasional unpopularity, they were a powerful influence in the society and government of each colony. "In no country perhaps in the world," Edmund Burke wrote of America, "is the law so general a study." Acute and inquisitive, American lawyers were full of resources and ready

to defend their interests at the first hint of attack. "In other countries,"
Burke continued,

> the people, more simple and of less mercurial cast, judge of an ill
> principle in government only by an actual grievance; here they
> anticipate the evil, and judge of the pressure of the grievance by the
> badness of the principle.[31]

The study of the law did not inevitably move men to revolt. There were
many Loyalist lawyers, and British lawyers were firm defenders of
imperialism, but the concept of fundamental law enshrined in the British
legal system did offer an important rationale to many revolutionary
leaders.[32]

In the course of the eighteenth century there was a general movement
to extend the English common law to America. The complication of
business and personal relationships developing in America required more
precise legal definition than provincial statutes could conveniently provide
and, since the decisions of colonial courts had never been printed, the
only precedents lawyers could argue were English. American lawyers,
however, came to regard common law in significantly different ways than
their British contemporaries. Sir Edward Coke, the dominant legal mind
of the seventeenth century and still the most influential shaper of colonial
legal ideas at the time of the Revolution, held that Magna Carta together
with the traditional common law made up a body of fundamental law.
Parliaments and kings were subject to it just as the people were, and the
people could justly disobey an act of their government that transgressed
it. These ideas had been transmitted to America in the writings of men
such as John Trenchard and Thomas Gordon and became a basic part of
the Whig ideology. They made colonists sensitive to ministerial conspiracy
and taught them to guard against the slightest inroads on traditional
constitutional guarantees. Ultimately they helped Americans to justify a
revolution against king and Parliament to preserve those fundamental
rights and privileges that the British government seemed to ignore. This
was the sort of thinking that had supported the English revolutions of
the 1640s and 1680s, but such ideas had been superseded in Great Britain.
Parliament had continued to garner more power at the expense of the
Crown, and most Britons (most notably, William Blackstone who in
the eighteenth century replaced Coke as the country's legal inspiration)
came to look at the Lords and Commons as the source of all law. Indeed,
with the fundamental law protected by tradition alone, Parliament could
change legal principles that had existed for hundreds of years by simple

majority vote. In England the distinction between fundamental and ordinary or statute law had been lost, but American lawyers still cherished the difference. For them the common law became a tool to use in defense of liberty against the designs of prerogative power in cases ranging from the Navigation Acts to the threat to trial by jury.[33]

Paterson was a conscientious student of the common law, and a belief in fundamental law followed naturally from his earlier studies, from his interest in British history and the Magna Carta, to his study of Coke and Blackstone. He had developed the concept of the right of revolution in the form of a college disputation and based his theory on the fundamental law. "Tyranny is the exercise of power beyond right," he explained. It appears "when the king makes his will, rather than the law, his rule." There was no question in his mind that "wherever law ends, tyranny begins," and he concluded that "the lawfullness of killing a tyrant: was evident and unquestionable." Revolution, he conceded, could not be taken lightly. Great caution had to be exercised because the killing of the king would tend to further disturb an already unstable society and perhaps open the door to even more misfortune. But the right of the law over the prerogative of the king was absolute. Here was the philosophy that would allow him to justify his own participation in rebellion.[34]

In light of his later success and fame, Paterson's decision to make a career of the law was a wise one. He was fortunate in having as his sponsor Richard Stockton, a member of the governor's council and justice on the Supreme Court bench, who would later be a signer of the Declaration of Independence. Stockton had many connections in England as well as in America and, perhaps most appealing for young Paterson, his office and residence lay just a few hundred yards down the road from Nassau Hall.[35] At Stockton's, Paterson received the best of legal training and was still able to retain his close association with family and friends.

His apprenticeship would last for five years, until he was admitted to the bar in November 1768. During these years he labored diligently, for he realized, as he said, that "application is necessary to achieve eminence in learning."[36] He studied alone into the early hours of the morning, but he still had the energy to discuss knotty problems in talks with his fellow clerks or in letters to his Philadelphia friend, MacPherson. He spent long hours doing chores for Stockton, especially when the master was out of town. He had use of Stockton's library, to supplement the few volumes he was collecting on his own. He also had the opportunity to help Stockton serve some of his most prestigious clients, such as William Alexander, the self-styled Lord Stirling, who during the Revolution would consign his monumental legal difficulties to Paterson's trusted hands.[37]

His own career did not begin with distinguished clients and large fees. Princeton was a small town, and its legal needs were already well served. So, in search of a clientele, Paterson moved in 1769 to New Bromley, a half-day's journey to the west of Princeton, and in 1772 to Raritan, less than a day's journey to the north. Perhaps it was family loyalty that kept him near the seat of his father's business, or the fellowship of his college friends in nearby Princeton, or a continuing doubt about his ability to successfully compete in more challenging surroundings, but Paterson seems not even to have considered setting up in New York, Philadelphia, or one of the centers of legal activity in New Jersey such as Burlington or Perth Amboy. It does not seem likely that he had business lined up in either of the two towns that he tried. Investigation of the records of the counties in which he did his legal work indicates that he had very few cases to look after.[38]

Soon the boredom of life in the country drove him to such desperation that in one letter he referred to himself in words reminiscent of Gray's "Elegy in a Country Churchyard" as "the rose in the wilderness that blooms unnoticed," its fragrance wasted on the desert air. In the same letter he explained that he had "scarce any amusement to resort to when I find my spirits flag." When he tired of the law, "and such is daily the case," he tried reading, dreaming of ladies, and always wound up envying MacPherson for the diversions that the city provided. When two acquaintances, one of whom excelled at the flute, came to visit his hermitage, he joined them in a frolic through the countryside in search of an echo: "I never heard any thing more enchantingly harmonious."[39] But as much as he thirsted for amusements and entertainments, Paterson cautioned his younger brother that it was high time in his life "that frothy merriment, unmeaning noise, and idle sportfullness should give way to thought more solid, and to actions more useful." He warned that young people are especially prone to be "carried away by fashionable amusements" and explained that "frothy amusements gradually weaken the mind, and give us a relish for others of a more criminal nature." Maturity came in being able to balance practical pursuits and diversions so that one did not indulge in the latter "to too great a degree. . . . Trust me, my Dear Brother, the life that will not bear reflection is full of pain and will infallibly render you forever miserable."[40]

Presumably as a result of dedication to his own aphorisms, some of the elements that contributed to his later career began to materialize. In August 1769, just a month after he settled in New Bromley, Paterson was appointed a surrogate of the province. In this capacity he could collect fees for representing the governor in actions on wills.[41] Undoubtedly,

Stockton, hoping that the new position would bring some business Paterson's way, had recommended him for the appointment, but still there was no noticeable increase in clientele. Indeed, after moving to Raritan, Paterson operated a branch of his father's store as well, overseeing the legal needs of the family's enterprise and making occasional business trips to New York and Philadelphia.[42]

To become known by his senior colleagues in the profession, a young lawyer had to attend the court sessions. Thus, while he waited for business to improve, Paterson found time for continued study and regularly attended meetings of the county court. The way he conducted himself on these occasions must have been an important reason why his colleagues in later revolutionary assemblies trusted him with important responsibilities.[43]

Most of the cases that he handled in his early career involved the collection of debts, and the single most complicated legal entanglement he was called on to unravel was his own father's financial difficulties. In January 1775, Richard Paterson placed all his property (house, land, stock of merchandise, and slaves) up for sale expressing his desire of "quitting business and of closing his affairs." The advertisement he placed in *Dunlap's Pennsylvania Packet* included a request for "all persons indebted to him on bond, note or book accounts, to make immediate payment," because, the ad continued, "to pay those to whom he is indebted, it is necessary that those should pay first who are indebted to him."[44] As it turned out, his creditors did not wait, and to avoid having his father's properties attached for indebtedness, William arranged to take a mortgage in his own name against his father's lands and buildings. Ultimately, his father was forced to declare bankruptcy, but much of his wealth had been protected through the legal assistance of his son. Before the whole affair was over, Paterson had represented his father in more cases than all the rest of his clients combined.[45] It must be assumed that young Paterson's economic position was due more to his business activity and his involvement with his family's fortunes than to attention to his meager legal practice. By 1776, when he was chosen for the Legislative Council (a position that required £1,000 of property), he was financially comfortable and beginning to be recognized as socially prominent in his neighborhood.

His association with the legal profession embroiled Paterson in the political protests of the 1760s. While he was serving his apprenticeship, the clamor over the Stamp Act swept through New Jersey. The Stamp Act, a futile attempt to raise revenue from America by requiring that newspapers, merchants' contracts and bills of lading, and all legal documents bear stamp duties, was initiated by Parliament in March 1765.

Since there were no newspapers and no major ports in New Jersey, the burden of the stamp taxes threatened to fall most heavily on New Jersey's lawyers. The members of the bar joined in a convention in September 1765, and resolved not to use the stamps in any of their transactions. In part because of the urging of Paterson's teacher, Richard Stockton, a delegation was sent to join the Stamp Act Congress that was meeting in New York.[46] Beginning in November when the law went into effect, the lawyers refused to do any business that required the stamps and thereby effectively closed the courts. Nevertheless, from the outset the tactics of protest they employed were cautious and conservative. They denounced "all indecent and riotous behavior," and, while they stood for principle, they restricted their protest to passive resistance. When they reconvened in February 1766, several hundred "sons of liberty" demanded that the lawyers resume business without the stamps. But such a direct affront to the government and the law was further than they wished to go, so the assembled lawyers simply put off a resumption of activities until April 1, by which time the legal machinery of the province had returned almost to normal, and Parliament had repealed the law.[47] Still only an apprentice, Paterson had played no direct role in the Stamp Act episode, but he had been able to observe the protest and the involvement of Richard Stockton at first hand.

Actually, the months during which the courts were closed provided welcome relief for many Jerseymen who suffered economic hardship and were persistently hauled into court by their unsympathetic creditors. Their woes were intensified by economic deflation in the wake of the French and Indian Wars, and a circulating medium that was steadily contracting as the province levied taxes to withdraw the currency issued during the war. The colony wanted to temper the effects of the withdrawal with new paper money outlays, but in 1764 Parliament passed a currency act forbidding any issue of paper money that required acceptance of the bills as legal tender. Despite all the pressure that paper money advocates would bring in the next decade, and even in the face of Governor Franklin's support for at least a limited legal tender provision, the laws were disallowed in England year after year. And each year the increased taxes needed to pay off the debt further diminished the currency in circulation.[48] No longer flushed with the prosperity of a wartime economy, the Jerseymen found themselves faced with plummeting prices and had to tighten their belts. No matter how much property a farmer owned, he could find no cash to pay his creditors. As Paterson explained to his friend Luther Martin, even the people who had the best collateral could not borrow money.[49] Creditors hired lawyers to bring their delinquent debtors into court to attach their property for public sale, but there were few buyers, so the debtor's farm and belongings might sell for a fourth or a fifth of their actual value. This may explain why Paterson went to such lengths to ensure that his father's property was not sold in this way. As a resident of Hunterdon County explained in 1770, "a man with an estate worth £5,000 will have it torn from him, tho' all his debts amount to but £100; a situation which will naturally make a man feel desperate."[50]

To be sure, many people were insensitive to the problem. While the debtors continued to push paper money bills through the assembly only to have them disallowed in England, others thought the only effective solution to the economic situation would be a retreat from what they saw as an artificially inflated wartime standard of living.[51] Austerity, however, could not help those already hopelessly entrapped in debt.

Though their plight may have been due to very complex economic phenomena, the oppressed debtors desperately vented their rage on the lawyers who brought down the power of the government on them. Their rage was not without reason. Considerable evidence suggests that lawyers were engaging in petty, even unnecessary, litigation to generate fees, and were overcharging clients shamelessly. Such respected attorneys as Bernardus LaGrange and Samuel Tucker were "summoned before the legislature to answer allegations of malpractice."[52] In 1765 a law for regulating legal fees was considered by the assembly, but it never went into effect. In 1769 and 1770, there were uprisings of the people in Essex and Monmouth counties demanding public regulation of the legal profession. Because sympathy for the rioters was so widespread, they were given only light fines or simply released when brought to trial.[53] This sort of popular agitation was not unique to New Jersey. In the election for the New York assembly in 1768 a popular slogan had been "no lawyer in the Assembly," and in Pennsylvania lawyers were attacked for being allies of the "merchant aristocracy."[54]

According to the portfolio of Paterson's cases, his early years as a member of the New Jersey bar earned him no special distinction. When public opposition arose, however, the young lawyer's defense of his profession was forthright and unquestioning, as could be expected from one who aspired to eminence within it. Paterson lamented that lawyers were thought to have "an inordinate desire of accumulating riches" and maintained that the charge was unjust.[55] "If there be dirty attourneys, who drive through thick and thin and stickle at nothing to promote their own designs," those few individuals should "be severely punished and dealt with in an exemplary manner." But, he cautioned, "do not involve the innocent in the punishment of the guilty." He admitted that a few might have participated in "unjust practices," but believed that the recent clamor was due in large measure to those people of the province who were notorious for groaning "under the burden of heavy debts, which they have no easy prospect of removing but by the interposition of an insolvent act."[56] Despite the evidence of Britain's refusal to consider the financial plight of the colonies, Paterson showed no sympathy for the debtors who, he suggested, had become "strained in their circumstances and reduced to the lowest ebb of poverty, by high living, riot, or sensuality." He wondered that such people "should ascribe this situation to the oppressive measures of cunning men" (which was how, according to Paterson, they characterized the judicious application of the province's laws), rather than blaming their own voluptuousness and moral degeneracy. The result from Paterson's distorted point of view was that reputations were ruined on the basis of total falsehoods or the "aggravation of real tho' petty offences," and justice was poorly served.[57]

The movement for the regulation of the legal profession, which Paterson so strenuously resisted, was unsuccessful, and it was not until the "exigencies of impending Revolution demanded their popular solidarity" that the lawyers voluntarily agreed to "prevent unnecessary litigation."[58] Paterson was interested in supporting the lawyers against what he considered an unfair attack. Presumably he realized that one way to earn the respect and trust of his professional elders was to make himself conspicuous in their defense. He was certainly not opposed to the principle of government regulation per se. According to his education and his evolving social philosophy, it was the responsibility of every society to encourage its people to live virtuous lives, and some groups might need more encouragement than others. Besides, as will be discussed later, Paterson openly favored the public regulation of the medical profession.

We must assume that Paterson's stance in defense of lawyers set him apart from many other people in the New Jersey countryside. Besides accusing some of them of "high living, riot, and sensuality," he was countering the hostility to the legal profession common among many of his Calvinist neighbors. Alan Heimert has recently shown that there was widespread agreement with both heralds of the Great Awakening, Edwards and Whitfield, in the "conviction that legal contention was essentially sinful" and that lawyers "encouraged men to use legal procedures to deny or circumvent their moral obligations." Whitfield had even gone so far as to suggest that the business of an attorney was unchristian, or "at least extremely dangerous" for one who sought to glorify God.[59]

The Raritan Valley neighborhood of rural New Jersey in which Paterson chose to launch his career was a hotbed of evangelical activity. Since

the area had been heavily settled with Dutch- and German-speaking farmers, the dominant sect was the Dutch Reformed Church, and the Calvinist
impulse had taken root there from its earliest days. Even before the Great
Awakening swept through the rest of the colonies, the Reverend Theodorus
Jacobus Frelinghuysen had been pressing his flock to return to a more
orthodox Calvinism. The evangelical spirit was continued by his son, John
Frelinghuysen, who succeeded to the ministry at his father's death, and
by John's student, Jacobus Rutsen Hardenburg, after 1758. For more
than fifty years, then, New Side Calvinist beliefs were reinforced there
time and time again.[60]

Paterson was one of the English-speaking minority in the neighborhood
of Raritan who, for the lack of a minister of their own, attended the
services in the Dutch church. But there were tensions. For more than a
decade, the Dutch had been trying to establish a divinity school to provide
preachers for their growing congregations. For proof of need all they had
to do was point to the duties of their own Reverend Hardenburg who,
although he had been relieved of some of his burden in 1761, still had to
minister to three churches (Raritan, Bedminster, and Readington). While
it was obvious that more ministers were needed, there was considerable
debate about whether or not a separate school was a good idea. Some
thought that future Dutch Reformed ministers might properly attend
Princeton before they went on to study divinity in the home of some
learned Dutch preacher. But others insisted on a school of their own,
and ultimately Queen's College, now Rutgers University, was established.[61]

Presumably all the time Hardenburg devoted to the establishment of
the college and service as a founding trustee had something to do with
the rumor that the elders were seeking an assistant to help with his
ministerial duties. The records of the church are silent about the confrontation that ensued, but Paterson's papers contain the draft of a
petition to the consistory that establishes his familiarity with the ideology
and his fluency in the rhetoric of evangelical Calvinism. It also provides
another example of Paterson's assumption of leadership in the community—at least in the religious community.

"We cannot but deplore our unhappy case," Paterson wrote, "that in
a Land, where the Christian Religion is taught in Purity, we cannot avail
ourselves of the preached word, because [it is] dealt out in a Language
of which the greater part of us are ignorant." Apparently the Dutch
members of three combined congregations were split themselves on whether
or not to recognize the English-speaking members as being in full communion with them, for Paterson went on to say that

it is rumoured that some of the members of the Dutch Church of which Mr. Hardenburg has the charge have openly declared that the English are not in Communion with them, & of consequence have no right to interfere in their ecclesiastical Polity. This we look upon as an assertion extremely harsh, & which, we take leave to say, has given us great uneasiness. Diversity of Language does not necessarily suppose Diversity of Sentiment. There are no differences between English Calvinists and Dutch; their religious principles are the same; and hardly anyone will be so absurd to say, that truth is not truth unless it be expressed in a particular Stile or Language.

Reflecting the belief in unity that Heimert has deduced as one of the hallmarks of evangelical Calvinism, Paterson emphasized that his group did not want to allow "a matter of mere form" such as language to "prevent a Union" of people of like belief. But if the Dutch were so uncooperative as to deny the English full membership and refuse to allow preaching in their own language, the minority would have no alternative but to set up a church of their own. "For our Importunity and Warmth on the present occasion we do not pretend to apologise," he went on, "our eternal Peace is at stake, and therefore we cannot forbear, we must be pressing."[62]

Answers to four questions were demanded: Would the English be admitted to full membership? Would they have a voice in the election of the proposed new assistant to Reverend Hardenburg? Would services be performed in the English language (in proportion either to the percentage of English in the congregation or to the amount they contributed to support the minister)? And, would the hoped-for new preacher be required to service any more than the three churches already under Hardenburg's care? Finally, Paterson closed with more assurances.

We do not desire to make a breach in the Communion of the Church; a national or Party Spirit is, in civil matters, when carried to excess, highly pernicious; in religious, no words can express its unhappy Effects; a national or party spirit be assured therefore has no influence over us on the present occasion. We desire, that divine worship may be performed in English as well as in Dutch, and in Dutch as well as in English; we desire, that difference in Language may not most absurdly create difference in Sentiment; we desire to be united with the Dutch Reformed Church; and finally, whether united or not, we desire & pray, that we may live as Brethren, as Christian Brethren with those in Communion with that Church.[63]

Because the records of the church show no evidence of this controversy, we cannot be sure that the petition was ever presented to the consistory, and there is no way to establish exactly when the English language became accepted. The wording of the petition clearly bears Paterson's measured and diplomatic legal style and, although this draft must have also reflected the ideas of others in the English-speaking community in the area, the document tells us more about Paterson's religious ideas than we can learn from his college essays. It indicates that he was influenced by his formal religious training at Princeton as well as by the history and the moral philosophy he learned there, and that it bred in him an appreciation of the "pure" Christianity that evangelical Calvinists preached and practiced all over the colonies, whether in English, German, or Dutch. It is possible that this controversy over the language to be spoken in the Dutch Reformed Church soured Paterson on matters of church government and congregational decision making and kept him from having the conversion experience required of full-fledged New Side believers. In the future, Paterson chose to attend religious services regularly, to contribute generously, and to offer particular support to evangelical activities (missions to the frontier, for example), but never to become a voting member of a congregation. In New Brunswick, for example, where he lived for more than twenty years (1783–1806), Paterson helped to build the church and supported it vigorously, but he declined admission to full communion and thereby avoided any involvement in internal congregational affairs.[64] Still, as his public pronouncements throughout his life attest, Paterson was a firm believer and vigorous supporter of religious institutions. His social and political philosophy continued to reflect certain values and attitudes that were consistent with the religious influences of his early life. Finally, the episode with the Dutch Reformed Church also shows Paterson presenting himself as a leader of men, testing his powers of argument on the community around him, and laying the foundations for more important leadership roles later on.

On at least one other occasion during this period of his life Paterson spoke out again in the interests of the community. In this case, he was concerned about doctors and their influence on public health. The state of the healing arts in the eighteenth century was not conducive to earning the confidence of the public. Only a small percentage of the practicing physicians had ever received training beyond apprenticeship, and "quacks, mountebanks, and midwives practiced 'physick' alongside trained doctors."[65] In his undergraduate commonplace book, Paterson had laid it down "as a maxim, that when a nation abounds with physicians it grows thin of people."[66] The founding of the first American medical school in 1765 and the establishment in 1766 of the Medical Society of New Jersey, the first of its kind in America, were signs of an increasing concern with professionalism, but there were still problems very disturbing to the public mind.[67]

One medical problem that was a continual concern in colonial America was the treatment of smallpox. In a letter to Aaron Burr, who was staying at Elizabethtown, Paterson expressed surprise that his friend had chosen to remain in that place for any length of time. Paterson was so convinced that the atmosphere of Elizabethtown might lead to smallpox infection that he always drove "thro' Eliz-town as quickly as possible, lest the soft infection should steal upon me, or I should take it in with the very air I breathe."[68] As a child Paterson had seen evidence of inoculation's dangers when Jonathan Edwards died of a reaction to the treatment shortly after taking over as Princeton's president. There is no evidence that Paterson ever allowed himself to be inoculated.

The process of inoculation—or variolation as it was then commonly called—was a new one in the eighteenth century, and many doubted its effectiveness. Some years before, Cotton and Increase Mather had sparked a controversy by supporting inoculation in Boston. The process of inoculation consisted of placing pus from "the pustules of a smallpox victim into an incision or puncture in the skin of a healthy person." The infection that resulted usually remained mild, but the inoculated person could pass on a full-blown case of the disease to anyone who came into contact with him. Some doctors were very careful in instructing their patients to remain at home and in effect quarantine themselves while the infection ran its course, but others allowed inoculated patients to carry on ordinary lives while their cures progressed. There is no doubt that, in this manner, doctors who practiced inoculation actually did spread the disease.[69]

In several essays, probably prepared for presentation to his Cliosophic brothers, Paterson feigned some very superstitious ideas about medicine (including the idea that listening to certain music—presumably not the same music that endangered morals—was the only cure for people "bitten by the tarantula").[70] His argument, which saw the practice of inoculation as being very dangerous to the community at large, was exaggerated for humorous effect.

"*Beware of Doctors*," he wrote, for many physicians seemed to be more interested in their fees than in their patients' health.[71] Paterson claimed to know of a conspiracy among certain doctors to spread smallpox intentionally throughout the community. "The doctors," he said, "have scented their snuff boxes with the smallpox," and "with quite a modish air" offered to pass them from person to person in company. Paterson explained that since in the instances he had observed all of those present had already had the disease and therefore could not contract it again, he had done no more than pass the box and warn his friends "with shrugs and expressive looks" to do the same. Later, he claimed, he repented not speaking up when two elderly women suffered bad reactions (one "flew upwards" with a "whizzing in her brain" and the other was "seized with a most violent fit of laughter").[72] The doctors had "done all in their power to introduce the smallpox among us, which otherwise never would have made its way into this remote corner of the province."[73]

Paterson was clearly exaggerating in proposing such a conspiracy theory. He seemed to go further still in giving credence to

some of the most elderly and sagest women whose opinion is much to be regarded in matters physical as well as ecclesiastik. . . . A certain set of men will, I know, laugh at the observation and call it the freak of a disordered brain; but for my part I freely declare, that I wholly agree with these old matrons, and look upon this spreading disorder to be as ominous to the full as the oversetting of a saltseller, the dreaming about a clergyman, or the howling of a dog.[74]

Paterson went on to describe an omen of the previous year when "a comet or blazing star" was sighted.

Those who are skilled in matters of this nature, (one of whom without vanity I count myself) looked upon it as a token of some terrible disaster, or sudden revolution in the lower world; such as the fall of a statesman, the death of a king, or the degradation of a field-preacher.

The spread of smallpox, Paterson concluded, "warns us of our approaching dissolution."[75]

Although he poked fun at irrational superstitions, Paterson thought there was real evidence for a societal decline and he did share a deep suspicion of medical practice. We know that he was serious about his distrust of doctors, for in 1771 he joined his father and others in petitioning the New Jersey assembly to pass a law regulating the practice of medicine. Although it was more sober in tone, the petition mentioned some of the same concerns Paterson had spoken of before

that many persons ignorant and unskilled in Physic and Surgery, in order to gain a Subsistance, do take upon themselves to administer the former and practice the latter; thereby endangering the lives and limbs of their patients, and greatly impoverishing their estates, to the

unspeakable injury of the Survivors, who frequently are composed of
a distressed parent and a miserable offspring.[76]

To remedy this "inconvenience," the petitioners pleaded that a standard
of medical knowledge be fixed, a mode of examination be prescribed, and
"the practice in general so regulated" as the legislators thought necessary.
When the legislature complied the following year with the requests of this
and many other petitions, the act was hailed as an important step in the
progress of the medical profession.[77]

Although Paterson's early career cannot have appeared very successful,
even to himself, it had provided him with some experience and enough ex-
posure so that when it came time to choose those who would sit on the
councils of rebellion, he was considered to be eligible by his colleagues and
the people. He had reinforced his belief in the concept of fundamental law,
found new evidence for his social philosophy, indicated his concern for the
state of religion, and spoken out to protect the community from the unregulated practice of medicine.

As Paterson's career developed, as he rose to high public office, and as
his associations with the rich and powerful widened, different forces came
to influence his social perspectives and political decisions—his defense
of lawyers is a good example. As he went on through the several phases
of his public life, however, there was a recurring dichotomy in the positions
he took on certain issues, especially those that admitted to a moral interpretation. This dichotomy can best be understood in terms of his early involvement with evangelical Christianity.

Finally, Paterson's confidence in his own abilities to lead men had
developed to the point that, in 1775 and 1776, when the Revolution
brought opportunities to his doorstep, he might accept them. It is difficult
to comprehend the personality of this self-effacing but ambitious young man
who chose to sit back where the action wasn't and wait for clients and
status to seek him out. He stated this sentiment most clearly in a 1773
letter to MacPherson: "Business, especially in the law way, seldom is
[great] at first: it increases little by little: its progress is slow and gradual.
. . . Have patience," he counseled his friend, "the Prospect will brighten
as you advance in Life."[78] This exceptionally tranquil, almost passive, attitude toward the growth of his practice supports the assumption that young
Paterson set his career objectives quite modestly. What is especially significant is the way the American Revolution propelled this country lawyer
into roles that he could never have expected, and that such a talented but
insecure and retiring young man was able to fulfill those responsibilities
as well as he did.

PART II

THE CONSERVATIVE DILEMMA AND THE AMERICAN REVOLUTION

By the time the war for independence had reached New Jersey, Paterson's personal revolution—his projection of himself into the local leadership elite—had already begun. During years of studying law and patiently waiting for his professional career to bear fruit, he had never questioned the conservative moral and social philosophy that he had adopted from the start.

As the Revolution approached, Paterson consolidated his basic beliefs into an attack on the political corruption and moral licentiousness of British society. He feared a war for independence and a change in the authority of government because of the tremendous social and political dislocation that might arise. Social distinctions might be confused, and the old assumptions of deference confounded while chaos prevailed. But Paterson feared even more the moral degeneracy and political decline that he considered inevitable if America remained tied to the corrupting influence of Great Britain. Here then was the dilemma that turned a conservative into a revolutionary.

Although he was ideologically prepared to support independence, Paterson could not forget the realities of his situation. He was still preening

45

himself for the future. For fear of casting himself as a troublemaker, he refrained from active participation in the movement until after Lexington and Concord, when even the most respectable social leaders could be found speaking out against the Empire. Once elected to represent his county in the revolutionary government, however, Paterson's support was genuine. Serving as a delegate and as secretary in all but one session of the several pre-Revolutionary provincial congresses, Paterson took part in the agonizing decision for independence. Essentially, shrinking alternatives finally left Paterson and his colleagues with nothing to do but allow themselves to be enslaved by the corrupt and degenerate British or make the break.

Paterson's experience forces us to consider some of the subtleties that historians must consider in drawing broad generalizations about historical causation. The "progressive" historians of several decades ago would have discounted Paterson's ideological pronouncements—as they did all revolutionary rhetoric—as simple propaganda, a false front to cover dreams of self-aggrandizement. In a 1950 article in the *William and Mary Quarterly,* Richard Haskett offered convincing support for this generally accepted interpretation, especially where Paterson was concerned. Although Haskett admitted in a footnote that he could not be sure of Paterson's real motives in supporting the Revolution, he ignored evidence of the young lawyer's ideological commitment and clearly suggested that Paterson took the risks associated with revolution primarily for the private profits to be gained: "He could gamble his own future on the success of the Revolution and prosecute both in the name of patriotism." Haskett is very effective in analyzing the ways in which Paterson's career and fortune did benefit as a side effect of the Revolution, but it is at the very least questionable to infer a man's motives from the outcome of events.

The more recent "neo-Whig" school has taught us that ideas expressed in the rush of events should not be casually dismissed in the search for more purely material motives. But their suggested alternative framework for interpretation is not entirely satisfactory either. Paterson's ideas do seem to reflect the dominant ideological perspective of the American intellectual elite. He fully perceived the threats to the balanced constitution; he eventually justified independence as a way of preserving the political and moral virtues of America from British corruption; he desperately feared the unsettling influence of designing men who would not hesitate to pervert the best interests of society for their own selfish motives. And yet, if we give any weight to Haskett's evidence, Paterson himself seems to be a prime example of this self-serving type.

The apparent paradox can be explained only when we remember that while by 1775 Paterson had not yet received any real professional recognition, he had spent more than a decade laying the foundations for future success. Those years of social climbing, legal training, and community service were precisely the prerequisites for a man like Paterson to be accepted among the traditional colonial elite—an acceptance that came, ironically, just at the time when the old elite was being split by the Revolution. A young man in Paterson's position could not disregard the influence his actions would have on his professional reputation. Therefore he delayed any public display of support for independence until the outspoken opinions of others made it safe. He justified the seizing of opportunities that revolutionary leadership and public office brought his way without stopping to consider those actions as comparable to the schemes of the social levellers whom he so openly criticized. Paterson's personal ambitions cannot be set aside in trying to assess his motives in 1775 and 1776, but neither can his ideas. His justification of the Revolution was made in ideological terms that he had begun to develop in college more than a decade before, and he would persist in his devotion to those same ideas as long as he lived. He must have meant much of what he had to say. Moreover, when these terms are understood in context—the frame of reference shared by New Jersey citizens in 1776—one can see how his ideas must have made sense at the time. It was this unusual combination of a developing personal career and an emerging rationale for independence that led Paterson to voice the traditional and conservative ideology of the old elite at the very time he rose to leadership in the Revolution. The fact that he benefitted personally from holding high public office should be no surprise. Neither should it be taken as an indication that he preferred his own interests to those of the public he served.

During the war, Paterson's duty as attorney general of New Jersey was to preserve as much order and stability as possible in the chaos of revolt. He devoted himself to the task with a passion and succeeded in revitalizing the effectiveness of the traditional system of county government. By the end of the war, when he was ready to resign from public office and return to full-time law practice, Paterson's dreams for financial security and social respectability had been realized. To the extent that it cleared the field of some of Paterson's major competitors, increased the general volume of legal business, and made Paterson the best-known lawyer in the state, he owed much of his success to the American Revolution. To the extent that a total disintegration of society and government had been avoided during the years of revolt, New Jersey in turn owed a great deal to William Paterson.

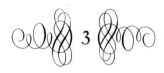

The Ideological Origins
of the Revolution in New Jersey

The moralistic social and political philosophy that Paterson drew from his Princeton education eventually drove him into a leadership role in the politics of independence. Unlike some of his colleagues in the councils of rebellion who tended to support the colonial cause as a way to break down the economic and social barriers of the old colonial elite, Paterson was moved more by his conservative ideas about the nature of a virtuous society and his desire to see them played out in America.

This view represents a new interpretation of Paterson's political perspective. Only a few years ago he was described as "more of a thorough-going radical than many of his fellows" in New Jersey's revolutionary leadership. By illustrating the dramatic way in which Paterson's career blossomed during the war years—overlooking his conservative social and political philosophy, and stressing the ways in which his public office benefitted his private fortunes—Richard Haskett made Paterson appear to be an opportunist seeking fame and fortune with little if any regard for the well-being of society. As Haskett told the story, Paterson even ignored the call to join the Continental Congress because he selfishly wanted to continue to feather his own nest.[1]

But Paterson was no mere opportunist. He was moved more by his conscience than by his pocketbook. A careful study of his personal and public papers suggests that the single most important element in his personality, and the factor that dominated his outlook on the American Revolution, was his deeply conservative political and social philosophy. He was well aware of the radical changes that could result from the Revolution, and he may have realized that such changes could be turned to his personal advantage, but the philosophy that allowed him to support the revolt and the spirit that drove him on to see it succeed was, paradoxically, a desire to keep things the same. In his own day the British or American Tories would have properly called him a revolutionary because of his stance against the royal establishment. But Paterson believed firmly in the deferential political system that had evolved in the American colonies. He cherished the society in which each man knew his place and in which an individual's upward mobility was a process of traditional education, moral self-discipline, and support for established social and political institutions. His scrupulously thought-out decision to support the movement for independence was made only after he became convinced that what he saw as the stable, orderly, and morally upright society of the colonies was more threatened by continuing as a part of the British Empire than it would be by the political confusion and social dislocation that would invariably accompany a revolutionary war.

Before 1775 Paterson had paid little attention to practical politics. While he was a legal apprentice, his teacher and friend Richard Stockton had played an influential role in opposition to the Stamp Act, but there is no evidence that Paterson became involved.[2] He wrote John MacPherson with regrets that he had not been with him in Philadelphia to witness a protest rally against the Townshend duties. But in fact he had no great concern for the issues involved; he only wished he had been able to hear a mutual friend "play the orator."[3] In another letter to MacPherson, Paterson did voice some opposition to the establishment of an American Episcopate, and he feared that the dissenters in America might be too disorganized to prevent it. But he was not very concerned, because "in the colonies," he explained, "few of the Church of England, except those who are stiled High Fliers, espouse the cause."[4] In all his writings until 1774 or 1775, allusions to American politics were exceedingly rare.

Paterson did not seem to be moved by economic problems either. The most serious economic problem in New Jersey during the decade before 1775 was the plight of the debtor, made worse by the British refusal to approve an issue of paper money in the colony. Although what little business Paterson had consisted of creditors seeking repayment of overdue debts, his reaction to the debtors was much more emotional and strident than one might expect from a man merely defending the interests of his clients. He railed against the debt-ridden farmers, claiming that their poverty was due more to their own "high living, riot or sensuality" than to any policy of Parliament.[5] As described in Chapter 2, his father was almost completely wiped out by his creditors in 1775 because a shortage of currency had made normal repayment impossible. But even this did not alter Paterson's critical view of debtors. There was no evidence that he was thinking of protecting the interests of business enterprise as the Revolution approached. Before the fighting began, he gave up all interest in the family business to concentrate on his official government duties.

The one selfish motive that might have influenced his decision was the recognition he could expect to gain from speaking out on important issues— as he had done before in defense of lawyers and in criticism of poorly trained doctors. The more secure his reputation grew as an outspoken and even-tempered community leader, the better his chances became for social status and professional success. By this time Paterson must have been impatient for success, but there is no reason to believe he could have foreseen the opportunities the Revolution would bring him.[6]

Substantially unmoved by the practical political issues and economic problems that drove others to the brink of revolt, Paterson became instead one of the prime spokesmen for the ideological origins of the Revolution in New Jersey. The philosophy he espoused proved to be the perfect ideological expression of his personal aspirations, but it was considerably more than propaganda or a simple cover for selfish interests. As the pressure of events that developed out of the Boston Tea Party propelled the colony toward rebellion, Paterson began to draw together the maxims of history and moral philosophy to which he had subscribed since his first years at the College of New Jersey and fashioned from them a rationale for the Revolution based more on abstract and spiritual principles than on political or economic interests.

The intellectual sources of this ideological orientation toward the Revolution were natural elements in the education that Paterson and his contemporaries had received. First there were the lessons of Whig history that taught Englishmen to jealously defend the "balanced constitution." Maintaining a constant equilibrium among the forces in society assured that selfish interests could not corrupt the virtuous political system that Britain had slowly evolved since the time of Magna Carta.[7] Ancient history and the classics provided colonists with case studies of the rise and fall of nations, stories in which liberty and tyranny were always contending with one another. By studying the history and learning from past mistakes, colonial leaders hoped to avoid the unfortunate fate of their

political counterparts in ancient times.[8] Enlightenment rationalism was
another source of these ideas.[9] In trying to formulate a science of society
similar to the science of nature, the philosophers of the day proposed that
natural or fundamental laws, beyond the authority of any parliament,
should be the final arbiters in a society.[10] Finally there were moral and
religious ideas that served as a stimulus to revolution. Ever since the
beginnings of New England, puritanism had taught that God would show
his displeasure toward a society that allowed its orthodoxy to slip away.[11]
Now, especially after the Great Awakening, New Side ministers (like
those that taught at the College of New Jersey) hurled jeremiads against
the luxury and moral degeneracy of colonial society. The treacheries of
the imperial administration were seen as signals of divine disapproval.[12]

Although he had long remained aloof from the complex issues of the
Empire, some time before the spring of 1775, Paterson made his personal
determination to support the colonial cause and began to articulate his
philosophy. It is impossible to identify precisely when Paterson's "decision"
came, but he did leave, written in his own hand, the text of an "Address
on the Rise and Decline of Nations" in which he expounded his revolutionary cosmology. Although the specific audience to which he presented the
address is not known, the topics discussed and the tone of the discourse
place it near the outbreak of hostilities (1774–1775).

We know that he spoke most often before his brothers at the Cliosophic
Society, and, since the address at times takes on the rather didactic tone
he often assumed before them, it is probable that it was presented there.
Some of the sentiments Paterson expressed were not uncommon around
Princeton. The September 1775 commencement included a Latin oration
entitled *De Luxuria,* a speech on the nature and pernicious effects of
luxury, and a disquisition on "The Growth and Decline of Empires."[13]
But Paterson's address is extraordinary in that in its ten pages the lessons
of Whig history, the classics, and eighteenth-century rationalism are all
woven together into a single argument that at times takes on the spirit of
a Calvinistic jeremiad. In the address, Paterson shows how even some of
the provincial issues of the preceding decade, which of themselves would
never have led to rebellion, contributed to the attitudes and emotions of
1776. It remains the fullest exposition that can be found of the ideological
origins of the Revolution in New Jersey.

"The rise and fall of empires compose the most curious and interesting
part of history," Paterson began. Moralists characteristically concentrate
on why things fall apart, and Paterson was far more interested in the
collapse of empires than he was in their beginnings. Like the writers of
ancient Greece and Rome, who dealt in idle fictions and "preposterous

fables" about the origins of their own states, writers who described the early history of England through the "traditions of the vulgar, the songs of the druids, the fables of canonized monks" were unworthy of regard. Every legend, "however groundless, that tended to please national vanity was dwelt upon with rapture," and even accounts that were at first "founded in truth were so worked up and coloured by the pencil of fiction" that they were now useless to the critical observer. "They may aid the flights of the poet," Paterson continued, but they "degrade the dignity of the historian; they may decorate the pages of the former, but they debase those of the latter."[14]

With a characteristic blend of rationalism and protestantism, Paterson turned to the decline of empires: "Though the existence of a state cannot be prolonged beyond the decree of heaven, yet its dissolution may in general be accounted for by natural means." Subscribing to the organic theory of politics then in vogue, he explained that the causes of decline were inherent in every state.

> Physicians tell us, that from our birth there is some peccant humour in the body, which gradually increases, and at length brings on its dissolution: so in the body politick; the principles of death are interwoven in the very frame and texture of every political establishment.

Invariably some "dead-doing principle" would creep in without the early symptoms being recognized to secretly debilitate and eventually destroy the government. And still worse, whenever a nation reached its crisis stage, "men of a pestilential turn" always arose to satisfy their own interests and "urge on the ruin" of the nation as a whole: "Like vultures they hover, to prey upon and devour it."

To illustrate his point, Paterson turned to the example of Great Britain and to a defense of the British constitution. In a limited monarchy like that of Great Britain, he explained, the way to keep the internal elements of destruction from taking over was to preserve the balance of the constitution and "not to suffer the smallest encroachment, as it will be an inlet to tyranny." He attacked in no uncertain terms the "shallow politicians and pretending patriots" who clamored about maintaining "the balance of power among neighboring and independent states," but at the same time struggled to destroy the balance within the state for their own objectives. It made no difference to him whether the balance was upset in order to increase the privileges of the king or those of the people, for "the first introduces despotism and the latter anarchy, which generally ends in the tyranny of a single person." Paterson propounded as eternal truth that all faction tends to tyranny; history evinces, that, whichsoever party prevail, the people are sure to be oppressed . . . [because] every party does more or less take humour, prejudice and passion for principle, and therefore the interest of a party and that of a state is for the most part totally different.

Totally detestable, then, "were those princes and men, who espouse or create a party in order to disunite the people." "Princes of this cast" could be found in the experiences of modern nations as well as in the annals of ancient history. They "always have some iniquitous scheme in view: They hope perhaps amidst the shock of contending parties to effect what otherwise they could not." This is an unmistakable reference to George III and his alleged attempts to buy the support of a party in Parliament and subvert the constitution.

The elucidation of this theme brought Paterson to the body of his address and to the explanation that the first "mark of declension" within a state occurs when

grievances though complained of and abuses though petitioned against, remain unredressed; when public defaulters, though accused, and ministers, though impeached, pass unchastized and even unnoticed.

A case such as this was an indication that one party had become so powerful that it "may deviate most grossly from the known rule of law, and make the most terrible inroads upon the constitution with impunity." In the tradition of Whig politics, Paterson saw it as the responsibility of the people to remain extremely vigilant and, by petitioning and using the press or whatever means necessary, "to restrain those in power . . . and in general to make them walk in the track prescribed by law."

Jerseymen did not have to look far to find examples of the failure of the imperial administration to consider seriously their petitions and grievances. Their petitions against the Stamp Act had been answered only after considerable and often violent agitation, and their resolves and protests against the Townshend duties (New Jersey upheld nonimportation until both New York and Philadelphia had faltered in their resolve) had been at least partially successful. But on the matter that most directly affected New Jersey's economy—the ban on paper money laws—the British had refused to budge. Although in the 1780s Paterson became one of the most outspoken critics of paper money, we have no indication of his stance before 1776, and he did not specifically mention this issue in his address. Still, for most Jerseymen this was perhaps the clearest illustration of his charge of

British unresponsiveness to American needs. When a 1768 loan office bill, passed by the New Jersey assembly with considerable pressure from the countryside, was disallowed by the British because of its legal tender provision, the act was rewritten to require that the certificates would only have to be accepted in payments of debts at the loan office that issued them. But the British Privy Council disallowed even that provision (although they had approved similar formulas for Maryland and Pennsylvania). To Jerseymen, the Privy Council's action was seen as so senseless and arbitrary that even Governor Franklin wrote Secretary Hillsborough to complain of its unreasonableness.[15] In 1770 the assembly tried to bring pressure by refusing to arrange for the provisioning of the king's troops. This method had worked for New York, but now Hillsborough held firm and eventually had the troops removed from New Jersey rather than give in to the colony's pressure. Finally, in 1775, faced with the rising storm of rebellion, the London government did consent to a £100,000 issue of New Jersey bills of credit,[16] but by that time British intransigence on an issue so crucial to Jersey farmers and debtors had already poisoned their feelings toward Britain.

In his address, Paterson severely criticized ministers who broke in upon the constitution in even trifling ways

> to serve a present expedient, or to supply a present exigency. . . .
> They do it perhaps to procure ease and quiet from some pressing disturbance, perhaps to rid themselves of an instant perplexity, or to allay the tumult and clamour of a vexatious and unreasonable populace.

But once a decision is made to breach the constitution, "one encroachment naturally leads to another, till at length the civil establishment is wholly overthrown."

Evil and designing ministers could advance their schemes only if the public let down its guard. Paterson himself underscored this key notion: "*Slavery is generally preceded by sleep.* All history confirms, that times of imaginary security are commonly times of the greatest danger." He thought that nations like Britain that "hath freedom to lose" should be especially vigilant, and he seemed to chastize his countrymen who were less concerned about the activities of their king and his ministers as he emphasized the "appearance of fatality when a people are at ease and thoughtless, inattentive to the conduct of their rulers, and sunk, as it were, into langour, and a state of insuperable lethargy." Paterson described how an artful prince, abetted by a set of obsequious dependents, generally prepossesses the people in his favor, and does everything in his power to beguile them into a belief of their security, and indeed fairly to lay them asleep. His first acts of oppression wear the semblance of law; he breaks in upon their privileges little by little, and is extremely cautious to clothe everything he does in the venerable garb of legal authority. . . . Danger is then imminent when the appearance of justice is maintained. The form of law is made use of merely to destroy the substance.

George III had proudly proclaimed himself a constitutional monarch, but, in Paterson's eyes, he was notorious for using Parliament to achieve his personal ends.[17]

Some years before, in trying to dramatize the dangers of unregulated medical practice, Paterson had imagined a doctors' conspiracy to spread smallpox intentionally.[18] Now he was completely serious in hypothesizing the premeditated "design" (the term used in the Declaration of Independence), carried out over a number of years, to lay low the British constitution. Any threat to the constitution was in Paterson's view a serious challenge to the well-being of the nation. Ordinarily, when the oppression was undisguised, it "shocked the public eye" into recognizing the danger. If, however, the menace was hidden so that the people continued in "imagined security," the peril was much greater. The belief that an intrigue against the constitution was being perpetrated in the highest circles of the British government was not an uncommon one in the 1770s.[19] But Paterson's suggestion that an indication of the existence of conspiracy was the absence of any real evidence for one was a fantastic piece of circuitous reasoning.

Putting aside constitutional questions, Paterson's address proceeded to consider several lessons of social and political philosophy that could also help to explain the decline of great nations. Among them were the ill effects of standing armies, the unequal distribution of wealth, the multiplicity of laws, and the domestic effects of foreign wars.

It was a most deadly symptom of decline when "a standing army is kept up in times of profoundest peace." Paterson must have been aware of the inconveniences caused by the British practice of quartering troops among the people. His boyhood village of Princeton, halfway between the two larger towns of Trenton and New Brunswick on the main road from Philadelphia to New York, was regularly called on to quarter troops. Petitions of the time indicate that citizens had complained bitterly when "families with not more than one room: were required to entertain some-times ten, twelve or fifteen soldiers."[20] But in 1758 barracks were built in several locations around the province, and the citizens were no longer in-convenienced. In fact, the presence of these barracks often brought money into the community, so that in New Jersey the quartering of troops might be seen as more of an economic windfall than a hardship.[21] There were a few instances of soldiers brawling with each other or damaging property, but nothing comparable to the troubles in Massachusetts. In fact, when the regiment that was primarily responsible for the massacre in Boston was transferred to New Jersey, the troops were accepted like any others and were commended for their behavior when they moved on in 1771.[22]

Even though the presence of British troops caused no real hardship for New Jersey in the 1760s and 1770s, Paterson feared a standing army as a matter of principle. "Were the present race of Britons like their ancestors of old, or the ancient Romans," he explained, "a standing army would not wear so terrible an aspect." In old England as in the early Roman Republic, only citizens with property had been allowed to become soldiers, so that they would be more likely to fight for glory or the public good than for selfish gain. However, soldiery was now the province of "mer-cenaries and hired troops," and Paterson warned of the consequences.

When the mass of common soldiers are made up of persons of no property, and profligate manners, and abandoned principles; when too they conceive themselves as a distinct body within a state, and look upon the interests of the people as opposed to their own; who can think of so mercenary or graceless a crew in any other light than as tools of oppression, and instruments in the hands of an enterprising spirit to work out the ruin of a state?

Next in his catalogue of "dead-doing principles" Paterson listed an unequal distribution of wealth. "The excessive opulence of some and extreme poverty of others" encouraged "perpetual clamour and discord." Classical examples again provided evidence to support his view: "A com-munity of goods was established at Sparta, and an equal distribution of land at Rome." The result had been "sufficient to make a nation happy, powerful and great." Every individual defended the nation with equal vigor "as the interest of every individual was seen as the same." At first glance this position may appear not to fit the upwardly mobile young attorney who had defended his wealthy colleagues at the bar against the public outcry of poor debtors. But these ideas were typical of many of his

New Side friends who showed a deep concern over the disparity of wealth in the society around them. Evangelical leaders had always cautioned against the avaricious attitudes necessary for the acquisition and preservation of great fortunes. Men of moderate means were thought more likely to give proper attention to the service of God. Charges that the Calvinists sought to level the differences in society were not uncommon. Some went so far as to suggest that a return to orthodox Christianity might include a divestiture of worldly possessions. In 1777, Abraham Keletas, a New Jersey evangelist transplanted to Massachusetts, preached that selfish accumulation of property was

> a shameful reverse of the example of the primitive Christians at Jerusalem, who sold their estates, and distributed the money arising from the sales, to supply the wants of their distressed brethren. All that believed (says the sacred Historian) had all things [in] common, and sold their possessions and goods, and parted them to all men, as every man had need.[23]

There was indeed a considerable social and economic distance between the rich and the poor in the colonies, and, instead of getting better, the situation was becoming more stratified. Eighteenth-century observers who warned of a growing tendency for the rich and the poor progressively to outnumber those of "middling wealth" were substantially correct. There seemed to be a mad scramble for the marks of social respectability, which was heightened by the realization that, as provincial society became more complex, the avenues of upward social mobility were increasingly difficult to traverse. Paterson had shown an avid interest in bettering his own social position. He ingratiated himself with certain college friends on the likelihood of their later rise to high station and adopted a superior air of mature sobriety toward the more flamboyant fun-seekers among his college contemporaries. But he also detested "solemn fops," "coxcombs," and other pretenders to social superiority whenever he saw them around him. This apparent paradox was common to many of Paterson's contemporaries.[24] It suggests that, even before the Revolution, some people were disquieted by the ambiguous doctrine of equality that has perennially plagued American idealists.

Paterson was not worried about wealth for its own sake. Wealth, after all, simply enabled men to educate themselves better for public service. He had noted in his college commonplace book years before that "knowledge and virtue, and a more eminent degree of service to God and man, ought to be the distinctive character of the rich and the great."[25] But society would benefit, he thought, if no individual was so rich and powerful or so poor and defenseless that the temptation might arise to prefer self-interest to the public good. "An immoderate desire of gain," he claimed in his address, led to a situation in which "patriotism, one of the most noble of affections, gradually declines, and at last wholly dies away." As Paterson saw it, when men who were interested primarily in personal wealth were fortunate to find that "the public good happens to run in with the spirit of selfishness, then indeed they assume the garb of patriotism, and are uncommonly active and clamorous, zealous and violent." But if personal and public interest come into competition, "then the happiness of the nation is wholly disregarded."

Another token of decline was the

> multiplicity of laws . . . [which] swelled to an enormous bulk, and multiplied to an almost endless variety have a natural tendency to elude justice, introduce chicanery, and keep up a spirit of contention. . . . When laws are too numerous or complicated, or, if they do not err on this score, too vague and obscure, a spirit of litigation will seize upon every class of people, and render life vexatious and troublesome.

America was renowned for its spirit of litigation, and some citizens of New Jersey had more than once blamed attorneys who used the intricacies of the law to increase their fees and unnecessarily harass unfortunate debtors. Paterson had defended lawyers against these charges, and one of his most fruitful enterprises in the years following the Revolution would be his updating, systematizing, and simplifying of the laws of New Jersey.[26] But responsible lawyers and revised legal codes notwithstanding, the state would suffer immeasurably if the offices of public trust were not filled with men of integrity and unimpeachable public-mindedness.

Finally, war could presage the internal degeneracy of the nation in a number of ways. If nations, he wrote,

> take up arms, (which at times is inevitable,) it should be on the best motives, and for the justest cause. For war however successfully carried on insensibly exhausts a nation, and endangers its destruction: war interrupts the course of trade, depopulates the country, relaxes the force of laws, and what is still worse, imperceptibly brings on corruption of manners.

Moving from these general propositions to the specific example of Britain, Paterson related some of the recent difficulties that had been faced by the colonies as a result of the mother country's penchant for war.

> A rapid succession of expensive wars, arising chiefly from continental connections, has, within less than a century, begot in the British government a new mischief of a terrible aspect. The national debt, the unhappy consequence of long and chargeable wars, is now swelled to an enormous sum, and must fill every breast with the most alarming apprehensions. Already its effects are severely felt; trade is burdened with heavy imposts, and taxes of every kind surprisingly increase. Look forward and a prospect still more dreadful opens to view.

As Paterson saw it, the debt was too great for there to be any hope of paying it off—national bankruptcy was inevitable. Disgrace, confusion, dissension, and ruin would be the result. The future for Britain seemed to offer little hope, but Paterson was reserving his most despairing predictions.

His address had been forceful and animated from the beginning, but he had saved the best for last. The final third of Paterson's address was devoted to an emotional, sermonlike discourse on "luxury and corruption of manners." As historical evidence for his argument, Paterson opened with a comment on how the "doctrines of Epicurus had pernicious influence on the genius and morals of the people towards the close of the Roman republick; and perhaps tended not a little to precipitate its fall." Important as luxury and corruption were to Paterson as signals of societal catastrophe, he was painfully aware that not everyone agreed with him, or rather with the rigorous protestantism on which some of his ideas were based. There were those rationalist cynics who could not perceive the moral dimensions of their own society. "It may not be amiss to observe," he wrote,

> that in our own country the tribe of deists, free-thinkers, etc. have conduced mightily to bring on corruption and dissoluteness of manners. What indeed can be expected from a set of men, who look upon virtue as romantick or nominal, and zeal for religion as superstitious or idle?

He then launched into a tirade against the evil effects of luxury.

> Luxury effeminates and torments the opulent, and tempts the indigent, who are destitute of the means of pleasure, to acquire them

by fraud and violence. Luxury turns the brave to cowards, and the industrious to thieves. Luxury begets profusion, profusion begets want, and want begets venality and dependence. A general depravity of manners is the necessary consequence of unbounded opulence, which poisons every rank in life and generally proves the bane of affluent states. The most chargeable superfluities are considered as the necessaries of life; these grow upon us every hour, and people now-a-days cannot subsist without articles, which a few years ago were wholly unknown.

Although luxury was "dressed up as a virtue" and given names such as "taste, elegance, politeness, fashion," Paterson was convinced of its sinfulness. In the tone of an evangelical preacher, he attacked the "contagion" that was, in a "soft and imperceptible" way, infecting the people. At the beginning "smooth and flowery," luxury and voluptuousness lull men so that "nothing is listened to but the musick of adulation and the song of pleasure." Conscience and reflection had been silenced "in the roar of obstreporous jollity." He could only hope for a rebirth of conscience, which "breaks in upon the hour of mirth, dashes the brightest joys with sorrow, and pours poison in the bowl of sensuality."

Luxury and moral degeneracy were related to each of the other marks of decline of which he had spoken. One reason for fear of a standing army had been the fear of luxury and voluptuousness in the military.[27] Temptations of a luxurious life were what led public officials down the paths of corruption. The "insuperable lethargy" he had noted before could be tied to the "enfeebling lull" of luxury.

These ideas were not new to Paterson; his education at Princeton had been intended to inculcate such notions. A few years earlier, when Princeton's President Witherspoon had addressed the people of the West Indies in search of students and financial support for the school, he had stressed the importance of a "prudent education," especially for "children of persons in the higher ranks of life." Wealth subjected young men to "dangerous temptation," and they had to be taught the virtues befitting those destined for public service, "the abhorrence of low riot and contempt for brutal conversation." Witherspoon had argued that the college in the countryside of New Jersey was much better suited to achieve this goal than schools in Britain, where "a constant succession and variety of intoxicating amusements, such as Balls, Concerts, Plays, Races, and others" might encourage unwholesome desires.[28]

While Paterson was not entirely immune to the frivolities that college

life offered, he had been careful to keep them under control, and he subscribed fully to the proscription of luxury. At one point in the address, he
borrowed the language of a talk "On Musick," which he had prepared
several years earlier.[29]

> Luxury lures from the path of duty, and beguiles into vice; luxury
> taints the morals, and vitiates the manners, sinks into weakness and
> effeminate softness. Luxury [like music] lulls only to enfeeble,
> soothes only to unnerve, and Circe-like, turns men into brutes.

Even "persons virtuously inclined . . . unable to resist the torrent, suffer
it gently to waft them along" on the path of degeneracy. Paterson was
insistent that this was "no imaginary description" and suggested that his
listeners look around them for the incontrovertible evidence.

> Lo! what splendid edifices, what costly furniture, what magnificent
> apparel, what voluptuous festivity, what luxurious banquets! The
> enfeebling lull of musick, sprightly dances, gay gardens, splendid
> theatres, gilded baths, intoxicating masquerades, luxuriant tables, and
> publick gaming houses are now looked upon as innocent and even
> necessary gratifications. How often are fortunes dissipated, and health
> impaired in loose festivity, and luxurious enjoyments? The ladies too
> have their amusements, their melles [parties], their visiting-days, their
> hurricanes. Day is turned into night, and night into day; all is mirth
> and sport and dissipation; all distinctions are lost, and all conditions
> are confounded. What rapid progress hath luxury made even in these
> infant colonies?

Writing in 1778, David Ramsey concluded in his *Oration on the Advantages of American Independence* that, were it not for the Revolution,
"our frugality, industry, and simplicity of manners, would have been lost
in an imitation of British extravagance, idleness and false refinements."[30]
But months before independence was even seriously considered, Paterson
had been able in his address to identify and trace the origins of America's
new and dangerously demoralizing tastes.

> We tread close upon the heels of our brethren in Britain; we imitate
> them in dress, in manners, in equipage, in riot, in voluptuousness, in
> every softening pleasure and degrading vice. Infatuated Americans!

so swiftly to lay hold of every luxurious habit, and so eagerly to lick up every foreign and pernicious vice. Where now is that simplicity in manners and in dress more enchanting far than the false glitter and borrowed refinements?

This intriguing, if exaggerated, picture of colonial society in the years before 1776 was not the meaningless flight of a disordered mind. Paterson's intellect was widely respected, and his capacity for practical and effective leadership would soon be proven. Those who shared Paterson's fears could point to more than a few historical precedents. If they associated luxury with the more wealthy elements of American society, as did Paterson, they would have feared with him the increasing polarization of the American economic spectrum. There was a likelihood that luxury would breed more luxury, but the most frightening possibility derived from the proposal to establish in the colonies a nobility on the Old World model.

Even before the Stamp Act crisis, Governor Bernard of Massachusetts had suggested to friends in England that a formal nobility should be established in America. It seemed to Bernard and others that the creation of some titled aristocrats in America would be the only practical way to give the upper houses of the provincial legislatures the prestige they needed in the political climate of America where so much popular attention was paid to the lower houses.[31] In New Jersey, too, there were problems that brought to mind the most galling practices of feudal nobles. A controversy raged in the *Pennsylvania Gazette* in January and February 1770, following the publication of a letter by a Jersey farmer. The letter complained of the damages caused by Philadelphia's "haughty gentry" who trampled the fields of farmers while fox hunting.[32] As late as 1775, Sir John Dalrymple wrote his *Address of the People of England to the Inhabitants of America* in order to soothe Americans who felt the English "assumed airs of superiority." Dalrymple insisted that every honor of England was open to Americans and suggested that [the British] would be happy to see you ask the establishment of a Nobility, and of ranks among yourselves."[33]

Paterson believed that certain men, usually well-educated and well-to-do men, were better qualified than others to lead society. But the deference he thought should be shown to members of this natural aristocracy was far different from the unnatural deference demanded by a formal nobility. Paterson had already listed the unequal distribution of wealth as a sign of social weakness. To translate the de facto aristocracy of wealth in the colonies into a formal nobility of the European kind would undermine any chances America had to achieve its full potential as a virtuous society.

In the words of one recent scholar, "Americans were repeatedly told that they represented the last outpost of English freedom, that they were the last sentinels of English virtue."[34] The idea that America was a "city upon a hill" with a peculiar opportunity to achieve as near as possible political and social perfection had come with the earliest Puritan colonists. Paterson was capable of similar utopian sentiments. Summoning up the picture of a pastoral arcadia where simple virtues persistently triumphed over scheming self-interest and corruption, Paterson seemed to look forward to the Jeffersonian image of a society of yeoman farmers whose very simplicity and lack of social pretension were marks of their own integrity and the nation's virtue. America was thought to have a unique opportunity to carry these dreams into reality. Europeans looked on the inhabitants of America as living in close approximation to a state of nature, uncorrupted by social or political contrivances as entrenched as their own. But now it seemed to many Americans that the evils were rapidly increasing, and worse still, they seemed to be abetted by a British conspiracy to spread immorality and aristocracy across the Atlantic. The view of America as a "city upon a hill" may have indeed encouraged the idea of a conspiracy against it. The English connection had been good—it had after all given them the blessings of the British Constitution—but now that constitution was being destroyed. It appeared to many Americans that if they had any hope of achieving their virtuous utopia, they must break with the British, who were too far gone for thorough redemption.[35]

Paterson then asked his audience a series of rhetorical questions.

Is not a nation far gone in luxury and on the verge of ruin, when places [in Parliament] are made merchandise and merely bought and sold, when most things are carried by a bare majority often procured by little arts, when electors "give up their dirty souls for pay," and when in short corruption is reduced to a system? Is not a nation far gone in luxury, when crowds of prostitutes set themselves up for sale, when the land swarms with spies and parasites and sychophants, when nothing is sought for but wealth to sate avarice, and titles to sate vanity? Is it not an evident token of degeneracy and mark of declension, when pensions are bestowed undeservedly, and taxes multiplied unnecessarily, merely to keep up a number of obsequious dependents, or a legion of rascally tax-gatherers? When trade is fettered with severe restrictions, when the people groan under an enormous national debt, when selfishness, venality, and licentiousness universally prevail, is not the prospect terrible, has it not an appearance of fatality?

Time was short and becoming shorter, for "swarms of pensionary vultures are hourly increasing, and prey upon the vitals of the Constitution." For them all things were "base and venal," and "so far from having the *virtues,* they have not even the *vices* of great men."

To conclude, he turned again to the ancient past to "let Rome, let Athens, let Sparta speak." The same sort of luxury and corruption had helped Cyrus to conquer the Assyrians, given Persia to Alexander, and enabled "Atilla, with his tribe of undisciplined barbarians, to lay the western empire" low. "Caesar mounted on luxury, triumphed over the liberties of his country, poured desolation, like a rapid torrent, over half the globe, and swam in Roman blood." In ringing tones, Paterson assured his fellow Americans that, ideologically at least, the odds were on their side: "All history declares, that the dissolute, the voluptuous, and effeminate have ever been subdued by the hardy, the temperate and the brave."

The perspective on events that Paterson assumed, colored as it was by his conservative and moralistic social philosophy, suggests one possible solution to a perplexing problem in the history of the revolutionary period. The trend in recent historical scholarship has been to suggest that New Jersey had no direct interest in the issues of the Empire and that therefore its citizens were among the most reluctant of the revolutionaries. It has been pointed out that, with no staple product, no major ocean ports, and no frontier, this primarily agricultural colony felt the inconvenience of Parliament's legislation far less than others. There were so few Anglicans in New Jersey that there was no real threat of their seeking power, and there were no troubles with British troops as there had been in Massachusetts. The only real hardship felt by Jerseymen had to do with the shortage of currency, and on this point the British had finally given way. Although there was no physical oppression, it has been argued that by 1776 rural New Jersey had become so dependent on New York and Philadelphia that there was no alternative other than to go along with their decision for independence. It was, these historians assert, primarily "a matter of following the leaders."[36]

This new interpretation does help to answer the vexing question of why New Jersey approached the ultimate decision for independence with such hesitancy and trepidation. However, it fails to comprehend and adequately explain the intense ideological commitment shared by many of the state's revolutionary leaders. Are we to assume, to use the words of the Declaration of Independence, that New Jersey's leaders were willing to pledge "their lives, their fortunes, and their sacred honor" primarily to defend the interests of some merchants from Boston, Philadelphia, and New York? This seems quite unlikely.

The pattern of revolutionary ideas that emerges from Paterson's address, on the contrary, suggests that Jerseymen did not have to look beyond their borders to find reasons for revolt. Many of the issues were intellectual and constitutional ones that appealed to thinking men in all the colonies. Despite his residence in rural New Jersey, Paterson was no purely provincial localist. He may not have expected his own career to bring him more than local fame, but he was clearly capable of comprehending the scope of affairs beyond his neighborhood, and his responses to events as the Revolution neared bear this out. Even some of the less theoretical issues, which may on the surface seem to have had little relevance to Jerseymen, took on new meaning when conceived in the context of Paterson's broader view of the world. True, New Jersey had suffered no special inconvenience from the presence of British troops after 1763, but the generalized fear of standing armies that was supported by the warnings of Whig pamphleteers could have been very important in the minds of potential revolutionaries. There may only have been a thousand communicants of the Church of England in New Jersey in 1775, but if plans for an American Episcopate were seen as a contrivance for "high fliers" (as Paterson called them) to introduce new aristocratic institutions into the colonies, the issue might appear in an entirely new light. New Jersey may have been less capable of maintaining "a viable existence outside the British Empire—i.e., as an independent state" in 1776—than the more self-sufficient colonies like Massachusetts or Pennsylvania, which may help to explain the "reluctance, hesitancy and misgiving" some historians have found.[37] But there were other Jerseymen who had studied the annals of the ancients, applied classical lessons to the problems of their own day, and ultimately concluded that the colony could not remain connected to an empire that hourly became more corrupt. The decisions of colonial neighbors and the tangible issues of imperial politics and provincial economics were of undeniable significance, but Paterson shows that New Jersey's revolution had its home-grown ideological origins as well.[38]

Paterson's philosophy contained several elements that reflected the popular point of view assumed by some of his New Side friends and neighbors: his concern for the confused state of the laws (a more common complaint of antilawyer groups than of attorneys themselves) and the inequality of wealth (a situation feared by some Calvinists, a few of whom went so far as to preach the benefits of a communal system). These were sentiments that seemed to contradict his personal aspirations, but Paterson's commitment to the public good, a theme pervasive in the literature of the day, helps to explain such apparent inconsistencies.[39] Aspects of

Paterson's ideas on politics and morality, which at other times might appear clearly contradictory, combined readily in deciding for revolution.

The conviction traceable to Paterson's college experience, that only men of virtue could govern well, was the uniting theme that made his ideas on everything from ministerial conspiracy and parliamentary factionalism to luxury and dissipation hold together. What were needed were men of public virtue who would set personal interest aside for the well-being of the community and men of personal virtue who could withstand the temptations that accompanied wealth and power. For a devoted believer in the deferential system of colonial America to stand for an overthrow of the long-respected old order was indeed a difficult decision, but Paterson believed that deference had to be earned. To deserve the approbation of the people, a leader must live a life of virtue and patriotism. At all times, he must prefer the public good to the interests of party or faction, defend the sanctity of the constitution even to the extent of self-sacrifice, continually provide an example of good personal conduct, and otherwise help to maintain the community's moral standards. It was clear that some of those to whom colonial Americans had entrusted their political leadership had failed the public trust by allowing their decisions to be governed by the favors of the royal establishment and their selfish desire for a life of material luxury. It was equally clear to Paterson and, as events would soon prove, to many of his neighbors as well, that he did possess the community spirit and sturdy moral conscience necessary to hold the people's faith. He sought to preserve deference as a political principle by replacing venal and corrupt leaders with others like himself who more properly deserved the respect and fidelity of the people.[40]

Paterson's "Address on the Rise and Decline of Nations" has a tone far more militant and uncompromising than any of his earlier statements. The words have a frenzied, almost frantic quality that his letters, essays, and speeches had never had before and would seldom have again. He believed firmly in the ideas he presented, and he clearly realized where those ideas were likely to lead him. His anxiety arose from his desperate fear of revolution, which he was coming to see as inevitable. Paterson's conservatism was not the kind that might cause one to remain loyal to the monarchy in defense of his station. Conservative though he was, Paterson embraced the idea of a republic from the beginning. But, in the absence of greater dangers, a revolution simply to change from a limited monarchy to a republic would not be worth the risk. In 1776, however, the stakes would be higher. He knew that revolution would raise the dangers of social dislocation, civil war, looting and rioting in the streets, and, worst of all, an insidious erosion of the respect for the traditional and stable institutions of established authority, but that without it moral decline and social disintegration seemed inevitable. This was the dilemma that made a conservative into a revolutionary.

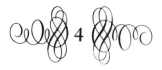

4

The Decision to Revolt

It seems ironic that a traditional and moralistic soul like William Paterson should receive his baptism in practical politics as a leader in a revolutionary war for independence. But if history weren't ironic at times, it wouldn't be as interesting. Paterson had made an eloquent intellectual commitment to protect America from the corrupting influence of Great Britain, but he had so far declined to participate actively in the protest movement. Although his ideological arguments presented a clear justification for American independence, a complete separation from Britain was an alternative he considered only when it was forced on him. Clinton Rossiter's description of a conservative eighteenth-century American Whig fits Paterson well: He was "an aristocratic, liberty-loving, lawmaking moderate rather than a democratic, equality-seeking, stability-shattering leveller."[1] It was the rush of events in the latest crisis of empire that so reduced the alternatives as to make independence the only acceptable path and to draw William Paterson into a position of leadership in the revolutionary movement. In taking on this new role, Paterson did not sacrifice his puritanical conservatism or his passion for stability and moral order. In fact, his role in the administration of revolutionary justice would later enable him to help New Jersey become a more virtuous society—or at least a more law-abiding one. Nonetheless, the decision for independence that Paterson and most of his colleagues eventually made was not the free choice of revolutionary patriots, but the grudging recognition that there was nothing else left to do.

The final deterioration of the imperial relationship began when news of the passage of the Boston Port Bill, one of the so-called Intolerable Acts, reached Massachusetts on May 10, 1774. Before three days had passed, the Boston town meeting had resolved to stop all import and export trade with England and the West Indies and directed Sam Adams so to inform the other colonies. In Virginia, after declaring June 1 (the day the port bill became effective), a "day of fasting, humiliation and prayer," the burgesses found their house dissolved by governor and council. Adjourning to Williamsburg's Raleigh Tavern, they resolved to boycott tea and to communicate with the committees of correspondence in the other colonies about calling a general congress. By August a convention of Virginians had vowed absolute nonimportation and an embargo on all exports to England (including tobacco) unless the grievances raised by the Intolerable Acts were soon redressed. But support for such uncompromising economic retaliation was not forthcoming from other colonies. In New York and Philadelphia, there was a considerable distrust of Boston's merchants and opposition to proposals for an embargo, and, in Boston itself, a large faction desired to settle their troubles by paying for the tea that the radicals had spilled into Boston harbor. Finally, Adams agreed to follow the suggestions for a congress that were coming from every corner of the colonies. In a locked chamber (so that the governor's order to dissolve could not be heard), the Massachusetts assembly selected delegates and set the date for the First Continental Congress in Philadelphia.[2]

New Jersey's colonial legislature had not been in session when news of the port bill and the other intolerable measures arrived. Mass meetings were held in eleven of New Jersey's thirteen counties to condemn the new British regulations and to vow support for beleaguered Boston. A colony-wide meeting at New Brunswick (July 21–23) chose a delegation to go to Philadelphia and selected a new provincial committee of correspondence.[3] While Jerseymen waited anxiously for news of the Continental Congress, many were brought closer to a feeling of involvement and intercolonial fidelity as they sent provisions for the relief of Boston, which was under a British blockade.[4] The Continental Congress met in September, and soon local watch committees and county committees of correspondence were springing up everywhere to enforce the continental association against trade with Britain that had been agreed on at Philadelphia.[5]

To this point, while the resistance to the Intolerable Acts was overwhelming, there as yet had been no serious talk of independence in New Jersey.[6] A few such as Jonathan Elmer, who later was Paterson's colleague in the Senate of the United States, were already speaking in terms of "slavery or independence."[7] But most Jerseymen, like Paterson, were still far from seeing things in such black-and-white terms. In fact, moderate and conservative colonists saw economic sanctions as peaceful alternatives to unwanted violence.[8] If Paterson played an active role in any of the mass meetings or organization of local committees, no evidence of it has survived. Paterson's only intimate experience with colonial protest had been during the popular clamor against lawyers in 1769, and, in that instance, he had described the protestors as a propertyless rabble unfairly rebuking an entire respectable profession for the sins of a few.[9] Such rabble were hardly the type of people he would now seek to associate with. He had never been very interested in extralegal resistance to imperial regulations, and even the events of the winter of 1774–1775 were not of a sort to draw him in. The current protest over Parliament's latest inequities had not gone much beyond the nonimportation agreements of a few years earlier. Moreover, Paterson now had a reputation to protect. Even if he had thought that this new turn in imperial affairs called for his active opposition to British rule, a young man trying to make a place for himself in New Jersey's established legal profession might ruin any chances for success if he were to be marked as a radical.

Along with other Jerseymen of mixed sentiments, Paterson was content to await the decisions of the Second Continental Congress scheduled for May 1775. But then the quiet Jersey springtime was shattered by the thunderclap from Lexington and Concord. Spontaneously, the local committees, which had been readying themselves for months, were galvanized into action.[10] Now moderates and conservatives who abhorred violence found their alternatives considerably reduced, while the radicals were reinforced in their beliefs. "Gunpowder is a great equalizer," observes Edmund S. Morgan, "and after the Americans had matched their muskets against the British, they were more confident than before in denying the authority of Parliament."[11]

Not knowing what to expect, local militia companies across the province put themselves in trim. In Paterson's Somerset County, a volunteer company was organized, and drilling became an everyday procedure.[12] In other areas of the colony, overzealous patriots had to be restrained from shedding the blood of local Tories or striking out aimlessly at symbols of British authority. On April 24, within hours after the news of Lexington and Concord reached Princeton, a meeting had produced a circular letter calling for an extralegal provincial congress to be held as soon as possible.

The proposal was well received, and the date was set for May 23. All eyes now turned to the meeting of this first full-fledged Provincial Congress within the colony.[13]

The flurry of political and military activity also moved William Paterson. He had previously written that standing armies represented "military vengeance" hanging "over the heads of the people, like a sword, that threatened them with extermination at a single blow."[14] Now that blow had been struck. There was no longer any need to worry about being singled out as a troublemaker. After April 1775, the number of prestigious men involved in colonial protest swelled continuously. Soon men as respected as Paterson's friend and teacher Richard Stockton and Princeton President John Witherspoon would be loudly demanding independence. When the freeholders of Somerset County met at the county courthouse on May 11, 1775, Paterson was among them. The meeting resolved

that the several steps taken by the British Ministry to enslave the American Colonies and especially the late alarming hostilities commenced by the Troops under General Gage against the inhabitants of Massachusetts Bay loudly call on the people of this Province to determine what part they will act in this situation of affairs.[15]

The part Paterson was to play was decided when, after an hour's adjournment, he was chosen by secret ballot to be one of Somerset's deputies to the upcoming Provincial Congress.[16]

Were it not for the extraordinary events going on around him, Paterson's introduction to practical politics might have been very different, but in this critical situation his was to be a baptism of fire. As the deputies began to queue up and present their credentials, it became clear that the Somerset delegation was among the largest and most influential.[17] Hendrick Fisher, chosen president of the assembly, and Jonathan Dickinson Sergeant, who became secretary, were both from Somerset. Sergeant, a lawyer, Princeton graduate, and member of the Cliosophic Society subsequently chose two other young Somerset attorneys with Princeton backgrounds to be his assistant secretaries. His nominees—his old college friend William Paterson and Frederick Frelinghuysen, the grandson of Raritan's famous revivalist—were promptly approved by the delegates.[18] A few days later, Sergeant stepped down from his post, and Paterson was moved up to take his place, leaving Frelinghuysen as the lone assistant.[19] The care with which Paterson had cultivated his friendships and groomed his reputation had been worthwhile. Before he could have realized what was happening, the young lawyer who had previously played no active role in the politics of protest had become an officer of the extralegal congress that was soon to become New Jersey's revolutionary government.

Before taking any concrete action, the assembled representatives proclaimed their "profoundest veneration for the person and family of George III," and professed "all due allegiance to his rightful authority and government." But without pause for further reflection they voted approval of the Continental Congress and congratulated the provincial legislature for having done the same.[20] They were hesitant about organizing the colony without suggestions from the Continental Congress, which was sitting at Philadelphia. But, when no guidelines were forthcoming, the Provincial Congress set out on its own.

First they adopted a provincial association. The spilling of blood had hardened the line between supporters of the administration of the Empire and its critics, but some formal means were needed to identify those individuals who might seek to undermine the patriotic cause. Through the county and local committees, the inhabitants of the province were asked over the following months to sign the association that spoke in terms of an arbitrary design by the British and proclaimed the abhorrence of slavery (presumably to Parliament). They might ardently wish for reconciliation, but subscribers swore to

> personally, and as far as our influence extends, endeavor to support and carry into execution whatever measures may be recommended by the Continental and our Provincial Congress, for defending our Constitution, and preserving the same inviolate.[21]

Fearing a breakdown of orderly local administration, the congress also asked Jerseymen to

> associate and agree, as far as shall be consistent with the measures adopted for the preservation of American freedom, to support the magistrates and other civil officers in the execution of their duty, agreeable to the laws of this colony . . . firmly determined, by all means in our power, to guard against those disorders and confusions to which the peculiar circumstances of the times may expose us.[22]

Those who refused to sign the association left themselves open to action by the congress, the committees, or the local patriots.

By June 3 the congress had moved on to formulate a plan for setting the militia on a ready footing. Secretary Paterson carefully recorded the purpose of their instructions: "That due obedience be paid to officers, and strict attention observed in learning the military exercise." Where militia activity had begun in earnest (in Morris, Sussex, and Somerset counties), the companies were congratulated "for their zeal in the common cause." Regulations instructed the other counties to follow suit quickly so that every township or corporation would have at least one company, and to be sure that drills were held regularly each month, if not more often. Then, to meet the financial needs of the county committees, the delegates agreed to raise £10,000 from the inhabitants of the colony and apportioned shares to the respective counties. Representatives of the township committees were ordered to break down the appropriate shares for each individual and to collect the tax. Finally, a new Committee of Correspondence was chosen with authority to reconvene the Provincial Congress, and the session adjourned.[23]

As Paterson traveled home to Raritan, he must have pondered the significance of his new position and wondered what could transpire next. If he had any doubts about the reports from Massachusetts, they were soon completely dispelled by the news of the valiant American defense of Bunker Hill where the Americans had inflicted over a thousand casualties on the British in a single day (June 17).[24] Meanwhile the Continental Congress had taken over the patriot force besieging Boston as a Continental army and sent George Washington to command it. John Dickinson, with whom Paterson's old friend MacPherson had been so closely associated, won support for a peace feeler called the Olive Branch Petition, and the Continental Congress agreed to send it to England. But they also made significant steps toward establishing themselves as a regularly functioning governmental body by agreeing to issue $2 million in bills of credit, empowering commissioners to make treaties with the Indians, and establishing a post office department under Benjamin Franklin.[25]

Probably as important as any of these events in influencing Paterson's commitment to the revolutionary cause was John Witherspoon's "Pastoral Letter," which was read on June 29 to assembled Presbyterian congregations from New York to Philadelphia. Witherspoon's invocation of God's protection for soldiers in the name of liberty could only reinforce the commitment of men like Paterson who saw their religious belief and their social philosophy as two sides of the same coin.[26]

When the delegates to the Provincial Congress reassembled on August 5, they were prepared to follow the example of the Continental Congress and proceed to take over more of the functions of the legally constituted legislature. Paterson was again sitting as secretary. The first order of business was to instruct the county committees to deliver to the congress the names of those delinquent in paying their share of the £10,000 tax and those who refused to sign the association. The assessors and collectors, it was decided, should be paid the same salary as the officers of the provincial government who fulfilled the same tasks.[27]

The most important business to be completed by this session was the establishment of a system of regular elections. The delegates thought it was especially important that the people have frequent opportunities to renew their support for the work of the congress since increased taxes and further military preparations appeared inevitable. Therefore it was decided that on September 21, 1775, and on the third Thursday of every September "during the continuance of the present unhappy disputes between Great Britain and America," elections would be held for the Provincial Congress and the county committees of observation and correspondence. The township committees were to be chosen each March.[28] The Provincial Congress thus put everyone on notice of their intention to supplant the colonial legislature and to assume the governing authority in the colony. By regularizing the establishment of the county and local committees, they were organizing the several levels of a revolutionary government. There was, however, no attempt to revolutionize procedure. Elections were to be held in the same manner as provincial elections had always been held, and anyone qualified to vote for the colonial assembly could participate.

Once the electoral machinery was set, the delegates moved on to more prosaic but no less important business. They promulgated a series of specific militia regulations that required all able-bodied men between sixteen and fifty to join their local company and set the amounts to be paid for service exemption and as fines for failing to appear on muster day. Quakers were exempted from military service, but they were expected to perform "all other services . . . consistent with their religious profession." Jonathan Dickinson Sergeant was made treasurer with the responsibility to receive the tax money as it came in. A Committee of Safety was formed so that there would be some patriotic authority in the colony even when the congress was not in session. Finally, the delegates referred complaints of price gouging to the Committee of Safety for action and then adjourned.[29]

New Jersey's First Provincial Congress had completed its tasks. Unlike the previous extralegal gatherings of Jersey patriots, the congress had taken significant steps toward assuming the government of the province. The colonists feared what might happen if a vacuum of authority developed, and their new provisions for taxing, electing representatives, organizing the militia, and supervising the activities of local administration were seen as required preconditions for repudiating the authority of the governor and his assembly.

Paterson's role as secretary of the congress was not an easy one. Perhaps Sergeant realized this when he resigned in Paterson's favor after only a few days of service. The secretary was relied on to carefully record the minutes of each meeting, to keep track of delegate attendance, and to maintain all the official correspondence of the congress with the Continental Congress, the other colonial governments, and the county committees. The amount of paperwork must have been unpleasant to the young man who had been moved to such frustration by the chore of copying advertisements a few years earlier.[30] It was a laborious and thankless job that others were unwilling to assume, but it did give Paterson an extraordinary opportunity to become known and respected. It also put him in a position where his future career, indeed his future life, depended on the success of the American cause. His name was affixed to every pronouncement of the Provincial Congress. If the king's troops were able to destroy the revolutionary forces and to punish those guilty of leading the treasonous rabble, Paterson's name would be high on their list.

The king had proclaimed the American colonies to be in open rebellion on August 23, but the vagaries of eighteenth-century communications kept this news from reaching America until early November. Meanwhile, elections had been held in New Jersey, and the newly chosen Second Provincial Congress had met. Somerset County, which had chosen nine delegates the previous May, now sent only three, and Paterson was not among them.[31] The press of personal business, not a relaxation of his commitment, influenced Paterson not to seek reelection. The leaders of the congress had hoped to retain him as secretary (even as a nondelegate), but a member who had spoken to Paterson reported that Paterson's "business and circumstances would by no means admit of his associating as secretary."[32] The largest part of his activity at this time must have been devoted to solving his father's financial problems, but he also remained active in Somerset's continuing military preparations.[33] John Carey was chosen to take over the secretary's chores for the three-and-one-half week session. The repsonsibilities of the office had been strenuous in the first congress. They became even more challenging as the second congress took on more and more of the business of governing the province. Carey found the job too much to handle along with his other responsibilities as a delegate, and, when the next session was called to order at the beginning of February 1776, he was pleased to hand the office back to Paterson.[34] The press of personal business had eased, and Paterson was again able to devote his time and energy to nurturing his fledgling political career.

Although the session of the Provincial Congress that Paterson had missed had been relatively uneventful, there were new developments in Philadelphia. John Dickinson, long a conservative and conciliatory influence in the Continental Congress, had embarked on a campaign to undermine those who were inclining toward a decision for independence. His native Pennsylvania, Delaware, and subsequently Maryland responded by instructing their delegates in Philadelphia to oppose independence at all costs. The result pointed up in bold terms the divisions that continued to exist within the Continental Congress.[35] New Jersey became associated with the Dickinson group when, by what turned out to be the final meeting of the legally constituted Provincial Assembly convened at Burlington in November 1775, its delegates in Philadelphia were instructed "utterly to reject" any bid for independence. Encouraged by the Privy Council's approval of their most recent paper money bill and a few petitions against independence, Governor Franklin was almost able to convince the assembly to send its own petition to the king. But the emissaries who were quickly dispatched from Philadelphia to change the mind of the assembly had the desired effect, and the Continental Congress, anxious to maintain the appearance of solidarity abroad even if it was deeply split from within, was spared embarrassment.[36]

From this point until February 1776, when Paterson joined the second session of the Second Provincial Congress, political opinions polarized dramatically. Soon Governor Franklin found himself under house arrest, and Attorney General Cortlandt Skinner was forced to flee after the interception of a packet of incriminating letters between the governor and himself.[37] In England, Parliament had passed the Prohibitory Act (December 22), really an authorization for piracy, which set the royal navy loose against American ships as if they were enemies and outlaws. In addition, the British had begun negotiations to hire Hessian mercenaries to quell the American revolt. By that time, the Continental Congress had directed an unsuccessful attack against the British at Quebec, had authorized the creation of an American navy, and had appointed a committee to seek support from America's friends abroad. Also important in the movement toward independence was the publication of Tom Paine's *Common Sense*, just weeks before the Provincial Congress reconvened.[38] To be sure, there were also private and personal motivations behind the decisions of many Americans to continue in support of the movement that daily became more and more revolutionary. Assuming that Paterson had received the news, the fact that his bosom friend John MacPherson had fallen at Quebec would have helped to dispel any lingering doubts he may have had about standing firm in the face of British intransigence.[39] However, while the pressure of unfolding events and arguments like Paine's made radicals more convinced of their righteousness, those apprehensive about the consequences of revolution became more fearful than ever before.

Within the next few months, it became obvious to more and more colonists that, as distasteful as the idea may have appeared a year before, a war for independence was the only alternative to total subjection to Parliament. New Jersey's Provincial Congress was called back into session by its Committee of Safety to answer the demands of the Continental Congress for a new battalion of troops and for more effective internal security and communications. Paterson was again the secretary, and the manuscript minutes that remain are written in his hand.[40] The Provincial Congress met through February 1776, as rumors spread that the British might abandon their positions in Boston and occupy New York. Detachments of Jersey minutemen "equal to a battalion in the Continental service" were sent to help build fortifications in the neighboring colony, and the official records and treasury funds stored in Perth Amboy were removed for safekeeping. In this session's single most important act, the Provincial Congress resolved to extend the franchise to "every person of full age, who hath immediately preceding the election, resided one whole year in any county of this colony, and is worth at least fifty pounds in real or personal estate." Here was a significant liberalization of the election laws that had long strictly adhered to suffrage by freeholders alone.[41] To give the newly enfranchised voters an opportunity to exercise their privilege, the election of a new Provincial Congress was planned for the fourth Monday in May, even though the election law did not call for one until the following September.[42]

Aware that the threat of war was close at hand, the delegates felt out of touch with the stream of events that seemed to be coming too fast. They found "the measures of the British ministry [to be] uncertain, extraordinary, and new almost every week." The situation appeared out of control, at least as far as the Provincial Congress of New Jersey was concerned. With this in mind, on March 2, they revised the instructions of their representatives in the Continental Congress to allow them "to pursue such measures as you may judge most beneficial for public good of all the Colonies" and adjourned.[43]

Although the new instructions superseded the orders of the previous November, which categorically rejected independence, most people in New Jersey were still unwilling to see the tie with Britain cut. A considerable number would remain loyal to the Crown in any case. Many found it hard to justify a far-reaching and irrevocable step when they had not personally felt the effects of Parliament's economic legislation or the intimidating presence of British troops. Others, like Paterson himself, could comprehend the tyranny of British legislation, the treachery of her military threat, and the danger of further moral degradation, but were nevertheless deterred by other considerations from reaching the ultimate decision for independence. One's commitment to the goal of freedom from Great Britain depended on how far one was willing to go in justifying the means for achieving it. Clearly, an extension of the war in Massachusetts to all the colonies was inevitable if independence were declared, and there was the frightening prospect of a continental war for independence turning into a social revolution. Such fears were not unique to Jerseymen; they were shared by people in every colony who saw how much they had personally to lose from an unsuccessful revolt, or even from a successful one that destroyed the stability of the social order in the process of establishing independence. To the chagrin of many radicals, John Dickinson and others were eloquently defending the interests of this group in the Continental Congress.[44]

Paterson had long recognized the dangers of internal revolution, and, although he seemed to think a republican form of government would serve America better than the British monarchy, the obvious dangers that would be imposed by the transition from one to the other were enough to terrify him. Paterson remembered his history. He had, for example, studied and carefully digested the history of the Puritan Revolution. In that case, "a few moderate men sought only to ascertain the liberties of the nation," but others wanted "an utter extirpation of hierarchy and monarchical government." This latter group had "at first concealed their designs under the profession of rigid Presbyterianism" and only later revealed their true intentions of leveling the traditional institutions of British society and politics.[45] Paterson's historical opinions about the English Civil War suggest his unwillingness to go as far as some of the evangelical Calvinists of his own day in converting simple religious orthodoxy into a stimulus for democratic egalitarianism. There was always in his mind the fear that factions of self-serving Americans might seek to capitalize on the troubles of their country as had the British levelers only a little over a century before.

Paterson's position was most clearly stated in his answer to the question, "Is It Lawful to Kill a Tyrant?" In this argument, Paterson had supported the absolute moral righteousness of doing away with a tyrannical king, but he seemed even more concerned with the means to the end. In the punishment of crimes, he had explained, even the heinous crimes of a tyrant, both the severity of the crime and the possible bad effects that the punishment might have on society had to be taken into account. He maintained that "the peace of society is of much greater importance than the peace, or even the life, of many individuals." Although revolutionaries might be morally justified in throwing over tyrannical rule, Paterson insisted, they "must consider whether the killing of the tyrant will be more hazardous to the state than permitting him to live." If assassinating him will in all probability be attended with the worse consequences to the state, it will follow that it is not always lawful to kill a tyrant, because "*salus populi suprema [lex]*" (the safety of the people is the supreme law).[46]

In the same piece, Paterson had turned to history for illustrations. Caesar had been overthrown, but immediately thereafter Rome was "plunged into greater misery." There "arose a triumverate of tyrants" where before there had been but one. English history also provided its "melancholy proof" of the dangers of revolt. The Puritan Revolution against Charles I, culminating in his execution in 1649, had been justified as a war to restore Britain to moral rectitude. But Paterson claimed that it did no more than exchange one tyrant for a worse one. "Cromwell," he explained, "beleaguered the nation with a standing army, which was no better than a brood of scorpions, besides [instituting] other infringements on the liberties of the people, which Charles never attempted." The killing of a tyrant had so often resulted in national misery and civil war that Paterson had suggested as an alternative solution the idea that "the king can do no wrong" but that his ministers may be prosecuted if they enforce the illegal orders of the Crown. This might save a kingdom from the great shock that almost always accompanied revolution. The ultimate act of justice toward a tyrannical king, though totally justifiable in moral terms, had to take second place to the "peace of the public and the security of the government," without which the cohesive forces of the society would begin to break down.[47] The situation was more real now than it had been in his student days, but Paterson's basic ideas had not changed. Law and order still came first.

Notwithstanding the relative quiescence of New Jersey's population and the fears of some of her leaders, the colony was inexorably swept into the decision for independence. This was partly the result of anxiety stirred by the preparations in New York for imminent invasion, and partly due to pressure brought on them by the Continenal Congress to formally constitute their new government.[48] There was also the realization that the decision for or against independence did not really belong to Jerseymen. Dependent on stronger neighboring colonies, New Jersey was bound to act as a satellite. As they moved toward independence, New Jersey was irresistibly swept along.[49]

In the final analysis, however, New Jersey was carried into the Revolution because the new Third Provincial Congress, which sent the sympathetic delegation to Philadelphia, approved the Declaration of Independence, and wrote the constitution for the new state, was considerably more Whiggish than the population at large. William Paterson was a leader of this newly chosen congress. Why the results of the May elections were so unrepresentative is not difficult to ascertain. Weeks before the election was held, it became clear that the vote would be a referendum on independence. The Continental Congress had proclaimed America's ports open to the ships of the world and on May 10 had instructed those colonies that had not yet done so to set up a govenment so that every kind of government under the Crown "should be totally suppressed and all the powers of government exerted, under the authority of the people of the colonies."[50] Some spokesmen for independence boldly made their appeals, but only a few Tories saw fit to risk the ire of their neighbors by denouncing the radicals. One citizen of Somerset County reported that the election gave the Tories an opportunity to "parade their troops," whose "appearance in some Counties was formidable."[51] Yet, even though suffrage requirements had been relaxed in response to popular petitions, when election day arrived, only a relatively small number of votes were cast. The vote was overwhelmingly for known Whigs.[52] Perhaps the small turnout was due to the fact that there were open Whig-Tory contests in only a few counties. It has been suggested that most voters, feeling that a Whig victory was a foregone conclusion stayed home.[53] But it is also likely that, in these days before the introduction of the secret ballot, many chose the path of prudence and refrained from publicly identifying themselves as moderates or Tories in the exercise of their viva voce right. A few months later, these timid Tories, emboldened by the presence of the British in New York, would plunge New Jersey into a civil war.

William Paterson was one of the relatively conservative Whigs chosen by Somerset County to sit in the Third Provincial Congress that later became the Convention of New Jersey. There were extremists, too. John Witherspoon, outspoken advocate of independence, was present, as well as several delegates from Bergen and Monmouth counties who would defend the authority of the king and Governor William Franklin to the end. But the continuing uncertainty and hesitation of men like Paterson set the tone for the congress. This was the body that would eventually commit New Jersey to independence, but it did so with none of the dogmatic determination that one might expect of a revolutionary assembly. In fact, the Third Provincial Congress was a rather passive body that was often influenced by external pressures in making what nonetheless remain memorable decisions. They took the steps necessary to ensure New Jersey's role in the independence movement, but they had to be pushed every bit of the way.

The first few meetings of the congress, which convened in Burlington on June 10, were given over to ordinary business. Paterson was unanimously chosen secretary, and Samuel Tucker was elected chairman. Resolutions from the Continental Congress were read and studied. Then on June 12 came a test vote. An obstructionist minority introduced a motion to require two-thirds of the deputies to constitute a quorum. Paterson joined the majority of 41 to 15 in voting down the proposal, which set the pattern for future decisions (the votes would never again be even as close as this).[54] The relative unanimity of their voting, however, did not encourage the congress to take precipitous or radical steps. They more often than not waited until decisions had been made for them.

The first really significant business they undertook was forced on them by Governor William Franklin. This devoted servant of the Crown had tenaciously clung to the thread of royal authority while his colleagues in other colonies and even his own attorney general had been forced to abdicate and flee.[55] Franklin had summoned the colonial legislature to meet on June 20 in Perth Amboy, near Staten Island where the recently dispatched Royal Peace Commission was to be headquartered.[56] Over the past months, without the necessity of an open confrontation, the Provincial Congress had assumed the powers of the governor and his legislators in almost every particular. Now that the governor was throwing down a direct challenge to its authority, the congress had no choice but to act. On June 14, they voted 38 to 11 that Franklin's order to the legislature to convene "ought not to be obeyed." Then, on the following day, they took a series of steps to keep the governor from interfering further in their affairs. First, by a vote of 41 to 10, he was declared to be in "direct contempt and violation of the resolve of the Continental Congress" which had called for the suppression of all vestiges of royal government. By 42 to 10, they agreed that he was "an enemy of the liberties of this country; and that measures ought to be immediately taken for securing" his person. In a final act of ingratitude, they voted 47 to 3 to cut off his salary.[57]

These charges were forthright and strong, but the congress hoped that Franklin would peacefully submit. One needs only to imagine what the patriots of Virginia would have done to Governor Dunmore (who had encouraged Virginia slaves to remain loyal to the Crown instead of their masters) if they could have laid hands on him in June 1776, to appreciate the kid gloves with which the Jersey congress had handled Franklin. Colonel Nathan Heard was ordered to carry out "the necessary business" of securing the person of the governor with all "delicacy and tenderness." But Franklin refused to sign the parole that would have left him "on his honour," and Heard had no choice but to place him under armed guard. The congress, now forced to take further action, ordered Heard to bring

Franklin to Burlington and appealed to the Continental Congress to arrange for the ex-governor to be moved to another colony where he "would
be capable of doing less mischief." On June 20, the reply of the Continental
Congress was received. If, after examining the prisoner, the delegates were
convinced that "he should be confined," an arrangement would be made to
move him to another colony. The next morning Franklin was brought
before the assembly, and again he made it impossible for his judges to be
lenient, this time by refusing to answer their questions and, like Charles I
in a similar situation, denying their authority to judge him. In the end the
congress grudgingly declared him "a virulent enemy" and placed him under
guard until the Continental Congress arranged for him to be moved, eventually to Connecticut.[58] Thus, this crucial step in bringing New Jersey into
the ranks of independence was forced on them by Franklin's intransigence.

Earlier that week the congress had appointed Friday, June 21, as the
day on which they would consider the propriety of setting up their own
government (according to the instructions from Philadelphia) and choose
a new delegation to represent New Jersey in the Continental Congress.
The arrest of the governor on the same day set the stage for what would
be the most critical day in New Jersey's movement toward independence.
Petitions had been coming in since the congress first met, and a number of
them had argued against independence. One that had been printed in the
New York newspapers was signed by nine hundred New Jersey freeholders.
Some Whig leaders still voiced their disapproval of independence, at least
until the people had spoken unequivocally.[59] But the petitions read on the
afternoon on June 21 "praying that the government of the Province of
New Jersey may not be changed," fell on deaf ears. Now that the last
vestige of royal authority, the governor's office, was unoccupied, some new
pattern of government was absolutely necessary. If there was anything that
Paterson and his colleagues feared more than despotism from Great
Britain, it was anarchy at home. The decision "that a government be
formed to regulate the internal police of this Colony" was made by a vote
of 54 to 3. New Jersey's reluctant revolutionaries had voted overwhelmingly to take another step toward independence, but the step actually reflected a conservative inclination. Like their conservative fellow patriots in
the Continental Congress, who, once independence became likely, argued
that a system of confederation and government be formalized first, the
New Jersey leaders were trying desperately to keep some semblance of
authority present in this time of great trial.[60]

June 21 had been so busy that the matter of choosing a new delegation
to go to Philadelphia had to be put off until the next day. Many of the
delegates may have preferred to delay still further any discussion of inde-

pendence, but there was now no alternative. A resolution for independence had been placed before the Continental Congress, and a committee was already at work framing the document of separation. There was no doubt that the delegates to be sent to Philadelphia would have to vote either for or against the break with England, and, as the New Jersey congress came to choose them, they in effect decided for independence. The dean of the new delegation was John Witherspoon, whose outspoken advocacy of independence was well known. Of the others (five in all), probably the least positive on the issue was Richard Stockton, Paterson's old friend and teacher, but like the rest when the time came he would be present to sign the declaration. The instructions given to the delegates were especially significant for they were specifically empowered to join the other colonies "in declaring the United Colonies independent from Great Britain," and setting up a "confederacy for union and common defense."[61]

The congress had spoken clearly and unequivocally, but it was hardly the choice of committed revolutionaries. On the matter of independence as on the matter of setting up a new government for New Jersey, the congress had waited so long that the decision was made for them. All Paterson and his colleagues had to do was to recognize that the actions of the king and Parliament, the British army, Governor Franklin, their neighboring colonies, and the Continental Congress had deprived them of any real alternative other than following the road to revolution. They may have prepared themselves ideologically so as to rationalize such dramatic actions when they became absolutely necessary—certainly Paterson had done so in his "Address on the Rise and Decline of Nations." But they had lacked the boldness to act before. Even now, their revolution was a passive and defensive one, less concerned with reorganizing society than in maintaining order, and less concerned with striking out in new directions than with not being left behind.

The following week was devoted to preparing the new constitution. Radicals are often accused of wanting to tear down the old order before they have anything to replace it with. New Jersey's revolutionaries could hardly be charged with this. They were rushing desperately to erect a new structure of government before the old one was wiped completely away. A committee drafted the constitution in only two days; then, after a few days' consideration before a committee of the whole house, the new pattern of government was speedily approved.[62] Actually there was not much new in it. The old structure of the provincial government remained intact, considerable property requirements were retained for officeholders, and the franchise was extended no further than had already been approved. The largest single innovation in this and all the new state constitutions was the increased power of the legislature. The governor of New Jersey would henceforth be chosen by the legislators for one year and would be essentially powerless.[63] The sentiments that led to this legislative supremacy were obvious, but legislative decision making was usually arduous and always inefficient. Could such a government operate effectively? There were other questions and doubts as well. This Provincial Congress had no specific authority to constitute a new government, and there were no plans to have the document ratified by the people. Only on July 18, two weeks after the constitution was promulgated, did the congress finally resolve to "assume the style and title of the Convention of the State of New Jersey."[64] Throughout the manuscript minutes Secretary Paterson consistently referred to the new government being considered as a "Charter of Rights" rather than as a constitution, suggesting that he and others viewed the document as something less than a permanent frame of government.[65]

The role that William Paterson played in the creation of New Jersey's first constitution has been a matter of confused debate. It has been claimed that, since he was the secretary of the congress and skilled in the law, he must have been the author of the document.[66] According to the official minutes, however, he was not even a member of the drafting committee, and in the only roll-call vote taken to confirm the constitution rather than defer it for further consideration, Paterson voted "no."[67] It has also been suggested that Paterson's objection was most likely based on his disapproval of the last paragraph of the document,[68] which stated in tones characteristic of New Jersey's reluctant revolutionaries that

> if a reconciliation between Great Britain and these Colonies should take place, and the latter be taken again under the protection and government of the Crown of Great Britain, this Charter shall be null and void.[69]

If one looks only at the limited evidence provided in the congressional minutes, this conclusion might seem satisfactory. On July 3, Paterson did join eight others in voting unsuccessfully to delay printing the constitution for a few days "in order to reconsider, in a full house, the propriety of the last clause."[70] This idea that he objected to the last clause is consistent with his later attacks against moderates and trimmers who would not unequivocally support independence. But Paterson had more substantial reservations, too. Just a few months after it went into effect, he was suggesting that the constitution be set aside since it was inappropriate to the critical conditions that required dynamic executive leadership.[71] Then too, the charter of rights did not protect rights very well, at least as far as Paterson was concerned. In the decade after the Revolution, he attacked the constitution time and time again for making what he saw as the sacred property rights of individuals subject to the whim of a majority at the polls.[72] It is not clear whether Paterson approved of the liberalized suffrage qualifications that were carried over into the new constitution, but, in February 1776, when the congress decided to ease the restrictions on voting and call a special election, the delegation from Paterson's Somerset County was the only one to vote against both proposals.[73] Even into the 1790s, Governor William Paterson criticized the constitution as being inadequate for effective government, in part because it was written in great haste to meet a crisis situation.[74]

Actually the crisis was more imminent than has been supposed. On July 2, the same day the congress voted on the constitution, the worst fears of New Jersey Whigs were realized as General Howe landed his troops on Staten Island.[75] Members of the convention sitting in Burlington were shocked that morning when Lieutenant Colonel Nathaniel Scudder of the Monmouth County militia, who had ridden through the night to reach them, reported that he had seen the enemy fleet approaching. At 6:30 the previous evening, he had counted "about 130 sail in the channel from the Hook to New York within nine miles from the Narrows." About 4:00 in the morning, after having already traveled fifty miles, he had heard "a very heavy firing of cannon," which he presumed to be either the British attacking New York or attempting to "cover the landing of their troops."[76] The news struck the delegates at Burlington like the crushing blow of a sledgehammer. In fact, the noise that Scudder heard must have been the result of a summer thunderstorm for there was no firing as the British landed that day.[77] But, for all the delegates knew, at that very moment their wives and children were being ravaged by the enemy.

The convention immediately sent word to Philadelphia and appealed to the Continental Congress to send assistance "without the least delay" to meet "this alarming exigency." The convention adjourned to inform absent delegates of the frightening news and convened again that afternoon to hurriedly finish their debates on the new constitution, approve a few amendments to the committee report, and vote. It is likely that some of the delegates did not even wait until the afternoon session, but hastened home to see to the safety of their families.[78] It is also reasonable to assume that many who did attend and voted to ratify the constitution were influenced by the immediate threat of enemy guns, which made a stable system for maintaining domestic order all the more necessary. This assumption is not meant to suggest that, in the absence of news from

Sandy Hook the delegates would have agreed with Paterson and placed limits on the legislature's authority. The eclipse of executive power was common to all the revolutionary state constitutions. The trend was inevitable. But analysis of the 1776 constitution must take into account Scudder's dramatic role as the Paul Revere of New Jersey's revolution.

Since Paterson was well trained in the law and familiar with history, we must assume that he foresaw at least some of his later objections in 1776, when the constitution was being framed, and that this accounts for his vote to reconsider it. Far from objecting only to the final clause, Paterson set himself apart from his less scrupulous colleagues who had sacrificed too many of what he thought to be the necessary and conservative protections of government in the face of British cannon and the need to assure that the people would accept the new formula.[79] His negative vote should be seen as a conscientious personal expression of his conservative philosophy, which the constitution had lamentably rejected. The more liberal elements of the new framework threatened to confound the orders of society and to undermine the assumptions of deference. He was correct: Once the people got a taste of governing themselves, once they realized that they could direct the decisions of their representatives, voters would no longer be satisfied to trust in the judgment of their betters. Much of Paterson's later career would be spent trying to convince the people of New Jersey that they had made a terrible mistake.

Meanwhile, despite his disappointment, Paterson remained at the forefront of New Jersey's revolution. It is ironic that the official copy of the constitution he voted against, on display to this day as the symbol of New Jersey's decision to break with its colonial past, is written in his hand and bears his signature as secretary.[80] Paterson was conservative, moralistic, and maybe even a little paranoid, but he was not stupid. Even if his scrupulous conservative philosophy was rejected in the haste of the moment, there would be other opportunities when his ideas might be more widely accepted and his skills in administration and legal work more appreciated. In this spirit he set aside his objections to the constitution, allowed himself to be chosen a member of the first Legislative Council under the new constitution, and faced anew the problems created by a nation at war.

On September 13, the newly chosen governor, William Livingston, spoke to a joint session of the new legislature and tried to reinforce their belief in the rightness of the American cause. *"America,"* he reminded them, "had deferred independence 'till the decisive alternative of absolute Submission, or utter Destruction" had been reached, "till the most scrupulous [conscience] could, on the maturest Reflection, find itself justified

before God and Man, in renouncing those Tyrants." Livingston must have
hit a responsive chord in Paterson's scrupulous conscience when he went on
in moral terms very similar to Paterson's to declaim against the British who
had "ravaged a great part of *Asia*; and dissipated in Venality and Riot,
the Treasures extorted from its innocent Inhabitants by the Hand of
Rapine and Blood"; and now "finally meant to prolong their luxury and
corruption, by appropriating to themselves the hard-earned Competance
of the American world." Paterson's conservative religious and social
ideology, which had led him to regret the corrupting influence the British
had had on American society, could be an effective force for mobilizing
men toward the hard work needed to win independence. Ideological and
practical political justifications for revolution continually reinforced one
another. Livingston closed his address by calling on his audience to join
him in "setting our faces . . . like a Flint, against the Dissoluteness of
Manners and political corruption, which will ever be the *Reproach of
any People*."[81]

5

Prosecuting the Revolution

William Paterson's reputation as one of the leading architects of independence in New Jersey was hard-earned. As attorney general of the infant state during the years of revolution, his position was crucial to the success of the independence movement there. His most significant contributions were the restoration of stability to the system of justice and the destruction of the loyalist opposition to the Revolution within the state. These were also the years in which Paterson married, started his family, and saw his professional career and personal fortune grow to considerable size.

The young man who, just a few years before, had been teasing his friend about the favors of the ladies of Philadelphia now had a lady of his own. While Paterson was struggling to set right the troubled legal system of the state, he was also making plans for marriage. His fiancée was Cornelia Bell, daughter of a Somerset County landowner, John Bell, and, if Paterson's letters to her are any token, she was quite a captivating young lady. They first met at the home of Anthony White where Cornelia was staying. Young Paterson was swept off his feet, describing her as "the sweetest pattern of female excellence." All through 1777 and 1778, when official business kept him traveling from one corner of the state to the other, Paterson would sit at 2:00 in the morning after all his paperwork was done and write to Cornelia pledging and repledging his devotion. Fearing that his characteristically reserved manner might be mistaken as an absence of passion, the attentive young suitor waxed poetic: "Roll on ye Hours; bring, bring the Happy Moment, when I shall hail Cornelia my wedded love."[1] Finally in February 1779, the two were married. In 1780, a daughter was born.[2] The years of the Revolution would eventually provide Paterson with an estate and a comfortable life for his family, but, in the meanwhile, the overwhelming demands of his office and the long periods he had to spend away from home caused him much frustration.

Revolution is a risky undertaking; to understand this is to understand why such reluctance and irresoluteness permeated the ranks of New Jersey's leaders in the months preceding independence. The most obvious danger was losing to the British, and, in the summer of 1776 with General Howe just landed in New York and numerous loyalists threatening retaliation, this outcome appeared a distinct possibility. There was also the danger of the side-effects that came with revolution: With the old institutions of government set aside, how could order be kept, lawbreakers brought to justice, and contracts enforced? Paterson believed that men of honor and station, like himself, who took their responsibilities seriously, could be relied on not to take undue advantage of the situation, but people of a meaner sort might raise havoc while society, occupied with fighting a war, relaxed its guard.

The American Revolution brought together extremists of every sort. These included those who sought a radical change toward a more open and democratic society as well as those who could justify radical means to defend the old social order against corruption from outside and deterioration from within. James Otis, an early leader of the independence movement in Massachusetts, stated the conservative view most clearly when he expressed his concern that "when the pot boils, the scum will rise."[3] If some turmoil was unavoidable in the process of breaking with Britain, so be it; but Paterson and others devoted themselves to holding the chaos to a minimum and keeping those whom Otis called the scum of society where they belonged. Now that the break with Britain had been made, Paterson seemed more concerned with keeping the great unwashed in check than he was with the degradation to be caused by aristocratic libertines. But regardless of Paterson's targets, the conservative impetus for his ideas remained the same.

The rejuvenation of the judicial and executive institutions and the stabilization of the legal system of the new state were the most important contributions that Paterson made to the success of the Revolution. In his capacity as legislative councillor, Paterson was involved in the preparation of legislation that confirmed most of the old court system, established the punishment to be paid by convicted Loyalists, and controlled the treatment of prisoners.[4] The critical state of affairs, however, forced Councillor Paterson to concern himself with military and administrative details as well. Some of these, such as arranging a military exemption for shoemakers, were insignificant. But others, such as intervening with the governor to recommend that the demoralized militia be sent home for the winter less than a month before Cornwallis led the first invading army into New Jersey, were potentially disastrous.[5]

Although the new constitution of 1776 left no doubts that the legislature was supreme, during the war government by legislature became all but impossible. The legislators had to concern themselves with all the minute details of militia appointments, with the flagging morale of New Jersey's soldiers, and with the critical problems presented by people disaffected with the Revolution while, at the same time, maintaining a full legislative calendar.[6] As a result, they did none of these jobs very well. With regard to the militia, for example, despite the military emergency, the legislators insisted on continuing the common practice of allowing people to avoid military service by hiring substitutes and paying exemption fees.[7] This policy must have been popular with their constituents, but, in the present state of affairs, it was a flirtation with disaster. In a letter to Paterson early in 1777 on the choice of brigadier generals, General Philemon Dickinson suggested that perhaps they should appoint a "baker's dozen" so that none of Jersey's thirteen counties would feel that its favorite son had been slighted.[8] Another of Paterson's correspondents during this period complained about the caliber of superior officers appointed. Officers and men, he reported, "must now have a high opinion of their leaders or they will not take the field." The letter, signed "Amicus," specifically suggested a few men of unimpeachable integrity, but one passage betrayed the author's secret doubts that the legislature was capable of choosing well: "Pray advise your body to commission only gentlemen *or as few others as possible*" (italics added).[9] The weaknesses of the system are evident in these illustrations. In these critical days, New Jersey simply could not afford the luxury of allowing all these decisions to be made by inefficient, inexperienced, and overworked legislators who were susceptible to pressures from the electorate.

Paterson was among the first to recognize these limitations and, with Governor William Livingston led the attempt to revitalize the executive power of the government. Since August 1776, when he had been appointed attorney general, he had been fulfilling the duties of this office at the same time that he was sitting in the legislature. This peculiar position (he was even charged with violating the state constitution by holding a post of profit under the government while a legislator)[10] made him particularly aware of the need for dynamic executive leadership. The failure of the legislature to act promptly and prudently when it came to the crucial issues of military preparedness and public safety became more and more clear during the first months of the fighting in New Jersey.

The Loyalists, or the "disaffected," as the legislators usually called them, presented the most pressing problem. At the same time that the Provincial Congress had been informed of the British fleet's arrival at New York, news came that the Tories were arming and organizing themselves in the cedar swamps of Monmouth. Local officers warned that Monmouth militiamen might refuse to go off to fight leaving "their wives and children to fall either Prey to the Enemy . . . or be murdered by the Tories in their absence."[11] This crisis was met by sending in troops from the surrounding area to disperse the Loyalist forces, but, throughout the summer and into the fall of 1776, evidence of Tory strength continued to surface all over the state.[12] Cornwallis followed Washington across the Hudson in November 1776, and for the next two years New Jersey fully earned its designation as the "Cockpit of the Revolution."[13]

Paterson thought the darkest hour was the winter of 1776–1777. In a subsequent newspaper essay he wished that "the Months of November and December 1776 could be erased out of the Calendar of Time."[14] To further complicate matters, the state was effectively paralyzed during December and January because the legislature, which alone had the power to call up troops and commit supplies, was not in session. Flagging morale was somewhat restored by the dramatic victories at Trenton and Princeton, but by January 1777, when the legislature met again, the customary institutions of justice had seriously deteriorated, Loyalism was as big a problem as ever, and most of eastern Jersey was still under enemy guns.[15]

In mid-March, as the legislators were readying themselves for another recess, William Livingston and William Paterson, the two most important executive officers, took steps to avoid a further erosion of governmental authority. On March 11, Livingston proposed the creation of a council of safety to investigate Loyalism, invigorate the justice system, and make necessary decisions while the legislature was not in session.[16] It was not a new idea—the Provincial Congress had resorted to a similar solution when it was faced with an emergency situation in 1775 and 1776[17]—but in March 1777, the emergency had become a matter of survival.

The assembly and council each considered the governor's suggestion, but decided that they needed a joint meeting to finally thrash out the critical matter. Councillors Paterson, Symmes, Scudder, and Cooper were instructed to meet with a committee of the assembly "in a free conference on the subject."[18] The conference, held March 15, 1777, proved to be one of Paterson's finest hours. In a forceful address, he described the wide scope of the domestic and military crisis facing the state and encouraged support for the governor's plan to revitalize the institutions of government. His argument began with a general discussion of the plight of the state, including the activities of Tories and indecisive patriots, then he criticized the state's failure to enforce the law vigorously, and came finally to place most of the blame on the vacillation of the magistrates in the local courts.[19]

According to Paterson's analysis, New Jersey was too late in getting its new government set up and operating smoothly: "The Irruption and rapid progress of the Enemy in this State has, with other causes of an internal Nature, prevented the Powers of Government from being established, & carried into Execution with the necessary force and energy." Part of the responsibility for this delay "in putting off the old rotten Constitution" and ushering in the "Hour of Independence and Separation" was laid at the feet of the Tories. But much of the blame went to "a class of Beings called moderate Men," and even "some honest Whigs, who were either of a timid cast, & of weak nerves, or who had a . . . foolish doting passion for Great Britain and the old Constitution." A year or so before Paterson himself might have been described this way, but now he went on about how this "set of puppets" and second-guessers had been used by the British in their imperial schemes of the last decade. They "were continually declaiming in Favour of Patience and Forbearance, and Tenderness, and all the soft-eyed Virtues." Yet, when the time for independence and setting up a new government came, they were "the most noisy and turbulent, and violent, and outrageous in their opposition." Paterson went on to describe how men of this sort could draw from deep wells of sympathy and compassion "whenever any Measure of a spirited stamp" was taken against the Tories. "They bewailed in the most pathetic Strains the misfortunes and Afflictions of a Tory, but I never knew one of them [to] lament over the miseries of a Whig." It was the continued widespread expression of such sympathies that made extraordinary action necessary on the part of the revolutionary administration of the state: "The period has at length arrived in which it behooves us to Mark the Complexion of Men, to view every Shade in their Character, and with an Eagle's Eye to look into their very souls."[20]

Paterson thought that failure to enforce the law adequately was at the heart of New Jersey's troubles. The exceptional executive powers that Paterson proposed went beyond the political theory that he and his fellows had studied from the great philosophers: "It is the grand truth of all the fine Writers on Government, that they do not distinguish between Theory and Practice." Paterson admitted that "it is easy to build up an ingenious system or Code of Law, which shall appear with singular Beauty on Paper, but which however will vanish the instant we attempt to put it in use." Extraordinary situations required extraordinary political solutions, and this was particularly true when the cause of the disorder in society was related to the insufficient administration of justice. "A little practical virtue," he went on, "is preferable to the finest theoretical system in the world, if it cannot be put into exercise." This was precisely the problem as Paterson saw it in New Jersey. The legislature passed laws, but they went unenforced because of the failure of the state constitution to provide for adequate executive authority. Not only were the laws disregarded, but popular respect for the authority of the government had never really been established. "I do not know of anything," Paterson declared,

> that can place the legislative powers and of course Government itself in a more debasing and contemptible Point of Light than the making of laws without Force sufficient to put such laws into Operation and use. Sir, if there be not energetick virtue in the executive Branch of Government to enforce Laws, we may at once take leave of each other, and go home. In the present state of warfare and confusion, we stand more in need of executive than legislative powers.[21]

With an absence of spirited administration on the state level, the organs of justice on the local level had failed to function properly. This was particularly true with regard to the county court system. Paterson asked his fellow conferees to "take a view of the bench of justices in the several counties of the State, and tell me where is the Magistrate who has acted up to the Line of Duty, and the Spirit of his Station." Then, presuming the answer his question would receive, he went on to say that

> there may be a few Exceptions; there may be here and there an individual, who has had Firmness and Fortitude sufficient to make him bear up under the pressure of Adversity and in the Face of Danger. But alas! the Bulk of them, be the cause what it may, have forebore to act, notwithstanding the Nature and Urgency of publick Affairs required the most vigorous exertions.

Paterson thought that several reasons might "be assigned for the vapid conduct of the magistrates." Partly, of course, the "invasion of the State by a cruel and rapacious enemy" was responsible, as was the acknowledged "Want of Knowledge and Want of Spirit in several of the persons in Office." But the chief factor, as he saw it, was

> the Want of a particular Council or Body composed of the most spirited persons and invested with large and extensive Powers, to act with all Vigor and Energy, to be an example to the inferior officers, and, if I may so phrase it, to set the Wheels of Government in Motion.[22]

From his central position as both member of the Legislative Council and attorney general, Paterson had eloquently professed his concern for the steadiness and stability of the county court system. New Jersey's leaders had realized from the beginning the importance of maintaining as much continuity in government as possible while undergoing the great transition from colony to state. For this reason, the new constitution had been rushed through the previous July, despite the opinion of some like Paterson that more time was needed to fully consider it.[23] Aware that the British threatened their families and eager to hurry home to protect them, the delegates first took time to agree to an instrument of government. Then, just two days later, "to prevent a failure of justice," the convention ordered "all judges, justices of the peace, sheriffs, coroners, and other inferior officers of the late government within this Colony" to continue in their offices "under the authority of the people." The convention ordered "that all actions, suits and processes be continued, altering only the style and form" to reflect the rejection of the king and Empire.[24] Now, a little over eight months later, the hastily adopted constitution had proved unequal to the test, and Paterson had identified one of its greatest drawbacks as the failure to encourage the strenuous enforcement of revolutionary justice in the county courts. Soon the state would take action.

The role of local government in revolutionary America, stressed by Paterson in his speech, has lately become a matter for debate among historians. Some have argued that, while the Continental Congress struggled to establish its authority and new governmental structures were set up in the states, local institutions remained virtually the same as they had been. According to Clarence VerSteeg, for example, traditional local institutions helped provincial societies to "bridge the transition from colonies to states with a minimum of disruption." However, other studies have suggested that there was upheaval on the town and county levels as well as everywhere else. Clearly the situation was different from state to state. As far as New Jersey is concerned, the evidence suggests that local institutions were more stable than not.[25]

Paterson's stress on the vitality of county courts underscores the importance of local institutions. New Jersey had town meetings like those in New England and county courts like those in Virginia. Dennis Ryan has recently documented how town meetings in several New Jersey jurisdictions presented unchanging responses to local needs during the revolutionary period. Ryan's detailed analysis of six towns is most convincing, but on the issue of the relative stability of state versus local government his scope is not broad enough to be conclusive.[26] The county courts were more important than the town meetings in this regard. To begin with, they possessed more direct authority over the citizens than the town meetings did. Holders of the most influential town offices (overseers of the poor, keepers of the roads, surveyors, and assessors) had less significance than county officials in preserving law and order. The county sheriff's enforcement of the county court's decisions and the official visits of the county tax collector were undoubtedly the most direct and memorable encounters with government authority for the typical New Jersey colonist.[27] In contrast, the more subtle pressures and unspoken social control exerted by neighbor against neighbor in the town meetings were not sufficient to counter the forces of disintegration unleashed in 1776. The county court's significance was partly a reflection of the practical problems of an earlier era when the inconvenience of colony-wide transportation and the absence of a New Jersey newspaper to report the activities of the colonial legislature made the regular meetings of the county court more important. They usually provided the only opportunity for leaders of the neighboring community—lawyers, litigants, and officials alike—to come together and exchange news and points of view.[28] Moreover, the basic component of revolutionary political activity in the colony had been the county committee, which was relied on by the Provincial Congress to collect its taxes, administer its oaths, and oversee the training of the militia.[29] Once reinforced and invigorated, as Paterson proposed, the county courts could serve along with the town meetings as forces of stability and order during the period of crisis.

During the first months of war, however, the county court system had (for reasons Paterson had noted) failed to prosecute justice with the energy and vigor the situation required.[30] Now, partly as a result of Paterson's speech, the conferees were convinced of the need for prompt action.

That same day, they reported to their respective houses, and the Council of Safety was authorized and set in motion.[31] For the next eighteen months, the Council of Safety would help Livingston and Paterson restore the executive leadership they felt was so sorely lacking in the infant state. The powers it had been granted were extraordinary, so extraordinary in fact that the legislature would only authorize the council to operate for three months at a time without a reconfirmation of its authority.[32] The legislation was renewed five times, and each time the powers of the council were increased or expanded. As first constituted, the council had twelve members who were all members of the legislature. Eventually its number was increased to twenty-three, and the percentage of legislators went down. Governor Livingston personally presided over almost every meeting, and Paterson was one of the few who were chosen as members for each of the six sittings. The council's primary responsibility was to seek out and indict the Loyalists who were becoming such a threat to peace and security. The council convened in one county after another, often calling on local justices of the peace to sit with them to investigate and try to identify the suspected Loyalists in the neighborhood. The county officials and militia officers were sent out to apprehend the suspects and bring them before the councillors for interrogation. If they were willing at that point to swear allegiance to the patriot cause, their cases could easily be passed over, but, if they refused, the council would either have them imprisoned until the next meeting of the county court or arrange bond to assure their presence at a later date.[33]

When it was not investigating Loyalists, the council acted out its general responsibility to see to the well-being of the state while the legislature was not in session. In that capacity, it encouraged the enforcement of the laws against profiteering, administered the distribution of passes necessary to travel across the state and cross the lines of the enemy, and even temporarily appointed officers to essential posts in the militia as they became vacant. It was given the power to move sessions of court from place to place for safety from the British and to grant exemptions from military service to people with strategic occupations.[34] But suppressing the Tories remained the council's most important task.

As a member of the Council of Safety, Paterson continued to argue for vigorous action against the Loyalists. Some weeks after the forming of the council, he tried to explain the reasons for the brazen attitude assumed by so many New Jersey Tories and to account for the fact that there seemed to be more of them than there were before. "Many of the Whigs," he claimed, "have of late cooled down, & become quite lukewarm; while on the Contrary the Tories grow upon our Hands in the most rapid manner." This was seen as partially due to the fact that the burdens of military service, commandeered supplies and wagons, quartered troops, and the like, were borne only by the Whigs. Meanwhile, the Tories went unpunished for their crimes, continued in business "asking the most exorbitant prices for everything they have to sell," and remained to plunder the property of the Whigs whenever invasion of enemy troops caused the patriots to flee. "We have taken the most effectual Way to *make* Tories," Paterson explained, whereas

> one well-timed & signal instance of public Justice in the Dawn of Toryism would have been attended with the most happy Effects. It would too have been the most successful Line of Conduct that could have been pursued. We shall be obliged to make an hundred Examples now, whereas one would have had the same, nay greater, Efficacy, in the Beginning.

Instead the "weak, timid, cruel [to the Whigs], and ill judged Policy" of the state had elevated the Tories "to a Degree of Boldness and Barefacedness" that threatened to "work out our ruin." In Salem County, for example,

> there is a group of Tories which threaten to give the State considerable trouble before they can be suppressed. Some parts of Hunterdon have been always infested with a Nest of disaffected people, of whom it is high time to get rid. The other Counties in the State are more or less pestered with them.[35]

Much of the blame could be traced to the inadequate administration of justice. "It is really a laughable sight to view the conduct of our public Bodies with Respect to the Tories," he claimed, not trying to be funny at all. By treating the accused with unnecessary kindness, the convention and some of the county committees had compounded the troubles with the Tories and endangered the very fabric of society under law. Confessed Tories who were called before them would "put on a sort of penitential trim" and be dismissed with no more than a reprimand. As a result, Paterson observed, "the rascal returned ten times more hardened than before." This laxity had been carried to the point where the Tories were "at ease" and grew in number, while the dispirited Whigs were left to "moulder imperceptibly away." It could all be boiled down to a basic political maxim.

Those who are in power should always so rule as to make it the Interest of People to side with Government. For it is a Truth which holds equally good in political and private Life, that interest is the Pole Star by which the Mass of Mankind steer their Course. Make it the *Interest* of People to be Tories, and my Life for it they will soon become so. And have we not made it the interest of the people to become Tories, and do we not find, that, in Consequence of it, they grow wonderfully upon our Hands?

The only way to deal with the problem of the Tories, Paterson thought, was to act swiftly and forcefully to make them pay for their transgressions. Otherwise the disaffected would never be put down, for "they have nothing to fear From the Enemy, if they should prove successful; and they have nothing to fear from us, for they laugh and push it in our very faces."[36] Apparently moved by Paterson's urgings, the council did act vigorously against the Tories.

Although its task was herculean, its time short, and the difficulties many, the Council of Safety was generally effective in its work. The legislature had been careful in granting powers to this extraordinary body, conservative in choosing appointees to the board, and vigilant in keeping the council within its bounds. Moreover, as thorough as its investigations were, the council always conformed to the formalities of legal procedure. This is a very significant point. Acting in his capacity as attorney general, Paterson could have sought authority to set up extraordinary courts to deal with the Loyalists. Instead he worked through the Council of Safety, which used the opportunity to invigorate and rehabilitate the institutions of local administration by calling on the county sheriffs to serve their orders and by referring cases to the county courts for adjudication.[37] By the time the Council of Safety went out of existence in October 1778, Toryism had not been crushed out, but the crisis situation that had existed a year and a half before had been brought under control, and the viability of the administration of justice on the county level had been partially restored.

No one was in a better position than William Paterson to know what was needed to restore the respectability essential to governmental authority. As a legislative councillor he had helped to write the laws, as a member of the Council of Safety he was responsible for investigating those suspected of wrongdoing and issuing indictments, and as attorney general he prosecuted the cases before the state's courts. As time passed, his duties as attorney general were becoming more and more important. After October

1777, Paterson left the Legislative Council, and after the early months of the Council of Safety he attended its sittings less regularly.[38] Of course, the better the job the Council of Safety did in flushing out Loyalists and other suspects, the more work there was for the prosecutor.

The cases that the attorney general was called on to prosecute included all the social evils. His notes on cases often recorded the evidence and legal arguments in a very matter-of-fact way. For example, when Paterson prosecuted Moses Beivers in a 1779 session of the Sussex County Court, the indictment was for fornication. His notes recorded Mary Davis's statement that the defendant "had carnal knowledge of [the] Witness 12 times in the County of Sussex." When she became pregnant, the witness went on, Beivers offered her £5 to swear that a servant boy was the father. The trouble was that Mary had told a number of neighborhood people that Thomas Brandine was the real father. Because of the confusion and the defense attorney's adept argument, the jury acquitted Beivers.[39]

Some people would steal and fornicate no matter what the political climate, and Paterson could bring these people to justice in the fullest spirit of his puritanical conception of right and wrong. In fact, there is reason to suspect that at times his spirit might have overridden his good judgment. Consider, for example, the case against Joseph and Catherine Brown. According to Paterson's notes on the trial, the Browns had seduced a sixteen-year-old girl, a minister's daughter, taught her the ways of sin, and used her to help them pilfer her father's home. Some time later the girl confessed and then told her story to the grand jury. Reverend John Light, the state's chief witness, explained at the trial that during "the winter after the British left Brunswick his daughter got acquainted with Brown's family." On one occasion, after she "lost the great Part of her Cloathes at Brown's," the father "whipped her." But soon things began to disappear from the house, and she admitted having taken them for the Browns, who tempted her with "spangles and lace." As a case for petty pilferage or endangering the morals of a minor, there may have been some merit here. But prosecutor Paterson was relying on the girl, Elizabeth Light, for the sole testimony against the defendants on two robberies and three counts of burglary. The defense attorneys called forth several citizens who testified that the Browns were some place else on the night of the crimes, and seven witnesses agreed that Elizabeth Light was a girl of very bad character—her father had even been forced to throw her out of the house.[40]

In summarizing his case for the jury, Paterson argued that the girl's testimony had "led to the most important discoveries, and has opened up a scene of Iniquity rare to be met with in civilized Nations." For a long time the "fingers of suspicion" had pointed at the Browns:

> common fame did not scruple to place Joseph Brown and his Wife on the Roll with those who had perpetrated the most atrocious crimes [a likely reference to the Tories], yet until the present Moment we have not been able to come at that Degree of Evidence which was Sufficient in the legal scale.

One is forced to wonder whether Paterson's passion to punish the immoral element in the community clouded his judgment. His address to the jury criticized the defense counsel for attacking the girl's character, pointed out that it was the Browns who were supposedly responsible for her fall in the first place, and reminded the jurors that Reverend Light had accepted his daughter's confession of sin and accepted her back under his roof. He seemed to have had no doubt that an admittedly errant teenager, still anxious to win back her stern father's approval, would tell anything but the truth when placed on the stand. In contrast, Paterson's own notes on the case clearly suggest that the Browns may have been falsely accused by a young girl trying to cover her own wrongdoing. Moreover, in the spirit of vigorously enforcing the law, the attorney general may have encouraged the miscarriage of justice.[41]

The more important legal problems, however, were those brought about by the war, and these were much harder to treat in absolutely moralistic terms. Profiteering, for example, was common, and trading with the enemy was encouraged by the presence of the British in nearby New York. The ease with which goods could be brought in from New York made enforcement practically impossible, especially when members of some of the most prominent Whig families succumbed to the temptation. Elisha Boudinot must have been embarrassed when the garments he had smuggled in from New York for his bride to wear at their wedding were confiscated by revolutionary officers.[42] The task of enforcing the laws against illegal trade was made even more difficult when a subsequent law providing punishment for the mere possession of goods originating with the enemy was, due to a technicality, declared unconstitutional by the state's supreme court.[43]

By far his most challenging task was prosecuting the Loyalists. In proportion to population, New Jersey's Loyalist problem was very serious. When the claims for Loyalist compensation were presented to the British government after the war, the fourth highest number were from New Jersey.[44] Cortlandt Skinner's New Jersey Volunteers were the largest Loyalist regiment to fight during the war.[45] The extent of support for the Crown in New Jersey can be explained in part by the large Quaker population and in part by the presence of the British in New York and Philadelphia. These cities had long been the economic and cultural centers of New Jersey, and the temptation for fraternization and trading in the old familiar channels was strong. The sight of the British army marching across New Jersey could only serve to encourage people of a hesitant spirit not to commit themselves too publicly to the American cause, and large areas of the state were forced to live in the shadow of the king's troops all during the war.[46] In fact, if the depredations by the British in the state had not alienated some sincere moderates, there might have even been more Loyalist Jerseymen. Cornelia Bell explained to her brother that the troops' actions were "very impolitic, as they make themselves many enemies who would otherwise have been their friends."[47]

Defining the number of active Loyalists in New Jersey has been a matter of some debate. The long-accepted estimate was that there were about five thousand throughout the state, and some historians thought this was much too high.[48] The latest scholarship suggests, however, that New Jersey's potential supporters of the crown may have numbered as many as fifty thousand or more, amounting to 36 percent or 37 percent of the population (men, women, and children), most of whom may never have been engaged in the service of the king due to age, sex, or distance from the fighting.[49] The debate is partly due to the difficulty of distinguishing between potential Loyalists and moderate Whigs. The Bridgeton *Plain Dealer,* one of the several false starts at newspaper publishing made before independence, reported in January 1776 that there were "great numbers of ignorant thoughtless beings who are one day Tories, and the next day Whigs; and the third day nothing at all."[50]

Paterson had bemoaned the fact that the policies followed by the state had encouraged the undecided to become Tories rather than Whigs. He spoke of "prudent, moderate, compassionate, and merciful Men—None of your violent, heels over head Folks; but quite cool and phlegmatick" Jerseymen who had now become leaders of battalions of Tories that made it so unsafe for good Whig families that in some areas they "dare hardly venture to sleep in their own houses."[51] It was an unusual situation where political allegiance was switched from one side to the other and then back again. Paterson's friend Richard Stockton, himself a signer of the Declaration of Independence, was captured by the British and prevailed on to sign "Howe's declaration" renouncing the American cause. Although he was never thereafter politically active, Stockton did reverse himself in 1777 and took the oath prescribed by the legislature of New Jersey.[52]

These factors make it practically impossible to place many people at any certain point on the political spectrum. Indeed, the final clause of the state constitution, which left open the way for reconciliation with the Crown, suggests that not even the Whig leaders of the revolutionary state were willing to burn all their bridges behind them.

The fact that many families were split by the Revolution makes it even more difficult to establish the political complexion of some who kept close contact with family members of opposing political views. Cornelia Bell, who was to become Paterson's wife, saw her family shattered by the conflict. The family homestead, called Bellfield, was in Bridgewater Township, Somerset County, but during the Revolution all except her father left home. Her mother went to live in Philadelphia, Cornelia stayed with the family of Anthony White at Union Farm in Hunterdon County,[53] and her brother Andrew went over to the British in New York.

Andrew Bell had studied law under Attorney General Cortlandt Skinner, a Loyalist whom he followed to the British lines. There he sought his fortune as confidential secretary first to Henry Clinton and later to Sir Guy Carleton. In 1778 he accompanied the royal troops across New Jersey keeping a daily journal for the general.[54] Much to Cornelia's relief, he resisted the temptation to seek a commission in the king's army and served the rest of the war as a civilian in the secure comfort of New York City. Brother and sister had been very close before the war, and now they maintained an intimate (and illegal) correspondence all through the seven years of his exile.[55]

Cornelia believed firmly in the American cause, but she seldom wrote about politics in her letters, partly because she thought too much political talk was unladylike, and partly because she knew her opinions were upsetting to her brother. Nevertheless, much as she opposed the king and his troops, her letters indicate an essential social conservatism that her young suitor would appreciate. She assured her brother that her life was not upset by the fighting. As long as the American general Philemon Dickinson was quartered in the same house where she stayed, they could enjoy his personable manners and would not be called on to put up common soldiers. When she forwarded Tom Paine's latest work to her brother, she called it "a mere piece of scurrility."[56] The devoted sister was continually concerned about her brother's welfare, tried again and again to arrange a meeting with him, and in the spring of 1777 went so far as to have his summer underwear carried to him across the British lines—a singular example of providing aid and comfort to the enemy.[57] When she decided to marry William Paterson, Cornelia begged for her brother's approval and added that "Mr. Paterson bids me to tell you his arms will always be ready to receive the beloved brother of his Cornelia."[58] Andrew Bell owned no property in New Jersey, so as long as he remained behind enemy lines any legal action Paterson might take against him would be of little effect. But the repeated written assurances of Paterson's affection for Cornelia's Tory brother do suggest a soft spot in the revolutionary armor he assumed against moderates and trimmers who condoned Loyalism.[59]

For the most part, however, Paterson's resolution to persevere in the American cause was firm and unshakeable. Like many others he had at first hesitated to become active in the colonial cause, but once the irreversible decision was made, Paterson threw himself into the fray with all his energies. The completion of the break with England and the establishment of a stable political and social structure in the independent state became for him a self-perpetuating motivation. The constitution of 1776 may have failed to provide all he thought it should, but now it was the only law that the state had. Once he was appointed attorney general, it became Paterson's personal responsibility to enforce the law and maintain the order of society as effectively as possible. He realized the significance of the role he had been asked to play and was aware of the opportunities for career advancement that his new fame would provide. His personality was such that he could do nothing but devote himself completely and unreservedly to the duties of his office.

The responsibilities of the attorney general as Paterson fulfilled them were enough to tax any ordinary man, and they took their toll on him. He traveled from one end of New Jersey to the other attending as many county court meetings as possible and personally seeing to the prosecution of wrongdoers. The schedule, which he described as "busy and fatiguing," was made more oppressive because, like Cortlandt Skinner before him, Attorney General Paterson continued his private legal practice at the same time. He complained about the court session at Newark in March 1779, that "besides trying causes of which we had a great plenty, I have written almost three quires of paper since I came to this place."[60] When the sitting at Newark ended, he was prepared "to take horse" for Bergen where the business promised to be "still more intricate and disagreeable."[61] The constant traveling and long hours also affected his health; en route from the Sussex to the Monmouth County Court in the Spring of 1778, he fell so sick that he was forced to stay over at Princeton for two days. Then, unable to arrange for someone to take his place, he pushed on to Monmouth where he continued to work "constantly under the doctor's care." The drudgery of the business, he had complained, was "of itself sufficient to bring on sickness even in the healthiest."[62]

Other pressures were more mental than physical. The last significant battle in New Jersey had been fought at Springfield in 1780, but it was not until much later that the attorney general could travel without fear. He reported from Monmouth in 1782: "We have passed our time here more agreeably than we have done at any former Court; as we have not been under the most distant Apprehensions from the enemy."[63] When the Revolution began, Paterson was a bachelor who might not have minded spending long months away from home, but once he had met Cornelia he began to regret the demands of his schedule. Much of their courtship was carried out in letters written while the duties of his office forced them to be apart. Once they were married, the long absences became worse. "My wish is ever to be with you my dear Cornelia," he wrote in February 1779, "would to heaven I could! But business prevents; my duty forbids; and I must submit."[64] A month later he told her, "this absence is torment-ing."[65] And, if anxiety about the presence of the enemy and the heartbreak of separation from his bride were not strain enough, he could be depressed about the very bulk of the work that faced him. "Indeed, with respect to Business," he admitted in 1779, "I dare not suffer myself to take a look forward; if I did, I should sink under it in pure despair."[66]

A great deal of Paterson's despair was related to his efforts to crush the threat of Loyalism. He came to blame the Tories for almost all the prob-lems that the state had to face. Later in the war, when some citizens com-plained about the salaries of state officials and the taxes necessary to pay them, the attorney general tried to change the subject by attacking the Loyalists.

> The publick would indeed be considerably enriched if those Railers [active Loyalists] were brought before the bar of justice and made to answer for their conduct in the close of the year 1776 & Beginning of the year 1777, when the Enemy had Possession of great part of this state.[67]

At the insistence of the attorney general and in the same spirit in which the Council of Safety was created, New Jersey adopted the same type of laws against the Loyalists that other states were trying to enforce.[68] Previ-ous legislation, some of it prepared by Paterson himself, was strengthened in June 1777 to include the death penalty for those apprehended on their way to the enemy lines.[69] Another act provided that anyone who had gone over to the British or otherwise made known his loyalty to the king could escape punishment by returning his allegiance to the state by August 1. Those who had not returned would soon have their personal property confiscated and disposed of by newly appointed commissioners of forfeited estates, some of whom quickly distinguished themselves for their ability to find personal profit in public service.[70] Between the indictments of the Council of Safety and the activities of the invigorated county magistrates and commissioners, the Loyalists of New Jersey were in for a bad time.

Earlier Paterson had criticized the magistrates for not being firm or thorough enough, and now he resolved to make himself a model for vigorous enforcement of the law. He seems to have devoted his personal attention to all sorts of cases involving the disaffected, however serious or trivial the charge. For example, on July 27, 1779, Paterson recorded the result of the prosecution of William Stout before a special session of the Court of Oyer and Terminer and General Gaol Delivery in Monmouth County. Stout had gone over to New York which was "then in the Possession of the Enemy . . . without any License, Permission or Passport previously obtained . . . to the evil example of others." Stout had been detained in the county jail under the watchful eye of the high sheriff of the county who had brought him to court for trial. The defendant pleaded guilty, was fined £50, and was remanded to the jail until the fine and fees were paid.[71] Presumably the punishment counteracted any bad example he may have given.

Some people never seemed to learn their lesson. From the beginning Paterson had openly criticized the county committees and magistrates who let offenders get off with light penalties, only to find the conduct of the accused became even more bold than before. The situation called for exemplary punishments that would deter potential troublemakers in the future.[72] Paterson's own experience seemed to bear this out. In 1779, he had prosecuted Edward Price for the same offense that Stout had committed. Price had been brought to Shrewsbury by his parents in August 1776, when the British invasion induced them to move from New York, and, in 1777, although he was only fourteen or fifteen years of age, he had borne arms in defense of the state.[73] In 1779, Price neglected to get the proper papers before he traveled to New York with his mother, and on his return he was arrested and brought to trial. A note on Paterson's bill of indictment indicates that a plea of guilty cost Price only a £15 fine.[74] At that time it must have appeared a suitable conclusion to an insignificant case, but Price had not seen the end of Attorney General Paterson. In May 1782, he and some of his friends found themselves in far more serious trouble. According to Paterson's charge, "not having the Fear of God in their Hearts, nor Having any Regard for the Duty of their Allegiance, but being moved and seduced by the instigation of the devil as false Traitors and Rebels," the accused had armed themselves with guns and bayonets and arrayed themselves near Middletown where they "did falsely and traitorously prepare, order, wage and levy a publick and cruel War against the State of New Jersey." They had ordered militiamen to surrender and committed other hostile acts with the intention to "raise and exalt George, King of Great Britain, to the imperial rule and government of this State." This time Price declared his innocence and was turned over for trial, resulting in still more work for the weary prosecutor.[75] But while a few troublemakers like Price would return to plague the state time and time again, others were dealt with more conclusively. Paterson prepared the formal judgment against Robert Whitaker, a propertyless man charged with high treason before the Salem County Court who was sentenced "to be hanged by the neck until he be dead."[76]

The evidence of tireless activity (to the extent of his holding three government posts at one time), his expressions of determination in the face of despair, and the resolute manner in which he pressed indictments all illustrate the firm and persistent prosecution that characterized New Jersey justice in the period of Paterson's service as attorney general. He had made it his personal duty to try to restore the viability of the system of justice, and his insistence on attending as many meetings of the county courts as possible and pleading many cases himself made it easy to supervise the activity of the magistrates. There are indications that in certain cases (like that of Joseph and Catherine Brown) Paterson's passion to restore a vigorous prosecution of the law may have pushed him too far. But with the number of cases he handled, the backbreaking schedule of court sessions he kept up with, and the psychological pressures he worked under, it is surprising that such errors of judgment did not occur more often.

In the midst of a revolution, one would expect the creation of special courts to meet the extraordinary situation with simplified procedures and swift punishments. Instead, the regular use of the traditional legal institutions gave them renewed public respect. The county sheriff and jailer and the county magistrate were the authorities who judged the guilt and enforced the sentences against Paterson's accused. When critical situations warranted (as was the case in Monmouth County in the summer of 1778), a special court session might be called, but the court itself was a familiar and legitimate arm of the law, not an extraordinary or military authority.[77] Even the order of execution against Robert Whitaker was to be carried out by the Salem County jailer, not by the military or some other extraordinary governmental power.[78] The people of New Jersey could clearly see that the establishment of new and revolutionary governments on the state and national levels had not materially altered the patterns of local justice that they had known and relied on in the past. Their willingness to accept the new political wine was encouraged by the old familiar bottles in which it was served.

Paterson's record of service was not without blemishes, but the type of indiscretions that might be traced to him were hardly scandalous. In 1779, for example, Aaron Burr, an old Princeton friend with whom he had maintained cordial relations, called on him to look after the interests of a Mrs. Prevost, the widow of a British officer living on land in New Jersey that had belonged to her husband. Paterson interceded with the commissioners who threatened to confiscate the land and send her to the enemy and assured Burr that he would keep him informed of anything that might arise that would affect her interest.[79] Paterson himself purchased a valuable estate that was forfeited by a fleeing Loyalist attorney, Bernardus LaGrange. Cornelia described the house as only "tolerable," but we must assume that the £12,324 in depreciated money that Paterson paid was something of a bargain price.[80] Paterson helped his sister's husband, Thomas Irwin, to accumulate some property in the same way, and it has been suggested that there was "at least a shadow of collusion" in the way the estate of Somerset Loyalist David White was transferred to Irwin during the war only to be returned to White in the 1790s.[81]

His wife's family presented some other problems. When John Bell died and Andrew became the owner of the family's property, Paterson had no alternative but to bring indictment against him and allow the commissioners to seize the estate.[82] There were a few things, however, that he could do with the help of some friends. He was able to save many of the movable articles by buying them at the appraised value without competitive bidding, thanks to the intercession of Frederick Frelinghuysen, who was the commissioner for Somerset. Then Paterson proceeded to assess the value of all the articles he had been unable to recover so that his brother-in-law could appeal to the king for compensation. "As to keeping possession of Bellfield," Cornelia wrote, "that was not possible," in part because of the ill temper of "the old woman" (her relationship to the Bells is unclear) who stayed on at the homestead and claimed right to part of the house and land.[83] Moreover, while the attorney general bore the responsibility for enforcing the laws against trading with the enemy, with the help of friends who traveled back and forth under military passes, his wife carried on a regular mail-order service with her brother in New York. Before the war was over, she had requested that he send English stays, gloves, hair pins, white sarsnet [silk cloth], materials for a cap, black calico for a petticoat, guitar strings, medicine for her newborn daughter, "and a half a dozen et cetera's."[84]

As before, after 1776 the attorney general was expected to retain his private legal practice while in office. The ways in which Paterson's personal business and his official duties overlapped raise questions about his otherwise virtuous public character. His presence before the judge and jury of a county court as the eloquent spokesman for the state supported by all the prestige of Governor Livingston and the Council of Safety could only be to his advantage when he also represented private clients in the same courts before the same judges and jurors.[85] This may help to explain his insistence on attending so many county court sessions. When he was unable to attend specific court meetings, he might arrange for the same lawyer who represented him in an official capacity to look after the interests of his private clients as well.[86] There was at least one occasion when he represented a man he was prosecuting in the name of the state in a private cause in the very same court session.[87]

Before long, Paterson's practice was flourishing with new and influential clients. Landholder Anthony White, who was later to become Paterson's second father-in-law, merchant John Neilson, Governor William Livingston, Chief Justice Robert Morris, and William Alexander ("Lord Stirling") all entrusted their personal legal business to counselor Paterson.[88] Such promising students as Robert Troup and young Aaron Burr chose Paterson as the master under whom they would serve their apprenticeship in the law.[89] While one must assume that such men recognized Paterson's considerable talents as an attorney, the implication remains that they may have given him their business or trusted to him their education in hopes that his reputation before the courts would rub off on them.

In the second half of the twentieth century, there has been an increasingly suspicious and critical public attitude toward the private interests of public officeholders. Assuming that the temptation to serve themselves would be too great, we no longer trust our officials to avoid conflicts of interest, but require them to divulge information about their personal financial holdings and to create blind trusts to control them. Still, no one expects a person who has held high office for a time to return to private life at a position lower than he enjoyed before. Two hundred years ago, before ethics committees and legislative regulations were at work, the virtuous public servant was expected to act on his own to keep the public interest foremost in his mind. In a deferential political system, men were chosen for office not so much because of their positions on particular issues but because of their wide experience, sound judgment, and trust-worthiness. If a conflict arose between public interest and personal con-cerns, the officeholder was expected to endure self-sacrifice for the well-being of the community. Loyalists, for example, who resisted colonial protests because of their personal interest in maintaining the old order, were eventually rejected by their constituents. But when public interest and private concerns coincided, no one seems to have minded if the official was able to benefit.

The number of cases in Paterson's private practice increased dramatically during the war (from 15 in 1775 to 73 in 1781 and 124 in 1782),[90] but much of this increase was due to the natural influence of his newfound fame, the multiplication of cases brought on by the ramifications of the Revolution, and the fact that some of his most powerful competitors in the legal profession had fled the state to continue to serve their king.[91] Such successful members of the bar as Cortlandt Skinner and Bernardus LaGrange had become Loyalists to the direct advantage of William Paterson, who inherited the office of one and the estate and practice of the other. There were few who could criticize Paterson for taking advantage of this opportunity, since Skinner had fled New Jersey with the militia at his heels and LaGrange, who had been cited by the colonial legislature for exorbitant fees and had long been the subject of widespread "hatred and aversion," was burned in effigy in his own New Brunswick in 1775. The loss of neither of them was mourned.[92]

Paterson was twice offered a position in the Continental Congress and twice turned it down. He explained to Henry Laurens in 1778 that he was very busy "trying disaffected persons, which at the present juncture sound policy, as well as social justice, renders particularly necessary."[93] In 1780, he told the legislators who again proposed him as a delegate to the Continental Congress that the business of being attorney general required all the time he could devote to it.[94] It has been suggested that at least in the latter case he must have been looking more after his own fortune than the well-being of the state, since the reduced number of Loyalist prosecutions might indicate that "1779 was the last year of real revolution as far as the attorney general was concerned."[95] When the nature of the cases that still arose is considered, however, this conclusion fails to stand. The brushfire crisis of 1776–1777 that had necessitated the forming of the Council of Safety had been extinguished, but the threat posed by New Jersey Loyalists continued on. Paterson prosecuted Edward Price and his cohorts for perpetrating an outright war against the state in 1781, and he did not feel free of anxiety about the presence of the enemy until 1782.[96] Even in that year the legislature was forced to alter the election law and do away with the secret ballot for fear that the disaffected would otherwise secretly intrigue against the government.[97]

To be sure, Paterson's personal interests would be served better if he remained in New Jersey rather than traveling south to Philadelphia, but there is no reason to doubt the sincerity of his concern for the safety of his constituents. Besides, serving on the Continental Congress would require still more long absences from his wife and family. Paterson remained in the office of attorney general, assiduously performing its duties until the treaty of peace was assured in 1783.[98] Surely a man who favored his private interests over his public responsibilities would have resigned earlier to concentrate on his personal fortune. Moreover, unlike many others of his experience and position, Paterson showed no interest in speculation. He purchased only one forfeited estate and immediately made that farm on the Raritan his home and office.[99] Paterson's compromises with the letter of the law were always matters open to interpretation. When he interceded for family or friends, for example, the decisions he sought to influence were always of an administrative nature and never judicial.

Paterson felt that he deserved a successful career, not particularly because of his devotion to the cause of independence, but because of his long and arduous training in the law and because of his patient devotion to professional pursuits before 1776, when his immediate returns had been so small. Paterson realized that success in the legal profession was something that came after years of patience and self-discipline. Now that independence was won and his career was at last bearing fruit, Paterson could relate his success to his long study, hard work, and public service rather than to an unpredictable side-effect of a social revolution.

Paterson represented the last generation of those who had struggled to earn their way into the old colonial elite through education, moral self-discipline, and attention to the manners of polite society. The problem was that his leadership qualities went unrecognized until the old colonial political structure had begun to break down. The fact that, like most upwardly mobile young men at the time, he chose to support independence, did not mean that he had set aside all of the lessons he had learned and the values he had nurtured in following the traditional and accepted path to elite status. He was, as James K. Martin has noted, one of the lower echelon colonial leaders who made it to the top because of the Revolution.[100] But Paterson did not have to seek out a rationale for his actions. Without realizing it, for more than a decade he had been bringing together the elements of a political and social philosophy that in a revolutionary situation would coincide perfectly with his ambitions for leadership. He certainly seems to have taken his virtuous self-image too seriously, but such problems must have been common among those to whom voters had deferred their political judgments. The threat to American society that he had perceived had led Paterson to defend his traditional beliefs by radical means, at least until the war was over and independence was secure. Had he been born and educated a decade or so later, things might have been different, but he had worked desperately to fit himself into the respectable ranks of the old deferential society, and he could never be comfortable with the assumptions of the new democratic one that would soon begin to emerge. Paterson had earned a reputation for leadership in the most innovative country in the world, but he had done so while preserving his moralistic conservatism.

Paterson has been accused of a willingness to "gamble his own future on the success of the Revolution, and prosecute both in the name of patriotism."[101] But the relatively minor indiscretions he committed while in office should not detract from his considerable accomplishments. Under his direction hundreds of Loyalists were efficiently prosecuted and hundreds of estates were confiscated. The problems with effective enforcement of the law that Paterson had identified in March 1777 had been solved, largely through the efforts of Attorney General Paterson. By the time he left government service in 1783, the popular respect for the authority of governmental institutions had been restored, the invading armies as well as the Loyalist enemy within had been defeated, and Paterson could rest assured that independence had been won without the radical political and social dislocation he had feared from the beginning.

PART III

INVENTING A NATION

The objective of independence had coincided perfectly with Paterson's personal ambitions, and his law practice was booming when he left the responsibilities of public office behind in 1783. With freedom from Britain won, his professional reputation and financial condition were also secure. Now he seemed satisfied with the social position he had attained and did not thirst for further advancement. He had the opportunity to become involved with some of his friends in large-scale speculation in land and public securities, but he turned their offers aside. Paterson's personality did not fit him to be a "high roller"; he was content to enjoy public respect and relative security and leave the higher stakes to the more adventurous. Thanks to the connections he had made during the Revolution, Paterson had all the legal business he could handle for the next few years. His self-satisfaction with professional success and material comfort, however, could not make up for the loss of his wife and infant daughter who died within a few weeks of each other soon after he had returned to private life, leaving him with two youngsters to care for on his own.

The public issues that most concerned Paterson during the Confederation decade were financial ones, especially the relief of debtors and the circulation of devalued state paper money, both of which he steadfastly opposed. Although each of these positions was clearly in line with what his creditor clients would have expected from Paterson, his arguments also reflected his own conservative political philosophy. He came to view the sanctity of contracts as a basic principle of republicanism, a principle that should be immune from any and all interference, even if it came from the popularly elected legislature. In order to guarantee this principle, Paterson joined the movement for a stronger national government and hoped that some new central authority might serve to circumscribe what he saw as the dictatorial tendencies of the popular will.

Paterson's role in the Philadelphia convention was crucial. He was largely responsible for formulating and carrying out a three-phase effort to assure equal representation for the small states in at least one house of the national legislature. The New Jersey Plan was no eleventh-hour attempt to obstruct the convention from breaking in on states' rights. Rather it was a sophisticated political maneuver that represented only one phase in the general struggle over representation. Paterson, the man most responsible for the plan, never intended it to be accepted item-by-item as an absolute alternative to the Virginia proposals that had already been debated. In fact, he would have opposed certain elements of it himself had they come to a close vote. What the New Jersey Plan succeeded in doing was to carry the debate over representation into a third and final phase that eventually resulted in the adoption of the Great Compromise. Paterson's Connecticut friends who proposed the compromise deserve certain credit, but were it not for the unshakeable arguments and the adroit procedural strategy of the delegate from New Jersey, the large-state representatives might never have accepted the compromise. In a sense, therefore, William Paterson should be considered the "father of the United States Senate."

Thus, it was fitting that Paterson should have been chosen to sit as a senator in the first Congress. In this capacity he was able to help fill in some of the gaps that the framers of the Constitution had left open. Paterson was directly involved in writing the Judiciary Act of 1789, which set up the federal court system and established the first rules for its operation. He also took part in the debates over Alexander Hamilton's financial plan and, as issues began to divide the delegates, Paterson emerged as an ardent supporter of Federalism. Finally, after two sessions of hard work in the Senate, he was chosen by acclamation to assume the governor's chair which, since 1776, had been filled by his old friend William Livingston. As he returned to New Jersey in 1791, it can be asserted without qualification that Paterson had contributed in a significant way to the creation of a new, distinctly American, form of government.

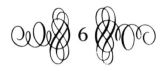

6

Hard Money and the
Dangers of Democracy

News of the coming of peace was greeted in April 1783 with a celebration in Trenton and services of thanksgiving and festive illuminations all across the state, but the feelings evoked were more those of relief than of jubilation. The cost of the war had been high in both physical destruction and psychological stress.[1] William Peartree Smith wrote to his friend and fellow Jerseyman, Elias Boudinot, then president of the Continental Congress, to share his feelings about the peace.

> The fine air of this illustrious morning . . . has set my silent bells into a little jingle. . . . They are very weak, I must confess. I am incapable of ringing the Grand and Noble chimes of Triumph.[2]

The news of the abortive Newburgh conspiracy of Continental soldiers to overthrow the congress was still fresh, and Smith was concerned about some of the problems that the infant nation would have to face in the near future. Not the least of them was "to set all the parts of the Great acquired machine" of the Confederation into order. He told Boudinot of his fear that the structure was "all going to Pieces, without sufficient force in the Commanding Spring." And if, as he thought, it would become necessary for some "Master Hand" to seize the reigns of government as Cromwell had in England, he only hoped it would be the great and meritorious general who had rescued the nation in war.[3]

The difficulties New Jersey would face in the years after the war were not very different from those of the years before. Continental politics was still of little concern to Jerseymen, and a great deal of their governmental business was still carried out on the county level. But there were new complications in the economic changes and political pressures brought on by the new climate of republicanism. For many popular leaders, the solutions to social problems would appear much simpler because of the political change, and they would expect the political institutions of the state to be more responsive to the needs of the people. For those who were more conservative, however, the decisions of the state government in these years would seem totally destructive to the true ideals of republicanism, and they would seek salvation in a reconstituted and more powerful national government of the type Smith had foreseen. Like any fine liquor, the spirit of stable republicanism had to be distilled in the fire of contention and discord before it could begin to strengthen and mature.

William Paterson's immediate reaction to the news of peace was a feeling of deliverance. He had not complained, except to his wife, of the rigors of his service during the conflict, but, now that it was over, he retired to private life at the age of 38 and looked forward to a period of relaxation. He had considered a move to New York, but soon decided against it because of the insecurity and confusion there. He wrote of his desire to "pass the Remainder of Life in Quietude and Peace," and he wished especially to make up for the long months that the war had forced him to spend away from home and hearth.[4]

Paterson's father had died in 1781 and had been buried at his son's farm on the Raritan. This made William the head of his father's family, a responsibility he would assume by assisting his brothers and brother-in-law to establish their business careers with helpful advice and financial support.[5] But his wife and children were closer to his heart. The war years had not been easy on Cornelia. It had been pleasant for her to move into a comfortable home, and she was certainly well provided for, but the long periods of separation from her husband were hard on her. She wrote to her brother Andrew about "the many tedious hours I pass alone" and told him how she looked forward to her mother's coming to stay at the Raritan farm, "for surely no one ever required the presence of a Mother more than I do, being frequently indisposed and entirely alone."[6] On Paterson's infrequent visits home, two children were conceived—Cornelia, born June 4, 1780, and Frances, born January 29, 1782—but the busy father had missed some of the most cherished moments of parenthood.[7] In the summer of 1783, as he set aside the responsibilities of his office for the last time, he could look forward to a fuller family life. Instead he met with personal tragedy.

Frances, his youngest daughter, fell ill and died in June 1783.[8] The shock would have been profound under any circumstances, but Paterson's wife was expecting another baby in the fall, and she took the loss very hard. A fleeting reunion with her brother managed to restore her spirits somewhat, but in October she, too, became ill.[9] In a few weeks she presented her husband with their first son, but the strain of childbirth proved to be too much for her weakened condition. Four days later, she died.[10] Cornelia's death was a traumatic experience for Paterson. He had loved her deeply, but they had been deprived of a normal life together. Now, just when it seemed that he would be able to spend time with her, she was taken from him. He mourned her loss and wrote verse to commemorate her death and its impact on him.

> Her person was delicate, full of grace and dignity
> Kindled by beauty and enlivened by sense
> She was loveliness itself.
> The beauties of her person were exceeded only
> By those of her mind. . . .
> Go Passenger
> Reflect upon your own mortality
> and learn to die.[11]

But if a part of Paterson died with Cornelia, he could not afford to mourn for long. With daughter Cornelia now three and his newborn son William to care for, he had scant time for self-pity. He explained to Cornelia's brother that, as deep as his grief had been, "yet what consolation do my sweet babes afford." He hoped that Bell and his mother would come and visit the Raritan farm before he broke up the house to move into the town of New Brunswick, to a more convenient home, one less crowded with poignant memories.[12] A little over a year later, he married Euphemia White, one of Cornelia's dearest friends and the daughter of Anthony White, who had provided a home for Cornelia in the early days of the war. Paterson's first wedding had taken place in the White home, and Euphemia had watched the beginning of Cornelia's married life as the newlyweds moved into White's Union Farm until they could find a place of their own.[13] Now, five years later, she stepped in to make a home for Paterson and Cornelia's children.

When Paterson retired from public life, he had never thought of giving up his lucrative private practice, and burying himself in work was a way to forget his grief. Paterson's legal practice in the years between 1783 and 1790 took him into twelve of New Jersey's thirteen counties, but it has been estimated that 65 percent of his cases were handled in either the county courts of Hunterdon, Somerset, and Middlesex, or in the New Jersey Supreme Court.[14] In these four jurisdictions alone, he took part in 947 cases over eight years.[15] Adding to that the cases he handled in other jurisdictions and routine legal business such as writing wills and consultations that were never reflected on the court dockets, Paterson must have been a very busy man.

As his business grew, naturally so did his income. It has been estimated that, even in 1787, when he was preoccupied with responsibilities at the Philadelphia convention, his professional income amounted to about £1,000.[16] His reputation led to his participation in some of the most significant legal actions going on in the state at the time. Aside from maintaining his professional prestige, these cases afforded generous fees and further increased his fortune.

The single legal question that occupied the attention of New Jersey's landed interests, almost to the exclusion of other critical issues, was the dispute over the boundary between East and West Jersey.[17] The two boards of proprietors jealously protected their political influence and their respective landholdings on either side of the dividing line. When the boundary between New York and New Jersey was changed in 1769, the exact location of North Station Point, which had been used as the northern terminus for the East-West line, had been set several miles to the east of where it was supposed to have been. The West Jersey proprietors, who stood to profit considerably if the East-West dividing line were shifted to the east, fought in the Provincial Assembly to have the new location of North Station Point accepted as the terminus for a new dividing line. The East Jersey group resisted, but the Revolution intervened before any action could be taken. The political influence of the proprietors had been dealt a shattering blow by the Revolution, but their residual lands, particularly those in the disputed area, were still of very considerable value. Soon the West Jersey proprietors renewed their long and vigorous struggle to have the dividing line changed in their favor. The authority to make such a change rested in the state legislature, and, from the end of the war until 1786, each of the respective boards of proprietors paid a team of lawyers to defend its interpretation of the boundary to the legislators. Paterson was a member of the East Jersey defense team, and with William Churchill Houston, Robert Morris, and John Rutherfurd, he appeared before the

legislature in a three-day hearing in 1784.[18] The result was a victory for
the East by a one-vote margin.

After this, Paterson appears to have stepped aside. He found it "inconvenient" to attend another legislative hearing in 1785.[19] By that time both
he and Morris were also representing the interests of the West Jersey
Society, an independent group of Englishmen with extensive interests in
West Jersey, and Paterson had probably decided that it would be improper
for him to again appear publicly for the Eastern proprietors.[20] In any case,
the interests of the East were confirmed in 1786.

Paterson's portfolio of clients also included the very lucrative business
of Sir Robert Barker. Former Loyalist sympathizer James Parker was
agent for Barker, an Englishman whose extensive lands in New Jersey had
been overrun during the war by tenants who now refused to recognize his
rightful ownership.[21] Parker, a considerable landholder in his own right,
was concerned that an "unrestrained licentiousness" in one area might
make it difficult for any landlord to keep his "tenants under proper behavior."[22] Once he received Barker's power of attorney, Parker hired a
distinguished legal staff including James Kinsey, Elias Boudinot, Abraham
Ogden, Frederick Frelinghuysen, young Richard Stockton, and William
Paterson.[23] Paterson's participation was partly in the form of consultation,
but he was personally involved in some thirty cases of eviction of farmers
in Sir Robert's name in 1785 and 1786.[24] Though the Barker business
"provided a field day"[25] for New Jersey lawyers, Paterson was no in-
discriminate fee grabber. To one of his clients, for example, he had recommended an out-of-court settlement because he had no desire to load his bill
down with costs. "The Play," he explained, "is not worth the candle."[26]
Every now and then in the lifetime of most lawyers, a case comes up in
which the legal fees pyramid to a point where they become truly a monu-
ment to the profession. For Paterson's generation, two of these windfalls
were the East and West Jersey boundary dispute and the Barker land case.
Paterson was influential and well connected enough to get in on both of
them.

His legal expertise and far-reaching reputation inevitably drew him back
into public affairs, this time in the services of the Confederation. He was
chosen in 1785 to be a commissioner in the settlement of a dispute between
the states of Massachusetts and New York.[27] When he accepted the appointment, he involved himself for the first time in the national affairs that
would in the future absorb more and more of his energies. But at least
until 1787 his concerns were still primarily centered in New Jersey.

The question of a policy toward Loyalists remained a knotty problem even after the war ended. Once the peace was secure, many Loyalists scurried to find passage on ships for England and Nova Scotia. In a letter to his brother, Paterson said he thought Loyalists were the only ones who were unhappy about the treaty; "speed them all," he wished.[28] Others who had remained loyal to the king now decided to make their ways back to New Jersey, and the problem of what to do with these returning Tories plagued the state all through the Confederation.[29] In some areas, there was tremendous popular resistance. In Monmouth County, Paterson explained, the people seemed "determined not to suffer any of the refugees to return and live among them."[30]

By the end of the decade, however, many of the wounds seemed to have healed. The policy finally decided on by the state was to encourage the repatriation of at least those who had not taken up arms against the United States, and, although their confiscated estates were never returned, all other legal restrictions against them were set aside. Some of the Loyalists were welcomed back and rose to positions of respect and prosperity in the postwar years. Paterson assured his brother-in-law, for example, that he needed no invitation to visit his niece and nephew. It is unknown whether Bell ever returned to the farm on the Raritan where his sister died, but he did give up his plans to follow his friends to England and instead returned to New Jersey. Eventually he settled in Perth Amboy where he became an active Federalist, collector of the port, and prominent representative of the East Jersey proprietors.[31]

During the Confederation, Paterson participated in attempts to breathe new life into the state's business community. In 1783, he signed a petition to establish a state impost to counterbalance the levies of New York and Pennsylvania and to encourage an independent foreign commerce for New Jersey—"that situation of Independence and Wealth, to which from their resources and local advantages they have a right to aspire."[32] When the state legislature in 1784 initiated legislation that carefully regulated lawyers and rigidly limited their fees, Paterson voiced his obvious displeasure.[33] And before the end of the decade he was drawn again into the mechanics of the state's political system, when he successfully defended the victors of a Hunterdon County election against charges of tampering with the ballot boxes.[34] The matters of public concern that earned Paterson's closest attention during the Confederation period, however, were questions of political economy—debtor legislation, paper money, and public finance.

By far the largest part of Paterson's legal practice was involved with the collection of debts. Of the 947 cases represented in his four busiest jurisdictions, at least 544 were debt cases, and of these he represented the creditor in 455. Moreover, it has been estimated that, thanks to his efforts in these four jurisdictions alone, between 1783 and 1790, £194,936 was collected by New Jersey creditors.[35] In the last years of the war the problems of insolvent debtors had been complicated by a series of economic factors that soon filled the jails with unfortunates who could not meet the demands of their creditors.[36] Despite conservative opposition, the legislature took action on behalf of the beleaguered debtors, and in 1783 and 1786 laws were passed to ease their plight. The 1783 law made it possible for any debtor, with the consent of a majority of his creditors, to turn over all his real and personal property (some clothes, tools, and a bed excepted) and thereby obtain his freedom. The 1786 code allowed the debtor to petition for bankruptcy on his own initiative. If the creditor wanted to keep the debtor in prison, it became his responsibility to pay the jailer for the detainee's support. Another piece of legislation, the notorious Bull Law, which was passed in March 1786 and repealed in November of the same year, sought to protect debtors from having their belongings sold off at a fraction of their real value. With a critical shortage of cash, the bids offered at public auction for the property of debtors were patently unfair. The Bull Law required creditors to accept sufficient property at appraised value to satisfy the debt. These laws appear to have been sincere attempts to save a considerable percentage of the state's population from "utter Ruin,"[37] but the creditors' influence was strong, and one of their willing spokesmen, William Paterson, thought the laws were misguided.

Paterson's statements on the debtor laws defined his position on the sacred rights of property. In one comment on the interrelation of property and the law, he explained that

> to the State it is immaterial in whose hands the property remains, but it is of the last importance, that its citizens should be faithful and punctual in the Performance of Contracts and Payment of Debts. The Legislature therefore should leave the parties to the law under which they contracted.[38]

He saw the Bull Law as particularly opprobrious. It was, he later claimed, "in direct contravention of contracts, and in open violation of every principle of honor, honesty and good faith."[39] Perhaps Paterson's attitude was hard-hearted. After all, his father had earlier faced some of the same misfortunes that Confederation debtors now had forced on them. But there was more at stake here than the financial future of some marginal farmers. As Paterson saw it, the legislature was setting aside some basic tenets of republican government in its haste to satisfy the desires of the people. He reasoned that

> the Legislature must have been sensible of the injustice and terpitude of the measure; but they supposed it would have been pleasing to the bulk of their constituents, and therefore suffered themselves to be carried away by what they conceived to be a popular current.[40]

He maintained that "the rights of private property were inviolable"[41] and that the debtor laws were only one way in which the state legislature was compromising this cardinal rule. Paper money was another.

The beginnings of New Jersey's paper money problems in the Confederation period can be traced back to March 1780, when New Jersey, like the other states, was called on to withdraw at the rate of forty to one for specie all the Continental currency then circulating in their state. The states were to replace Continental bills with a new issue of state paper money, which they would redeem in taxes within six years. In June 1780, New Jersey complied with Congress's request, guaranteeing the new notes as legal tender. It soon became clear, however, that the problem of depreciation had not been solved. Within a year, the new issue "was being reckoned at three to one for specie in spite of the tender laws."[42] By June 1781 the legislators were forced to recognize the problem. In an attempt to straighten out the tangled financial situation, they enacted a new law that repealed all the legal tender provisions relating to paper currency within the state and suspended the sale of confiscated estates, which were being sold at a fraction of their real value because of the depreciation. Here was a simple declaration by the assembly that the guarantee they had given a year before was no good. To ease the blow to New Jersey debtors, the legislators granted a one-year grace period in which creditors who forced their debtors to pay would have to accept the paper at face value. Thereafter they could insist on being paid their debt in full either in specie or in paper money at market value equal to the full specie amount.[43]

Creditors were angry because they could not insist on full repayment of debts for one year. Debtors were angry because they would eventually have to pay back their loans at face value (unless their creditor for some reason forced payment within the year's grace period). William Paterson was very angry, too, but he was most upset about the legal tender guarantee, a promise that the legislators had broken. "What a master stroke this in politicks!" Paterson sarcastically remarked. "What a splendid display of honesty and skill."[44] "What encouragement can there be for industry," he asked, "when a man, having gleaned together a little money . . . has put

it out upon use in expectation of receiving a full return of the principle
. . . is paid in paper . . . which represents not a third of it?"[45] Paterson
recalled that, when the state currency issue was first put forward, the
"faith of New Jersey was solemnly pledged for its redemption. The voice
of our legislature declared that every Bill wore the Face of Truth, and not
the mask of deceit and falsity." But, in repealing the guarantee, the legislators had broken their promise.[46]

In the haste of the moment, the authors of the 1776 constitution had
accepted as a matter of faith that the omnipotent legislators would not
abuse their authority. Now, as Richard P. McCormick has pointed out, it
began to appear that "public contracts might be voided by a simple majority
vote, and that the rights of property, in fact, were insecure in an unrestricted democracy."[47] Apparently Paterson believed that depreciation could
have been avoided, or at least minimized, had the legislature stuck to its
word and maintained the legal tender guarantee (not that he would have
supported the legal tender provision in the first place). It was perfectly
clear, however, that this act of irresponsible devaluation would damage
public faith in the state, particularly in matters relating to paper money.

The issue arose again in 1785. Prompted by a shortage of currency and
a hard-felt depression, hundreds of Jerseyans petitioned their legislature to
establish a loan office or land bank with authority to lend £100,000 in bills
of credit. The proposal was not a radical or unrealistic one. Colonial New
Jersey had repeatedly turned to the paper money expedient to ease its economic problems, and its record of fiscal responsibility had been a generally
good one. But there had always been a conservative group who opposed
paper money, and now they were stronger than before, "reinforced by the
conviction that the legislature could not be trusted to adhere to its
promises."[48]

Paterson became one of the prime spokesmen against the new loan office.
Among the arguments he advanced was the contention that the scarcity of
money did not in fact exist. "Money cannot be scarce," he claimed, "when
the Commodities of a Country find a ready Market, and sell for a good
Price."[49] People might find it difficult to borrow cash even though they
offered the best security, but this should not be taken as evidence of a
scarcity of money. There would be plenty of money to lend, he thought, if
the creditors did not fear that the legislature would again somehow undermine their investments. The problem was not a shortage of money but a
shortage of moral integrity, he said.

The indolent and dissipated may clamour about the Scarcity of
Money; the one will not toil to get it, & the other squanders it as

fast as he receives: their clamour would be the same, if they possessed all the mines of Peru.[50]

Now "Labourers, Tradesmen and Mechanics demand for their Work and Services at least one fourth more than they did before the War." And, as still further evidence that there was no scarcity of money, the legislators had been collecting such high salaries that most were able to "lay up at least one half of their wages."[51]

While he was in the government, Paterson had defended the legislators against charges of overspending. Now he could not resist taking the opportunity to remark sarcastically to the antilawyer interest that the wartime assembly that had kept salaries low might have "pickt up perhaps," their spirit of economy "from some pidling Attorney, or some business hunting, wonder-working Justice of the Peace." Now, however, any "spirit of saving" was gone, and the "Yea and Nay men" of the legislature were playing "pernicious patriots" trying to exact whatever salary and expenses they could from the public treasury.[52]

To accentuate his argument that there was no real scarcity of money, Paterson tied it together with his old ideas on luxury and moral corruption. Far from being destitute, "people of all Ranks purchase foreign Manufactures, and are emulous to excel in Dress, in Equipage, in living, and in all fashionable and expensive Amusements." Paterson had returned to the puritanical moralizing that had influenced his political decision making in the past. His proposed solution must have appeared incredible to those threatened with foreclosure and imprisonment by impatient creditors or the county sheriff, for Paterson proclaimed that

it must be the Wish of every good Man, as it is in the interest of every wise man, that Money should decrease and not increase among us. A decrease of Money will introduce a Spirit of Industry & Frugality, will restrain luxury, Extravagance and thoughtless Profusion, and will compel people to work for the Bread they eat, and not go about seeking whom they may devour.[53]

In deciding against both the "justness and utility" of new paper money legislation, Paterson was quick to admit that colonial precedents had not worked badly.

Before the Revolution, Paper money within certain confined limits retained its value, & was equal to coin. There was then no violation of Faith public or private; Credit had received no wounds; but on the contrary Honesty and Truth were considered as the basis of all Contracts, whether they respected Individuals, or the Community at Large.[54]

Since the Revolution, however, the actions of the legislature had raised grave doubts.

While the people remember the catastrophe of the Continental money, while they contemplate the Fate of the State money, While they bear in memory the act for inforcing payment in certificates [the wartime legal tender law], While the legislature of Today may break in upon and destroy the Contracts formed and ratified by the Legislature of Yesterday, while all property has become uncertain owing to the mutuable principles of legislation heretofore practised to serve the Interest of the Moment or a present Exigency, it is the Height of political Frenzy to order a new emission of Paper, and by the compulsive edict of the Law to make it pass in payment equal to gold & silver.[55]

For the state legislature, which had already proved itself unworthy of trust, to issue bills on the assumption that they would circulate without depreciation was, in Paterson's word, "preposterous."[56]

But the most effective arguments used by the opposition to the new loan office and paper money outlay were political rather than economic.[57] For Paterson, the whole question came to rest in the political principles that were at the heart of republicanism.

In Legislation the following principles are clear, that All the Citizens of a State ought to be viewed with equal Eyes; That one order of *Citizens* ought not to be preferred to another; that Property ought to be secured, and rendered inviolate, that Industry ought to be encouraged, Honesty and good Faith inculcated and promoted, and Deception, Fraud, and Perfidy detected and punished.[58]

The application of these principles was easy and direct.

The Sum which the Debtor owes makes up Part of the Substance of his Creditor, and ought not to be taken from him without his Consent; nor ought it to be paid in any other Kind of Money than that which was stipulated between them. If the Legislature interfere, and invent a new Species of Money to serve the Purposes of the Debtor,

Though at the Risk of ruining the Creditor, is it not an Act of Partiality, and causeless Preference?[59]

In other words, Paterson felt that, unless the popular will, as expressed through the elected legislature, was limited with respect to property rights, the essential principles of republican government would be destroyed.

As a result of the public debate, the assembly tabled the paper money bill in the fall of 1785 on the resolution of Abraham Clark, the state's paper money champion, who probably sought to find more support before putting it to a final vote.[60] When the legislators convened again in early 1786, the bill was approved by the assembly, but was turned down by the council. According to Paterson, the measure was then "committed to the saddlebags of Mr. Clark," who carried it to a special session called in New Brunswick in May, where it was passed into law.[61] The tyranny of the majority seemed to be at hand.

Paterson's disapproval of the popular posture of the state assembly would ultimately lead him to favor a strengthening of the Confederation government at the expense of the states. But New Jersey's support for the nationalist group in Congress, which had come early, was based on other issues as well. Once the war was over, the nationalists agreed that their best chance to invigorate the powers of Congress was to win for it an income independent of the voluntary state requisitions called for in the Articles of Confederation. The result was the financial plan of 1783 that had as its main feature the establishment of a national impost to raise revenue for the repayment of the war debt.[62] New Jersey's leaders saw in the impost an opportunity to be free from the unfair burden placed on them by New York and Pennsylvania. With no major port of her own, New Jersey was forced to import through these neighboring states, whose tariff duties were passed on to New Jersey buyers in the form of increased prices. New Jersey had her own contributions to pay to Congress, but, as it was working out, Jerseymen were paying a sizeable share of their neighbors' contributions as well as their own. It was unlikely, however, that the financial plan would receive the required unanimous support, and, before 1783 was over, New Jersey had arranged to pay the interest on that portion of the Continental debt held in the state directly rather than continue to honor the inequitable requisitions of Congress.[63] This could only disappoint the nationalists who wanted the public creditors to look directly to Congress for satisfaction.[64]

Nevertheless, New Jersey continued to support the movement for a national impost. In 1785, the legislature required its implementation as a precondition for the state to pay its share of the new congressional requisition. This 1785 requisition had a new twist. One-third of it was to be paid in specie and two-thirds in indents (certificates given for interest due on the federal debt).[65] New Jersey citizens held a disproportionately large share of the debt and would therefore receive more than enough indents to satisfy two-thirds of the state's quota. The catch was that Congress would issue no indents in states that did not agree to comply with the entire requisition, and New Jersey refused to pay any specie as long as the 1783 impost was still not in effect.[66] Then, to increase the pressure on the nationalists to win approval for the impost, the state assembly ordered its congressional delegates to vote against any resolutions involving expense for New Jersey from which the Confederation as a whole or New Jersey in particular received no specific advantage.[67] A delegation from Congress tried to convince the assembly to withdraw the order on the grounds that it seemed to be an attack on the national government rather than a tactic to encourage the extension of its authority. The special delegation suggested to the New Jersey lawmakers that if they were so concerned about the state of the Confederation, they should "urge the calling of a general convention of the states for the purpose of amending and revising the federal system."[68]

The problems that the federal system posed for New Jersey were already clearly in focus. A strengthened national government might help protect New Jersey from the unfair burdens imposed by selfish neighbors, but a more powerful central government could become a threat in itself. The problem would be to find some middle ground where New Jersey was protected but the central government was limited from encroaching on the state's authority. Although Abraham Clark's opposition had not been altered and there appeared to be no intention of actually paying the requisition, the assembly quietly agreed to rescind its obstructionist resolution.[69]

Paterson was one of the few who publicly spoke out in support of the requests of the Congress. In a petition prepared in May 1786, he assumed a position diametrically opposed to the legislators who chose to isolate New Jersey's problems rather than rely on the as yet unfulfilled promises of the Confederation. "The more the interests of the states are intertwined," he reasoned, "the more close and perfect will be their Union; the more sure and permanent will be the Basis of National Credit & Honor."[70] He went on to point out "that New Jersey has a surplus of certificates," and the surplus indents collected by Jersey creditors could be sold in the states that needed them to fill their obligations. It was therefore "emphatically in the Interest of New Jersey to adopt the resolution."[71] To make full use of every opportunity to score the popular assembly, the petition concluded with demands that the doors of the assembly be thrown open for "the Admission of all Persons who are disposed to attend," and that the wages of the state's legislators be reduced.[72]

Notwithstanding these criticisms of the legislature's secrecy and costs, the popular branch of the New Jersey government was considerably more popular than it had been before the war, and this was at the heart of Paterson's worries. The suffrage qualifications that had been carried over from the Provincial Congress into the 1776 constitution called for a mere £50 of personal property as an eligibility requirement, but currency depreciation since 1776 had made the £50 provision practically meaningless.[73] Not only were there many more voters from the lower ranks of society than before the Revolution, but they were electing a new type of representative who was more ready to respond to popular political interests. Before the Revolution, "four out of five members [of the assembly] were either well-to-do or wealthy." But, by 1785, "fully two thirds of the representatives were ordinary farmers," and lawyers and merchants "were all but eliminated."[74] The people's willingness to defer the making of political decisions to their "betters," which was common before the Revolution, had undergone a shattering blow.[75] The upper house was still more conservative, but the aristocratic character it had cherished in colonial days was lost forever during the Revolution. It might delay the passage of paper money legislation for a while, as it had with the loan office bill in 1785, but it could not hold out forever.[76] Ultimately the councillors, like the assemblymen, had to answer directly to the people.

The laws for debtor relief and state paper money that Paterson had spoken against so vigorously were economic in nature, and Paterson, because of his clients, had good reason to line up with the conservative opposition. But despite the generous income he was able to collect from his legal business, his personal finances do not suggest large landholding or speculation, and at least some of his income was eaten up in expenses related to his practice. Township tax records indicate that in 1788 he maintained two riding chairs and a chariot to enable him to do the traveling he had done on horseback in his younger years.[77] He was invited to join R. R. Livingston and Elias Boudinot in a series of land investments in 1789, but Livingston had to report to his partner that "Mr. Paterson rather declines joining in our purchase."[78] Paterson seemed to feel that the spirit of speculation had a hint of immorality to it. One of the arguments he had made against a new paper money issue was that the new notes would "bewilder Conscience in the Mazes of dishonest speculations."[79] In an age when great fortunes were to be made in land and securities, there is no evidence that Paterson participated in any of it. He was far from poor, owning a house and lot, twenty acres of improved land, two horses, four cattle, and one of the thirty-six slaves in the entire township in 1788.[80] But his wealth was not expended in the investments and speculations that were common to some others who shared his conservative opinions on the issues of the day.

The profits that he made from representing landlords and speculators in court could be rationalized in terms of political principle. The debtor laws and the loan office controversy of 1785–1786 were simply the clearest examples of the willingness of the legislators, if pressed by popular demands, to set aside the basic and traditional rights of private property. "In a free Government," Paterson explained,

> men expect to live under equal and certain Laws, which like the sun will diffuse their Virtue, and operate alike on every Member of the Community. Where the Guards of Property are liable to be removed at the Whim or pleasure of the Supreme Power in a State, a Person has not any Thing that he can call his own, or is sure of for a Moment.[81]

Submitting the rights of property to the transitory desires of the people created a new kind of tyranny, according to Paterson.

Along with the other basic tenets of the British political system, Paterson's education had impressed on him the concept of a fundamental natural law to which every virtuous society should conform. Much to the distress of the colonists before 1776, the British relied on Parliament balanced between king, lords, and commons to maintain the fundamental as well as the statutory law of the society. The American colonists resisted what they saw as aristocratic attempts to set aside their fundamental rights as Englishmen by the edict of Parliament. But when it came time to write the wartime constitutions for their new states, the American leaders placed the same kind of faith in the people that the British had placed in Parliament. For many men like Paterson who harbored serious reservations about the state constitution, it did not take long to find proof that their faith had been undeserved.[82] For these men, the legislature's handling of the debtor laws and the loan office bill clearly showed that the government of New Jersey was insensitive to its fundamental responsibilities.[83]

The realization that the state legislatures could not be trusted to preserve the basic principles of republicanism brought men such as Paterson to seek new and more specific limitations on the authority of government. In what has been called the most distinctive political idea of the American Revolution,[84] they sought to separate the fundamental law from the purview of everyday government and enshrine it as absolutely superior to the provisions of statute law produced by the legislatures.[85]

For Paterson, the right of a man to his property was not an issue that could be left to statutory law. The same stimuli that had brought Paterson the moderate to assume leadership in the movement for independence now moved him toward the argument for a new constitution. Whig history and the classics had constantly warned that the unrestrained rule of the popular will would be as undesirable as that of a despotic parliament or an absolute king.

At one point in the loan office controversy, Paterson had wryly commented that "opinion regulates Politics and governs the World."[86] The fundamental law had obviously been betrayed, and there were signs that the same kind of moral corruption and passion for "fashionable & expensive amusements" that had inflamed Paterson before the Revolution were again at hand.[87] To be sure, his legal business might prosper and his friends' speculative investments might be guaranteed if a new and stronger government were set up, but, as with his decision to support the Revolution, such material motivations made up only a small part of his rationale. To debtor-farmers, Paterson's feeling that a decrease in money was needed to restore the spirit of industry must have appeared ridiculous, and, to more tolerant men, his tirades against fashion in "dress and equipage" must have seemed overly passionate. These were the ideas, however, that he continually returned to, and these were the ideas that drew him into the movement for a new federal constitution.

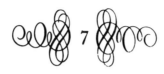

7

The Federal Convention,
the New Jersey Plan, and the
Politics of Nation Making

William Paterson's finest hour came in the federal convention of 1787. Most histories mention his name with reference to the Paterson Plan or the New Jersey Plan as it is also called, but until now the full extent of his contributions to the American Constitution has not been completely recognized. In the dynamics of debate and compromise that gave birth to a new and durable formula for American government, Paterson proved himself a consummate politican as well as a great lawyer and statesman.

The hopes and fears that were represented in the Philadelphia convention had long been brewing. The years between 1776 and 1787 had been eventful. The decade had offered numerous opportunities for the independent sovereign states and the Congress to test their power and influence, and by and large the record had not been a bad one. Many of the problems relating to the Loyalists had been settled, the postwar economy had begun to show signs of recovery, and after years of distress some matters of serious interstate rivalry had been brought to amicable conclusion—all considerable achievements for a new nation so recently ravaged by war.[1] But New Jersey's experiment in independence, like the experience of her sister states, had not been entirely successful. Two issues in particular irked Jerseymen: the unsettled ownership of the land between

131

the seaboard states and the Mississippi River (which potentially gave an unfair advantage to other states), and the intricacies of Confederation finance (which represented a distinct disadvantage to New Jersey).[2] Paterson, who had complained long and loud about Confederation financial affairs, later described it as "a low and wretched situation," in which as a result of the schemes of neighboring states and the "mischievious" policies of New Jersey's own legislators "an air of despondency had spread itself over the face of the country."[3]

As early as 1778, three years before the Articles of Confederation were adopted by the states, New Jersey recognized that the Confederation would be too weak unless additional powers were granted to Congress. In that year a "Representation" by the state legislature suggested that the "sole and exclusive" authority of Congress to regulate foreign trade and dispose of western lands was crucial and hoped that the income from customs duties could be utilized for the general concerns of the Confederation.[4] New Jersey cooperated with the nationalists in their subsequent attempts to strengthen the government through amendment, at least until 1785 when, in desperation, the state withheld support of a new requisition until a national impost was agreed to.[5]

In the course of the Confederation decade, Paterson also came to favor the nationalists' cause, influenced no doubt by his experience as a congressional commissioner and by the "poverty and distress" he saw resulting from financial chaos.[6] But more important in Paterson's evolving political conscience was his concern for the "sacred rights of property." Before it had really had a chance to take root, he thought, America's experiment in virtuous republicanism had begun to degenerate because property was unprotected from the whims of the people. The more effective the paper money party became in pushing through their popular legislation—culminating in the 1786 loan office—the deeper became his fears. While many of his worries were based on what might happen if, at some time in the future, the new currency were to be devalued, his gloomy prospects betrayed a fear that all the idealism of the Revolution might soon be lost forever.

Many of the men who had sat in Congress from 1781 to 1783 had tried to infuse the Confederation with more power. A financial program to guarantee public credit and encourage stable economic growth had been conceived by Robert Morris, Alexander Hamilton, James Madison, and other leaders who worked to win the necessary taxing power for Congress, but their labors were in vain.[7] When the war ended in 1783, many of the leaders left Congress, partly because, like Paterson, they sought to return to their ordinary lives, but also because the war's end brought shrinking chances for a strengthened union. Disheartened as they were by earlier failures, these nationalists nevertheless maintained their concern for the state of the Union. Some had mercantile and speculative interests that tied their attention to national affairs, others were moved by more selfless patriotic concerns, but whatever their motives the precarious health of the new republic became more and more evident to them as time passed. On top of the financial prostration of Congress, the ultimate failure to win unanimous state approval for a national impost in 1786 and the potential dangers exposed by Shays's rebellion seemed to threaten impending doom. A few men such as Madison and Hamilton realized that these ominous events presented them with a unique opportunity to seek once more an exalted national government. It seemed somehow ironic that these ultra-nationalists who had campaigned without success for partial reform through congressional impost, now sought to bring about a thorough and organic change. If the impost had been approved, an opportunity for more sweeping reform might not have arisen until much later, and then under very different circumstances.[8] But if the situation of 1786–1787 was unique and fortuitous, it was also critical; if they failed now, the Confederation might simply dissolve.

The 1786 Annapolis convention, convened at Virginia's request, was the first act in what became a carefully orchestrated plot to reconstitute the American republic. New Jersey was not passing up any chance to improve her position and sent three delegates to Annapolis (William Churchill Houston, James Schureman, and Abraham Clark). Their instructions were to seek "a uniform System in their [the states'] commercial Regulations and in other matters . . . effectually to provide for the Exigencies of the Union."[9] Wary New Englanders, on the other hand, doubting the sincerity of Virginia planters who invited them to discuss commercial affairs, refused to attend. In fact, only five states sent representatives, and there seemed little reason to go on with the conference. Alexander Hamilton, the most nationally minded of them all, proposed, with Madison's moderating counsel, to issue the call to a new and more general convention. The Jersey delegates enjoyed the most generous mandate from their state government, so they were asked to make the formal motion. As fate would have it, the task fell to Abraham Clark, the leader of the popular paper money faction back in New Jersey, who was senior member of the state's delegation.[10]

As the New Jersey legislature jumped to approve the Annapolis recommendations and choose its commissioners, Paterson's political star again began to rise. He had held no state office since 1783, but the legislature now chose him along with David Brearly (chief justice of the state

supreme court) and William Churchill Houston (who had been at
Annapolis) to go to Philadelphia. John Neilson (a merchant and one
of Paterson's clients) and Abraham Clark were also chosen, but both
declined.[11] Clark claimed that his current position as representative of
New Jersey in Congress was reason enough to disqualify him, but his
later lukewarm attitude toward ratification and subsequent opposition to
Federalist positions in the Congress (1791–1794), suggest that he might
have felt uncomfortable in the company at Philadelphia.[12] William
Livingston, the respected governor, and Jonathan Dayton, a rapidly rising
young businessman and financier, agreed to serve in place of Clark and
Neilson.[13]

When he arrived in Philadelphia, Paterson found himself in a very
respectable company of men, the vast majority of whom shared his concern
for the state of American society and government. For Paterson, most of
the financial problems of New Jersey had been translated into political
terms: He saw the inflation of paper currency and the expedients for
debtor relief as challenges to the sacred rights of property that should be
protected in a republican system. Delegates from other states would
perceive the needs of the nation in a different context, and some may
have been thinking more of themselves than they were of the public
interest.[14] But almost all of them were prepared to see considerable new
powers lodged in the central government.[15]

William Pierce, a delegate from Georgia who recorded capsule sketches
of the assembled gentlemen, described Paterson as

> one of those Men whose powers break in upon you, and create
> astonishment. He is a Man of great modesty, with looks that bespeak
> talents of no great extent,—but he is a Classic, a Lawyer, and an
> Orator;—and of a disposition so favorable to his advancement that
> everyone seemed ready to exalt him with their praises.[16]

There is no record of any of these other praises spoken of by Pierce, but,
by the end of his stay in Philadelphia, Paterson would have earned the
respect, if not the praise, of his colleagues. Unlike Livingston, who was
described by Pierce as seeming "little acquainted with the guiles of
policy,"[17] Paterson was to prove himself one of the most cunning and
effective politicians in the hall.

Once the assembled delegates had chosen officers and established rules
of procedure, Madison's faction seized the initiative. The Virginia Plan,
presented on May 29 by Edmund Randolph as the first act of business,

was the result of long months of planning. Madison had corresponded widely in support of the scheme and had prevailed on the other Virginia delegates to caucus before the formal sessions began so that they could present a united front.[18] The result of their labors must have been a shock to Paterson and his colleagues.

The plan called for a consolidated national government with legislative, executive, and judicial departments. The first branch of the legislature would be chosen directly by the people and the second would be chosen by the first. They were to be empowered "to legislate in all cases to which the separate States were incompetent," and they were to enjoy a veto power over all state laws that the national legislature considered to be "contravening . . . the articles of union." A national executive was to be chosen by the legislature and, with members of the judiciary, would sit as a council of revision to check the decisions of the legislature. Specific articles also covered a guarantee of the territory and republican government of each state, the admission of new states into the Union, and so on.[19]

While most of these proposals would become the object of heated debate in the ensuing months, the provisions for proportional representation in both houses and the very wide power of Congress to veto state laws were the most crucial challenges placed before the delegates. According to Robert Yates, Randolph had "candidly confessed" his intention to set up a "strong *consolidated* union," very unlike the Articles of Confederation. Such total reform had not been discussed before, at least not in the open.[20] Although they had not been able to come up with the unanimous approval of the states required to amend the Articles, the nationalists had found growing support for granting additional powers to Congress. Now they put all that aside and struck out for much more.[21] Randolph stated his fear that the country was "on the eve of [civil] war" and explained how he saw "incontrovertible" evidence of the dangers of democracy in the recent experience of the various states. Congress, as constituted by the Articles, now seemed too democratic to be infused with further powers— unless some radical changes were made.[22]

New Jersey's leaders had given consistent support for supplementing the powers of Congress, but had always meant them to be *supplementary*. There is no evidence that they had even given serious thought to a total change that might cost their equal vote in Congress.[23] But this was precisely what the Virginia Plan proposed, and Madison and his colleagues came to Philadelphia prepared to stand absolutely firm on that principle. Madison's followers, referred to as the large-state group, and their opponents in the small-state group, which was led by Paterson, quickly assumed battle lines for what turned out to be a six-week struggle over the principle of representation. Recent scholarship suggests that the issues behind the division were based less on relative state population and more on sectional location and whether or not the states possessed considerable amounts of unoccupied land (thereby making them potentially large states).[24] But whether their differences were potential or actual, the confrontation between the two groups came at several points to the brink of destroying the convention.

From the beginning, the leaders of the large-state group, even though they could muster a clear majority on some questions, were aware of the diplomacy that might be necessary to bring success to their cause. For example, Madison and his supporters talked the Pennsylvania delegates out of demanding that even the deliberations of the convention be carried out according to proportional representation; presumably they realized that the small-state delegates would never even take their seats under those conditions.[25] Throughout the long struggle over the basic issue of representation, each side would hurl threats at the other, some concealed in the language of legal technicality and some brazenly obvious to everyone in the hall, but the ultimate threat was to walk out of the convention and destroy what appeared to most to be America's last chance for preserving national peace and unity. In the end, both groups had to be convinced that this was the only alternative left before they could be brought to compromise.

The notes that Paterson took during the convention, while sometimes quite revealing, were usually sketchy, uneven, and (unlike the fine paragraph summaries prepared by Madison) clearly intended solely for his own reference.[26] His first cryptic lines, penned on the day the Virginia Plan was presented, were no exception, but they do provide clear evidence that Paterson understood the large-state challenge from the first. The Virginia Plan was unclear about what would happen to the states under the new system. They were not specifically denied their existence as sovereign entities, but neither did they have any place in the new government, which was apparently to be formed directly on the authority of the people rather than on the authority of the states. In his list of the basic resolutions of Randolph's plan, the only objection Paterson inserted was beneath the provision for proportional representation: "Sovereignty is an Integral thing." There could only be one sovereign authority, he believed, and to grant that sovereign power to the central government directly on the authority of the people could only destroy the states. If, as Paterson also noted, Randolph believed that "We ought to be one nation" rather than a union of states, the issue of representation was clearly at the heart of it. The idea that sovereignty might be divided up among different and distinct governments ruling the same people made sense to no one, at least not yet. That idea, unique to American political thought at the time, would eventually emerge from the struggle that the large and small states were about to take up. Paterson also noted the firmness with which Randolph phrased the demand for proportional representation. "This," he wrote beside the resolution on representation, is "the basis upon which the larger States can assent to any Reform."[27] It was clear to Paterson, even from the first day of debate, that, if the large states could not win support for this principle, they would refuse to take part in any other proposals for revising the government, even at the risk of dissolving the Union.

For the next ten days, the deliberations of the convention were directed to Randolph's other resolutions, but it became evident that the real drama would begin when the question of representation came up. The Virginians had maneuvered the convention into a serious and formal consideration of a total change in the Articles of Confederation and also the method of representation within that government. Paterson was already convinced of the need for a strong and consolidated national government. Like other small-state nationalists such as George Read from Delaware, he was clearly committed to organic change and certainly had no relish for the prospect of continuing with the popular legislature of New Jersey as the only protector of public and private rights in his state.[28] His objection was to the unfair representation that the Virginia Plan proposed for the less populous states. The reason he voiced no objection to Randolph's other proposals was probably that he had none serious enough to deserve immediate attention. Whatever other questions he had could wait for the essential matter of representation to be settled.[29] Until this all-important matter came up for debate, Paterson bided his time.

The large-versus-small-state division began to impinge on every issue, whether it was the means of choosing the senators, the relative size of the Senate, or the congressional veto over acts of state legislatures. When John Dickinson suggested on June 7 that the Senate be chosen by the state legislatures, Madison and James Wilson of Pennsylvania were immediately on the defensive. They wanted representation in the Senate to be proportional, but also wanted the number of senators to be kept small. If the legislature of the smallest state elected even only one senator, then, to keep the figures proportional, the largest state's delegation would become huge.[30] On the previous day it had been decided to have the lower house chosen by popular ballot, and now Dickinson argued convincingly that the states would be completely extinguished if they were allowed to play no role in the new national scheme. Deciding to leave aside the volatile issue of apportioning the seats, even Virginia and Pennsylvania gave way and voted to have the state legislators choose the Senate.[31]

Tempers rose again on the following day (June 8) as Delaware's Gunning Bedford correctly identified a proposal to grant absolute power to the new government to veto state laws as an integral threat to the small states. If "Delaware would have about 1/90 (for its) share in the General Councils, whilst Pa. & Va. would possess 1/3 of the whole," there was nothing to stop the large states from vetoing every act of the small state's own legislature.[32] This time Madison and Wilson were able to deliver the votes of their respective delegations, but the absolute veto proposal was defeated nonetheless.[33]

Paterson took no part in these early debates until June 9, when he placed the central issue squarely before the convention. With Brearly seconding, Paterson moved that the committee turn to consider "the rule of suffrage in the Natl. Legislature." Drawing on all the oratorical skills he had practiced as a son of Clio, and all the political knowhow he had absorbed during the turbulent years since, Paterson put together a forceful and convincing speech. Beginning with the argument least likely to change many minds, he reminded the delegates that the official instructions issued by Congress to the convention specifically limited the scope of their powers to the "sole and express purpose of revising the Articles of Confederation." As must have been clear to the large-state leaders, Paterson was taking the same type of unshakeable position that they had assumed. Paterson's legalistic argument constituted a potential threat: The small states might use the limits imposed on the convention as a legitimate basis for repudiating the convention entirely if it overrode their interests. To reinforce his point, Paterson had the instructions of Massachusetts, which contained the same restrictive phrases, read from the floor. He reminded the delegates that the Virginia Plan went far beyond this legal mandate, and in the process he laid down a challenge equal and opposite to the one posed by the large-state men a week before.[34] In one sense, it was a gamble that the large states would compromise on the matter of representation before they would see the entire convention flounder. In another sense, it was no gamble at all, because any new government that did not preserve the sovereign authority of the individual states would be quickly rejected back home in New Jersey.

Moving directly from legal technicalities to practical political realities, Paterson stressed that the present plan could never be ratified; the "people [were] not ripe" for it. "The idea of a national Govt. as contradistinguished from a federal one, never entered into the mind" of the people. In the same words he had used at a critical juncture in 1777, he suggested that sometimes "a little practicable Virtue [is] to be preferred to Theory." The convention should limit itself to proposals

> that will meet with the Approbation of the People. We must follow the People; the People will not follow us—the Plan must be accommodated to the public Mind—consult the Genius, the Temper, the Habits, the Prejudices of the People.[35]

These were not words usually found on Paterson's lips. It is likely that he was only throwing the idea of the "sovereignty of the people" back at Wilson who, arguing in support of proportional representation, had made himself the passionate spokesman for "the *mind or sense* of the people at large." "The democratick Spirit beats high," Paterson intoned (but just one line away in his notes for the speech was the injunction that it be "properly regulated and modified").[36]

In a rhetorical flourish that served to introduce the meat of his argument, Paterson referred to a comment made by David Brearly a few moments before. If the government they planned was to be truly national, then the present state boundaries should be completely erased, and new equal districts established in their stead. Calculating to raise apprehension among the landed states jealous of their claims to western territory, and hoping to win over some of the loyal sons of the Old Dominion and the Massachusetts Commonwealth who wished to retain their traditional borders, Paterson claimed "the whole must be thrown into a hotchpot, and when an equal division is made, then there may be fairly an equality of representation."[37]

Then he launched into a carefully reasoned argument on the integral nature of sovereignty, how it must exist either completely in the states or in them not at all, and how sovereign states were by definition equal. In answer to Wilson, who on the previous day had phrased an argument against state sovereignty by comparing the state to an individual citizen, Paterson asked if "a rich individual citizen should have more votes than an indigent one?" If so, the poor would be "entirely at the mercy" of the wealthy in the same way that the small states would "have everything to fear" from the large states if they lost their equal vote. Paterson granted that the Articles of Confederation had to be amended "to mark the orbits of the States with due precision," but said that otherwise he was "attached strongly to the plan of the existing confederacy." Why could not the new strong national government act on the states rather than directly on the people? As he saw it, the argument for "representation from the people at large," rather than from the existing state legislatures, was purely a maneuver to justify proportional representation for the larger states. Whether the authority of the national government emanated from the people or the states would make no difference in its operation. The new government's effectiveness would depend on the "Quantum of Power" lodged in it, not on the source of that power. The large states—Virginia, Massachusetts, and Pennsylvania—were concealing their real purpose, which was the destruction of the smaller ones. It was not a strong government he was worried about; indeed, he admitted the necessity of centralized coercive power. But "why not operate on the States—if they are coerced, they will in Turn coerce each individual." The "democratick spirit" could be restrained without wholesale destruction of the existing political system.[38]

Paterson put aside his notes and concluded his remarks with an extemporaneous challenge to the supporters of the Virginia Plan. The large states had already made it known that they would only agree to reform if it were based on proportional representation. Wilson had gone so far as to threaten that, if their proposals were not approved, the large states might set up their own confederation. Now Madison carefully wrote down what Paterson had to say in reply.

Let them unite if they please, but let them remember that they have no authority to compel the others to unite. N. Jersey will never confederate on the plan before the Committee. She would be swallowed up. He [Paterson] had rather submit to a monarch, to a despot than to such a fate. He would not only oppose the plan here but on his return home do everything in his power to defeat it there.[39]

Paterson's speech of June 9 was the first open challenge to the position of the large-state nationalists, and it incorporated every argument that the small-state faction would use in the next five weeks to have Randolph's resolution on representation thrown out. Paterson's opening argument, the challenge to the legal authority of the convention to discuss reform as far-reaching as the Virginia Plan, was a bombshell. It may have appeared petty, unimaginative, and obstructionist to committed nationalists from the larger states, but it was the best legal argument that the small-state delegates could have mustered, and, if necessary, it would deal a lethal blow to hopes for a new national system. The principle of state equality was at the heart of the old system that Paterson's position sought to retain, and events would show that, once equality was restored, at least in one branch of the legislature, Paterson and his small-state colleagues would calmly agree to set aside any legal technicalities. Each and every one of his points of analysis on June 9 was aimed directly at the matter of representation: the proclaimed attachment to the principles of the confederacy, the definition of sovereignty, the total subjugation of the small states, and his belief that the source of authority was inconsequential to the exercise of governmental powers. Each of these points would remain at the core of the small-state position.

Paterson had also identified another challenge to the small states that the authors of the Virginia Plan had apparently failed to notice. Randolph's eleventh resolution, which was poorly worded, read:

Resd. that a Republican Government & the territory of each State, except in the instance of a voluntary junction of Government & territory, ought to be guaranteed by the United States to each State.[40]

On June 5, when Paterson asked that discussion of this article be left until after the matter of representation was decided, no one objected. It is likely that he was primarily concerned that the large states could use the territorial guarantee to cheat the small states out of a fair share of the value of the western lands.[41] But Paterson's devious and legalistic mind had also noticed that, theoretically at least, it would be possible for several of the smaller states to join themselves together for defense against the larger ones. Now he pointed out that if they did so, the unfortunate wording of Randolph's eleventh resolution would make them run the risk of losing all of their territorial and political guarantees from the national government. It appeared to be an attempt at intimidation to "prevent a Consolid[ation] of Gov[ernment] and Territory" of the lesser states for their own protection.[42] The point was minutely academic, and it couldn't have gained the Jersey lawyer any praise for magnanimity. It does, however, illustrate the degree of careful concentration that Paterson had given to the threat of proportional representation and all the possible repercussions that might come with it. Paterson was acknowledged as the prime spokesman of the small states on this central issue, and, at every crucial step on the long road to the Great Compromise, he would be at the forefront.

He had spoken boldly, in the uncompromising terms he thought were necessary. He sincerely believed in most of the arguments he presented. The only obvious exception was the first point, that the convention did not have the legal authority to go beyond the precise boundaries of its instructions. Once an acceptable compromise was finally agreed to, Paterson quickly dropped that objection and, in the end, signed the Constitution,

which clearly represented more than a revision of the Articles.[43] But otherwise he was being forthright and honest; his justifications of the small-
state position were real and significant.

He was probably right about the practical matter of ratification; there
was scarcely a chance in a thousand that the small states would have gone
along with the Virginia Plan. And, when it came to ratification, the small
states would also include New Hampshire (whose delegates had not yet
reached Philadelphia) and Rhode Island (who had refused to appoint any
at all).[44] Paterson knew that if he could convince the large-state leaders
of this point, they might feel themselves backed into a corner. If the
convention represented a last chance to save the Union, and if the emergency was as serious as they claimed, then they had to report out a plan
that at least had a chance of ratification by all the states.

There were very real and tangible reasons why the small states' interest
required equal representation. Paterson had described how the large states
would theoretically be able to overrule the small states on any question
in the proposed new government. The argument had been phrased in a
general way, but, in fact, there were specific issues that the small states
were concerned about and that they were certain would be decided against
them if proportional representation became a reality. Paterson had been
involved at least symbolically in the attempts of New Jersey merchants to
win protection from the unfair imposts of the neighboring states.[45] The
small states had had previous experience with the central government's
decision making in commercial matters—all of it bad. They had promptly
agreed to send delegates to the commercial convention at Annapolis, and
the instructions New Jersey issued to her Philadelphia delegates also made
specific reference to "the State of the Union, as to trade." New Jersey and
Connecticut were in a similar position: Both were without major ports of
their own and were taxed by their commercial neighbors. There was no
way they would agree to a program that did not give them at least an
equal role with New York, Pennsylvania, and Massachusetts in making
commercial decisions.[46]

The other potential conflict was that of the western lands. Since the
outbreak of the Revolution, New Jersey's spokesmen had stood firm for
the joint ownership by all the states of the former Crown lands east of
the Mississippi. This great resource, they reasoned, had been earned by the
efforts and expenditures of all the states during the war against England
and so belonged to them all. They wanted the land sold to pay the war
debts of all the states, not just to serve the selfish interests of those that
had previous charter claims. New Jersey had been unhappy with the way
the land question had been handled under the Confederation,[47] but, like

the other landless states, she had had an equal say over the Northwest Territory that did finally fall under undisputed Confederation control in 1784. By the time of the Philadelphia convention, the only trans-Appalachian lands still claimed by individual states were those of Virginia (the area south of the Ohio that later became Kentucky), North Carolina, and Georgia, and much of that territory was already in the hands of speculators. But, as Paterson had suggested in his speech, there were also grounds for argument about the vacant or unoccupied lands that lay within the boundaries of the large states. If the Virginians wanted a truly national government, Paterson had suggested, they should be willing to see all the states' boundaries erased, have all the land thrown into a "hotchpot," and then reorganize the states on an equal basis.

This type of proposal might win serious support from land speculators in New Jersey, Maryland, and Delaware, which had no vacant lands of their own,[48] but Paterson saw the lands issue more as a matter of state interest than private concern. For him it was primarily another argument for equal representation. What if the large states ever did agree to turn over the remainder of their trans-Appalachian lands? Under the Randolph proposal for proportional representation, little New Jersey would have no real say over what happened to them. The "hotchpot" idea was one that would be brought up again in the convention, especially by Maryland's Luther Martin, and some may have taken it seriously.[49] For Paterson, however, it was merely one more sensitive point on which he could apply pressure in search of an equitable solution of the representation issue. Madison saw the point immediately.[50] Here was a veiled threat from Paterson to the large states: Either give in on proportional representation, or risk having the explosive western lands issue fought out on the convention floor.

There were probably other matters in Paterson's mind when he rose to defend the equality of the small states. His tie to the state of New Jersey was more than that of a concerned citizen or elected representative. With William Livingston, who sat by his side in Philadelphia, Paterson had nurtured the state into independent existence. Many of the most ardent nationalists at the convention had established their political careers in the service of Congress and had achieved their first public reputation through their identification with the Continental war effort.[51] Paterson, on the other hand, while he had several times been asked to serve in Congress, had remained in New Jersey, striving throughout the war to establish and stabilize the legal authority of his state. To be sure, he had lost some of his benign feelings toward the state legislature during the paper money fights of the 1780s, but he was not prepared to see the sovereign state of New Jersey simply written out of existence. This was a matter of philosophy as well as paternal affection. Rapid changes in government or society, he thought, presented a threat to stability and order.[52] As attorney general of New Jersey, he had gone to considerable trouble to reinforce the people's faith in the institutions of local county government. This had served to ease the transition from colony to state and made the shift in governmental authority—from royal governor to popular legislature—less apparent on the surface.[53]

He had come to Philadelphia in search of some absolute guarantees, which he thought were essential to a virtuous republican system, but found men who wanted total innovation instead. If complete constitutional revolution could be so easily rationalized on the basis of a supposed emergency situation and ratification by popular conventions could supersede the state legislatures in a manner totally different from the legal procedure for amending the Articles of Confederation, what was to stop some cabal from calling yet another convention in a few years and sweeping away the whole system again?[54] He agreed that thorough reforms were called for, but he hoped that, even if a new system rather than a revision of the old were needed, whatever emerged from the convention would not be so different from the Confederation as to be totally unrecognizable. On this score as well as on all the others, state equality had to be retained. Practically everything Paterson did during his time in the convention was directly related to achieving equal representation for all the states.

Paterson's speech of June 9 had presented all the small-state objections. James Wilson of Pennsylvania and Hugh Williamson of North Carolina spoke in answer to him, but Paterson asked that a decision on the question be postponed "as so much depended on it." The following day was a Sunday, putting off the vote for at least another twenty-four hours and, although the fate of his argument seemed clear, Paterson may have taken advantage of the time to seek support informally among other small-state delegates. It has been suggested, for example, that he may have been closeted with Roger Sherman of Connecticut and others to discuss strategy.[55] Although there is no solid evidence that such a meeting actually took place, the hypothesis is intriguing. When Sherman spoke to the convention before the vote was taken on June 11, he could add nothing to Paterson's argument, but he did suggest an alternative conclusion—a compromise that would make representation in one house equal and in the other proportional. Here, in germ, was the Great Compromise to be thrashed out over the ensuing weeks.

Proof of a small-state caucus on June 10 would provide more evidence toward an understanding of Paterson's overall contribution to the convention and a clearer assessment of whatever cooperation existed among the small-state delegations. Unfortunately, however, no such proof can be found. Sherman's suggestion was passed over and a vote was taken on proportional representation in both houses. The small states lost the issue in the lower house (by a vote of 9 to 2) and in the upper house as well (by a vote of 6 to 5). The 6-to-5 vote for proportional representation in the Senate was too close to call overwhelming, and there was still the problem of limiting the size of the upper house. Paterson's notes were terse. They did not even record the final verdict.

Two days later, the Virginia Plan was reported out of committee, and the resolutions already agreed to were read aloud to the delegates. These basic principles were supposedly agreed upon. All that was left was to fill in the details. However, the operating rules of the convention did allow for the delegates to change their minds on any particular issue and reopen debate.[56] Since he had already threatened to walk out if equal representation were not retained, Paterson must have thought that a change of mind was at least possible or he would have left at this point. But, if Paterson's arguments had not been convincing enough before, how could they have more weight now, especially with the already approved Randolph resolves spread out on the table? The only recourse was to rephrase the same arguments and try to present them again, this time with some new twist. The new twist would be called the New Jersey—or the Paterson—Plan.

Paterson conceived of the plan as a way to present his ideas on representation again—this time giving them the added weight of a complete plan of government. Paterson's resolutions could be laid on the table next to Randolph's, and the small states could argue that they deserved the same degree of serious attention that the Virginia Plan had already been given.

The resolutions as they were presented on June 15 were not all written by Paterson. The coalition that came together to write and present the New Jersey Plan was very loose and unstructured. Some of the ideas in Paterson's speech of June 9 had apparently been worked out by Brearly and Paterson acting together.[57] June 9 was also the date on which Paterson's old college friend Luther Martin took his seat for the first time.[58] It is likely that Paterson helped to fill the Marylander in on what had happened up until then, and perhaps the idea of presenting a complete alternative plan came up in these conversations. It is possible that Sherman of Connecticut or Lansing of New York, also contributing authors, came up with the idea and presented it to Paterson and others. A likely occasion for such a discussion would have been the previous Sunday, June 10, but as I have said, we cannot be sure. Whoever contrived the scheme, however, the first mention of it before the convention

came on June 14 when Paterson asked for one day's time so that several
of the delegations, "particularly that of New Jersey . . . might . . .
contemplate the plan reported from the Committee of the Whole,
and . . . digest one purely federal, and contradistinguished from the reported plan." The large states could hardly object, and Randolph himself
moved an immediate adjournment until the next day.[59]

As it emerged from several preliminary drafts into the form in which
Paterson presented it on the floor, the plan was a hodgepodge of different
proposals with a little something for everybody who had collaborated in
it.[60] The first article defined the proposals as revisions, corrections, and
enlargements on the powers of the Articles—clearly to be distinguished
from Randolph's preface to the Virginia Plan "that a national government ought to be established." The powers of the government were
to be vested in a unicameral legislature where each state would have an
equal vote. The powers of Congress were expanded to allow it to levy
an impost on foreign trade, collect a stamp tax, and regulate trade, as
well as to compel the payment of future requisitions levied on the
states. Congress was to elect a plural executive, and the executive would
appoint judges of a supreme court. The only provision of the plan that,
after being altered in several crucial respects, was actually incorporated
into the final version of the Constitution was the one declaring that the
acts of Congress as well as the treaties of the United States "shall be
the supreme law" of the land [61]

The differing interests of some of the individual members of the small-
state faction can be found here. Martin, the author of the supremacy
clause, was clearly looking out for factions and special interest groups in
his home state.[62] Marylanders who had paid off their debts to British
creditors in depreciated state paper money were not anxious to see the
possibility of the Treaty of Paris being enforced to the letter,[63] and Martin
still hoped for an opportunity to ply away a share of the rich lands of
Virginia and the other landed states for Maryland speculators.[64] The
supremacy clause, as Martin phrased it, was an ingenious blend of those
interests in a form that gave the impression of being a sincere attempt to
assure the rest of the convention that the small-state group did not seek
to completely emasculate the new government. Martin used the words
"supreme law" as a smokescreen to conceal his real intentions.

The precise wording of the clause as recorded by Madison is as follows.

Resd. that all Acts of the U. States in Congs. made by virtue &
in pursuance of the powers hereby & by the articles of confederation
vested in them, and all Treaties made & ratified under the authority

of the U. States shall be the supreme law of the respective States
so far forth as those Acts or Treaties shall relate to the said States
or their Citizens, and that the Judiciary of the several States shall
be bound thereby in their decisions, anything in the respective laws
of the individual states notwithstanding; and that if any State, or
any body of men in any State shall prevent ye carrying into execution such acts or Treaties, the federal Executive shall be authorized
to call forth ye power of the Confederated States, or so much thereof
as may be necessary to enforce and compel an obedience to such Acts
or an Observance of such Treaties.[65]

Since the New Jersey Plan included no provision for inferior federal
courts, any judicial enforcement of federal acts or treaties would have
to be carried out in the appropriate state courts, but while the proposed
clause did proclaim the supremacy of such laws and treaties "respective
laws of the individual states to the contrary not withstanding" (italics
added), it said nothing about the state constitutions. A state court could
not be compelled to enforce a federal law or a treaty if it was contrary
to the provisions of that state's constitution. This meant that Marylanders
could not be deprived by federal act or treaty of their right under their
state constitution to pay debts in Maryland paper currency.[66] Conveniently,
the state courts were the only place in which the state constitutions were
still to be superior to acts of the federal government. Martin's intentional
misrepresentation of the words "supreme law" did not go unnoticed.
Madison quickly pointed out that in reality the New Jersey Plan offered
no more assurance of state adherence to treaty provisions than the Articles
of Confederation did.[67] When the phrase "supreme law" was ultimately
included in Article 6 of the completed Constitution, it was immediately
followed by the injunction that "the judges in every State shall be bound
thereby, anything in the *Constitution or Laws of any State* to the contrary
notwithstanding" (italics added).

No one in the hall could have doubted that the latter part of the
supremacy clause as included in the New Jersey Plan was intended to
grant specific authorization for whatever drastic measures might be
necessary to put down popular uprisings in the states. The specter of
Daniel Shays was too vivid in their memories for the delegates to think
of anything else when they read that if "any body of men in any state"
prevented the execution of a federal law or treaty, the "power of the
Confederated States, or so much thereof as may be necessary to enforce
and compel" obedience could be called out. But, as Irving Brant has
observed, there were other implications to these phrases as well. If (as

Martin would propose later) new states might be carved up out of the
present landed ones (Virginia must have been his special target), and if
the Congress passed a law to such effect, the supremacy clause called for
the joint military force of the Confederation to be used to enforce the
law. The wording of Madison's proposals as they lay on the table did
not rule out such a situation.[68] The constitutions of the individual states
guaranteed their right to exist, but the state courts were the highest tribunal in which such a guarantee could be secured. As Brandt has suggested,
Martin's wording of the supremacy clause was double-edged. The Maryland courts might block any move to force payment of debts in hard
money, but if an attempt should be made to break in upon the boundaries
of a large state like Virginia, her state courts could offer no protection
against the armed forces of the United States and would have no recourse
but to cooperate in the state's dismemberment.[69]

New York's Lansing also made contributions to the plan that were
shaped by the peculiar interests of his state. The powers of Congress as
he proposed them would concern only commercial matters and would
have to be enforced through the state courts, though he did allow appeal
to the federal judiciary. An earlier draft of Lansing's proposal would
have specifically maintained the right of the individual states of "laying
Embargoes in Times of Scarcity" and stated a certain percentage beyond
which the income from the federal impost would "accrue to the Use of
the State in which the same may be collected." While not spelled out
in the New Jersey Plan as presented, the plan did not specifically deny
the states' right to collect trade duties collaterally with Congress, nor
did it close the door on the future enactment of a revenue-sharing proposal,
such as the one Lansing had in mind.[70]

Paterson was interested primarily in the matter of representation. That
he accepted the contributions of Martin (which would protect paper
money) and Lansing (which would allow New York to continue to
profit unfairly on taxes from New Jersey) should be taken as a measure
of his desperation in seeking allies in the representation debate.[71] Tying
together this group, which also included Roger Sherman, John Dickinson
and the Delaware men, Yates from New York, and the rest of Paterson's
Jersey delegation, was no easy job. Sherman's proposals for the plan
included a guarantee for payment of foreign debt that must have made
Martin from Maryland squirm, but Paterson was apparently able to
soothe both his Connecticut and Maryland allies. The only contribution
that seems in the end to have been taken from Sherman was a guarantee of
equal rights for citizens of one state charged with committing a crime
in another.[72] Since they were not mentioned in his colleagues' proposals,

Paterson appears to have been primarily responsible for the clauses on the executive and the judiciary which were significant only in that they filled out the plan as a complete alternative to Randolph's.[73]

The fact that Paterson was willing to include the provisions of Martin and Lansing, each of which went against his personal belief and the interests of his state, is an indication that he did not seriously expect all of his resolves to be adopted. To Martin and Lansing, the New Jersey Plan provided a convenient way to further their own special interests, but, as Paterson planned it and as the most important people in the convention read it, the plan was simply intended to be a stalking horse for equal representation. Paterson knew that few, if any, of the men in the convention would even consider letting the positions of Martin and Lansing stand, but he had to get support from somewhere for the larger question, which he hoped at least had a chance of passage. It may seem, especially when one notes their later Anti-Federalist staunchness, that Martin and Lansing used Paterson and forced him to compromise his political principles. But Paterson believed that this was one time when expediency and a little common sense should prevail over the scruples of theoretical principle.[74] Here he used Martin and Lansing to press every advantage he could in defense of state equality.

While the newspapers continued to report that "the greatest unanimity" existed between all parties at the convention, Paterson was steering it to another showdown.[75] After he submitted his nine resolutions on June 15, a day was allowed for the delegates to copy them, and an interval of time granted so that "the friends of the plan . . . wd. be better prepared to explain and support it."[76] But when Lansing and Paterson arose to present their arguments on the following day, they said nothing fundamental that Paterson had not already brought up on June 9. Lansing mentioned the insufficient authorization and the impossibility of the Virginia Plan's receiving popular approval. Paterson echoed these themes and, claiming that he would avoid "repetition as much as possible," proceeded to say almost exactly what he had said a week before. He referred to the precedent of state equality in the Articles of Confederation[77] and the argument that the authority of the new government depended on the "quantum of power" in it, not the source of that power. He brought up the "hotchpot" again. This time he asked more explicitly whether, once proportional representation were implemented, Pennsylvania would be voluntarily willing to "admit a participation of their common stock of land to the citizens of New Jersey" and then provided the reply himself—"I fancy not."[78] His own notes indicate that he also argued for the solemnity of the Confederation as a contract entered into by all the states. If that contract were simply wiped away now, he reasoned, "why [could] not the new or present one be broke in the same Manner?"[79] Paterson closed his speech with some window dressing aimed at maintaining the fiction that his plan was intended to be a complete form of government equal to the Virginia resolutions—Randolph's bicameral legislature, he claimed, would cost the government too much to maintain.[80]

Wilson, Hamilton, and Madison each took their turns in destroying whatever credibility the new resolutions had. Hamilton was primarily interested in presenting his own candid sentiments about the needs of the Union and in disassociating himself from the other two New Yorkers, but Wilson and Madison tried to deal with the small-state proposals point by point. Madison particularly emphasized the devious loopholes left in Martin's wording of the supremacy clause.[81] When they were through[82] and the votes were taken, the New Jersey Plan took its place in history.[83] The plan had failed, and with it went all hopes of keeping the convention from setting the Articles completely aside.

But had the preservation of the Confederation really been the intention of the scheme? As far as Paterson was concerned, his dogged defense of the Confederation was essentially another tactic for winning equal representation. He saw it as a means to the end of state equality, not necessarily as an end in itself. Aside from the idiosyncracies of Lansing's and Martin's contributions, there were many matters in the jointly authored resolutions that Paterson believed in—that there was no need for two houses in Congress, for example—but none was so crucial in his mind that he would not willingly have sacrificed it in order to achieve state equality.[84]

To the extent that the New Jersey Plan had been intended by Martin or Lansing to protect their special interests or perhaps even to break up the convention, it was a dismal failure. But to the extent that Paterson and some others (especially Dickinson, Sherman, and the Connecticut group) saw the resolutions as another attempt to convince the convention of their firmness on the matter of representation, the desired result was achieved. As early as June 16, while Paterson's words still rang through the hall, C. C. Pinkney of South Carolina realized what it was all about. "If New Jersey was indulged with one vote out of 13," he explained to the convention, "she would have no objection to a national government."[85] Dickinson is said to have told Madison that the New Jersey Plan represented "the consequence of pushing things too far" in pressing for proportional representation in both branches of the Congress.[86] Madison himself saw that equal representation was the crux of the whole business. "The great difficulty lies in the affair of Representation," he said, "and if this could be adjusted, all others would be surmountable."[87] To have Madison even contemplate changing his position was quite an accomplishment. The fact that Connecticut shifted its vote just before the question was called and voted against the plan it had helped to form suggests that by then its delegates thought compromise on the representation matter was at least possible and that Connecticut was ready to meet the others halfway.[88]

After the vote was taken on June 19, the debate continued. While Martin could not be stopped from being as obstreperous as ever, Wilson was trying to appear friendly and was assuring the small states that he would not go as far as Hamilton in supporting a national government "that would swallow up the state governments" in their entirety.[89] As if to soften the blow of the day before, on June 20 the convention agreed to change the wording of the first Virginia resolution from "national government" to "the government of the United States."[90] The change was only cosmetic. Madison and Wilson would not be prepared to give in to compromise until they had carried on the fight for a completely proportional system for another month. For that matter, Paterson may not have yet been ready to accept equal representation in only one of two houses. The verbal battle for state equality was far from won. But, as a skirmish between the contenders, the debate over the New Jersey Plan stimulated movement in the right direction.[91] Madison and Wilson certainly knew they had not heard the last of the small-state arguments, and all Paterson and his colleagues had to do was prepare for the next confrontation.

The third and final phase of the representation struggle included the formulation of the Great Compromise and the process of getting the convention to agree on it. Paterson had some part in the formulation of the compromise, but he was especially influential in winning the delegates' support for it. Madison and his followers knew they needed a wider margin of support than they had in the convention if they expected the constitution they were writing to be ratified by all the states. New Jersey and Delaware were firmly against a proportional system; Connecticut and Maryland were not quite so firm but were unlikely to ratify on the basis of inequality; no one knew what would happen in New York; and, with nobody to speak for them, it would have to be assumed that New Hampshire and Rhode Island would stand with the small states, too. With all these states outside of the system, a national government would be national in name only. During the debate on the New Jersey Plan, the large-state men realized that a compromise on the matter of representation would be sufficient to bring Paterson and most of the others over to support a strong central government, but they thought the issue was so important that they wanted to try every other possible means of persuasion before they gave it up. When Connecticut changed its vote on June 19, and Paterson and his colleagues did not walk out after their decisive defeat (even Lansing and Yates stayed on until the 10th of July),[92] it might have been taken as evidence that the small-state delegates were not unshakeable in their determination. On the other hand, the strategy of the small-state delegates was to make it absolutely and unmistakably clear to the large states that equality and only equality would bring them around. This was the task that fell to Paterson.

Meanwhile the convention went back to a step-by-step reconsideration of the Randolph resolutions. The apparent reduction in tension was short-lived, however, and by June 27 the convention had returned to the seventh and eighth of Randolph's resolves—the ones that dealt with the composition of the House and the Senate, respectively. Luther Martin had been cooling his heels for a week, and now he exploded in a two-day harangue on state equality. The speech "might have continued for two months," Ellsworth later said, except for the expressions of "fatigue and disgust" evident on every face.[93] As soon as Martin stepped down, Lansing and Dayton began to squabble with Madison and Wilson, and the debate became so animated that Franklin wound up suggesting that prayer might help to temper their tongues.[94] The next morning, the Connecticut men were talking compromise again, and Ellsworth claimed that he at least did not despair for the fate of the convention. The same might not be said of Madison, however; he begged the small-state men "to renounce a principle . . . which cd. never be admitted, & if admitted must infuse mortality into a Constitution which we wished to last forever."[95] Then it was resolved (6 to 4 with one divided) to reject state equality in the first house, and Ellsworth immediately moved for equality in the second.[96]

Paterson had never tried to conceal the firmness of his belief in the need for equality, and, on the morning of June 30, he and Brearly tried to remind the others of where the small-state men still stood. They proposed that Washington be instructed to write to the governor of New Hampshire and request the "immediate attendance" of that small state's delegates in Philadelphia. Only New York was willing to go along with this idea.[97] One whole day of animated debate was devoted to Ellsworth's proposal for equality in the Senate. Madison and Wilson were still adamant, Dayton called the proportional alternative an "amphibious monster," and Delaware's Gunning Bedford got a little carried away. According to Madison's notes, Bedford practically dared the large states to break up the Confederation: "If they do the small ones will find some foreign ally of more honor and good faith, who will take them by the hand and do them justice."[98]

July 1 was a Sunday. When the tally was taken on Ellsworth's motion on Monday morning, the vote was tied. It seems that Luther Baldwin had

decided to vote with his friends from Connecticut (thereby dividing
Georgia), and Martin's colleague from Maryland was late that morning,
allowing Martin to place Maryland solidly with the Paterson group. Even
though the tardy Marylander showed up a few moments later, the large
states dared not try to have the vote taken again.[99] Madison's and Wilson's
hold on the convention seemed to be falling apart. There were dangerous
signs of weakening within their own delegation as well. For the first time
since the New Jersey Plan was introduced, the convention had come to a
dead stop. What cool heads there still were realized that if compromise
were to come, it had to come now. Over the objections of Madison and
Wilson, they set up a grand committee with one member from each state
"to devise & report some compromise." Paterson was chosen to represent
New Jersey.[100]

The members of the committee were carefully chosen to encourage the
likelihood of compromise, and the delegates were not disappointed. On
July 5, as the convention was called to order again after a two-day recess
for Independence Day celebrations, Chairman Elbridge Gerry reported that
a middle ground had been found. If an equal vote were allowed to each
state in the Senate, the small states would allow proportional representation in the House and, to make the arrangement more palatable to the
large states, they would also preserve for the House the sole power to
write money bills.[101]

From July 5 to July 16, the delegates debated various elements of the
proposal, aware that the fate of the whole convention hung in the balance.
To be sure that no one forgot just how precarious the situation was,
Paterson spoke three times during this period, and each time he made it
clearer and clearer that no other grounds for compromise existed. On
July 5, he defended Bedford who had been criticized for his idle threats
of a few days before and took the opportunity to reply in kind to the
challenges of Madison and Gouverneur Morris.

Madison had been venting his spleen at the committee's proposals. He
thought that granting the House sole right to initiate money bills was no
compromise at all, and he ended by suggesting that it might be best for
"the principal States comprehending a majority of the people of the U.S."
to agree on a plan they thought was just, whether or not the minority
delegates in the convention went along. Madison claimed that he had "the
firmest hopes that the other States would by degrees accede to it."[102]

Gouverneur Morris carried the emotion still further.

> This country must be united. If persuasion does not unite it, the
> sword will. . . . The scenes of horror attending civil commotion can

not be described, and the conclusion of them will be worse. . . .
The stronger party will the make traytors of the weaker; and the
Gallows and Halter will finish the work of the sword.[103]

Paterson acknowledged that the warmth of Bedford's argument might have
been "improper; but he thought the Sword and the Gallows as little calcu-
lated to bring conviction," and he complained of the manner in which
Madison and Morris "had treated the small states."[104]

The release of emotion in rhetoric was not sufficient to calm tempers.
For the next two days, the debate continued at fever pitch. The exact pro-
portions of representation in the lower house were to be decided by a
special committee. Meanwhile, the large-state men argued the insignificance
of the money bill provision, and the small states (represented by Ellsworth,
Sherman, and Bedford) urged acceptance of the compromise.

When Paterson spoke up again on July 7, it was to balance the scales
again. It did not matter to him whether the matter of money bills was
thought to be important or not, but he reminded the delegates that the
small states had already agreed to proportional representation in the lower
house and that now they would accept nothing less than equality in the
upper. Madison recorded: "There was no other ground for accommoda-
tion. [Paterson's] resolution was fixt. He would meet the large states on
that Ground and no other." And then to further impress the opposition
with his steadfastness, Paterson added that "for himself he should vote
agst. the Report [the compromise] because it yielded too much."[105] According to King's notes, Paterson was even stronger: "If we cannot agree
in this, . . . we had better divide & lose no longer Time."[106] The only
way to negotiate a compromise was to keep trying to convince the large
states that they were not the only ones doing the compromising. Just to
show how accommodating his small-state colleagues were being, Paterson
stuck to the opposite extreme. If the small states were going to convince
the large-state men of the firmness of their position, they needed someone
to act the unbending and dogmatic role being played by Madison and
Wilson on the other side. Paterson filled the bill.

When they came back together on Monday, all was confusion. The
special committee reported its proposed figures for representation in the
lower house, but, when asked whether population or wealth had been their
guide, the committee would give no straight answer. Morris and Rutledge
tried to side-step the problem by postponing discussion of the exact numbers
and taking up the second paragraph of the committee's report, which allowed the Congress to regulate its own representation in the future. As it
turned out, Gouverneur Morris was most worried about the back-country

men who might come to dominate the Union as new states were created,[107] but Paterson dropped another bombshell when he flatly challenged the counting of slaves in the proportioning of representation: "He could regard negro slaves in no light but as property." Madison, counting on at least a three-fifths clause, must have gulped as he wrote down those words. "What is the true principle of Representation," Paterson asked?

> It is an expedient by which an assembly of certain individuals chosen by the people is substituted in place of the inconvenient meeting of the people themselves. If such a meeting of the people was actually to take place, would the slaves vote? They would not. Why then shd. they be represented?[108]

This was a good point. Paterson also noted that such a provision would be likely to encourage the slave trade as southern states tried to increase their representation.[109] But, besides speaking his mind, Paterson was opening a wedge between Wilson and Madison. On July 10, New Jersey quietly agreed to the percentages suggested for the first house (including slaves), but, from July 11 to July 13, things went from bad to worse for the large-state men. Wilson and Morris of Quaker Pennsylvania argued against any formula for counting slaves, while Madison's allies from South Carolina held out for slaves to be counted in their full number. By July 13, Gouverneur Morris was wondering if equality in the Senate would not be the only way the northern states might defend themselves against the South, and other delegates from large northern states began to weaken.[110]

On the morning of July 14, Ellsworth moved that the delegates vote on the whole report of the committee, that is, to accept or reject the entire compromise. One more day of cajoling the moderates and warning the opposition had to be endured until the tally was taken. Paterson sat back and let Sherman, Martin, and Dayton carry the debate against Madison, Wilson, and Charles Pinkney, who tried once more to undercut the compromise with a proposal for a partly proportional Senate. But the sides did not budge. After what could hardly have been a very restful Sunday, the delegates reconvened on Monday morning, and the vote was taken. The small states won. William R. Davie and Hugh Williamson had swung over North Carolina to the side of the compromise, and Elbridge Gerry and Caleb Strong split the vote of Massachusetts because they realized that not to compromise now was to give up all hope of agreement on a new government. New Jersey, Delaware, Connecticut, Maryland, and North Carolina outnumbered Virginia, Pennsylvania, Georgia, and South Carolina, thanks to Strong and Gerry who had paralyzed Massachusetts.[111]

There was no doubt where the votes of New Hampshire, Rhode Island, and New York would have gone had they been cast.

The large states took the defeat as though in a state of shock. For the first time in weeks, neither Madison, Wilson, nor Morris had anything to say. In an atmosphere of disbelief, the delegates moved on to the next of Randolph's resolutions, at the point where they had left off back on June 27. Butler, Gorham, and Rutledge began to bicker about the wording of the clause that would grant powers to Congress. The vote on whether or not to submit the question to a committee came up a deadlocked 5 to 5. Then Randolph rose to speak. "The vote of this morning (involving an equality of suffrage in 2d. branch) had embarrassed the business extremely." He claimed to have come that morning with another plan for compromise whereby equal votes might be allowed to the small states in certain cases,

> but finding from the preceding vote that they persist in demanding an equal vote in all cases, that they have succeeded in obtaining it, and that N. York if present would probably be on the same side, he could not but think we were unprepared to discuss the subject further. For these reasons he wished the Convention might adjourn, that the large states might consider the steps proper to be taken in the present solemn crisis of the business, and the small States might also deliberate on the means of conciliation.[112]

It is clear that Randolph, like Madison, Wilson, and the other large-state delegates, was unhappy with the morning's decision. But it was also clear that he wanted the rest of the day free for the different factions to put their heads together and decide where to go. The large states had probably not given serious consideration to what they would do if they lost, especially after July 10, when the New Yorkers left and seemingly crippled the small states' chances. If the large-state men should decide to stay on, they wanted to reconsider some important provisions in their plan. They obviously would not grant the same powers to a legislature representative of the small states as they would to one directly representative of the people. As Randolph said in his comments that morning, all the resolutions in his plan "were founded on the supposition that a Proportional representation was to prevail in both branches of the Legislature."[113] Now the large-state delegates needed time to rethink their position.

But Paterson was not going to allow them to browbeat the small states into accepting anything less than had been won that morning. As Randolph finished, the angry Jerseyman was on his feet, twisting the meaning of Randolph's words and creating a situation more emotionally charged than any moment in the convention so far. Here are Paterson's dramatic words as Madison recorded them.

> Mr. Patterson thought with Mr. R. that it was high time for the Convention to adjourn, that the rule of secrecy ought to be rescinded, and that our constituents should be consulted. No conciliation could be admissible on the part of the smaller States on any other ground than that of an equality of votes in the second branch. If Mr. Randolph would reduce to form his motion for an adjournment sine die, he would second it with all his heart.[114]

In seconding Randolph's resolution, Paterson had purposely twisted the Virginian's meaning. Randolph had apparently only intended to take the rest of the afternoon to caucus and discuss matters informally, but Paterson's call for adjournment *sine die* (indefinitely, with no date set for reconvening) amounted to a formal motion that the convention give up and go home. Had they rescinded the secrecy rule and consulted their constituents as Paterson suggested, most delegates realized that a storm of opposition would make it impossible for them to pick up the pieces and start again.

A month before, when he was trying to hold together the loose faction that presented the New Jersey Plan, Paterson had proved himself a master at subtle political maneuvers. Since the opening of this third phase of the struggle for equal representation, however, he had become increasingly blunt in stating his position. The Connecticut men who had proposed the idea of the compromise and worked for it all through the detailed and unpleasant negotiations deserve a great deal of credit for their labors, but convincing the large states of the need to give in on this critical point required more than the skillful yet friendly manner of debate exhibited by Ellsworth or Sherman. There had to be someone standing absolutely firm— as intransigent as Madison and Wilson remained on the other side.

Paterson, of course, did not do this alone. There were others who occasionally took a decisive stand. For example, in the closing hour of debate on the compromise, his New Jersey colleague Dayton reiterated firmly that he would "in no event" give up state equality.[115] It was Paterson, however, who provided the constant backstop on which the compromisers could base their efforts. His stance had become firmer and firmer as the days went on. Veiled threats to broach openly the matter of

unoccupied lands had given way to flat refusals to consider the three-fifths
formula for representation. Now the victory had been won, and he was
telling Randolph in no uncertain terms to take it or leave it.

Randolph dared not call his bluff. He said he "was sorry that his
meaning had been so readily & strangely misinterpreted," but he was
thinking only of adjourning

> till tomorrow in order that some conciliatory experiment might if
> possible be devised, and that in case the smaller States should con-
> tinue to hold back, the larger might take such measures, he would
> not say what, as might be necessary.[116]

Paterson had made no mistake. He knew that the further conciliation
Randolph and the Virginians wanted would have given New Jersey and
the others less than they had won fairly and squarely on the floor of the
convention. Paterson now seconded the motion for "adjournment till
tomorrow, as an opportunity semed to be wished by the larger States to
deliberate further on conciliatory expedients."[117] But his downright non
sequitur of a few minutes before had made its point. There could not be
many delegates who believed that the small states would do any more
compromising. Apparently, quite a few of them thought Paterson was
absolutely serious. Broome from Delaware joined Gerry in opposing Paterson's suggestion: "Adjournment sine die . . . would be fatal." Rutledge
from South Carolina, allied from the beginning with his neighbors from
Virginia, now saw "no chance of a compromise: beyond the one that had
already been voted on. The little States were fixt.," he at long last
observed.

> All that the large States then had to do, was to decide whether
> they would yield or not. For his part he conceived that altho' we
> could not do what we thought best, in itself, we ought to do some-
> thing. Had we not better keep the Govt. up a little longer, hoping
> that another Convention will supply our omissions, than abandon
> everything to hazard. Our constituents will be very little satisfied
> with us if we take the latter course.[118]

Then it was voted to "adjourn till tomorrow."

Rutledge was unhappy with the situation, but not as unhappy as
Madison, Wilson, or Randolph. Madison described in his notes a meeting
that was held by "a number of members from the larger States" on the
following morning. There was a group, no doubt headed by Madison, that

was prepared to break from the convention and propose its own plan—which, as Madison pointed out to the meeting, would have the support of the principal states and the majority of the people. But that any such forceful conclusion should emerge from this meeting was made impossible by the others present who

> seemed inclined to yield to the smaller States, and to concur in such an Act however imperfect & exceptionable, as might be agreed on by the Convention as a body, tho' decided by a bare majority of States and by a minority of the people of the U. States.[119]

Here then was the last meeting of that large-state caucus that Madison had begun to put together even before the convention met. Fearing that without compromise they would have to go home empty-handed, many of the large-state delegates had finally acquiesced to the small states' demands, and any realistic chance for overturning the Great Compromise approved the day before disappeared.

In the long struggle for representation, Madison and Paterson had led the opposing factions in heated debate. More than a few times during those weeks the fate of the entire convention hung in the balance, but both Madison and Paterson realized the importance of their task and persevered. Actually they were closer together than this struggle implies. They both agreed, unlike many outside the convention, that a new and vigorous form of national government was needed.[120] After July 17, with the question of representation settled, both of these men and their colleagues from large and small states alike concentrated on the 'more delicate matters of shaping a government that could govern firmly yet not get out of control.

In the course of their struggle over representation, Paterson and Madison had acted as the main agents in the development of the most unique aspect of the American Constitution. In the Randolph plan, the role of the states in the new system was left purposely vague, but, if representation were to be proportional and based directly on the people, then, by definition, sovereignty would be placed wholly in the new government. There was no explicit denial of the states' sovereignty, but, as everyone would agree at the time, the sovereignty had to be either in one place or the other, not both. Paterson had noted at the very outset of the convention that sovereignty was "an Integral thing" and could not be split up or divided between different governments. Thereafter, when Paterson spoke of a "federal" system (as opposed to Randolph's "national" system), he meant one that had no sovereignty of its own, but was delegated powers by the sovereign states. Inherent in the arrangement that became known as the Great Compromise (which called for a representation of states as well as of the people at large) was a basic theoretical change in the nature of sovereignty. No longer an integral thing, it was to be shared by the central and the state governments in their various capacities. From here on, the term "federal" took on new meaning, and ever since it has been used to represent this unique concept of shared sovereignty in the American Constitution.[121]

Ultimately the Great Compromise was a victory for the nation and the states. Madison, Wilson, King, and the other large-state people had finally been convinced that "New Jersey was almost as real a political entity to Jerseyites as was Virginia to Virginians."[122] Moreover, once the Great Compromise helped the small states to feel important in the new system, they no longer looked with fear on the proposed new and more powerful central government. To the extent that Paterson was responsible for forcing the large-state delegates to recognize these political facts of life, he deserves credit for the ultimate success that the convention achieved. And to the extent that his firm stand won acceptance of the idea of an upper house of the legislature where the states would be equally represented, Paterson deserves the title "Father of the United States Senate."

His contribution made, Paterson wrote to his wife on July 17, telling her that he expected to be home by the end of the month and asking her to send money so he could settle accounts for his Philadelphia expenses.

The business is difficult and unavoidably takes up much time, but I think we shall eventually agree upon and adopt a system that will give strength and harmony to the Union and render us a great and happy people. This is the wish of every good, and the interest of every wise man.[123]

He remained in Philadelphia and continued to attend the sessions until July 23. Ironically, on the same day he left for New Jersey, the long-awaited New Hampshire delegates arrived in Philadelphia.[124]

During August and September, as the convention labored over the details of the document, Paterson was looking after his business at home. Explaining that he was "under the necessity of being absent," he had asked that Dayton be present to help Brearly and Livingston with the work.[125] Even when Brearly wrote on August 21 to report that the business was dragging on terribly because "every article is again argued over, with as much earnestness and obstinacy as before it was committed,"

and to ask if Paterson could not possibly join them, he declined to
return.[126] A few days later, he wrote to Ellsworth to ask what was
happening at the convention.

> Full of Disputation and noisy as the Wind, it is said, that you are
> afraid of the very Windows, and have a Man planted under them
> to prevent the Secrets and Doings from flying out.[127]

He went on to hope that they "would not have as much Altercation upon
the Detail, as there was in getting the Principles of the System." Paterson
closed with earnest good wishes, but no offer of help. "I wish you much
Speed, and that you may be full of good Works, the first mainly for my
own Sake, for I dread going down again to Philada."[128] He did return,
though, in September to sign the completed document.[129]

The completed Constitution was reported to the Confederation Congress
and sent out to the states with instructions that it be ratified by special
conventions to be chosen for the purpose.[130] There is no indication that
Paterson played any role in winning support for the ratification in New
Jersey,[131] but there was no significant opposition to be worried about.
Surely the situation would have been very different had the Virginia
Plan, as originally proposed, been fully implemented, but the Great Compromise was easy for most Jerseymen to accept. Other obvious benefits to
New Jersey were to be found in the provisions that gave Congress the
sole power to impose import taxes and to establish congressional regulation of interstate trade.[132] There was the likelihood that the state's taxes
could be dramatically reduced because the Congress had been empowered
to take over the debts of the Confederation, and, although there was no
explicit mention of it in the completed document, the Constitution did
not deny the new government the power to assume the debts of the
individual states.[133] The farmers who had borne the brunt of the state
taxes over the years could only breathe a sigh of relief.

Undoubtedly these factors made the farmers and the paper money
party less interested in fighting ratification on the grounds that it made
the loan office and debtor relief schemes they had tried before impossible.[134]
Paterson and his fellow hard-money men could rest assured that the state
governments (deprived of the power to abrogate contracts and meddle
with paper money) could not cause too much trouble. With many
Jerseymen and others from all over the nation, he could put to rest some
of the apprehensions he had felt about the future of the American experiment launched so auspiciously in 1776. Just a few years after the
adoption of the Constitution, he looked back on it as America's salvation.

Great and glorious transition! Perhaps, history does not afford an instance of the kind. My fellow citizens, let us be grateful for the benefits and blessings, which we enjoy. Highly does it become us to support and preserve the constitution and government of the United States, from whence, under Heaven, all our prosperity proceeds.[135]

The Constitution, Paterson would maintain, represented "the ark of safety and the palladium of our liberties."[136] And, as long as the Constitution was followed, and the government used its power wisely, the opportunity to establish a great and glorious American Arcadia might finally be realized.

The rest of Paterson's life would offer numerous opportunities for him to look to the Constitution and to apply its principles as he understood them. Serving on the Supreme Court during some of its most creative years, he would help to clear up a few of its inconsistencies and see the nation over some of the most troubled of her early national years. And all the while he could maintain the belief that the service he had given to the success of the Revolution and the writing of the Constitution had brought America closer to the great and virtuous prospects he had in view.

Federalism and the Senate

Paterson's participation in the federal convention had been a public duty that he had accepted with some reluctance. To judge from his letters, he had not been anxious to become involved in state or national politics and sincerely preferred to stay at home and practice law. Nevertheless, he seemed unable to resist the call to public service. Since his college days, he had considered virtue, personal and public, to be the most important factor in political life. If men of virtuous public spirit (as he considered himself) were unwilling to make sacrifices in the interest of society, then offices of public trust would fall to men who looked out for their own interests first. This was a belief that was not only to involve him in a whole new career in national politics, but would also shape his responses to the development of the first political party system in the new nation.

If there was any doubt that Paterson and his fellow delegates in Philadelphia had written a constitution that would satisfy New Jersey, it was dispelled as soon as the document was made public. Up until that time, the convention's secrecy rule had limited newspapers to editorializing about their hopes for the new system and publishing selections from John Adams's recent *Defense of American Constitutions*.[1] But starting in early October as the text of the new Constitution appeared in the public press, the near unanimous praise of Jerseymen was to be heard everywhere. The provision that forbade state imposts, which would finally free the state from the unfair burdens placed on it by New York and Pennsylvania, pleased everyone, and the granting of an independent revenue to the national government would relieve the state of the heavy taxes needed to pay congressional requisitions and to carry the interest on the Continental debt.[2] To be sure, the story would have been different if Paterson and his collaborators had not succeeded in winning equal representation in the Senate. Lambert Cadwallader who called the new constitution "a very excellent one," wrote to a friend that

> when I reflect that the smaller States are admitted to an equal Representation in the Senate with the larger it appears to me a Circumstance much more favorable than I could have expected.[3]

Unlike the situation in many other states, the process of ratification caused no serious public debate, and the ratifying convention gave its unanimous approval before the year was out.[4] But, even after the ninth state ratified it the following July, the new Constitution was only the framework of a new system of government. If that system was to be a sound one, more than efficient electoral procedures and judicial institutions would be required. That public virtue of which Paterson spoke so fondly would be necessary, too, and his fear that this spirit was being lost was to dominate Paterson's political perspective in the years to come. The editor of the *Brunswick Gazette* sounded this note of concern early on. On September 11, 1787, a week before the convention at Philadelphia finished its task, he wrote that

> great things are expected from the federal convention, to whom we would willingly consign the task of lessening our burdens, curing our vices, removing our grievances, and making us a happy people. There can be no doubt of the ardor of their exertions; but we must not impose the whole work upon them.—They may, and we are persuaded will inform us of the real situation of the American States, will point out to us the true road to national felicity; how we may extricate ourselves from our present difficulties, and conduct our governments in future, on the most economical republican principles. But it remains with us to be virtuous—This must be the exertion of every individual.—Resolves on paper or the best draughted schemes of legislation will be altogether ineffectual, unless we ourselves put our hands to the plough, and resolutely determine to practice the

homely and necessary virtues of industry and frugality. We must work out our political salvation with fear and trembling.[5]

Back in New Jersey, Paterson resumed his busy legal career. His business was still primarily a matter of collecting debts and bringing suit against those who could not pay.[6] His inability to settle his own accounts must have been distressing enough for a man who preached the sanctity of contracts so fervently, but it hurt all the more because the source of his troubles was his own family.

It all started when his brother Edward and his brother-in-law Thomas Irwin, the husband of Paterson's sister, set off for Europe in July 1786, to seek their fortunes. In preparing for the trip and arranging passage, they established the partnership of Irwin & Paterson and indebted themselves for a considerable sum to Philadelphia businessmen. In the absence of collateral, the loans were made only when the partners promised that William Paterson would underwrite them. When one of the creditors, William Bell (no relation to Cornelia or Andrew), wrote Paterson to explain the arrangement, he hoped the young men would have a "quick passage and arrive to a good market."[7] But the market was not as good as it could have been. By early 1788, they returned to Philadelphia, and Paterson's brother Tom also became involved in the business. In February of that year, Tom signed for £1,326 worth of goods delivered to Irwin & Paterson and again listed William as the guarantor.[8] Within a few months, they all went to New Orleans to set up business there. Their elder brother seems not to have objected to the financial arrangements until later when the bills became due.

By the end of 1788, the creditors were pursuing Paterson to have him make good on his brothers' debts. Irwin had written in June[9] enclosing a copy of the letter he had sent Bell to explain the delay in paying, but there was no word from Tom. Paterson wrote to them at New Orleans explaining his situation and insisting they pay at least some portion of the loan to keep the creditors from his door, but there was no reply and no payment. Edward, who had apparently made some arrangement with William beforehand to settle his part of the account, wrote in October, but, by the time the letter reached New Brunswick on December 10, his usually well-composed brother was beside himself with apprehension and dismay.[10] William's depression was evident in his reply to Edward on the following day.

Fortune frowns on me; my life has been a chequered one. I have been industrious and uniformly endeavored to promote all my friends and connections to the utmost of my power; and it is with a heart full of grief and the most poynaunt anguish, that I tell you, that I owe all my misfortunes to such endeavors. Farewell; kiss your bible, and swear, that you will never be security for any man—it has ruined thousands and me among the rest.

By that time, Tom had written from New Orleans with the news that he could send no money at all. "When I received Tommy's letter," Paterson went on, "I was obliged to leave the room." He was upset about the situation in which the financial pressures would place his wife and children: "I shun them; my soul is tortured when I think of them, and what they will be soon, very very soon." He could not understand why Tom or Irwin could send nothing: "Had they nothing to sell—no lands, no Negroes, they should have sold had they brought but half the price."[11]

William was more sympathetic toward Edward, but he had to be firm. Edward still had not learned his lesson when it came to paying his bills.

> Mr. Shields sent me an acct. of things you bought from him, and which, it seems, you told him I would pay. I have refused. I cannot do it. I am unable. Mr. Drake informed me, that he had let you have upwards of £10 in cash, and expected that I would pay. I gave him the same answer. Then your barber called on me; I told him he must stay until you settled—for you must pay your own accts. As to the two first I was astonished; because you know well my circumstances, and as to the last I supposed you would not go away without paying him of all people in the world, because it is disgraceful to be in debt to one's barber.

William was still willing to wish Edward well in whatever line of business he had decided to undertake, and he closed his letter dramatically with a piece of advice: "My soul is on the rack—again farewell—Oh think of a brother ruined, and forswear suretyship."[12]

As far as his other brother was concerned, Paterson's feelings were more severe.

> I am harassed and prosecuted for your debts and those of Irwin and Paterson. My credit is ruined; my reputation is blasted: I and my wife and children are beggars; and, gracious heaven, all this dire calamity is owing to men called Brothers. I may perhaps keep out of Prison during the Winter, but in the Spring a Jayle must be my

> Doome—unless I experience more Lenity from Creditors, who are
> strangers, than I have justice from you, who are a Brother.[13]

The situation seemed all the more unjust because what little money the
debtors had been able to raise in New Orleans had been applied to other
accounts, for which William was not responsible. "I am here, on the
spot," he wrote, while the creditors will not "give themselves the trouble
of sending after you to New Orleans; there you are, out of their reach
and here I am at their mercy." Resigned to his fate, Paterson bade farewell to a brother he hoped never to see again.

> The reflection is at once terrible and true, I should have been worth
> thousands, and easy and contented, happy in my children and the
> prospect of providing for them in the world If I had never had a
> Brother. Farewell—You will not have another brother to ruin.[14]

Although he tried his best to put off the creditors and delay payment
of the accounts, over the next two years Paterson was obliged to pay
over £1,400 to John Donaldson of Philadelphia to settle the largest
portion of the debt. While he had to do some borrowing himself to meet
the payments and the household budget must have been strained, Paterson
was neither brought to court nor forced to sell his estate.[15] There is some
evidence that Thomas Irwin, who was later able to straighten himself out
and resume a profitable business, eventually made some restitution to his
benefactor, but Paterson seems never again to have been interested in his
brothers' lives.[16] A decade later, both Thomas and Edward were struggling
as school teachers in Pennsylvania, and even though Tom made an
overture to his estranged brother, who by then was in comfortable circumstances as a Supreme Court justice, there is no indication that William
responded.[17] The resentment endured, and the brothers remained apart.

Throughout 1788, the year in which Paterson foresaw the destruction
of his personal estate, New Jersey was playing its part in erecting the
new edifice of national government. As an essay reprinted in the *Trenton
Weekly Mercury* in January had put it, the Constitution was like a
replacement for the defective roof of a mansion house that had been
supported by thirteen rafters of unequal size and strength. According to
the essay, a group of "skillful architects" chosen to consult on the problem
recommended that, since the old roof was beyond repair, it should be
"entirely removed, and that a new roof of better construction should be
erected."[18] By July 1788, the required nine states had approved the archi-

tect's plans, but the framework still had to be assembled and the structure put into place. In October, the legislature began planning for the selection of the state's two senators and four representatives.

The choice of senators was relatively easy. A joint session of the legislature met on November 25 and from a field of four nominees— William Paterson; Jonathan Elmer, a well-known Cumberland County physician; Abraham Clark, leader of the state's paper money party; and Elias Boudinot, devoted patriot and president of the Continental Congress during the war—chose Paterson and Elmer. If there was any contest it was between Elmer, who garnered 29 votes, and Clark, with 19. Boudinot, who got only 7 votes, seems to have thrown his support to Elmer, preferring to be a candidate for the House as long as Clark was not chosen for the Senate. Paterson overwhelmed the others with 45 votes.[19]

His success had been a foregone conclusion. Months before, when he was drafted for the nomination, he wrote to his wife explaining the need to clean up as much old business as possible "especially if I shall be obliged to leave New Jersey in the first spring month."[20] He had second thoughts about accepting the nomination, in part because he feared that the job would force him to give up much of his legal practice. He even tried to retract his promise to run, but his friends were insistent.[21] Federalist leaders in the state saw in Paterson a candidate of solid conservative opinions who would support their interests in Congress and, best of all, was sure to win the seat with no trouble. John Chetwood, an outspoken supporter of the Constitution, member of the New Jersey ratifying convention, and political confidant of Boudinot, assured Paterson that he would be unanimously elected; "a grateful country cannot forget you." In response to Paterson's hesitation to seek the appointment, Chetwood played on his vanity and his sense of public duty: "If to any, surely to such a man, the country under peculiar circumstances, ought to have a right to look up."[22] This type of pressure was too much for Paterson to resist. By the time the appointment became official in November, he had resigned himself to taking on the new responsibility.

There is no evidence that Paterson took part in the successful campaign to elect Boudinot and his friends to the House. The election was a very irregular one in which several counties kept their polls open weeks longer than planned, in order to build up the margin of votes for Boudinot and the rest of what was called the "Junto ticket."[23] By the time the state-wide balloting was finally closed late in April, Paterson had already occupied his seat in the Senate chamber for over a month.

In March 1789, as the new senators and congressmen began streaming into New York City, where the new government was to reside, the city was bustling with excitement and anticipation. The new Congress was scheduled to convene there on March 4, and, after proper verification of the electoral votes, George Washington was to be inaugurated president of the new republic. Office seekers hurried about as the new senators and representatives settled themselves in their lodgings and made introductory social calls on one another. William Paterson did not take his seat in the Senate until March 19, but since the necessary quorum of twelve senators failed to arrive for almost three more weeks, there was still plenty of time for social activity. "Great works are going on here," Paterson reported to his wife on March 24, "and there will be marvelous doings when the Pres[ident]-Gen[eral] arrives. . . . The Fed[eral] building is elegant," he went on. "It far exceeds anything of the kind I have seen & all join in declaring that there is nothing equal to it in this country "[24] Within a few days, though, he complained to her of all the time spent in "idle ceremony and show" and described

> the round of visitants with which I have been honored. I have returned the greater part of them and so there will be an end of this kind of ceremonious conduct. All are sick of it and yet all follow it. Such is the prevalence of fashion, and the force of custom.[25]

The hectic social life of the capital city abated somewhat as the Congress got down to work. The Senate finally filled its quorum on April 6 when Richard Henry Lee arrived from Virginia and presented his credentials. The first day was spent in the formalities of electing a president pro tempore and counting the electoral ballots for the presidency. Paterson acted as a teller on behalf of the Senate in totalling the votes and then was appointed to help prepare the certificates of election for George Washington and the vice president, John Adams. Now that the national legislature was in operation and the leaders of the executive branch were set, the Senate took on the task of organizing the third branch of the federal government. On April 7, a committee made up of Oliver Ellsworth of Connecticut, William Maclay of Pennsylvania, Caleb Strong of Massachusetts, Richard Henry Lee of Virginia, Richard Bassett of Delaware, William Few of Georgia, Paine Wingate of New Hampshire, and Paterson was ordered to "bring in a bill for organizing the judiciary of the United States." The bill they reported was placed at the top of the Senate docket and eventually became the Judiciary Act of 1789.[26]

The charge of the committee was to fulfill Article 3 of the Constitution, which vested the judicial power of the United States in "one supreme Court, and in such inferior Courts as the Congress may from time to time establish." The issues involved were delicate ones, because a considerable part of the Anti-Federalist opposition to the Constitution had been directed against Article 3, and the Congress was now trying to calm the fears of those who expected the new government to run roughshod over state sovereignty and individual liberty. Much of the debate in the state ratifying conventions had centered around the judiciary article, and many of the constitutional amendments proposed by them sought to limit the jurisdiction of the federal courts and guarantee jury trials in civil as well as criminal cases tried there. Even some supporters of the Constitution agreed with the criticisms of the judiciary article and supported the movement to restrict the authority it granted.[27] These amendments to limit the scope and power of the courts were being debated in Congress at the same time that the judiciary plan was under consideration, which complicated the committee's task. Moreover, the committee included an outspoken critic of the Constitution, Richard Henry Lee,[28] who worked in and out of the committee meetings to undermine plans for a comprehensive federal judiciary. Next to Ellsworth, Paterson's acquaintance from college days and his fellow delegate at Philadelphia, Paterson was the most influential member of the committee. When the more than two months of preliminary discussions were done and the draft bill was finally reported on June 12, the first nine sections of it were in Paterson's handwriting.[29]

Compromise in the committee resulted in a bill that did not fully satisfy either the proponents or the opponents of a strong federal judiciary, although the latter group found more in it to please them. In order to accentuate the spirit of conciliation, Lee was chosen to present the final draft proposal to the Senate. Rather than confront those who wished to limit the courts through constitutional amendment with an open challenge, the committee had prepared a bill that did not go as far in impowering the judiciary as the Constitution allowed it to. Those who preferred that Congress create only a supreme court and go no further were chagrined at Sections 3 and 4 of the bill (sections written by Paterson) which established both federal district courts in every state and federal circuit courts as well. They could, however, take relief in the limited jurisdiction granted to those courts.

According to the draft bill, the federal district courts would have jurisdiction over "all crimes and offences that shall be cognizable under the authority of the United States, and defined by the laws of the same."[30] In other words, federal courts were to have criminal jurisdiction only over specific laws passed by Congress, specific provisions of the Constitution, or treaties of the United States.[31] The same courts would have exclusive original jurisdiction over all civil cases dealing with admiralty and maritime law; of all seizures under the laws of impost, navigation, and trade of the United States; and of certain suits involving foreign diplomats. The circuit courts were to have concurrent authority to hear the same cases as the district courts as well as appellate jurisdiction over district court decision. Moreover, they would have concurrent jurisdiction with the state courts in civil suits of more than $500 involving the United States as a plaintiff or petitioner, or when "a foreigner or citizen of another state than that in which the suit is brought is a party."[32] In short, the lower national courts were authorized to deal only with criminal cases except under specific circumstances, particularly when prejudice might be expected to arise in a civil action.

The draft bill limited the Supreme Court, too. Most cases that arose under the Constitution, laws, or treaties of the United States were assigned in the first instance to state courts. Section 23 of the draft bill (Section 25 of the judiciary act after it became law) provided for the appeal of state court decisions to the Supreme Court of the United States only if a claim of right under the Constitution, a treaty, or the federal law was denied there, but in the great majority of cases the states' highest tribunal remained the court of last resort.[33] Rather than grant a comprehensive jurisdiction to inferior courts, Ellsworth, Paterson, and the other framers of the bill were relying on this limited appellate jurisdiction of the Supreme Court to keep the states from challenging federal supremacy.

Paterson, though open to compromise, was a believer in a strong federal judiciary, and he voiced his opinions loud and clear in the Senate debate on the bill. The debate began on June 22 with the question of whether or not there should be any district courts at all. If they were to be set up, Richard Henry Lee, who himself had just introduced the draft bill, proposed that their jurisdiction be limited only to maritime and admiralty cases.[34] Paterson collected his thoughts on paper, and on the following day he rose and spoke with conviction. "Ever since the adoption of the Constitution," he proclaimed, "I have considered federal courts of subordinate jurisdiction and detached from state tribunals as inevitable."[35] They were necessary, he believed, for both theoretical and practical reasons. In terms of theory, Paterson spoke of the principle of shared sovereignty that the Great Compromise had built into the Constitution. He went on to address the point as to whether or not there should be district courts.

Who are we. How compounded. Of what materials do we consist. We are a combination of Republics, a number of free states confederated together, and forming a social league. United we have a head, separately we have a head, each operating upon different objects. When we act in union we move in one sphere, when we act in our individual capacity, we move in another. . . . The State tribunals consist of judges elected by the States in their separate capacity to decide upon state laws and state objects, they are not elected to decide upon national objects or laws, except as they may come in incidentally in a cause. The union has no vote in their election, no voice in their appointment. They are strangers, creatures of the state, dependent on the state for their very subsistance.[36]

On the practical side, the state judges were appointed by the states for various terms of office and "in most depend for their salary upon the legislature from year to year." If the state courts were left to assume the entire responsibility for subordinate federal jurisdiction, then the state judges could consider themselves to be in fact federal judges entitled to the term of good behavior and the permanent salary guaranteed by Article 3 of the Constitution.[37] The dilemma, as Paterson called it, was this: Either the state judges would require from the national government the term and the salary of federal judges even though the federal government had no voice in their appointment, or else the judges would remain dependent on the states, thereby destroying the judicial independence that the Constitution had sought to provide and prejudicing the only courts with jurisdiction over federal laws in favor of the states.[38]

Paterson insisted that the creation of independent federal district courts was not, as had been claimed, "casting a stigma on the state courts" or doubting their virtue. It was only "a proper precaution against dependent men." Paterson explained that,

> however I may value a man, yet if he be dependent on another, I should not like to submit to his decision a dispute in which that other is concerned. We have as men individually our Interests, connections and Ambitions. So as to States. Shall we suffer men so situated to mingle in the federal administration for their [the states'] interest?[39]

In more specific terms, Paterson asked: "Suppose New Jersey was to make suit against a Rep. of Virginia." Could the New Jersey state courts be trusted to adjudicate such a suit with total impartiality? He advised his colleagues in the Senate: "Do not give up the power of collecting your own revenue." The authority for the federal government to tax had been at the heart of the struggle for the Constitution; now it could be thrown away by trusting its enforcement to the state courts. "There must therefore be district judges of more extent of jurisdiction than maritime causes." The circuit courts would be important, too, but he thought that circuit courts could not "pervade in a country so extensive as this." District courts with significant authority were needed to "carry [federal] law to their homes, Courts to their doors—meet every citizen in his own state." If there were any who doubted whether this man from New Jersey who had fought so hard for the equal rights of the states at Philadelphia now saw things in national perspective, they were convinced by this statement near the end of his speech: "To become one people, we must have one common national tribunal."[40]

The district courts were agreed to, and Lee's proposal to further restrict their jurisdiction was turned down. This had been the most crucial element in the whole debate on the judiciary. Later votes guaranteed jury trials and approved Supreme Court review of state decisions. In the final act, the jurisdiction of the Supreme Court was limited to "controversies of a civil nature where a state is a party" (except between a state and its own citizens), to cases involving ambassadors or other public ministers or their servants, and to appeals from the district and circuit courts.[41] But, as Paterson had pointed out, to create no subordinate federal courts would be to effectively destroy the whole idea of an independent judiciary. While he differed from other proponents of the bill on certain particulars, such as his defense of the right of a defendant not to testify against himself and his opposition to the extension of equity jurisdiction in the federal courts, Paterson had proven himself both a Federalist and a nationalist.[42]

There was other important business in the first session of Congress. For one thing, the long-sought federal power to tax was exercised in a national impost law. Like the Judiciary Act, this first federal tax legislation represented an attempt to ease the fears of Anti-Federalists and even of some supporters of the Constitution who had disapproved the extent of the taxing power granted in the Constitution and had called for amendments to limit it to indirect levies. The proposed amendments were turned down by Congress, but no one had immediate plans for instituting a direct tax, at least until the new government was more firmly established. For the present, taxation would be confined to duties on imports and an excise on liquor.[43] Among his other responsibilities, Paterson served on one committee concerning customs house oaths, another to revise the Senate journal before publication, and yet another "to provide for safekeeping of the Acts, Records, and Seal of the United States."[44] Paterson also spoke out against granting titles to government officials.

William Maclay, a senator from Pennsylvania who was a savage critic of the Federalists, noted a speech by Paterson supporting the power of the president to remove heads of executive departments without interference from Congress.[45] For Maclay, who often "allowed his bitterness to get the better of his discretion"[46] and his judgment, Paterson's support of the removal bill was the last in a series of positions that convinced him that the Jerseyman was corrupt.

> Of all the members of the House [Senate] the conduct of Patterson surprized me most. He has been characterized to me as a staunch Revolution man and a genuine Whig; yet he has in every republican question deserted and in some cases betrayed us. I k ow not that there is such a thing as buying members, but, if there is, he is certainly sold.[47]

Maclay's insinuation that Paterson took bribes was mistaken, but he was correct on his analysis of Paterson's politics. Paterson's conduct in the first session of the Senate had shown him to be a loyal Federalist and supporter of the administration.

The Congress adjourned in September, and Paterson returned to his family and his clients in New Jersey. But he was back in New York the following January as the Senate resumed its business and was soon immersed again in the details of legislation. In this second session, he served on committees for setting up the census, framing copyright laws for "the encouragement of learning," and for reporting "a bill defining the crimes and offences that shall be cognizable under the authority of the United States and their punishment."[48] Each of these bills was then debated and passed on by the Senate, the last only after an amendment was added by Ellsworth to provide that surgeons looking for cadavers to dissect might be given the bodies of executed convicts at the discretion of the sentencing judge.[49] Paterson was active in the debate on the naturalization bill, defending the rights of aliens who declared their intention to become citizens, and supporting the amendment to the bill that would assure them of property rights and the protection of the laws.[50] His other senatorial duties included the investigation of nominees for executive appointments and the study of proposed treaties before confirmation.[51]

With the work of the Senate in full swing again, Paterson wrote to his wife on February 6, 1790, that he spent most of his time in his room, partly because of the cold weather and partly because "reading and business keep me employed." Judging from the round of dinner parties and receptions to which he was invited, the social life of the capital had not waned at all. He claimed to "have four or five invitations for Tuesday next to say nothing of other days." When the occasion demanded, such as when the French *chargé d'affaires* gave a banquet "to celebrate the alliance" or when the president called the senators to dine with him and discuss matters of legislation, Paterson went along and had "fine times." But whenever possible, he chose to "send an apology" and remain at home.[52]

There was personal business that had to be looked after, especially with his brothers' creditors still breathing down his neck. Irwin, his brother-in-law, had not been heard from in two years, but Paterson had learned that some of the creditors (not the ones to whom he was responsible) had been paid off. Paterson was left holding the bag to the tune of £3,000, and he didn't hesitate to complain about it when Irwin's son John wrote from Philadelphia to ask for help in winning appointment as an army surgeon. Paterson advised against it on professional grounds, suggesting instead that his nephew try to set up a private practice as soon as possible. But the letter also suggested that financial irresponsibility ran in the Irwin family. John had purchased £15 worth of supplies in Philadelphia by explaining that he was Paterson's nephew and that the senator would guarantee his credit. Once burned already, Paterson was shocked at the young man's behavior and enjoined him to make the repayment of the debt a matter of honor.[53]

While in New York, Paterson also tried to keep abreast of his clients' affairs, taking three days off to attend a chancery session in Elizabethtown, for example, and attending other New Jersey court meetings whenever he was able. He even took the time to carefully instruct his wife on finding the proper tenant for their Raritan farm: "He must also put in English grass seed with the winter grain and not plough more than a proportion of the land in any one year."[54]

The most sensitive issues in the second session of Congress, and the ones that demanded the most time, were involved with the plans of the secretary of the treasury for the funding of the national debt and the assumption of state debts. Alexander Hamilton, who had been disappointed in the unwillingness of the delegates at the Philadelphia convention to create a much stronger national government than the one set up by the Constitution, now saw a second chance for increasing the power of the federal government at the expense of the states and for encouraging people to think of themselves first as citizens of the United States rather than Virginians, New Yorkers, or Jerseymen.

The occasion was his proposal to put the public credit of the country on a solid footing. This had been impossible as long as the national government had no independent taxing authority, but now the government had the authority and was obliged to do something about repairing its financial reputation or lose whatever international respect the new nation could muster. The repayment of revolutionary war loans from France and Holland had been neglected, and Dutch bankers had lately been involved in heavy speculation in United States securities with the expectation that the new government would make good on them. Speculators at home were important, too, not only because some of them were Hamilton's personal friends, but more significantly because they represented the business class of America and, as Hamilton saw it, these were the people whose loyalty it was most important to attach to the new federal government. To convince them of the new nation's financial reliability, Hamilton proposed to fund the debt (to renew it by exchanging new securities for old) at face value. Several of the states had dealt with similar situations by offering security-holders compensation at or near the market value, which had the advantage of saving the government a lot of money. Some argued that, besides being very expensive, Hamilton's funding plan was a slap in the face to farmers and Continental soldiers who had bartered away their wartime securities for a fraction of their face value to speculators who now expected to make a killing. But Hamilton thought the only interest of his opponents was to get the debt settled as inexpensively as possible, regardless of the possible effect on the nation's financial respectability.[55]

Faced with such opposition and hopeful of winning approval for his plan to assume the state debts as well, Hamilton sent a compromise proposal to Congress. Rather than demanding a full compliance with the pledges made by Congress during the Confederation (6 percent interest and full repayment of the principal in specie), Hamilton suggested a number of options to be offered to Continental creditors that would result in bringing the overall interest charges down closer to 4 percent and even reducing some of the principal. To accomplish this, creditors were to be encouraged (but not required) to take part of their principal back in western lands, or be offered full interest on only two-thirds of their capital, exchanging the additional one-third for deferred stock that would only begin to earn interest in ten years.[56]

The House took up the funding proposals first. The main trouble there came from James Madison who, despite the absence of any previous opposition to the scheme, now suggested a plan whereby secondary holders would receive only a portion of the face value of their securities (near the current market price) and the original holders would be indemnified with some of the monies saved. Few took him seriously, however, and there is reason to believe that he had no real expectations that his proposal would get through. There were more radical members who preferred to buy up the whole debt at the market price and offer only 3 percent interest, and they tried to sway Madison to their side. But the Virginian seemed uninterested.[57] The House passed the bill on to the Senate in substantially the same form in which Hamilton had presented it to them.

Paterson's support for the funding proposal in the Senate was based less on any desire shared with Hamilton to increase an economic interest in the central government than it was on his continuing belief in the sanctity of contracts. He, Ellsworth, Maclay, and King were formed into a committee on July 11 to consider the bill sent in from the House. The following day, Maclay took space in his diary to comment on his fellow committee members. He thought Ellsworth was an eloquent man "of great faculties," but by trying "to reconcile the Secretary's [Hamilton's] system to the public opinion and welfare" he was attempting the impossible and stood to lose the confidence of both the administration and the people. For King he had only two words, "plausible and florid." But for Paterson there was more: He was "a *summum jus* man"; he could not see beyond the letter of the law. Paterson was thought "more taciturn and lurking in his manner" than the others, "yet when he speaks he commits himself hastily."[58] Maclay's opinion of Paterson was perceptive. Paterson had no reason to hesitate on the question of whether or not to fund at face value or pay the full 6 percent interest that had been promised when the certificates were first issued. He had been through this before back in New Jersey, when the state legislature had devalued its own legal tender notes. He recognized that it was possible for the law to be unjust, but, in financial matters, law alone was important, even if such a stand put him in a more conservative position than the compromise stance taken by Hamilton himself. The point was made succinctly on June 16, when, in the midst of an open debate on funding, Paterson spoke out. The committee on the debt bill had reported a further compromise that would have reduced the quarterly paid interest on the domestic debt to 4 percent. Paterson had sat on that committee, but now he spoke out against its recommendations and called for the full 6 percent.[59] As Maclay described it,

> now rose up Paterson with a load of notes before him. To follow him would be to write a pamphlet, for he was up near an hour. Near the beginning he put a question: "What principle shall we adopt to settle this business? If we follow Justice, *she says three per cent or even two is as much as the holders of the certificates can demand.* But what says law?—six per cent," and he was a *summum jus* man to the end of the chapter.

Maclay answered Paterson on the floor. It was not, as Paterson had suggested, a situation where the government was one party to a contract and the securityholders the other. Instead, Maclay saw "the people at large as being the debtors and the holders the creditors, and the Congress the umpire." He favored justice over the letter of the law and "reprobated his [Paterson's] position even with acrimony as the Shylock doctrine of 'my bond, my bond.'" But Ellsworth, who then stood to defend Paterson's view, made the point again: "Every continental bill carries a contract on its face—Why not observe it?"[60]

Those like Maclay who were concerned with economy and Madison who sought to discriminate between the speculators and the original holders lost in the end. The bill the Senate passed on to the president to sign into law called for a reduction of Hamilton's several options to only one. Creditors could exchange two-thirds of their securities for 6 percent bonds and the remaining third for deferred 6 percent notes that would begin to earn interest in 1800.[61] Paterson's letter-of-the-law stand, even stronger than that taken by Hamilton himself, had not convinced his colleagues, but it had proven him to be a loyal and self-motivated Federalist.

Hamilton's proposal to assume the debts of the states found even tougher sledding. At the heart of the assumption question was the belief that various states stood either to gain or lose from it. New Jersey, for example, still had some debts to be paid, and Massachusetts and South Carolina had much larger obligations that assumption could relieve. Virginia, on the other hand, had already paid off much of the money she had borrowed and saw the assumption proposal as directly contrary to her interest. In fact, the real matter of settling the accounts of the states and reimbursing those who had given more than their share in the war was already under way. A bill calling for such a final accounting was in Congress at that very moment. But Virginia and most of the other southern states were concerned that such a final accounting might never be made, and the ardor with which Massachusetts and South Carolina sought to push assumption through could not help but heighten their concern.[62]

Hamilton's idea was to increase the importance of the federal sphere by increasing its debt responsibility, thereby increasing the need for federal taxes. At the same time the states, which no longer had to service their debts, would lose the necessity to tax, and their former creditors would then see the security and authority of the federal government as the best protection for their investment. Then too, speculators who had turned to buying state securities when the Continental ones had become too expensive hoped that the federal government would take over the state debt and fund it on the same terms as their own. Assumption was thus a very knotty issue.[63]

According to tradition, a deal was made to break the deadlock between Hamilton and Virginia's Madison and Jefferson. Since the previous session, fruitless debate had continued about the location for the permanent seat of national government. The Pennsylvanians and New Yorkers opposed the southerners, who wanted the capital nearer to them. There is no evidence that Paterson participated in this debate, but he did keep several pages of notes on the various arguments. Now, in return for the votes of several Virginians for the federal assumption of the state debts, Hamilton is said to have promised to intercede in favor of moving the capital south.[64] In any case, the funding and assumption plan became law, and the banks of the Potomac were designated as the site of the nation's capital. When Paterson supported Hamilton's position on the southern capital, Maclay claimed he had been "retained by the Secretary," called him a "despicable character," and listed the Jerseyman as one of Hamilton's "gladitorial band" of followers who regularly went to battle in support of property and privilege.[65]

There is no question that the opinions Paterson expressed and votes he cast while he was in the Senate placed him firmly in the Federalist camp. Federalism was natural to Paterson. It was not an ideology that he had to learn. The sanctity of law and the Constitution, the stability of government institutions, and the importance of fiscal responsibility—all hallmarks of Federalist political philosophy—had been his basic beliefs since his training at Princeton. No matter what William Maclay thought of him, Paterson believed he was simply living up to his personal creed. It is not surprising, therefore, that he denied any association with a political party. It was an irony common to most political thinkers in the late eighteenth century that, notwithstanding their de facto allegiance to one set of political ideas or another, they attacked the concept of political parties and refused to admit loyalty to any party or faction.[66]

There has been considerable debate among historians over the beginnings of America's first two organized parties. In recent years, most scholars have tried to answer the contention of Charles Beard that the Republicans of the 1790s were directly related to the Anti-Federalists who opposed ratification of the Constitution. Most scholars now agree that, while the Anti-Federalists were moved primarily by state and local interests to oppose ratification, the origins of the Republican party were based on national issues instead.[67] It is easier to see the ties between many of the nationalist supporters of the Constitution and the Federalist party of the 1790s. They had been thinking in terms of national issues all along, and for many of them the work of the first Congress in legislating the impost, creating an independent federal judiciary, and adopting Hamilton's program to restore public credit was the fulfillment of their attempts since the mid-1780s to create a stronger national government.[68]

Although formal party organization would wait a few years until even more controversial issues such as neutrality in foreign affairs and the Jay Treaty had cemented public opinion, basic elements in each party's ideology could be found in the debates on the financial plan. Madison, former leader of the nationalists, had posed as a defender of the common man. He did not oppose the reestablishment of credit, but was apparently trying to accommodate the mass of the people to it by offering to give them a share. Hamilton's followers, on the other hand, feared the mass of the people and were trying to strengthen the new government against possible popular uprisings in the style of Daniel Shays. They feared that Madison was encouraging such opposition by pointing up how one class (the speculators) and one section (the North) stood to profit more than the others from funding and assumption.[69] Although Madison and the other leaders of the future Republican party were themselves descendents of the old colonial elite, they did not see themselves as threatened by the people at large as did some of the Federalists, who became quite transparent in defense of their elite status.[70]

Paterson enjoyed wide popular support at home in New Jersey, but his confidence in the average citizen was far from complete. He knew how an ill-informed electorate could be swayed by political charlatans; he had seen it happen back in his home state during the paper money crisis of the 1780s. He was not worried that they would vote him out of office; he was still complaining about the rigors of the public responsibilities he had been asked to assume and wished he could be left to live his private life and practice law. But he did fear that unscrupulous men who would sacrifice the principles of honest republicanism to the whims of popular desire might be elected in his place. The Revolution was over, and with it the peculiar dangers to public order that in his mind invariably accompanied such rapid changes in the situation of states. But there would still be challenges to the constitutional rights of property, and there were still men whose passions got the better of them. The new republic needed protection against these.

During his time in the Senate, Paterson acted according to his own persistent beliefs. Because these beliefs came so naturally to him, he failed to recognize the irony in his refusal to style himself as a member of the Federalist faction. Now Paterson was leaving the Senate and returning to New Jersey to become governor. Nevertheless, his political essays written throughout the 1790s indicate a continuing concern with national issues and an abiding Federalism in the way he perceived them.

PART IV

SERVING THE PUBLIC TRUST

The last fifteen years of Paterson's life were spent in service to New Jersey and the new nation. As opposed to his more ambitious early years, during the Revolution, for example, this final period in his life seems almost completely free of desire for personal advancement or further social recognition. As he returned to New Jersey to become governor in 1791, Paterson gave up his private legal practice. He never resumed it again. His financial security had been threatened by his brothers' failure in business, and for a time he feared that all would be lost. But he managed to weather the storm, and over the next decade and a half, through judicious investments, he was able to put together a sizeable estate to pass on to his children.

The popularity Paterson enjoyed in every corner of the state was phenomenal. In a period when party divisions were beginning to solidify, his favorite-son status allowed Paterson to remain aloof from factional strife. As governor, Paterson presided over the auspicious beginnings of the Society for Establishing Useful Manufactures, and the new company named their planned industrial community after him. Although the immediate experience of the SUM was disappointing, the project was to be remembered as one of the most important early chapters in the history of American industrialization. Another of his contributions to New

181

Jersey, second only perhaps to his service at Philadelphia, was the revision of the laws he began in 1792. It involved him in almost every aspect of society and politics and brought forth in him a motivation for reform.

His self-image had been reinforced by continual statements of public praise and his feelings of pride deservedly bolstered by his appointment to the United States Supreme Court. But Paterson still retained his somewhat pretentious moralistic style and his conservative view of politics and society. Although he forswore loyalty to any party or faction, thinking such divisions inimical to the public interest, his ideas naturally coincided with those of the Federalists. Maintaining in his mind the fiction that the Federalists represented the distilled best interests of the nation at large, rather than a political faction, Paterson based his avid support for the Sedition Act and his attack on Jeffersonian Republican newspaper editors in the crisis of 1798 on his aversion to the Republicans as a party.

Paterson served on the Supreme Court until his death in 1806. During those years, he had several opportunities to make further contributions to the interpretation of the Constitution he had helped to write years before. His most important cases reinforced the supremacy of the federal government over the states and laid the foundations for the principle of judicial review. Associated with the most conservative side of the court because of his decisions enforcing the Sedition Act, Paterson's Federalism did seem to soften in his later years. Everything in his personality, for example, made him tremble at the thought of Jefferson in the presidency, but he accepted the change with the same stoicism he maintained toward the decision in Congress to overturn the Judiciary Act of 1801. By the time of his death in 1806, the fears of many Federalists had begun to wane as President Jefferson adopted more and more of their positions on national issues.

Paterson could not disavow the Federalist party, because he had never openly avowed it in the first place. His ideas ran deeper than those of most party loyalists, making him appear to some a "Federalist among Federalists." But in reality his support for Hamilton's financial plan, the crisis measures of 1798, and all the other Federalist positions were based almost solely on his long-held desire to see the democratic impulse unleashed by the Revolution held in check.

Paterson the Governor

The genesis of Paterson's political career had come in the turbulent days of 1775 and 1776, just at the time that the public life of William Livingston was entering its final phase. Livingston had moved to New Jersey a few years before, seeking retirement from his active participation in New York affairs, but as the Revolution approached he was inevitably drawn into the fray. He served in the Continental Congress until he was appointed commander-in-chief of New Jersey's militia in June 1776. Two months later he became the new state's first governor. The fifty-year-old governor and his thirty-year-old attorney general, William Paterson, worked together throughout the war years to maintain as much order as possible amid the chaos of revolution.

The two had shared an intense commitment to their duties. Paterson had twice turned down appointments to the Continental Congress, explaining that his responsibilities at Livingston's side were more important. Although it does not shine through in their official correspondence, Paterson later described their relationship as one of "friendship and intimacy."[1] After Paterson had left state office in 1783, there was little contact between them. But when the older man died in 1790, Paterson wrote an elegy in his memory—something he had not done since the death of his wife Cornelia years before. In the poem Paterson described Livingston as a man of humanity and courage, of genius and learning, a man of religion who sought after "the noblest interests of man" and who, in devotion to public service, emerged "second in fame to Washington alone."[2]

Livingston's fourteen consecutive one-year terms as governor had provided an important measure of stability to the state's politics and government. Paterson's admiration for him was based on this accomplishment, as well as on the fact that the two men were identical in their conservative social and political philosophies. Livingston, like Paterson, had justified the Revolution as a moral struggle against the dissolute British. He agreed that the 1776 constitution was unsuited to the wartime situation, and, during the paper money struggles of the 1780s, he sounded the same arguments as Paterson against an unlimited acquiescence to the popular will. On the sanctity of contracts, the responsibilities of debtors, and concern for the erosion of the traditional deference in politics, Paterson and Livingston were as one.[3] This explains why, in 1790, many conservative Jerseymen thought immediately of Paterson as the next governor.

More important than his philosophy, however, Paterson was known and respected across the state. After his well-publicized service in the federal convention and his overwhelming election to the Senate, Paterson was clearly New Jersey's most favored son. Even though his conservative ideas on politics and society might have been distasteful to many, there was nothing they could do to keep him from taking over Livingston's position—if he would accept it.

Less than a week after Livingston's death, John Chetwood, Nicholas Bayard, and others were already pressing Paterson to take over the post. But Senator Paterson was still expressing his desire for anonymity and relief from the pressures of public office. He wrote to his wife about his continuing unhappiness at being separated from his law practice and expressed his hope that the legislature would find someone else better qualified. "Public life has always been disagreeable to me," he complained, "I would much rather pursue the line of my profession." This kind of talk is not unusual among politicians, of course, and James Young has recently shown it to be especially common among political leaders of Paterson's generation, but Paterson was apparently sincere.[4] Anyone who knew Paterson also knew that he could not resist a draft, but the rumors of his disinclination spread nonetheless.

By mid-August Jonathan Dayton was writing to beg Paterson's assurance that the stories were untrue, and a biting piece of satire had been published in several of the state's newspapers. The essay, in the form of a proclamation, was signed in the name of Captain Triumph (who was intended to represent Paterson). The captain explained how the loss of the "illustrious Livingston" had placed him in the position of deciding between his love for his country and his personal "prospects of shortly *eclipsing* the glory of all my [his] contemporaries in a certain learned profession." The struggle had been a tough one, but "thanks be to your stars, my countrymen," Captain Triumph continued, "*patriotism* hath at length prevailed, and your Governor I consent to be." Paterson and his supporters were aware that unless he agreed to accept the offer, the choice of another would result in an unpleasant political battle. As Captain Triumph explained it, Paterson's "*gracious* and *condescending*" decision was meant "to quiet the uneasiness" and anxiety of his countrymen, "and to prevent the vain aspirations of all worthless men."[5]

Captain Triumph had not been very gracious to Paterson, but his perception of the political situation and Paterson's response to it was perfect. Paterson had always had a passion for order in the political as well as the social world. He finally went along with the nomination to avoid the likelihood of a political struggle from which the state could only suffer. His boosters insisted on his choice, because they realized the extent of his popularity. Paterson was the only one who could win the office without a fight. Despite Captain Triumph's cynical barbs, the outpouring of support was tremendous. The new governor was elected unanimously when the legislature met in October, and he spent weeks thereafter in answering the dozens of congratulatory addresses that came from all over the state. They praised him for his public service, his wisdom in the law, and his moral fortitude.[6] At least one friend of the governor was so carried away that he lost all semblance of taste and penned the following poem, "On seeing Governor Paterson on board his barge the *Cornelia,* at the last celebration of Independence."

> On Raritan's smooth gliding stream we view,
> Enraptur'd view the man whom we admire,
> On this auspicious day, with laurel crown'd,
> How gracefully the honor'd barge moves on.
> See Neptune's hardy sons all clad in white,
> Timing their oars to the melodious flutes;
> Not Cleopatra's celebrated barge,
> When she full arm'd with each bewitching charm,
> A tyrant bound in the soft chairs of love,
> More elegantly, or pleasing could appear;
> Nor did contain a jewel of such worth,

> Nor freighted with a proud intriguing Queen;
> She nobly bears *New Jersey's* fav'rite son,
> Our guardian chief, our friend, ah Paterson.

Despite the poet's bad verse, the editor of the *New Brunswick Gazette* saw fit to print it.[7] Although such unctious paeans eventually came to embarrass Paterson, they serve as convincing evidence of the literally boundless admiration that some people had for him.

There was little reason for those who opposed Paterson's conservatism to fear him now. The 1776 constitution had effectively stripped the governor's office of any real independent authority. Moved by the same democratic impulses that motivated most colonies at the time, the framers of the New Jersey constitution had provided that the governor be chosen by a joint meeting of the assembly and council every year. Despite the appearance of power, they loaded on the responsibilities of the office to the point where it became nearly impossible for anyone to do an effective job. Besides sitting as the president of the Legislative Council, the governor was to "have the supreme executive power, be chancellor of the colony, and act as captain-general and commander in chief of all militia, and other military forces." Moreover, as president of the council, he was also chief officer of the Court of Appeals, the court of last resort for all legal causes.[8] The scope of the position was essentially the same as it had been for the last royal governor, except that in reality the authority that came with it was severely circumscribed. Although the governor still announced many appointments to state offices, he had little control over who was chosen. He was required to consult on a regular basis with a privy council, which consisted of at least three members of the upper house. No longer free to make criminal pardons on his own authority, the governor now needed the agreement of this privy council. The power to call together and adjourn the regular meetings of the legislature was reserved for the lawmakers alone.

In many respects, therefore, the governor's position was that of a figurehead. It carried with it a number of prestigious titles, but it allowed neither the independent authority nor the time necessary to do a very good job. With Paterson's help, Livingston had been able to take a dynamic hand in administration during the war, but once peace had returned, as respected as he was, the governor was forced to quietly take a back seat to the legislature. The greatest influence Livingston had during the contentions of the Confederation period was through the anonymous newspaper essays he continued to turn out.[9] During his own tenure, Paterson never assumed a real leadership role in the government. He could do little more than set the tone of administration and exert his influence indirectly from time to time.

The type of state problems that had interested him most in the past were those concerning paper money, debtor-creditor laws, and public finance. The paper money laws that he had so vigorously opposed during the Confederation were no longer a problem. Paterson rejoiced that the federal Constitution had in effect reaffirmed his arguments for a conservative fiscal policy. Later he described how the state had been in a "low and wretched situation" and suffered from an "air of despondency," partly because of the unfair trade dominance enjoyed by neighboring states and partly because of the "mischievous system of paper money" supported by the popular legislature with an "ardor bordering upon frenzy." The Constitution had ended all that and had immediately restored the confidence of investors and creditors by denying the states authority to print money or abrogate contracts.[10] Popularly elected legislators might still be irresponsible, but at least the sacred rights of property were now protected from their flights of fancy. With Paterson's obvious approval, New Jersey acted in 1788 and 1789 to retire the paper currency in circulation, and it was gradually withdrawn over the next decade.[11] In what one scholar has called a "mild counterrevolution," the majority in the legislature had shifted to the conservatives, but, by the time Paterson became governor, the passion to reverse the popular measures of the 1780s had begun to dissipate. In 1791 and 1792, for example, the legislature reinstated the debtor law of 1783, which had been repealed, and regularized the practice of allowing insolvent debtors to initiate their own bankruptcy proceedings without the previously required agreement of a majority of their creditors.[12]

Problems of state public finance had also been eased by the time Paterson took office, but he still had no faith in the judgment of New Jersey's legislators when it came to money matters. He had participated in the passage of the bill by which Congress proposed to assume the debts of the individual states. In 1790, New Jersey security holders were allowed to subscribe to a United States loan, by which they would receive federal certificates in return for state ones.[13] Like several other states, New Jersey had not reached its quota for subscriptions by September 1791, so Paterson was instructed by the legislature to petition for an extension of the time limit, which was granted. When the final accounting was announced in June 1793, it was found that (by proportion of population based on the first census) New Jersey had paid only $49,000 more than her fair share (five states had overpaid more, and only Georgia was owed less) in supporting the revolutionary war, and the state was awarded that amount in federal securities.[14]

But Paterson still claimed that the state legislators were "penny wise and pound foolish." They had not yet risen above the "ignorance and mismanagement" that, during the war, had cost the state hundreds of thousands of pounds. Paterson reminded the lawmakers how they had approved the devaluation of bills of credit and the sale of confiscated estates in return for inflated currency. He was not volunteering to return the estate that he himself had purchased under these conditions, but Paterson did point out that the state might have taken in as much money by simply renting the lands for three or four years rather than turning over title to them. If New Jersey had followed the lead of New York and waited prudently until peace had returned, the sale of confiscated property would have yielded far more for the treasury. Even after "the reestablishment of good faith" that followed the adoption of the new constitution and the assumption of state debts, New Jersey's legislators had neglected to "provide against a stormy day."[15]

The newest and most promising economic prospect in New Jersey while Paterson was governor involved the state's encouragement of domestic manufactures. The story of the Society for Establishing Useful Manufactures (SUM), set up under the guiding hand of Alexander Hamilton, is one of the most interesting chapters in the early history of American industrialization, and Paterson could not help but become involved. During his term in the Senate, Paterson came into contact with the men who promised to put New Jersey on the map as a manufacturing state, and he was suitably impressed by them.

One of these was Tench Coxe, a Philadelphia business promoter who soon became Hamilton's assistant in the treasury office. These two men were responsible for planning the SUM, but Coxe became the chief popularizer of the scheme. Even before the idea for the SUM began to take shape, Coxe was the president of a manufacturing society in Philadelphia and had written a number of pieces for the journals there.[16] Before long he was adapting these arguments for New Jersey readers and placing them in the Jersey papers. Early in 1790, for example, he wrote Senator Paterson asking for his assistance in forwarding one of these essays to the press. His accompanying letter summarized many of the arguments that would be used a year and a half later in seeking a corporate charter for the SUM.

Coxe started by touching one of Paterson's most sensitive spots. "If New Jersey intends to maintain its proportion of respectability within the union," Coxe said, they would have to turn to manufactures. He explained that there remained "few vacant tracts of tolerable farming lands" in the state and that, with the expected increase in population over the next twenty years, they could expect to have to "send out annually near 7,000 souls" unless something was done to provide work for them. Moreover, suitable raw materials and accessibility to the sea made New Jersey's prospects for manufacturing good. Coxe realized that the state's legislators were already "turning their attention to the promotion of manufactures," but he thought that the first step should be to permanently fix the state capital at some place suitable for industrial development. New Brunswick, where his family owned some land, was Coxe's first choice. Laying his cards on the table, the Philadelphian admitted that "two or three families here, and ours among them, have had serious conversation upon the subject of your manufactures, as they may be promoted to aid our lands." He begged Paterson to keep their communication to himself, because "state jealousies prevail more or less in every mind," and asked him to forward an essay on the benefits of manufactures to the "East Jersey *Gazette,*" without identifying him as the author.[17]

New Jersey was buzzing with talk about manufactures. Popular societies had been founded in Newark and Burlington to encourage their growth. In fact, a newspaper, the *Burlington Advertizer,* had been set up for the express purpose of serving the local society for scientific agriculture and useful manufactures. Every issue carried one or more articles explaining some new farming practice or industrial process. When Paterson became governor in the fall of 1790, the legislature already had before it a bill "to Promote Arts, Agriculture and Manufacturing" within the state. The bill was passed in the assembly by a vote of 21 to 11 and lost in the council by only one vote.[18] Proponents of industry were heartened. Tench Coxe took to his pen again and, in a series of articles published first in the *American Museum* and reprinted in the *Burlington Advertizer,* he proposed the incorporation of a company with

> its stock transferable as in a bank, to receive subscriptions from 400 hundred dollars upwards, to purchase 500 or 1000 acres of land well situated, to receive imported materials, and to export their fabrics— were they to erect works in the centre of such a body of land, to lay out their grounds in a convenient town-plat, and proceed with judgement and system in their plan, they would be sure of success in their manufactories; they would raise a valuable town upon their land, and would help to support the value of the public debt.[19]

At about the same time, Coxe forwarded to Secretary of State Jefferson a more detailed "plan for a manufacturing establishment in the United States" and explained to the secretary that such a scheme was soon to be introduced in New Jersey.[20]

When the preliminary organization of the SUM was set up in the summer of 1791, Governor Paterson was at the center of it. He attended the organizational meeting held in New Brunswick on August 7 and 8, where plans were made for the submission of the petition for incorporation to the state legislature. The success of the SUM's plans required that certain special privileges be granted in its corporate charter, so the phrasing and presentation of the petition had to be handled discreetly, with careful attention given to the sensibilities of the legislators. The list of petitioners was to be headed up by prominent Jerseyman Elias Boudinot, and Alexander Hamilton himself agreed to personally assume responsibility for preparing the document. As Theophile Cazenove reported to one of the Dutch financial houses he was representing in America at the time: "Toutes ces dispositions requierent le sécret." Cazenove, who seemed to have firsthand knowledge of the meeting, continued: "Cette importante partie ne sauroit être confiée à plus de prudence et d'habilité que n'en à Mr. Hamilton."[21] But Hamilton's diplomacy and skill could not guarantee that the legislature would go along. Here is where Cazenove believed Paterson's involvement to be crucial. With the governor's participation in the planning, he thought there was little doubt that the lawmakers would "accorde les faveurs qui sont indiquées dans le prospectus commes des préliminaires nécessaires."[22] Hamilton and Paterson together were sufficient to assure success.

Paterson's family did have a direct interest in the financial success of the project. One of the SUM's most active local supporters was John Bayard, formerly a successful Philadelphia businessman and Pennsylvania delegate to the Continental Congress, who had retired to New Brunswick in 1788 and who had taken as his third wife Johanna White, Euphemia Paterson's sister. In 1790, the citizens of New Brunswick elected him mayor. Although Paterson himself never owned stock in the SUM, Bayard did purchase $1,000 worth ($400 on one occasion and $600 on another) in trust for his sister-in-law Euphemia.[23] It is unclear whether the stock was a simple family gift or a feeble attempt by Paterson to cover up a possible conflict of interest. He was still trying to bounce back from the financial loss caused by his brothers' bad debts and may have seen the SUM as a unique business opportunity.

While personal profit may have been a factor, the SUM was worthy of support because it promised to be of considerable benefit to the state. As early as 1784, Paterson had joined others in petitioning the legislature to encourage the development of trade and manufacturing so that New Jersey might escape some of the unfair taxing policies of New York and Pennsylvania.[24] The Constitution had solved part of the problem, but

Paterson realized that the state would still benefit from a solid base of domestic industry and commerce. On his own, the governor might not have gone to great lengths to propose such a project to a skeptical or uncooperative legislature. But, with others urging him on, with much of the capital already raised, and with Secretary Hamilton, the defender of the nation's financial stability, personally involved, Paterson's assistance in fostering the enterprise was to be expected.

As it turned out, the lawmakers did not need much convincing. As mentioned earlier, in the previous session a bill for the encouragement of manufactures had passed the assembly and failed in the council by only one vote. When the SUM's petition was presented to the legislature in the fall of 1791, there was hardly any popular opposition to it.

It is interesting to note, however, that the one criticism that did find its way into the public press was a particularly perceptive one.[25] Writing under the pseudonym Clitus, a Middlesex County observer presented practically every argument that the later critics of the project would muster. Not only did he point out the unfair competition that such a large manufactory might provide to the industrious mechanics of the state, he also argued against the proposal for blanket permission to run lotteries and construct canals and opposed the request for tax exemption. Most importantly, Clitus recognized that some of the promoters might be more interested in financial speculation than industrial development. He defended many of the small mechanics of the state who had fought "faithfully in the militia," only to be "obliged, through necessity, to sell their hard earned certificates for a half crown in [to] the pound, to some of the very men who now come forward with them at more than twenty shillings" to invest in SUM stock.

Despite Clitus's convincing argument that the mechanics would not appreciate having to pay taxes while their huge competitor was exempt, no one joined his public denunciation of the scheme. The charter, with all of the desired privileges, was granted in November, and the legislature even agreed to purchase $10,000 worth of stock in the name of the state.[26] The promoter's decision to name the company's town after Governor Paterson was not a guileless gesture. It dramatized to the legislators as well as the people at large that their very popular favorite son approved of the scheme. Once that was known, Paterson didn't have to do much else to assure passage of the charter. The state's purchase of stock became a virtual vote of confidence in him.

The venture was disappointing, to say the least. The first set of directors was made up of seven New Yorkers and six Jerseymen. New Jersey was represented by such influential figures as Congressman Elias

Boudinot, whose name had led the list of petitioners for the charter, but the New Yorkers controlled most of the money.[27] All the New Yorkers, with the possible exception of Nicholas Low, were veteran financial manipulators. One perceptive observer wished that there were not "so many speculators among them,"[28] but, at their first formal meeting in December 1791, the directors chose the dean of speculators, William Duer, to be the governor of the company. While Paterson viewed the SUM as a step toward New Jersey's economic self-sufficiency, and Hamilton saw it as a showcase for the ideas he presented in his Report on Manufactures just two weeks after the corporate charter was granted, Duer and friends thought first of the opportunities for paper profit. They bid up the value of the SUM stock on the New York exchange market and set the stage for the company's financial collapse.[29]

Meanwhile, Tench Coxe was still trying to turn a profit with his family's landholdings. His efforts to have the SUM's industrial district set up at New Brunswick, or on the Delaware near Trenton where his people also owned land, helped delay the final choice of a site until May 1792.[30] Despite Coxe's efforts, the decision was made for the Great Falls of the Passaic River because of the superior water power. At last, with the site chosen, plans could be drawn for the factory buildings and the network of canals that would be necessary to direct the force of the river. Pierre L'Enfant was employed to lay out the district, but before he could even get started the financial foundation of the company was practically destroyed when the speculative bubble burst.

Duer had brought his fellow manipulators together into a scheme to corner the New York securities market but, because of his need to borrow money at usurious rates just at the time when the market took a sudden dip, this "King of the alley" (as Jefferson called him) was ruined.[31] His affairs were so intertwined with those of other financiers that his failure was bound to affect them, and, within a month, three of his fellow SUM directors had sued for bankruptcy. The direct financial loss to the company was considerable: $65,000 entrusted to Duer and John Dewhurst was never seen again. But more important was the psychological blow to public confidence in a company that boasted three bankrupt directors and a governor who was rotting away in a debtor's prison in New York.[32]

Evidence suggests that by this time Paterson's shares (those in his wife's name, that is) may have already been liquidated, but Paterson had to keep in touch with the SUM's affairs in order to protect the $10,000 investment made by the state.[33] He continued to attend stockholders' meetings and even presided at least at one of them.[34] But it is clear that he disapproved of the directors' financial manipulations. In mid-1792, at just about the time the perils of stock manipulation were being made crystal clear to the company, Paterson prepared a sermon to attack the passions of speculation.

"What Bustle and Stir, what busy faces, and anxious days, and sleepless nights." In the past several months, Paterson explained, speculation had become the rage. To illustrate his point, Paterson alluded to the case of Isaac Whippo, a former oyster shucker who had become a speculator and was recruited into Duer's scheme. "Whippo, Whip," he wrote, "has everybody turned speculator?" The objects of speculation seemed endless. There were "the 3 per cent stocks, the 6 per cent stocks, the deferred stocks, Condict's notes, Thomson's notes, Pierce's notes, and state notes without end." He also listed the "manufacturing scrip" that represented shares in the SUM. In his distrust of speculators and his feelings that the passion for trading in paper distracted people from really productive enterprises, Paterson was different from most other Federalists. He saw overtones of immorality in the business, too.

> Ye men, who count your guineas oftener than you say your prayers. Ye good folks of New Ark, Eliza[beth]town, & Brunswick, who had rather take even 2 per cent a month than pay your Parson a groat a year. Ye honest Farmers of Long Island, of Staten Island, and of New Jersey, come hither, sell your farms, quit your ploughs, and lend your money. Here is the place to make your fortune, to turn a Penny into a Pound, and Pounds into thousands.[35]

According to the ethic of the speculator, merchants, farmers, doctors, and lawyers were all wasting their time.

> What is merchandising & ploughing, and dealing out drugs, and pouring over Littleton and Coke, and plodding on in the common road of industry to the bold and adventurous Spirit of Speculation. Lo, the Speculator rises on the golden wings of others, casts a momentary blaze, shoots like a Meteor, and is gone.

The careers of Duer and the other SUM speculators had been bright indeed, but now they were gone, and the company was desperately weakened by their undignified end.

At the first word of Duer's fall, the directors of the SUM appealed to Hamilton for advice and assistance. As one recent author has said, they "called upon the St. George of the Treasury Department to slay the dragons of malfeasance and inefficiency."[36] The secretary responded by encouraging the directors to go ahead with setting up the cotton manufactory and hiring full-time officers (superintendent, accountant, cashier) and workmen to run it. He also indicated that, if necessary, he would help procure a loan to see the SUM over its troubled time. When the board met, Hamilton joined them and lent his personal reputation to their efforts to survive.[37]

Hamilton's aid was instrumental in getting them over the initial shock of the Duer affair, but his intimate involvement with the company led to other trouble. The SUM was inevitably drawn into the Jeffersonian criticism of Federalist financial measures such as the funding scheme and the national bank. Newspaper essayists argued that the company had been created to satisfy large investors and that its charter gave it an unfair advantage over competitors. Such public opposition may have hastened the demise of the company by discouraging prospective investors and by helping to generate complaints from the neighborhood. In response to petitions from people living near the company's land, the proposed charter for the city of Paterson was modified in November 1792. On December 17, the governor signed the official scroll, but the charter was not put into effect—the legislature never appointed the officials required by the document.[38]

The SUM remained a potent issue into the mid-1790s as the Federalists and Jeffersonians drew their lines of political demarcation more and more clearly. Meanwhile the company struggled fruitlessly to survive. Finally, in 1796, it halted all efforts at manufacturing.[39] The special privileges of the original charter, especially the company's right to exclusive use of the power generated by the Great Falls, proved valuable later on. Until 1945, when the operation was turned over to the city of Paterson, the SUM was in the business of providing electric power to industrial northern New Jersey. But, as long as Paterson was alive, the SUM story remained a tragedy. The state legislature did not charter another manufacturing company until 1809. With its buildings boarded up and empty, the place to which Paterson had lent his name became, in the words of one observer, "a ghost town."[40] It would be well into the next century, long after William Paterson was dead, before the city of Paterson was officially incorporated and finally began to fulfill the dreams for its industrial greatness shared by the SUM's original promoters.

Though their plans for encouraging manufactures had failed, Governor Paterson and the legislators could look to other, more successful projects. Perhaps the most obvious one was the establishment of the permanent state capital at Trenton and the construction of the original statehouse there.[41] Of greater importance was the decision to finally get on with the business of organizing the laws of the state and replacing the old British statutes that had been carried over as a temporary measure in 1776. (This monumental task was entrusted to William Paterson. Because of its significance, it will be treated in a separate chapter.)

The governor's executive chores were largely routine. He certified the appointment of scores of minor officials, from surrogates to oyster inspectors. He cooperated in the capture and extradition of criminals to neighboring states and heard pleas for commutation of the death penalty and executive pardons. Since 1787 he had been a trustee of his alma mater, the College of New Jersey; now, as governor, he presided at the trustees' meetings. Each year he publicly proclaimed the list of candidates for election in the several counties. He carried on the practice of officially proclaiming a day of public thanksgiving and prayer and, as chief of the state militia, he issued a proclamation specifying the uniforms to be worn by officers and men.[42]

Because of his first-hand experience in the national legislature, Governor Paterson felt qualified to advise New Jersey's representatives in Congress. Aside from the financial questions related to assumption, the issue that most interested him was the reapportionment of the seats in the House of Representatives. The original number of representatives assigned to each state was designated by the Constitution with an eye toward keeping the body from becoming too large. Consequently the total membership of the House in the first and second Congress had been a workable 65, only two and one-half times the size of the Senate. But the Constitution also provided for the establishment of a new proportion to be based on the results of the first census, and, when the figures were released, two problems immediately became apparent. First, there would have to be some dramatic changes in the size of some of the state delegations. In relation to the delegations of the small states, the number of large-state representatives was to become much greater.[43] The second problem concerned the overall size of the House, which some feared might become too big for business to be conducted efficiently.

Little could be done about the relative representation of the states—the results of the census were clear—but there were several attempts to keep the House from growing too large. The first plan to remedy this situation was a proposed constitutional amendment. In trying to assure as compact a body as possible, the Constitution had specified that each congressman must represent at least 30,000 constituents, but many thought that even this proportion was too large. They feared that representatives so distant from the people might look on themselves as a new aristocracy. Moreover, there was no assurance that the proportion would not be increased later to 40,000 or 50,000. Although the proposed amendment appealed to the popular desire for greater representation by guaranteeing the 30,000 figure, a more important provision circumscribed the guarantee by establishing the maximum number of representatives at 100. Once this ceiling was reached, a new proportion would have to be agreed upon and passed into law.[44] Since the amendment had not been ratified by the time the second Congress met, a bill was introduced to satisfy the popular will by simply allocating seats for the third Congress at a proportion of 30,000 to 1. The bill made no mention of a maximum size for the House. Quick computation showed that by this law the House would have to be increased to 112 members—almost twice what it had been, nearly four times the size of the Senate, and twelve more than the limit provided by the still-pending amendment. After considerable debate, the bill passed the House and was sent on to the Senate.[45]

Paterson was appalled. The main intent of the amendment, he observed in a letter to Representative Elias Boudinot, was to limit the size of the House; those who now "adhered rigidly" to the 30,000 to 1 proportion "violated its spirit, and also the principles of policy, of equality, and of the constitution."[46] It seems that when the seats were apportioned at 30,000 to 1, significant fractions were left unrepresented in several northern states, and large states such as Virginia, Massachusetts, Pennsylvania, and New York were overrepresented in comparison with their smaller neighbors. "From the experience I have had in Congress," Paterson continued, "I well-know, that extrinsic motives and improper passions have too often mingled in decisions." He saw the bill as a plot by the large states to aggrandize themselves at the expense of the small. Some argued that to limit the size of the House was undemocratic and smacked of aristocracy. Paterson gave these critics no quarter. The fear of aristocracy, he charged Boudinot, "is the scarlet whore, fly from the bitch as fast and far as possible." The only real aristocracy to be feared was the power of the great states over the smaller ones. Alluding to the particular benefits that Virginia would derive from the pending legislation, he wrote of "elysian fields bordering the mighty Potomack, the king of floods, and the grand reservoir of all the western waters." Paterson's old resentments against the large-state delegates in Philadelphia welled up in him again as he envisioned the large states, forced against their will in 1787 to accept the principle of state equality in the Senate, now trying to dominate the small states in the House and threatening to upset the delicate equilibrium of the Constitution by overshadowing thirty senators with more than one hundred congressmen, each of whom would claim that he more directly represented the will of the people.[47]

The reapportionment question became embroiled in a battle between the two houses, as each refused to accept the amendment of the other. When a compromise bill was finally arrived at in March 1792, President Washington exercised the only veto of his administration.[48] Eventually the 30,000-to-1 figure was agreed to, in spite of the governor of New Jersey's attempt to add his influence to the debate. Spurred on by the acknowledged champion of small-state interests, New Jersey's representatives had fought to the end and finally did succeed in forcing the large states to sacrifice at least a part of their new-found advantage. Minor reductions were made in the delegations of the six largest states, and the total number of representatives was kept to 105.[49]

Over the three years that he sat in the governor's chair, Paterson deepened his perspective on many issues. Most of his basic ideas (opposition to party, sanctity of contracts, the importance of financial stability) were not shaken, but he came to consider all sorts of new questions, from the organization of the militia and the preponderance of beggars in the community to the advisability of chartering toll road companies. These new and varied interests were reflected in several series of newspaper essays he wrote during the 1790s. Paterson had written for the press before, but his previous essays were never as comprehensive or organized as were those of the Federalist decade. There were at least forty-six of them, published at various times beginning in February 1793. Since they cover such a wide range of issues relating to specific aspects of his revision of the laws as well as to national political concerns, the discussion of them is divided between this chapter and Chapters 10 and 11.

The earliest essays in his Aurelius series began to appear in the *Brunswick Guardian* during the final months of his third term as governor.[50] The first piece set the tone for all the rest by calling on his fellow citizens to foster the same "candid and liberal sentiments" on public questions that Paterson was proud to claim for himself. He thought that political diversity was basic to free government. To the extent that it flowed from a candid inquiry into the truth regarding public questions and willingness to acknowledge one's error once the correct information was found, it was a natural feature of the type of system "where men enjoy the right of judging for themselves." The trouble was that some men were driven either by selfish views or party interest so that, however erroneously their opinions were formed, "no course of reasoning nor of facts" could open their minds.[51] Here was the key to the political frame of mind to which Paterson adhered for the rest of his life.

In his second essay, the governor lectured New Jersey's militiamen about the importance of "a well regulated militia" and the care with which they should go about the election of their officers. "To be prepared for war is the way to prevent it," he observed, "to be ready in arms to meet and resist tyranny never fails to deter its approach." He warned the veterans of the Revolution that, since "dark days may return" and "again may the oppressor arise, and attempt to enslave," they should instruct their sons in "how to secure and preserve the inestimable gift" of freedom. It seems, however, that the commander-in-chief had very little faith in the inherent good judgment of most of his men. Paterson thought it necessary to openly caution them against electing drunken, lazy, or ignorant officers and even went on to explain the obvious—why a drunk, a sloth, or a fool would make a bad leader. The last man to vote for, he warned, was the candidate who campaigned for his office by passing out free drinks. "Esau sold his birthright for a mess of pottage," Paterson preached. "Baser ye, if you barter your suffrages for a glass of brandy, or a can of grog."[52]

The most perceptive essays of the Aurelius series were those that analyzed certain weaknesses in the state constitution, one on the office of the governor, and another on the state judiciary. In the first of these, Paterson called for a complete revision of the constitution of 1776: "The constitution was framed at a very critical conjuncture, and, as it were, on the spur of the occasion." No one knew this better than Paterson who had sat as the secretary of the convention that wrote the document and who had even voted to delay its implementation until it could be more fully discussed. "It was at the time considered as a temporary thing resulting from the exigency of the moment, and [it was] expected," Paterson remembered, "that when we settled down with calmness and tranquility, it would undergo a dispassionate and thorough revision." As governor, Paterson had acquired first-hand experience in administering the state government in peacetime as well as in war, and he was convinced that changes were necessary. The problem with the governor's office was that the constitution required that he be both chancellor and commander-in-chief as well as chief executive officer. The duties of commander-in-chief, Governor Paterson argued, "require a turn of mind, and sentiment, a cast of genius, a facility and boldness of execution very different from what may be fit and appropriate to the functions of a

judge." Similarly, the judicial role of the chancellor as the final arbiter
of all cases in the Court of Chancery suggested that the governor should
be chosen from among the "professors of the law." But Paterson held
that the governorship should "be open to every class of citizens," not to
the lawyers alone.[53]

Another problem with the constitution concerned the appointment and
the salaries of judges. According to the Declaration of Independence, one
of the usurpations of the king was that he "made judges dependent upon
his will alone for the tenure of their offices and the Amount and payment
of their salaries." In attempting to remedy this, the framers of the New
Jersey constitution had assured the judges on the state supreme court
a term of seven years, but Paterson argued that this did not go far
enough. Not only were the judges chosen by the legislature every seven
years where "secret management, bargain-making, and other improper
motives are apt to mingle in the business," but, since the constitution was
"totally silent as to the amount and payment of the salary" of the judges,
this matter had to be debated by the legislature every year. To preserve
the independence of the judiciary, it was necessary, as was the case in the
federal Constitution, to keep the power of appointment and the control
of the judges' salary separate from the body that made the laws. The
influence that the New Jersey legislature held over its judiciary had
stemmed from the demand for popular participation in every particular
of government. But, "no scheme is so pregnant with mischief," Paterson
observed, "as that which, having the appearance of being friendly to
liberty, is at bottom opposed to it." The appointment of the judiciary
should be entrusted to the governor and a minimum salary for judges
should be set, a salary commensurate with their duties and the prestige
of their office.[54]

Paterson had a personal interest in the nature of judgeships. In February 1793, just about the time the Aurelius essays began to appear,
President Washington had called on Paterson to serve as a member of
the United States Supreme Court. Although Washington had chosen a
learned lawyer of universal respect for the position vacated by the death
of Thomas Johnson, there was one technical problem with Paterson's
appointment. The Constitution made it impossible for any member of
Congress, "during the time for which he was elected," to be appointed to
an office created during his term. Washington's original nomination of
Paterson was returned by the Senate because, even though Paterson had
resigned over two years before, the term of his Senate service had not yet
officially ended. On March 4, the date on which Senator Paterson's

original four-year term would have come to a close, the nomination was submitted again and promptly approved.[55] Before the month was out, Paterson had resigned as governor of New Jersey, taken his oath as a judge, and was preparing to depart on a tour of the southern circuit of the federal court.

Most of Paterson's service as governor had been routine. Only two major developments stand out: first, the creation of the SUM, which turned out to be an embarrassment for Paterson, and, second, the revision of the laws, which did represent a remarkable accomplishment, but was not completed until seven years later.[56]

Paterson had not taken on the governor's office with any specific goals in mind. He wanted simply to keep the government from becoming a battleground for parties and factions, and in this he was largely successful. Basically, however, it was the universal respect he enjoyed rather than any sensitive perception of politics that enabled him to maintain an administration free from debilitating factional controversy. But times were changing, and, had he remained in office much longer, New Jersey still would have come to reflect the evolving political climate of the nation. Moreover, as the controversial issues of the 1790s developed (the Whiskey Rebellion, the Jay Treaty, the Alien and Sedition Acts, and so on) Paterson would find it more and more difficult to conceal his own growing partisanship—a trend easily discernible in his numerous newspaper essays.

His constituents, particularly his neighbors in New Brunswick, were sorry to lose him as governor, but they were also proud to see him honored with appointment to the high court. As he prepared to travel to Georgia, where he was scheduled to serve his first term on the circuit, the citizens of New Brunswick held a dinner in his honor. Never one to pass up a compliment, Paterson graciously attended and accepted the praise of a sizeable crowd. The following Monday morning he was met at his house in Burnet Street and escorted to the dock by "the New Brunswick company of Light Infantry and a large number of respectable citizens." There, as he embarked for New York on his way south, a local poet penned the following tribute, called "On the Departure of Judge Paterson."

> See the once father, ruler of our State
> Throng'd by the rich, the poor, the great.—
> Why all this bustle? was it to revere
> A crested monarch, not with love but fear;
> The patriot's merits with his deeds combin'd,
> Their hearts united, and their voices join'd:

> While gratitude sincere inspires their praise,
> With sorrow the parting ship they gaze.
> Ye gales propitious!—to the destin'd shore
> Waft him—kind heav'n protect him evermore.

Although the printer of the *Brunswick Guardian,* which published the ode, kept his own editorial comments more in bounds, he was similarly eulogistic when he remarked simply that "Virtue will have its reward."[57]

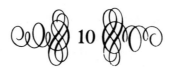

The Reformer of the Laws

After his service during the Revolution and his role in Philadelphia, Paterson's greatest contribution to his state was his revision of New Jersey's laws. Begun in 1792 while he was still governor, this project took up much of the time he could spare from his Supreme Court business for the following eight years. In the process, he did more than rationalize the legal system, which had been so confused before. He also took part in active efforts to reform social and political institutions and make them more just. In different circumstances, practical ideas for social reform might have made little, if any, impression on his legalistic mind, but, when he saw such problems in the shape of laws, his humanitarian side was allowed to show through.

When New Jersey launched herself onto the perilous ocean of revolution in 1776, William Paterson had been one of those who stood most firm for the preservation of the institutions of law and order. As discussed in Chapter 5, Attorney General Paterson worked tirelessly to reinforce the effectiveness of the county courts and suppress the opposition of Loyalists. He had earlier joined the chorus of complaint about the fragmented and confusing condition of the laws in the colonies, which often tended to unnecessarily complicate litigation, but, like many other newcomers to revolution, he was more concerned about maintaining the continuity of the legal system than he was about reforming it. With continuity in mind, the framers of the 1776 constitution had specified that, besides the colonial laws of New Jersey, both the common law and the statutes of Great Britain (at least those not repugnant to the constitution) should "remain in force, until they shall be altered by a future law of the legislature."[1] For more than twenty years the laws of New Jersey remained in this confused transitional state.

In 1790, the most recent compilation of the colonial laws of New Jersey was by Samuel Allinson. Allinson's laws as published in 1776 by order of the legislature comprised all acts passed in New Jersey through December 1775 that were still in effect.[2] In 1784 a supplement compiled by Peter Wilson was published, including all of the then valid laws that had been passed by the state legislature from 1776 through the end of 1783.[3] After 1784 there was no attempt at compilation. The result was that the New Jersey lawyer had to refer constantly to Allinson, Wilson, and the session laws for each year after 1783, as well as to all of the British statutes that had not yet been repealed by the legislature. The situation remained that way for nearly a decade, until the legislators finally resolved to do something about it.

In November 1792, the legislature authorized Governor Paterson to "collect and reduce into proper Form" all the relevant British statutes and all the acts of New Jersey "both before and since the Revolution" and to present them to the legislature for reenactment. The idea was to reform the legal system by digesting and consolidating the myriad colonial and state laws, which often overlapped and sometimes contradicted each other, while at the same time incorporating the desirable provisions of whatever British statutes still applied so that the original statutes could finally be repealed. The legislation also empowered Paterson to hire assistants and to arrange with a printer for publishing the final work.[4] New Jersey was not, of course, the first of the states to attempt the task of revising its laws; Thomas Jefferson had labored between 1776 and 1779 with a law revision committee in Virginia, while Samuel Jones and Richard Varick had done the same in New York.[5] But the New Jersey experience is particularly interesting because of the scope of the changes proposed there and because newly discovered manuscript sources reveal the rationale behind many of the proposed revisions.

The least difficult part of the procedure was the consolidation. Paterson would sit with Allinson, Wilson, the session laws, Blackstone, and in some cases with the laws of other states, decide what provisions of each law should still be in force, and digest them into a single act. For example, for an Act for Preserving Oysters, Paterson studied the three laws that were already on the books—one passed in 1719, one in 1774, and another in 1775. Both of the later laws had been allowed to expire, so the 1719 law was the only one still in effect. Paterson included what he thought to be the most significant provisions of the first and the last in a draft bill for the legislature that established a specific season for the gathering and selling of oysters and forbade nonresidents of the state to participate. Retaining the enforcement provisions of the 1719 act, the draft bill called for those disobeying the law to have their boats seized and sold at public auction with half the value received after court costs to be granted to the arresting officer or citizen. Paterson's observations, sent to the legislators along with the draft bill, noted that if the legislature thought such a law to be unnecessary they had only to repeal the 1719 statute and let well enough alone. The legislature, however, approved of Paterson's draft and passed it into law without alteration. Like most of the other acts Paterson drafted, the final section of this one provided for the repeal of all the former laws "coming within the purview of this act."[6]

Other draft bills were drawn from farther afield. His proposed Act for the Preservation of Morality, actually a blue law restricting activities on the sabbath, was drawn from at least three New Jersey statutes as well as British laws dating back to the reigns of James I, Charles II, and George II. In his draft for an Act for the Prevention of Frauds and Perjuries, he referred to statutes passed under Henry VII and Elizabeth I, in addition to specifying the relevant pages in Blackstone's *Commentaries*. An Act to Prevent Routs, Riots, and Tumultuous Assemblies was drawn in part from the laws of Massachusetts. These sources were clearly spelled out in the margins of Paterson's manuscript workbook on the revision, which runs to nearly 800 bound pages.[7] His Act for the Prevention of Waste (protecting landlords and minors from having their property destroyed by rapacious tenants or guardians) and his Act Concerning Wrecks (defining the procedure involved in the salvage of wrecked ships) appear there in draft form with no indication that they were drawn from any previous statute at all. They apparently represent Paterson's personal effort to draw some elements of the unwritten common law into the form of specific statutes. Like many other laws of the period, these two laws were not automatically enforced by civil authorities. It was the injured party's responsibility to seek redress in the civil courts.[8]

The legislators could not agree with all of Paterson's proposals. For example, they increased the fees he proposed for litigation in the court of small causes, decreased the fine for selling illegal lottery tickets, and ruled out a loophole in the law against horse racing that would have allowed two justices of the peace to sanction a race when such "public exercises" were deemed to improve "the breed."[9] But generally the elected representatives were willing to go along with Paterson's recommendations. In most cases, the new laws were enacted exactly as he drafted them.

As the work progressed, Paterson became convinced that consolidating and digesting the laws was not enough. Some of the old British statutes required complete revision. This was particularly true with respect to the criminal code. As Paterson explained to the assembly early in 1793, "the system of penal jurisprudence which prevails in Great Britain is complicated, and sanguinary in a high degree. It is written in blood," he wrote, "and cannot be read without Horror." He thought the most effective punishments for criminals were those that fit the crime, and he expressed his firm conviction that "the Impolicy, Inadequacy, and cruelty of the existing system of penal law" necessitated a "thorough reform."[10] Perhaps moved by the knowledge that neighboring Pennsylvania had already updated its criminal code, the legislators quickly agreed on a supplementary act that authorized Paterson, "according to his discretion," to prepare a reformation of the criminal laws and submit it for approval.[11] Even though there was the Pennsylvania experience to build upon, Paterson knew that the real reform would take far longer than the simple digesting of the laws. When he stepped down as governor in 1793, he realized that the responsibilities of the Supreme Court would consume most of his energies and suggested that the legislature appoint someone else to finish the task.[12] But they wanted no one else, and Paterson consented to work ahead on the project whenever time allowed.

His reform of the criminal statutes began with an Act to Punish Crimes, which was enacted with only minor alterations in 1796 after more than two years of discussion between Paterson and the legislators, including close comparison of his proposals with the systems of other states as well as the reforms Jefferson had unsuccessfully put forward in Virginia some years before. Criminal penalties in New Jersey, as in most of the other colonies, had relied on corporal punishment or fines in noncapital offenses. The death penalty was specified for a number of crimes beyond murder and treason including larceny, robbery (with threat of violence to the victim), burglary (with breaking and entry), rape, arson, counterfeiting, and horse stealing. The courts had no hesitation in inflicting corporal punishments, but the death penalty was rarely carried out. A first offender almost always could plead benefit of clergy, which called for him to be branded with a symbol that indicated his offense, but even second offenders were usually not executed.[13]

Since the Revolution, a movement for humanitarian reform had taken hold in several states, resulting in the abolition of slavery, the relief of imprisoned debtors, and reform of the penal codes. New Jersey had acted in the 1780s to ameliorate the condition of slaves, and the English practices of primogeniture and entail were modified. But there had been no movement to reform what one scholar has called "the barbarous criminal code."[14] The first significant steps made in that direction came in Pennsylvania in 1790 when a new code of criminal justice was adopted that did away with corporal punishments and replaced them with sentences to be served at hard labor in a state prison.[15] Early in 1796, the editor of the *New Jersey State Gazette* made note of a recent pamphlet, "On the Prisons of Philadelphia," and summarized its contents. Due to the institution of a "novel and humane discipline in prison," he explained, the crime rate there had declined considerably. Suggesting an enlightened social philosophy, he concluded that the reason 135 of the 243 serious crimes reported in Philadelphia over the preceding four years were committed by foreigners—and 92 of those by Irishmen—was that they had suffered under tyrannical oppression in Europe.

> Tyranny and bad government have made three fourths of the criminals that ever existed. Good laws, equal rights, human institutions and mild punishments with rigid discipline, will some time or other supercede almost wholly, the use of the gibbet and the halter.[16]

Paterson appears to have been convinced of the need to pay more attention to rehabilitating those found guilty of crime. His revised criminal code adopted by the legislature only a few weeks after the *Gazette* article appeared represented a real effort to humanize the correction procedure.

In Paterson's new law, an automatic sentence of death was reserved only for murder and treason, though a person found guilty of a second offense of manslaughter, robbery, burglary, sodomy, rape, arson, or forgery might also be hanged. The benefit of clergy was abolished and, for all but "negro, Indian, and mulatto slaves," corporal punishment was to be replaced with a sentence at hard labor. The penalties were less severe, but they were to be rigidly enforced. The hope was that a sentence at hard labor would be more effective at rehabilitating a rapist, arsonist, or forger than a letter branded on his thumb or cheek.

Specific penalties for dozens of offenses were detailed in Paterson's draft bill and approved by the legislature.[17] Counterfeiting, for example, had been for years one of the few capital offenses for which the benefit of clergy was specifically denied.[18] The death penalty was now reduced to a term at hard labor not to exceed ten years. Until the 1790s, grand larceny had also carried the death penalty, though it was seldom, if ever, carried out.[19] A law passed in 1791 had eliminated grand larceny from the list of capital crimes and instead provided for as many as 76 stripes at the public whipping post—a patriotic, if not humane, punishment.[20] Now, five years later, Paterson's code (after defining grand larceny as the theft of goods valued at $6 or more) replaced the corporal punishment with a fine not to exceed $500 and/or a maximum of ten years at hard labor.

Horse stealing was an offense that received special attention in colonial days. The traditional death penalty had been eased in 1769 in the hope that citizens would be more apt to perform their public duty and turn horse thieves over to the law. According to the preamble of the 1769 statute, "long experience" had shown that the "extreme severity" of the old law had "destroyed that Vigilance usually exerted by them in the apprehending of criminals." Thereafter the court could order "such corporal or other punishment . . . (not extending to life) as they in their discretion" judged most proper.[21] The strategy of the lawmakers did not work, however, and the theft of horses became such a problem during the Revolution that the automatic death penalty without benefit of clergy had to be reinstated in 1780.[22] In Paterson's 1796 reform, the death penalty was dropped for good along with the corporal punishment. Horse stealing was thereafter treated as grand larceny, and the penalty associated with it was likewise reduced.[23]

Some of the punishments were eased perhaps too far. A still valid 1741 law on the murdering of bastard children placed the responsibility of proof on the mother. If she could not prove that her dead child was stillborn, she was to suffer execution as a murderess. This statute was based on English practice, even to the point of requiring that it be read aloud in the churches of the colony at least once each year.[24] Paterson's reformed code removed the burden of proof from the defendant and reduced the penalty to a mere $200 fine and/or one year at hard labor. Since merely giving birth in secret without killing the baby was to be punishable by a $100 fine and/or four months in jail, some women may have thought it was worth the additional risk to destroy the evidence once and for all.[25]

Only in a very few cases were the criminal penalties increased. One example was for those convicted for a first offense of manslaughter. Reversing the trend of the 1791 law that had required only that such persons be imprisoned for a maximum of one year or give security for their good behavior during that time, Paterson's code called for a hefty fine of $1,000 or a term of up to three years at hard labor.[26]

Paterson intended the serving of time at hard labor to be a positive element in the rehabilitation of criminals. As he explained in subsequent observations to the legislature, which were also released through the major newspapers,

> punishment by hard labor was introduced with a view to bring on habits of industry, and to lessen crimes. A lazy knave dreads nothing so much as work. Set him at labour and you make him at least useful. Industry may thus grow up into a habit. But if he be suffered to remain in prison without employment, he will acquire a habit of idleness and will when liberated, be less disposed to pursue an honest and industrious course, be more prone to vicious practices, and be a worse man and more dangerous to society, than he was before.[27]

Unfortunately, however, the state's previous reliance on fines and corporal punishment meant that there were no facilities for incarcerating large numbers of prisoners and supervising their work. The new criminal code led to the construction of the first state prison at Trenton and the provision for a series of workhouses in the individual counties.

Paterson's draft of the bill regulating the state prison was approved by the legislature in February 1798, even as work continued on the prison building begun the year before. The detailed rules of operation spelled out in the statute were meant to protect the physical well-being of the prisoners and assure that the goal of rehabilitation was not forgotten. Offenders sentenced to a term of hard labor longer than six months were to be sent to the state facility within twenty days after their conviction. On arrival, the prisoner was to be washed and cleaned and kept separate from the rest of the inmates until a doctor could examine him. At the discretion of two inspectors (the act called for the appointment of eight), the new prisoner's clothes were to be either "burnt, baked, fumigated, or carefully laid by" until the end of his term. Inmates were to be fed and clothed at the expense of the state and were to labor each day except Sunday from eight to ten hours, depending on the season. The act went on to specify that the lights were to be extinguished and cells locked at 9:00 P.M. The walls of each cell were to be whitewashed twice each year, and the floors washed at least once a week. One or more rooms were to be set aside for an infirmary where sick prisoners were to be attended by a physician. There were also detailed regulations to check the inspectors, the jailkeeper, and his deputies to be sure that they carried out their duties properly. Furthermore, "to encourage industry, as an evidence of reformation," each prisoner was to have a separate account in which he could share in the profits of his labor after the cost of materials and expense of his food and clothing were deducted.[28]

Paterson's proposals, as they were enacted into law, reflected a trend that was taking shape across the young nation. Similar regulations were enforced in the Walnut Street jail in Philadelphia, which had been converted to serve as the Pennsylvania state prison. New York legislators voted in 1796 to set up similar institutions there, and, during the following decade, most of the other states followed suit. Under the influence of each other's experiments and the ideas imported in works such as Cesare Beccaria's treatise *On Crimes and Punishments,* which first appeared in 1764, Americans were beginning to develop a more enlightened attitude toward criminal behavior and a more humane method of dealing with it.[29]

Because Paterson figured that the expense of transferring prisoners to the state prison would be too high to justify sending petty offenders there, he planned for a subsidiary system of workhouses around the state. In a subsequent draft bill to incorporate the chosen freeholders of the various counties, Paterson had included the establishment of workhouses as one of their duties, but the legislators had left this authority out of the law they enacted.[30] Early in 1799 Paterson set out to convince them of the importance of these subsidiary facilities. "It is worthy of notice," he wrote,

> that persons, who are guilty of enormous crimes, and, perhaps, are incorrigible, are to be provided with materials, set to labour and encouraged to be industrious; while petty offenders, less callous, because little hackneyed in the path of iniquity, more yielding to advice and discipline, and easy to be reformed remain in the county gaol, inactive and unemployed, useless to the world, and a burden to themselves, nourishing bad passions, and evil designs, and becoming daily more and more averse to industry. Idleness debilitates the body, vitiates the mind, and is the parent of many crimes and disorders in the moral and political world.[31]

The new statute that Paterson prepared instructed the freeholders of the respective counties to immediately see to the establishment of a workhouse. It specified that the workhouse was to serve as the place of rehabilitation for criminals sentenced to hard labor for a term of less than six months, as well as for other disorderly persons and any "stubborn, disobedient, rude or intemperate slave or manservant" sent there by a justice of the peace. Rules for the everyday regulation of the workhouse were to be formulated by the freeholders, but the intention of the legislation was clear. Paterson's only fear was that, if given the opportunity, "weak, selfish and shortsighted" people would convince the counties to save the money rather than set up the workhouses right away. And indeed his fear was well founded.

The law, as passed, directed the freeholders to act only when they saw fit
and, as a result, this aspect of the reform was delayed until the last third
of the nineteenth century.[32]

In addition to the penal reform, Paterson saw the revision of the laws
as a way to introduce reforms into politics and society. In an interesting
twist from his usual comments on mass participation in politics, he spoke
out on a bill before the legislature and argued for election days to be arranged for the convenience of the electorate. Of course, this was not necessarily a departure from his old belief in deference. Once elected, the representative was bound to govern by virtue, not by popular opinion. As far
as can be found, Paterson played no part in preparing the statute passed in
February 1797—An Act to Regulate the Election of Members of the
Legislative Council and General Assembly, Sheriffs and Coroners. But
this did not stop him from making his thoughts known. On this question,
as on several other issues relating to the laws, Paterson went directly to
the people and chose to voice his opinions in the press. In the same week
that the bill was debated and passed, Paterson began to publish a series of
six essays in the New Brunswick *Guardian* criticizing the legislators and
encouraging the electorate to play a more active part in state affairs. His
main contention was that the assemblymen and councillors had conspired to
assure that the elections for Congress and the elections for state-level
offices did not take place at the same time. Paterson argued that if the
elections were held on the same day a considerable expense could be
avoided and voter participation would likely be increased. The legislators
were ignoring this, he charged, in order to give themselves the opportunity
to run for both federal and state offices in the same year.[33]

One of Paterson's most often repeated political ideas was his hatred of
political factionalism. He saw the revising of the laws as one way to discourage the growth of party spirit, and he planned several of them to
avoid opportunities for patronage and party strife. When it came to an
Act Respecting Bridges, Paterson sought to standardize the procedure for
building and maintaining the bridges in all the counties in order to avoid
the likelihood of party or individual interests becoming involved.[34] Similarly, in his proposed law for the maintenance and repair of highways, he
argued that all such work in the state should be hired out. This would
avoid the necessity of having individual town meetings decide on their own
whether to hire a contractor or to let the citizens contribute their labor—
something that was sure to open "the door for continual controversy and
party spirit." But Paterson's proposal had the drawback of seeming anti-
democratic, and so the legislature turned it down.[35]

In his observations to the legislature on his draft bills to incorporate townships and to incorporate the chosen freeholders of counties, Paterson became more philosophical. "Men are not born republicans," he said, "they must be made such by a course of discipline and education." Local government could serve a significant role in the process.

> Incorporate townships for certain purposes, and you establish schools for legislation of an inferior kind; incorporate counties for certain other purposes, and you form schools of a grade somewhat higher. Thus we proceed, step by step, from one object to another, and advance by regular progression in the line of legislative and political knowledge. . . . Called upon to act the part of legislators as to certain points, they soon feel the importance and necessity of exercising the trust in a proper manner. In this way they become good citizens and useful members of society.[36]

The revised laws therefore could be made to foster a stronger feeling of republican public spirit at the same time they helped avoid opportunities for the "endless altercation" of parties, which "embitters, agitates, and distracts the public mind."[37]

As far as social reform was concerned, the revised laws reaffirmed some of the changes that had been occurring since the Revolution and introduced some new ones. For example, the new laws reaffirmed the abolition of primogeniture and entail and moved toward ameliorating the conditions in which slaves lived.

Since J. Franklin Jameson was taken to task for failing to note that, although primogeniture and entail had been written into law in colonial America, they were generally ignored there, historians have played down the significance of their abolition. Paterson's ideas on the subject were interesting, however. He was never a social leveler in any sense of the word, but he did recognize that the legal protections of the old English aristocracy had no place in republican America. Laws passed in 1780 and 1784 had done away with the practice of primogeniture and put severe limits on the entail of inherited estates. These two British practices, which had allowed men with vast holdings in real estate to pass on their landed wealth to their eldest sons with the legal restriction that it never be split up into smaller parcels, were seen as totally irreconcilable with a republican social system.

In a 1793 newspaper essay, Paterson wrote that the "political prosperity and happiness" of a republican nation would be encouraged if landed property was "pretty equally diffused among the people." The farmer who owned his own land made a far better citizen. Land ownership, he thought, "naturally produces independence of sentiment, emboldens the spirit, and invigorates the mind." He could not sanction the "equalization of property by the strong hand of power," because it would amount to "a tax upon the active and industrious man for the support of the sluggard." But insofar as eliminating practices of primogeniture and entail would encourage the diffusion of landed wealth, he thought it to be characteristic of "the enlightened policy of the present republican age."[38] Although Paterson's reaffirmation of the earlier laws abolishing the old legal principles of primogeniture and entail really changed nothing, his thoughts on the topic represent another curious departure from his normally elitist philosophy and his frequent position as defender of the rich.

Questions of social philosophy were complicated with matters of morality where the issue of slavery was concerned. From time to time, Paterson had acted as attorney for blacks in his New Brunswick neighborhood, taking little, if any, fee. He had also seen to the manumission of at least one of his own slaves, making sure that he had first been taught to read, write, and ply a trade.[39] But Paterson was no abolitionist, and his lack of any burning desire to free the blacks from their chains was evident in the Act Respecting Slaves that he drafted for the legislature.

The movement to abolish slavery in New Jersey had gotten a slow start, despite the early and continuing support of the Quaker minority. Their first taste of success came in 1786 with the passing of a bill that forbade the further importation of slaves into the state and encouraged the manumission of able-bodied slaves between the ages of 21 and 35 by relieving the former master of any future responsibility for them. The 1786 act also provided for the indictment of masters for mistreating their slaves, but the penalties only amounted to "five pounds for the first, and ten pounds for the second offence." Another act adopted in 1788 forbade New Jersey ships to participate in the slave trade, made it illegal to remove a slave from the state without his or her consent, and required owners to see that their slaves were taught to read by the time they were 21 years of age.[40] In 1790, a committee of the assembly considered a petition that called for the gradual abolition of slavery by the freeing of slaves who had reached the age of 28, but the report of the committee was discouraging. The struggle of the abolitionists dragged on until 1804, when a program of gradual abolition was finally enacted into law.[41]

Paterson's attempt to digest the various laws involving slavery was bound to become embroiled in the continuing controversy. In January 1797, abolitionists in the assembly succeeded in amending Paterson's Act Respecting Slaves to require the manumission of all slaves born thereafter when they reached the age of 28, but the victory had come only with the speaker's tie-breaking vote. The lawmakers then decided to publish the bill "for the information of the public" before they took further action.[42] But Paterson was anxious to see his statute passed. In a letter to the speaker of the assembly, he expressed his hope that the abolition amendment would not be "the means of losing the whole bill" and suggested that they "form a distinct and independent bill for the purpose."[43] By November when the assembly reconvened, a reapportionment of the delegates had taken effect, and by a close vote the abolition amendment was removed from the bill. All attempts to have it reintroduced failed, and, on March 14, 1798, Paterson's revision was finally adopted without it.[44]

As was required, the statute consolidated and digested the previous laws concerning slavery. The main provisions of the acts of 1786 and 1788 were restated with only a few changes, and the impact of these changes was minimal. The penalty for importing slaves into the state was set at $140. This represented an increase of more than two and a half times the previous fine but another provision of the 1786 law laying a larger £50 penalty for importing a slave brought from Africa after 1776 (presumably because they were more likely to cause trouble) was dropped. As long as the fine for importing slaves remained far below the price that could be gotten for them on the open market, the penalties would be a poor deterrent.[45] The new law also extended the period during which a slave could be freed without a bond being paid by the owner until the slave's fortieth birthday. While this did make it more likely that a slave might eventually achieve his freedom, it also enabled masters to exact another five years of labor from their slaves before turning them out and to avoid the responsibility of caring for them in their old age.

Most of the sections of the act concerned the everyday rules respecting curfews and runaways. Slaves could now remain at large until 10 o'clock in the evening (instead of 9 o'clock) before they risked arrest, and they could travel up to ten miles (instead of five) from their masters' homes before they became subject to treatment as runaways. By deleting the restrictive thirteenth section of the act of 1714, Paterson made it possible for slaves to own real estate if their masters gave permission.[46] However, despite the humane intentions made clear in the reform of penal laws, slaves were still subject to whipping.

Paterson's attempts to introduce new social reforms through the revision of the laws extended to his concern about the multitude of beggars he claimed to see everywhere. For a newspaper, he wrote that

scarce a day passes in which beggars do not accost us, bewailing their misfortunes, and imploring charity. . . . Such as are really poor and entitled to relief ought to be provided for in a decent manner, and not suffered to wander up and down the country in search of bread.

The trouble was that "the far greater part of the beggars" were "beggars by profession" to whom begging was "an ease and a pleasure" because, "though able, they are too lazy to work." Critics of today's welfare system would be heartened to hear him say that

> nine out of ten of these sturdy beggars are from other states, they migrate, because they have been guilty of crimes; they come hither, because they are unknown, and may more safely enter a new course of villany.

Paterson thought workhouses were the answer. Workhouses could "whip them into activity and honesty, and teach them, that they must earn their bread before they can eat it." Like the laws of other states, even in the colonial period, most elements of Paterson's proposed regulations concerning the poor were intended to assure that relief was provided only for the "impotent poor" who belonged to the local community (having resided there for at least one year) and to guarantee as full as possible reimbursement of expenses to the city or township (for example, by auction of any property owned by the poor person). Workhouses were rare in early America, and Paterson's recommendation to build them attests to his belief in the possibility of rehabilitation. But such institutions were also meant to serve as a deterrent for wandering vagrants who would choose to inflict themselves on some other community rather than risk incarceration at hard labor.[47] When he drafted the bill concerning workhouses, Paterson proposed that they be used for the idle as well as the disorderly. He explained in his observations to the legislature that other states had done the same. "We see a score of beggars and vagrants in the little towns of this state for one in Philadelphia," he claimed, "because in the latter place they are sent to the workhouse." He recommended that the legislature consider "that common pipers, fiddlers, and common railers, and brawlers, wanton and lascivious persons, and such as are guilty of reviling, or profane speaking" be sent to the workhouses along with those accused of such noncriminal offenses as "neglect[ing] their callings" or "misspend[ing] what they earn."[48] The legislators declined.

The laws of colonial New Jersey, like those of Massachusetts and the other colonies, had tended to equate crime with sin. Therefore the statutes included punishments for all sorts of offenses that today are considered matters of personal moral judgment. Many of these older rules were carried over into Paterson's laws, but changes in the punishments prescribed indicate that New Jersey was caught up in the early stages of a national trend away from trying to enforce morality through legislation. This development has been most closely analyzed in Massachusetts, where William Nelson has traced the abandonment over some thirty years of the idea that "there was any one ethical standard that all men ought to obey," but the trend was at work in the other states as well.[49] In New Jersey, the penalties for blasphemy were reduced, and fornicators and adulterers no longer had to fear the pillory or the whipping post. The punishment for fornication was reduced to a $14 fine, and adulterers would henceforth have to face a fine of $100 and/or a maximum of six months in prison. In general, private offenses were to be punished less severely than "open lewdness."[50]

In a few cases, it appears that Paterson was more willing than the legislators to enforce moral standards. For example, he wanted to outlaw billiards. He thought that the game was such a threat to the moral well-being of the community that his draft bill on the subject, had it been enacted, would have authorized justices of the peace to enter any premises where they thought they might find a billiard table and, with help if necessary, to break it up on the spot.[51]

Paterson went to the people to argue for two other proposed laws that he perceived in moral terms. In one newspaper essay, he called on the legislature to defend the Christian sabbath against the criticisms of those who argued against traditional religion. He was sarcastic in his description of the Deists in France who had tried to abolish the sabbath and treat patriotism as their religion.[52] But his fears were unnecessary. New Jerseyans were not ready to follow the lead of the French and proved it by passing Paterson's proposed regulations for the sabbath into law. Paterson also spoke through the press on the issue of regulating taverns. His bill that was enacted instructed the courts to license

> no more inns and taverns in their respective counties than shall be necessary to accommodate and entertain travellers and strangers, to serve the public occasions of the said counties, and for the convenience of men meeting together to transact business.

In his newspaper essay on the topic, Paterson noted that every unnecessary tavern "is injurious to the person who keeps it, prejudicial to such as are in the same business, and mischevious to the neighborhood." The last matter concerned him most. "Unnecessary and ill conducted taverns" were public nuisances.

They encourage idleness, gaming and intemperance; they serve as lures to decoy people from their business, families and homes; they promote dissipation, alienate the heart from laudable and generous pursuits, debase the mental faculties, prostrate morals, and destroy all the finest feelings and noblest energies of our nature. Like Circe they convert the man into a brute.

According to Paterson's estimate, there were between one-third and one-half too many taverns in the state, and he hoped the courts would heed the provisions of the new law and reduce their number. In the same issue of the *Guardian* in which Paterson's essay appeared, "an Inhabitant of Somerset" congratulated that county's last court of quarter sessions for "resolving to pull down all supernumerary taverns, and like true guardians of society, refusing to listen to the interference of interested men."[53] Paterson's attempts to legislate his concern for morality were, therefore, partially successful. If the billiard tables of New Jersey remained intact, at least the sabbath was secure, and the number of taverns reduced.[54]

By late 1797, the revision of the laws had been under way for five years, and the legislature was becoming impatient. The speaker of the assembly wrote Paterson to ask how much longer he thought the project would take to be completed. With some resentment, Paterson replied by pointing out that the printer could not even begin to set the volume in type until the legislators acted on several bills they had been putting off for some time.[55] But the delay was partially Paterson's fault. The revision of the laws establishing procedure in the courts and regulating the practice of the legal profession had been left until last.

Paterson was first confronted with the problem of the courts in 1796, when he was sent the report of a legislative committee on the organization of the Supreme Court and the circuit courts of the state. He disapproved of the report on several grounds involving the jurisdiction of the respective courts, the advisability of setting up district courts, and the proper salary to be paid to judges. The disagreement was so significant that Paterson flatly refused to draft the bill as they wanted it. "A person, who is averse to the principles of a bill," he wrote, "ought not to draw it. . . . The heart and the head should concur or the chance is, that the work will be badly done."[56]

Then in January 1798, he was asked to undertake the drafting of a bill "for regulating the practice in the Court of Chancery, the courts of common law, and the Orphans Court, and for ascertaining the taxable costs in the same." Paterson first suggested that the legislation of specific rules for the courts was unwise and should be left for the courts themselves—each court should be left with considerable latitude, at least with respect to its own rules. But finally he agreed to do his best with regard to the first two, explaining that since he had never practiced in the Orphans Court and knew nothing of its proceedings, he could "not think of undertaking to draw a bill for regulating practice" in it.[57]

It was over a year before he was able to complete the drafting of the Chancery Act, the one that he considered most important.[58] The High Court of Chancery had begun in England as an expression of the prerogative power of the king and had emerged as the ultimate court of equity in which appeal could be made on the basis of justice to remedy defects in the common law, supply omissions in common law jurisdiction, and offer suitable legal procedures where statutes and common law were silent.[59] In each of the royal colonies, the governor and his council were authorized to sit as a chancery court, but the application of chancery jurisdiction in early New Jersey was spotty at best. Only one of the eighteenth-century royal governors (Lewis Morris) was a lawyer, and most of the others appear to have chosen not to exercise the chancery powers granted in their instructions.[60]

Several years before, Paterson himself had made some observations about the colonial chancellorship. Before the Revolution, he explained, "the business of equity was inconsiderable." But, even so, "the few suits that were instituted moved on heavily" because the governor

> had not perhaps one legal idea in his composition; he hated to decide upon what he did not understand; the business was irksome and odious; he put off the day of the hearing and the day of determination as far as possible; till at length by procrastination and expense and the risk of injustice arising from the ignorance of the judge, the remedy became worse than the disease.

The framers of the 1776 constitution, "predicting the future from the past," had provided that, as before, the chancellor and governor should be the same man. The problem was not immediately evident because very few civil cases were instituted during the war. As soon as independence was won, however, causes respecting property and civil rights, particularly those in the chancery court, had "wondrously increased."[61]

Paterson's Act Respecting the Court of Chancery passed by the legislature in 1799, outlined chancery jurisdiction and specified the manner of serving processes and subpoenas and the terms for granting injunctions. The mode of proof by witnesses and fees paid to them were to be the same as in the Supreme Court, and chancery decrees were guaranteed the same authority as judgments of other courts. One important difficulty with the poorly prepared chancellors of the colonial period, as Paterson had noted, was that their decisions were final and absolute. To remedy this, Paterson's 1799 law allowed appeal from chancery to the Court of Appeals and Errors, where the governor sat with the members of the Legislative Council.[62]

The bill that Paterson wanted least to draft, and the one that he thought would be most controversial, was the one that regulated the practice of law in the courts. Before the Revolution, Paterson had been part of the group that had successfully opposed a law to regulate practice, but after the war popular demands for limitations on legal practice and especially on legal fees in suits for repayment of debts were irresistible to the legislature. The 1784 Act for Regulating and Shortening the Proceedings in the Courts of Law was an expression of the influence debtors had over the New Jersey assembly. It was framed and ushered through the legislature by Abraham Clark, the leader of the paper money party.[63] The law's primary purpose was to protect debtors from what they thought to be artful contrivances of the law. For example, the 1784 law required that the creditor's declaration of what was due (which had to be submitted within thirty days of his bringing the action to keep the charges from being summarily dismissed) must be phrased in "as plain and concise a manner" as possible rather than being couched in the complex terminology of the law.[64] Perhaps if he could understand the charges against him, the defendant could do something on his own without going out and hiring an attorney. The lawyers had the debtor over a barrel when it came to fees for their services, too. The plaintiff's attorney could build up an astronomical bill including retaining fees, term fees (when an old case was continued to a new court term), and charges for drawing all sorts of documents that might or might not be necessary. If the defendant lost the case, he was responsible for the plaintiff's lawyer's fees as well as his own, and it was not impossible for the costs to mount up to more than the amount of the debt itself. "Clark's practice," as the procedure set up in 1784 became known, had severely limited the types of fees that could be charged in the court's approved bill of costs. The lawyer was still free to charge his own client for all sorts of services (though not exceeding the item-by-item list of acceptable amounts for each service laid out in a law of 1747–1748), but very few of them could be foisted on the opposition when the case was won. Moreover, a fine of £10 was established for lawyers who falsified their lists of costs or attempted to charge for services not allowed in the new law.[65] Naturally the lawyers had been dismayed. In a letter to his colleague John Lawrence soon after the passage of the act, Paterson had quipped: "Huzza, Boys! for the new Law."[66] But he was anything but pleased.

By the 1790s when Paterson took up his revision of the laws, popular sentiment against the legal profession had not abated. The traditional sources such as Charles Warren's *History of the American Bar* and more recent studies such as those of Richard Ellis and Maxwell Bloomfield are agreed that much of this antilawyer feeling had to do with a popular distrust of the common law.[67] Aside from the fact that it was English, enough to win a good many enemies for any institution in postrevolutionary America, critics pointed to the "mysterious and ambiguous character of the common law" and argued for simplification and codification of the laws so that they could be easily "understood by every individual" in the community. "Common sense and common honesty," they argued, should take the place of the common law.[68]

Paterson saw the call to revise the practice law as his opportunity to set straight some of the aberrations he perceived in the statute of 1784. As he explained to the legislature when taking on the task: "Instead of creating a system tending toward order and dispatch it [the 1784 law] engendered a monster, which it is impossible to mould into shape." As justification for his decision to rebuild the system from scratch, Paterson argued: "It is better to begin anew than to build on so bad a foundation."[69] During the intervening years, another act had dropped the restrictions on the services that lawyers could include in bills of cost, while reaffirming the charges authorized in the 1747–1748 law, but a good deal of confusion still existed in the legal system.[70]

The bill that Paterson prepared satisfied the legislature in almost every particular. It set down the basic rules for the operation of the courts. Among its provisions, the law established how infants were to be treated before the law, laid out the regulations regarding bail, and specified dozens of other details of general legal procedure. Paterson was careful, however, to leave most of the rules relating specifically to the Supreme Court or the Court of Common Pleas up to those courts themselves.[71] Where the 1784 law had favored the debtor-defendant wherever possible, Paterson's revision was more protective of the rights of the creditor-plaintiff. In his observations to the legislature that accompanied the bill, Paterson explained that

it frequently happens, that the sheriff somehow or other, conceives or finds it his interest to favor the defendant to the delay or danger of the plaintiff. In the above bill, I have endeavored to guard against this evil. The debtor is entitled to no indulgence but such as his creditor will voluntarily grant. He ought to have performed his contract, he ought to have paid at the day; good faith required it, and it was his duty to have done so. Every indulgence to the debtor is at the risk, expense and loss of the creditor. There is no point, whether regarded in a moral or political view, that deserves more attention than punctuality and good faith in the performance of contracts.[72]

What Paterson's practice bill did not do was to set the amounts of the fees to be allowed to lawyers and officers of the court. In arguing that this should be treated separately, Paterson explained that otherwise unwise changes in the practice might be made, as they had been in the past, merely as a cover for "the real, but latent" purpose of reducing lawyers' fees.[73] The legislature adopted the practice law and, in the absence of a fee bill from Paterson, appointed a committee to prepare one for themselves. Lawyers were panic-stricken. Several of them, including Matthias Williamson, Aaron Ogden, and David M. Ogden, wrote Paterson in March 1799, explaining that, because of current "prejudices and misconceptions" about lawyers, no just and long-lasting fee bill could be passed unless he drafted it. They thought that the amounts specified in the 1747–1748 law, which had been set down "in much cheaper times," were "too low," and they pointed out that there were some errors and omissions in the old bill that should be corrected. The lawyers' greatest concern was that if the legislature came up with its own bill, it might include a maximum sum for all the lawyers' fees in a particular action, something they thought to be "exceedingly unjust."[74] Paterson wrote to Williamson and his colleagues asking for specific recommendations, and he did turn out a draft bill of fees as they asked without provision for a maximum charge per case, but the amounts he settled on were little more than the old law provided.[75] He realized only too well that the matter was very sensitive and chose to avoid a confrontation by setting fees that no one could call too high. "Temperence and wisdom," he explained to the legislature, were necessary in order to calm the traditional clamor against lawyers.[76] Paterson urged Williamson and the others to pay strict attention to "legal correctness in bills of costs." Practitioners of the law, he wrote, should "adhere strictly" to the established fees in order to "preserve tranquility in the public mind." If there were "great disparity" of fees in similar causes, it might be "just occasion for complaint," he warned them.[77] By refusing to allow an inflation of fees over those already a half-century old and retaining the penalties for lawyers who falsified bills of costs or otherwise tried to overcharge the public, Paterson had created the impression that his concern was for the common man, but the weight of the law fell invariably on people of modest means. The new rules placed the law more on the side of the creditor and represented a conservative shift back from the pro-debtor philosophy followed by the legislature in the 1780s.

The culmination of his legal revision came in 1799 with passage of Paterson's Act Relative to Statutes, which provided that no English statute would ever again be recognized as law in New Jersey.[78] The section of the 1776 state constitution that had maintained the English laws in effect until they could be replaced had finally been fulfilled. All legal authority granted at any date by act of Parliament was null and void unless it had been reintroduced by Paterson and reenacted by the state legislature. The same new law also directed that common law opinions rendered in English courts after July 4, 1776, were not binding as precedents in any New Jersey court. In the almost seventy years since Charles Warren represented this law as a capitulation to popular sentiment against the common law, "the prejudices of the people crystallized into radical legislation," no one has challenged his judgment.[79] But it appears to me that the real effect of Paterson's law was to guarantee the continuing relevance of the great body of English common law that had come into existence prior to 1776. Some of the mysteries and ambiguities that upset critics of the common law were avoided by this limitation, but in the long view what was more significant was the preservation of the English common law tradition.

The recent studies of William Nelson and Morton Horwitz have added in great measure to our understanding of the reception of English common law in the early years of the republic and the ways in which it was adapted to meet the needs of an emerging capitalist economy and democratic political system.[80] There were radicals such as Boston's Benjamin Austin who called for the scrapping of the entire colonial legal tradition and the construction of a new simplified code to take its place. But most lawyers and political leaders, including almost all Federalists and a large body of Jeffersonian Republicans, were moved by a concern for stability and order to support the reception of the English common law in American courts and to oppose tampering with the traditional judicial system unless there was good cause.[81] In a comment on his proposed revision of legal practice in New Jersey's courts, William Paterson made a classic statement of what has come to be known as the "reception ideology."

There is a danger in departing from known and established regulation and usages, whenever this happens the law is perplexed, and
at a loss how to advise or proceed, and the client in consequence
is liable to injury or delay; everything is thrown as it were on the
ocean, and afloat for a time; and it requires much litigation, a series
of decisions, and a length of practice before certainty and order can
be restored.[82]

Here, in essence, was the same conservative philosophy fully expressed
forty years later by Kent and Story. American institutions had been kept
flexible enough to allow adaptation to new economic and social forces
without rejecting the common law tradition. But it was no coincidence
that the place of the trained attorney as the only person qualified to
interpret and articulate the law was preserved intact.

Once Paterson had seen to the publication of the revised laws in 1800
and collected his $2,500 fee from the state treasurer, his contribution to
the legal development of New Jersey was essentially complete. On at
least two later occasions, Paterson did make recommendations to the
assembly concerning additional changes in the law (to encourage corporations to build turnpikes in the state and to assure that manumitted slaves
could not be deprived of their freedom because of a technicality regarding their papers.)[83] But from 1800 until his death in 1806, almost all of
Paterson's professional attention was devoted to his responsibilities as an
associate justice of the United States Supreme Court.

Although almost every major element of his reform and revision of
the laws represented the same forces at work in other states, to some
extent Paterson had infused the new statutes with his personal prejudices—
on criminal punishments, local political bodies, tavern operations, and
debtor-creditor relationships, to name a few. The sensitivity Paterson
showed in reacting to the popular sentiment against the legal profession
and the compromise he achieved in formulating a practice law that would
protect creditors without creating a backlash from debtors and those who
defended them were noteworthy accomplishments.

The court records of the early national and antebellum periods in New
Jersey are still to be studied, but Paterson's cautious restructuring of the
judicial system and legal practice there represents in itself a significant
chapter in the development of American legal institutions and the reception of the English common law.

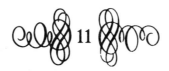

11

Parties, Politics, and
the Crisis of 1798

The mark that William Paterson left on the infant republic was primarily due to his long and devoted application to public service. As one group of New Jersey citizens wished when they toasted their former governor just a few months after his elevation to the United States Supreme Court: "May his usefullness increase his fame."[1] Appointment to the Court brought with it great prestige and a handsome salary of $3,500 per year, but the demands the job made on Paterson's time and energy were tremendous. The judges had little time to themselves, since they had to ride the circuit twice each year as well as hold two sessions of the Supreme Court. By 1793, when Paterson joined the Court, one of the original justices, complaining of overwork, had already resigned, and several nominees had declined appointment on the same grounds.[2] But Paterson seemed to thrive on work.

Paterson returned to national office just at the time when the first deep fissures were beginning to appear between the dominant Federalists and the emerging Republican party. The earliest signs of trouble had been visible to Paterson when he sat in the Senate and took part in the debate over Hamilton's financial plan, but, in the intervening years (1790–1793), sensitive domestic issues and questions of foreign policy had added more

fuel to the fires of discord. Paterson had definite opinions on many of
these issues and made them clear in the newspaper essays he was to write
in years to come. In addition, the record of the judicial cases he heard
during this decade of party struggle shows that on at least several occasions
Paterson's personal convictions and his passion for stability and order
influenced his judicial decisions in unfortunate ways.

The distinctive Federalist tone apparent in the Supreme Court during
the 1790s was not surprising. Washington chose his judges carefully,
"drawing the first characters of the Union into the Judiciary."[3] Besides
sharing a proven expertise in the law, all those he appointed were ardent
supporters of the national government and the powers it derived from
the federal Constitution. The president knew that the decisions of the
Supreme Court would be a crucial element in establishing the authority
of the new system. When he wrote to inform the original justices of
their nomination in 1789, Washington referred to the Court as "the
chief pillar upon which our National Government must rest."[4] The
political evaluation of the nominee was necessarily a factor in making such
significant appointments, but after 1792 the lines of political division
became obvious, and the president took even more care to appoint to
high office only those who were friendly to the policies of his administration. To do otherwise, he wrote, "would be a sort of political
suicide."[5] In 1793, when he asked Paterson to be a justice on the Court,
Washington noted that Paterson was "professionally qualified" and that
the public knew him and approved his conduct. But Washington also
knew that Paterson's views on most social questions and his devotion to
the Constitution were directly in line with those of the Federalists and
that he staunchly supported their political beliefs.[6]

Even though Paterson's ideas paralleled those of the Federalists so
closely, he continued to deny his association with any political party or
faction. In fact, the theme to which he returned most often in his
political essays of the 1790s was his opposition to parties of all sorts as
inimical to the best interests of the republic. This aversion to parties,
based on the assumption that true public spirit among leaders would
make them averse to factional divisions, was built into the mainstream
of Anglo-American political thought. Trenchard and Gordon, the authors
of *Cato's Letters* which were so widely read in America before the
Revolution, had attacked parties as engines of private interest and tools
of designing ministers. In his college commonplace book, Paterson had
traced the evil effects of parties back to the English Civil War, and he
repeated the criticism of parties as tools of corruption in his "Address
on the Rise and Decline of Nations." In defending the new Constitution,

both Madison and Hamilton had argued that the size of the country and the diversity of interests here would discourage the development of parties, an idea Paterson later reaffirmed. But even though the new nation inherited this wariness of political factionalism, the republican system required checks on power and freedom of opposition that would inevitably lead to the form of dissension that leaders like Paterson feared so much.[7]

In the very first newspaper essay of his Aurelius series, published while he was still governor of New Jersey, Paterson wrote about this inherent contradiction in the American political system. As undesirable and dangerous to the public interest as parties were believed to be, he saw that differences of opinion were unavoidable in a free government. If such a "diversity of sentiment" was based on "honest and candid" inquiry, then there was no real danger; the critic could be reasoned with, and once convinced would "think it no dishonor to retract, and acknowledge his error." On the contrary, however, "if his mind be darkened by prejudice, be guided by selfish views, or actuated by party spirit," no course of reason could bring him to admit his mistake. "He may be refuted, but will never be convinced." All Paterson could do to discourage such unfortunate and potentially destructive dissension was to call on all men to exercise what he called "candid and liberal sentiments." Otherwise they could never form "right opinions" by the "scale of principle and justice."[8]

A few weeks later, Aurelius warned his readers that party zeal could threaten the very heart of the political system. To the party follower "truth is falshood, and falshood is truth, as may best serve a present turn, or the politics of the moment." Paterson used the term "party lie" to describe the deceptions and misrepresentations that were used to destroy the reputations of public men not allied to the proper faction. If such a leader were "hunted out of office," Paterson asked, "will any hostile traducer fill it better, or act with more honesty and fairness?" No detractor was fit for public life. Paterson's faith in the judgment of the people would waver later in the decade, but in 1793 he argued that American citizens were "not prone to run into violent measures, or to be heated and worked upon by factious and designing men." This was thought to be due in part to the availability of newspapers carrying "much political light and useful information" and in part to the presence of "schools and seminaries of learning." Paterson shared the conviction with other contemporary leaders that without education in literature and science, without a knowledge of history and political philosophy, without a patriotism that "comprehends towns, counties, and states" as well as

226 SERVING THE PUBLIC TRUST

the little nieghborhood in which one lives, good citizenship was impossible. "Persons ignorant and uninformed," Paterson explained, "are easily imposed upon and led astray." Without "mental and moral improvement," Paterson closed the essay, "neither order, nor republicanism, nor civil liberty can long be preserved. Ignorance is freedom's worst foe."[9]

Paterson's distrust of parties and his concern for the "mental and moral improvement" of the people through education were common to the times and appealed to people of almost every political persuasion. National political alignments were new, and the line between the parties was not as clear-cut as it would be in later years. Devoted followers of both Federalist and Jeffersonian philosophies would still agree on specific questions, even when more partisan interests or more controversial issues were involved. On most matters of importance, for example, Paterson's natural impulses drove him to the same conclusions as other Federalists, but still there were some anomalies. For example, he never shared the Anglophilism common to most Federalists, and from time to time he voiced opinions on the moral and social problems associated with vast accumulated wealth, speculation, and luxurious aristocratic living, which sounded strangely like the rhetoric of the Republicans. Two points are especially important in explaining Paterson's departure from the typical Federalist mold: first, his political training in New Jersey during and immediately after the Revolution, and, second, his early association with New Side evangelism.

Few, if any, New Jersey Federalists relied on British markets or English businessmen for their livelihood, and, like the other Middle Atlantic states, New Jersey's population was ethnically diverse with relatively few residents maintaining family connections in England. This set New Jersey political leaders apart from the many Massachusetts merchants or Virginia planters whose efforts toward fostering a friendly cooperative relationship between the United States and Great Britain served a more personal interest. Jonathan Dayton, a steadfast Federalist representative of New Jersey throughout the 1790s and later a booster of Paterson's candidacy for the chief justiceship, had gone so far in expressing his lack of concern for such matters as to propose in 1794 the sequestration of all debts owed to Englishmen as the only suitable response to the depredations of the king's navy. Paterson was not driven this far, but, in the context of New Jersey Federalism, it should not be surprising that he was just as critical of attempts made by Britain to influence American foreign policy as he was of similar efforts by England's enemies, the French.[10]

Had the Revolution not widened Paterson's horizons and lifted him out of his little law practice in the Raritan Valley of New Jersey, the New Side religious associations he made there might have made a different man of him. For one thing, he would have been isolated from the influence of other more cosmopolitan and free-thinking men. During the summer of 1787, as Paterson labored in Philadelphia over what was to become the new federal Constitution, only a few yards from Independence Hall a new building was being erected to house the American Philosophical Society. Soon thereafter he accepted the invitation to become a member of that select fraternity, which was respected as an American equivalent of England's Royal Society. A few years later, while serving his first term as governor of New Jersey, he was admitted to the rank of Master Mason in the Order of Freemasons. Both of these associations were primarily important for the opportunities they offered for social relationships with other men of prominence. This was especially true of the Masonic lodge, which united in its bond of secrecy many of New Jersey's most influential citizens—John Cleves Symmes, Elias and Jonathan Dayton, Richard Howell, and Joseph Bloomfield, to name just a few. But Paterson's membership in such groups also implies a degree of open-mindedness and respect for unrestricted intellectual inquiry uncommon among those who were true believers in orthodox Calvinism.[11]

It is difficult to assess the exact influence of religious ideas on Paterson's thought in the later years of his life. His New Brunswick neighbors respected his knowledge of theology and the scriptures: "Few men, not of the clerical profession, appeared better to understand the doctrines of both natural and revealed religion." They enjoyed his fellowship as a "constant and serious attendant" at services and other church activities. He was especially interested in supporting a local campaign to encourage evangelical activities on the frontier. But church leaders were disappointed that such a distinguished citizen never chose to make, "in the usual manner, a public profession of religion" and join in the communion of the church. Since it was completely out of character, we must question whether Paterson actually made the deathbed confession attributed to him by the local Presbyterian minister in New Brunswick. Although there is no indication that he attended Paterson's bedside, the clergyman recounted in great detail how the dying man requested holy communion, openly regretted his failure to concern himself more with his spiritual well-being, and cautioned his son not to be so delinquent where his own soul was concerned. Such an occasion, real or imagined, certainly provided the minister with an opportunity to preach to everyone in the community on the importance of their individual relationship with God: "Ye that have hitherto thought too lightly of religion, let a death so instructive teach you its infinite importance." Nevertheless, while the desire to steer clear of internal church squabbles (such as the one he had been through years before in the Dutch Reformed Church in Raritan), the distractions of public office, the skepticism that his association with such groups as the American Philosophical Society and the Freemasons may have bred, and what his minister referred to as "certain doubts respecting himself" might have discouraged Paterson from maintaining his personal spiritual life, they could not expunge certain deep-seated religious beliefs from his personality.[12]

Like Elias Boudinot, the leading Federalist congressman from New Jersey (1789–1795) and Washington's appointee to direct the United States Mint (1795–1805), Paterson's religious ideas fit perfectly with his social philosophy. David Hackett Fischer has recently written of Boudinot that "the anchor of his conservatism was evangelical religion," which he hoped would "ameliorate the manners" and tempers of the people at large. In 1801, Boudinot's *Age of Revelation* was published in Philadelphia as an answer to Paine's *Age of Reason,* and later he became the moving force behind the American Bible Society. For Boudinot, as for Paterson, and for others, too, the popular passion for political power and material wealth seemed to threaten society by leading some men to forget their more important responsibilities to both God and their fellow men.[13] Devotion to duty may have distracted Paterson from attending to personal religious affairs, but an evangelical moral strain was often evident in his political and social rhetoric. When he railed against speculation, warned of wide variations in wealth, and condemned licentious living, he almost always did so in moral terms—the speculators, for example, were men who "counted their guineas more often than they said their prayers." His early religious training goes a long way toward explaining some of the apparent inconsistencies in his later political philosophy.

Paterson disapproved of parties as much as any of his political contemporaries, and he was a good deal louder than many of them in proclaiming his own spirit of independent judgment. But political issues invariably penetrated into the business of the Supreme Court, and in 1795 and 1798, when political and social pressures seemed particularly acute, his partisanship made itself clear. In several famous cases he appears to have earned the epithet "hanging judge" for the way he handled himself in the courtroom. He was, however, usually governed by a sense of moderation in his political career as well as in his personal life. Eventually his belief in principle and moderation brought him back from the brink of despair over the crisis of 1798, encouraged him to maintain a philosophical perspective as anxiety over the election of 1800 drove other Federalists into a frenzy, and thereafter allowed him to help develop an atmosphere of understanding between moderate Federalists and moderate Republican supporters of the new administration.

In his early Aurelius essays (1793), Paterson's natural tendencies to the Federalist side were already clear. The fifth article of the Aurelius series recalled the controversy over the adoption of the Constitution a few years before. To him, the critics of the presidency and the judiciary had been ridiculous. In the president, they saw "the fetus of a monarch . . . , an infant Hercules in his cradle," and the Senate was seen as "a very house of lords." The judiciary had been criticized as "unfriendly to liberty, and repugnant to the spirit of a free people" because it tended to make men honest and forced them to honor their contracts. "What a system of tyranny," Paterson quipped, "that the freeborn soul should be fettered with such trammels." Tongue in cheek, he continued: "All compulsion is odious; but to compel men to pay their debts is downright oppression and not to be endured." While he recognized the possibility, perhaps even the likelihood, that political parties would eventually establish firm lines of opposition in America, it was still a chimera to him in 1793. "It is pretended," he wrote, that various parties "have arisen under the present government." He noted some of the names given to them—democrats, mobocrats, equality-men, and liberty-men—and pointed out the absurdity of supposing all New Englanders to be "monarchy-men and aristocrats; while the mightly land-holders, and slave-holders of the south are sure to be fast friends to equality and the rights of man." He made no further mention of the "equality-men," but, like a typical Federalist he went on to label the charge that an aristocratic party existed as absolutely preposterous. "I verily believe, that we have suffered more, and have more to dread from the Hessian fly [a pest that was then taking a terrible toll in New Jersey's wheat fields] than from all the monarchy-men and monarchy makers, that now exist or ever will exist in the United States." For the present, he was content to defend the establishment and poke fun at the opposition; later on, however, his temper would rise.[14]

Paterson's initiation as an associate justice was a rigorous one. His first assignment in the spring of 1793 was to cover the southern circuit, the most inconvenient of all because it required traveling for long distances over the worst roads in the country.[15] Paterson left New Brunswick at the end of March by boat for New York and thence to Charleston. It would be late June before he returned, somewhat the worse for wear.[16]

Each time a new session on the circuit opened, the presiding justice led things off with an address to the grand jury. An important element in the rationale for having Supreme Court justices ride the circuits in the first place had been the opportunity it would provide for these illustrious supporters of the new national system to explain the nature of good government to the people of the various states, and these grand jury addresses were the most obvious opportunities for getting such points across. Special significance has been attributed to the presentations of Chief Justice Jay and his associates to the first meetings of the circuit courts in 1790, and, to the extent that they endeavored to justify the first expressions of national judiciary power, they were especially important.

Those copies of Paterson's grand jury addresses that remain in his papers indicate the same didactic tone. Typically, he began with an explanation of popular sovereignty and the responsibilities that the system delegated to each branch of government, then moved on to argue that the legislative and executive authorities were meaningless unless the judicial system fulfilled its role. Since the United States enjoyed "a government of laws and not of men," crimes against the government had to be considered as "pointed against the well-being, the political existence, and . . . the majesty of the people themselves." The order in which he made these points might be different from one grand jury to the next, but he usually stressed the same ideas. He would go on to explain that the laws of the United States were mild and in accord "with the spirit of benevolence and humanity," assure the grand jurors that the punishments were "duly proportioned to their [the criminals'] respective crimes" and tempered by mercy, and conclude with a short survey of the types of offenses scheduled to come before them.[17] Usually the grand jury's reply amounted to little more than a note of appreciation for the judge's wisdom and guidance.

Paterson's first trip on the southern circuit, however, proved unique. His appointment to the Court had come just a few weeks after the decision in the controversial case of *Chisolm* v. *Georgia,* in which a state was held liable to suit by a citizen of another state.[18] When Paterson got to Savannah the following spring, Georgians were still upset about it. The grand jurors took the opportunity to lay out their complaints to the circuit court in the form of six specific grievances including federal involvement in local Indian affairs, the method of assumption of the state debts, and the extension of national bank branches. They closed with a compliment to Paterson, whom they praised for his "elegant, concise, and republican charge" to them, but this cannot have diminished the judge's surprise at their unusually long and pointed reply.[19]

On several occasions, Paterson lectured grand juries on preventive justice and the importance of education for children. Reaffirming some of the ideas brought forth in his newspaper essays, Paterson explained that when the mental faculties are "overshadowed by ignorance" they are unable to resist the "fallacies and artful impositions of designing men." But when knowledge is diffused throughout the state by "proper and well-conducted schools," then men can begin to "discern moral and political sentiments, operations, and characters as they really are. . . . Before the torch of science," he concluded, "all illusive appearances vanish, like darkness before the dawning of day."[20] Although his remarks were veiled beneath the desire for more public education, Paterson was clearly speaking under the assumption that those who opposed the current administration did so out of ignorance. If only all the people were politically astute and morally sensitive, they would all be law-abiding Federalists. Such opportunities for the subtle expression of political opinion were not uncommon, but before long Justice Paterson and the Supreme Court were embroiled in one of the most controversial political questions of the day: How would America react to the progressively more radical French Revolution?

An answer to this question had been forced on the administration by the activities of Edmond Genêt. Early in 1793, the new French republic had declared war on Great Britain and sent Citizen Genêt as its minister to America. The Frenchman arrived in Charleston at about the same time that Paterson passed through the city on his southern circuit. Genêt was cheered by the people as he traveled to Philadelphia, where President Washington formally received him, despite the objections of Secretary Hamilton. But soon the welcome cooled. Even before he had presented his credentials, Genêt had been at work commissioning American ships to act as privateers in the service of France. On April 22, three weeks before Genêt reached Philadelphia, Washington had issued a proclamation of neutrality that declared that the United States was at peace with both Great Britain and France and warned Americans not to engage in acts of hostility against either of the belligerents. Ignoring messages from the president, Genêt proceeded to commission a total of twelve privateers, which raised havoc with British shipping. Despite orders to the contrary, some of the prizes were brought into American ports where they were sold after summary trials conducted by French consuls. Popular support for the Frenchman ran high, particularly among the Democratic-Republican societies that were beginning to spring up in several states, but the Federalist administration feared war with England if Genêt were allowed to continue his provocative activities.[21]

The first involvement of the Court came in July 1793, when Washington asked the justices for their interpretation of the treaty of 1778, upon which Genêt justified his actions. The justices declined to give an opinion

on the grounds that it was improper for them to decide questions of law
extrajudicially. They would wait until a specific case involving that particular problem was brought before them.[22] The August 1793 term of
the court was cancelled because of the prevalence of smallpox in Philadelphia, but when the justices came together the following February, with
Paterson among them for the first time, they found just such a case on the
docket. In *Glass* v. *Sloop Betsy* (3 Dallas 6), the Maryland district court
had denied that it had jurisdiction over French prizes, thereby issuing a
serious blow to Washington's attempts at stopping Genêt. The decision was
soon reversed by the Supreme Court.[23]

Through 1795, the Court was faced with a series of cases that concerned
American relations with the French Republic. Although it seemed to dis-
pense even-handed justice with regard to each—*The United States* v.
Judge Lawrence (3 Dallas 42), *The United States* v. *Richard Peters* (3
Dallas 121), and *Talbot* v. *Jansen* (3 Dallas 122)—the effect of the
Court's decision was to give added support to the administration's policy
of neutrality.[24]

Paterson's feelings about the French Revolution had been transformed
from expressions of public support at the beginning of 1793 to absolute
revulsion by 1795. On the first day of 1793, Governor Paterson had attended a banquet held at the White-Hall tavern in New Brunswick "to
commemorate the late success of the arms of the French republic." Along
with a "large and respectable company of gentlemen from different parts
of the state," Paterson had wished "reunion to the patriots of America and
France" and defeat "to the King of Prussia and the Duke of Brunswick."
The toasts went on to praise "General Dumourier and the French Army,"
the "rights of man," and the "cause of liberty throughout the world."[25]
It did not take long, however, for America to hear reports of the excesses
of the republic—most notably the execution of King Louis XVI on January 21, 1793. While most Americans continued to support the Revolution,
the activities of Robespierre and the Committee of Public Safety were
alarming to some of them, including Paterson. His change of heart can be
traced through the scattered newspaper essays he wrote between 1793 and
1795. As word of the Reign of Terror reached America, Paterson began
to see in the French Revolution all the fearsome social disintegration that
America had been able to avoid. The last straw for him was the official
rejection of the Christian religion and the abolition of the sabbath. The
"modern and mortal deists" were to blame for convincing their followers
that Christianity, hell, and the devil were "cunningly dressed" fables in-
vented by "artful and interested priests." The solution for the French was
simple:

Destroy these bugbears and their conscience will be easy and at peace.
Proceed, ye sons of sensuality and riot, eat, drink and be merry,
curse and swear and lie, cheat and slander, and steal and murder,
gratify every vicious appetite, and do every evil thing, for tomorrow
ye die, and death is an eternal sleep.[26]

The recurring theme in most of the essays he wrote in this period was
the threat of foreign influence. Paterson was concerned that Americans
would divide themselves into pro-French and pro-British parties. He referred specifically to the insolence of Genêt's advising the president in
July 1793 to call a special session of the Congress, which the minister assumed would be more friendly to his objectives than to Washington and
his cabinet.[27] By the following year, however, the British were causing as
much trouble as the French. British seizure of American ships trading in
the French West Indies had generated such popular opposition that Paterson's friend, Jonathan Dayton, had risen in Congress to propose the
sequestration of debts owed by Americans to British merchants until satisfaction was made.[28]

There is no record of Paterson's opinion on Dayton's proposal, but he
clearly wanted the United States to stand up for its rights and defend its
dignity as a sovereign power. It appeared to him that the nation was being
played for a fool by foreign agents from both sides. Emigrants from Britain
and France, who had taken up temporary residence in the United States
because of "commercial or other interested motives," were interfering in
American politics. "As soon as they set foot on the shore of America, they
begin their hostile career; and vilify the administrators of the government, the people, their manners, and laws."[29] Paterson was quick to point
out that such behavior would not be tolerated in either Britain or France.
On another occasion, he wrote that "the English and the French seem to
look upon us as men of straw, liable to be blown about and carried away
by every whim of European policy." He was forced to admit that the
nation "had been strangely managed for a year or two past," as various
foreigners and "their hot-headed adherents have exerted every art & influence to attach us to their respective systems and schemes." But he was
insistent that the nation stick firmly to its policy of neutrality. Otherwise
America's spirit of independence would be doomed: "Americans, your sun
of glory is set," he warned, "Ye are [again] to be slaves."[30]

The susceptibility of many Americans to the arguments of irresponsible
and even rebellious troublemakers was made painfully obvious in the
summer of 1794 by news of the Whiskey Rebellion in western Pennsylvania. Seeking to make an example of the insurgents, Washington had

sent Alexander Hamilton to command the federal force, and those rebels it had been able to catch were paraded through the streets of Philadelphia and imprisoned there until the next scheduled meeting of the U.S. circuit court for Pennsylvania in February 1795.[31] Justice Paterson was presiding, and he took the opportunity to regale the grand jury with a recitation of the evil influences of "disorganising spirits." Obedience to the law, he proclaimed, "is the first political maxim and duty in a republican government." It was the "thoughtless and ill-informed part of the community" that mistook the "salutary restraint" of the law for "slavish subjection" and looked on "irregularity and licentiousness, as sure symptoms of freedom, and certain indications of republican virtue." The target for his moralizing had changed since his prerevolutionary criticisms of the British aristocracy, but the puritanical tones were still the same. "Oh licentiousness! Thou bane of republics, more to be dreaded than hosts of external foes. The truth is, that civil liberty and order consist in and depend upon submission to the laws." The political principle was the same, too. It might have been permissible to ignore the laws of England in 1776 because Americans had played no part in making them. But now the law represented the nation's collective will. As Paterson often pointed out in his addresses to grand juries, those who broke the laws were committing crimes against the very "majesty of the people."[32]

The grand jury returned more than thirty indictments for treason, but many of the trials were delayed because of technicalities. The prosecutor, William Rawle, took advantage of the delay to have bills of indictment printed on which the grand jury had only to direct that the blanks be filled in with the defendants' names. But Rawle acted rashly. The grand jury decided that there was too little evidence even to charge eleven of the prisoners, and prosecution was eventually dropped against many of the more than thirty who had been indicted for treason. Only the first two defendants brought to trial, Philip Vigol (or Weigel) and John Mitchell, were convicted. The record of the other trials suggests that these two also could have won jury acquittal if they had presented any reasonable defense. The state called five witnesses in the first case and eleven in the second, but no one spoke for the accused except their lawyers and, rather than denying the allegations, the defense attorneys seem to have simply stated that their clients were forced to act as they did.

Paterson's forceful and animated address to the grand jury suggests how emotionally agitated he had become. In much the same way that his carefully reasoned legal judgment had failed him in the overcharged atmosphere of the Revolution (leading the attorney general in at least one case to seek to make public examples of two defendants despite the paucity of evidence against them), he lost control again. All of his concerns about the political stability of the new nation seemed to be summed up in these treason trials, and, once the lawyers had finished their presentations and the jurors had looked to the bench for instructions, Paterson held forth.[33]

At this point in a trial it is the responsibility of the judge simply to clarify any complex points of law and to instruct the jury on their deliberative duties,[34] but Paterson went beyond this and made it all but impossible for the jury to bring in anything but a verdict of guilty. In the case of Philip Vigol, Paterson told the jury that there were two points to be decided: First, has it been proven that the defendant did commit the acts charged in the indictment, and, second, was his intention a criminal one. But then, rather than properly leaving the decision to the jury, he went on to answer both questions strongly in the affirmative.

> With respect to the evidence, the current runs one way: it harmonizes in all its parts: it proves that the defendant was a member of the party which went to Reigan's house, and afterwards, to the house of Wells, in arms, marshalled and arrayed; and who, at each place, committed acts of violence and devastation.
>
> With respect to the *intention*, likewise, there is not unhappily, the slightest possibility of doubt: to suppress the office of the excise, in the fourth survey of this state; and particularly, in the present instance, to compel the resignation of Wells, the excise officer, so as to render null and void, in effect, an act of congress, constituted the apparent, the avowed object of the insurrection, and of the outrages which the prisoner assisted to commit.
>
> Combining these facts, and this design, the crime of high treason is consummate, in the contemplation of the constitution and the law of the United States.

As if he had not already gone far enough, Justice Paterson then proceeded to nullify Vigol's contention that he had acted under "duress and terror." The defendant's lawyers had tried faithfully to support such a defense, "but in this they have failed," Paterson concluded. As Paterson saw it, the whole treasonous affair exhibited "a disgraceful unanimity," and the accused was "distinguished for a guilty pre-eminence in zeal and activity." Then, after rejecting the defense out of hand, he went on to tell the jurors that

> the fear, which the law recognises as an excuse for the perpetration of an offense, must proceed from an immediate and actual danger

threatening the very life of the party. The apprehension of any loss
of property, by waste or fire; or even the apprehension of a slight or
remote injury to the person, furnish no excuse. If, indeed, such
circumstances could avail, it would be in the power of every crafty
leader of tumults and rebellion, to indemnify his followers, by utter-
ing previous menaces; an avenue would be forever open for the
escape of unsuccessful guilt; and the whole fabric of society must
inevitably be laid prostrate.

Paterson was telling them that the defendant must be made an example
for those who might foment rebellion in the future.[35] A prosecutor in
summation could not have done a better job of convincing the panel both
of the guilt of a party and of their duty to convict him. Almost as an
afterthought, Paterson closed with the reminder that, "if the jury enter-
tains any doubt upon the matter, they may find it specially."

Paterson's charge to the jury in the second case, that of John Mitchell,
was nearly the same, but this time he closed with the outright injunction
that

the prisoner must be pronounced guilty. The consequences are not to
weigh with the jury: it is their province to do justice, the attribute
of mercy is placed by our constitution in other hands.[36]

In this charge he had even forgotten to remind the jury of their right to
decide "specially."

In these cases, Paterson's concern for quieting dangerous political opposition evidently overshadowed his legal judgment and caused him to deny
the defendants their right to a fair trial. It was not unusual for judges
to summarize and clarify the evidence for a jury, especially when the case
was an involved one (numerous examples can be found in the records of
other trials). What was unusual was Paterson's apparent failure in these
two cases to leave the decision up to the jury. Not surprisingly, both Vigol
and Mitchell were found guilty of treason, and Paterson sentenced both
of them to die.

Paterson had not cornered the market on political bias. In November
1794, when President Washington presented his annual message to Congress, he blamed the Whiskey Rebellion on the Democratic-Republican
clubs that had been founded in recent months in various states. He attacked them as "self-created societies" joined together in a "diabolical

attempt to destroy the best fabric of human government and happiness"
that had ever been known and came close to charging any voluntary
political organization that opposed his administration with treason.[37] As
long as the Federalists retained control of the government, this attitude
would be their ultimate defense against political opposition. Richard
Hofstadter has observed that, like the first party in power in any newly
organized state, the Federalists naturally tended to think of themselves
"not as a party that had taken the reins of government but as the government itself." They saw the opposition as a "wholly unconstructive faction,
an anti-government." When the opposition criticized the policies of their
administration, it was taken as an attack on the very nature of republicanism.[38] Before long, the Federalists would be framing extraordinary laws
meant specifically to quiet their critics, laws that made a mockery of their
avowed commitment to republican principles. But, in the meantime, some
believed they could still afford to be magnanimous, as Washington proved
by pardoning the two prisoners found guilty of treason in Paterson's
court.[39]

The single most controversial issue to arise during either of Washington's two terms as president was the treaty negotiated with the British by
John Jay. Up until then, the discussion of foreign policy had been kept
pretty much on the official level because the questions involved in defining
neutrality and the prize jurisdiction of the admiralty courts were too
esoteric for popular debate. But when Jay returned from England early
in 1795, he carried with him the first really explosive political issue of the
decade. Almost everyone could find something dissatisfactory about the
Jay Treaty. It provided for the British withdrawal from the Northwest
forts, something promised twelve years before, and allowed American
ships to participate freely in trade with India. The treaty also allowed
American ships to have limited access to the British West Indies, permitted
the referral of prerevolutionary debts to joint commissions, and placed
British trade with the United States on a most-favored-nation basis. In
return for these dubious gains, the United States agreed to the British
definitions of maritime rights (setting aside the principle that free ships
make free goods) and contraband (broadening the list of prohibited articles) and promised to bar Britain's enemies from using American ports
as a base of operations for their ships and privateers. American supporters
of the French would have been sufficiently upset by this alone, but in
addition the treaty contained no guarantees against the continuing impress-
ment of American sailors by the British navy. When the provisions of the
treaty leaked out in March 1795, the popular clamor against it was im-

mediate. But this did not stop the Senate from ratifying the treaty in
June, after expunging Article 12, which would place more restrictions on
American trade in the West Indies than the British accommodations could
have made up for.

By secretly confiding to the British minister that the administration
had no intention of associating with France, Alexander Hamilton had
undermined Jay's bargaining position, but the brunt of the popular criticism for the lackluster provisions of the treaty was leveled at Jay himself.[40]
The president delayed signing the treaty until, over the summer, news
broke of a scandal involving Secretary of State Edmund Randolph. Then
Washington decided to formalize the treaty immediately rather than have
it look as though the secretary's indiscretions had in fact amounted to a
sell-out of the administration to France. But even this did not silence the
opposition. They complained all the more loudly because Washington had
signed the treaty at the same time that numerous popular meetings were
petitioning him to reject it.[41]

Washington was criticized by opponents in every corner of the Union.
They launched vicious personal attacks against him and charged that he
had forfeited his claim to the people's confidence.[42] With an eye toward
earning back some of that popular trust and firming up the loyalty of his
cabinet, the president set out to find an irreproachable replacement for the
unfortunate Randolph. Washington was truly in a desperate situation.
The country's leaders in foreign affairs were all either currently serving
the administration or were politically unreliable. John Adams was vice
president, John Jay, who was too unpopular anyway, was already serving
as chief justice (and was also governor-elect of New York), and others
like Jefferson and R. R. Livingston were in the vocal opposition. Forced
to turn to people whose impeccable reputation and loyalty might make up
for a lack of experience in diplomacy, Washington first chose William
Paterson. "The affairs of this country are in a violent paroxysm," Washington wrote in tendering Paterson the portfolio of the State Department.
Comparing the nation to a ship on a storm-tossed sea, Washington reminded Paterson that it was the duty of "its old and uniform friends to
assist in piloting the vessel in which we are all embarked between the
rocks of Scylla and Charybdis."[43]

To both Washington and Paterson, America's becoming embroiled in
the disputes of Europe seemed very likely, and both felt that the nation
needed help. But uncharacteristically, Paterson turned down this particular
call to duty. He was prepared to champion the cause of the administration
in his own way, but he wanted to avoid the center stage if at all possible.
He favored his place in the judiciary where controversy was usually

handled more soberly. What was more important, he knew practically nothing about foreign affairs. His decision to decline was a wise one.

Paterson did defend the Jay Treaty and attacked its critics, but he did so in purely political terms. The earliest of his Horatius essays, which began to appear in the Jersey newspapers in October 1795, relied on rhetoric and sarcasm to undermine the administration's detractors. To begin with, he accused most critics of the treaty of not having taken the trouble to read it, and he recommended that George Hopkins, the editor of the New Brunswick *Genius of Liberty,* publish the expunged Article 12 along with the proceedings of the Senate respecting it.[44] The most vituperative of the treaty's opponents were incensed that the president had ignored the public expressions of scores of town meetings against his signing the treaty. In response, a flood of Federalist defenders had taken to the newspapers challenging the right of the public to exert any influence at all over foreign policy, which, they said, the Constitution had expressly reserved for the president and the Senate. Paterson chose not to develop this particular argument, which was bound to excite even more clamor in the country. He turned instead to sarcasm. Although he granted to the people the unquestioned right "to assemble in town-meetings about politics, and to talk them over, and to argue pro and con, and to resolve and re-resolve upon them," they should reserve such meetings for those seasons of the year when the "scorching rays" of the sun did not beat too harshly on their heads and disorder their brains. During the dog days of summer, he pointed out, "in a rarefied, or thin state of the air, persons are apt to see strange sights, such as spectres, ghosts, hob-goblins, and the devil. . . . Indeed the brains of certain persons were miserably scorched, and almost burnt up, if we may judge by town-meeting speeches and resolutions" against the Jay Treaty.[45]

Paterson had never had much faith in the untutored judgment of the public at large. The storm over the Jay Treaty confirmed this belief and led him to worry more than ever before about the political parties which, in his view, threatened to destroy the stable republican system. Except for a few "choice spirits [himself among them, no doubt], who watch over the liberties and happiness of the people without fee or reward," he saw little real virtue among American politicians. The opposition party had been "rocked in the cradle of Jacobinism." Its followers could see nothing but bribery, corruption, and aristocracy stalking the face of the earth. "Genius of Robesspiere," he prayed contemptuously, "descend from thy blood-encircled throne, and with one stroke of thy guillotine smite the hideous monster dead." The one whose reputation had suffered most at the hand of these American Jacobins was John Jay himself: "Oh the sick

traitor—seize him, drown him, hang him, burn him, flay him alive."
Paterson went on to belittle the attacks that had been made on Jay. One
critic, no student of anatomy, said that Jay deserved to have his lips
"blistered to the bone" for having kissed the hand of the Queen of
England. Paterson answered that "kissing is a dangerous thing. An aristocratic kiss is the very devil; for lo! in about nine months after the kissing
business forth passt into the world that imp the treaty. No wonder," he
concluded, quoting from a Philadelphia critic of the treaty, that "town
meeting folks" should have been advised "to kick the damn'd thing to
hell."[46]

Paterson carried his criticism of America's Jacobins on through the
rest of his Horatius essays. Some men were "naturally turbulent and un-
ruly," he claimed, "nothing pleases them and everything disquiets and
offends." They are envious of men with talents and temperaments superior
to their own "and feel pain at the excellence, success, felicity, or exalted
station of others." Unable to think for themselves, they "attach themselves
to men at the head of a party" and "drive on furiously" to attack the
nation's leaders, often with "a brick-bat or a stone" as their only argument
against a "reasoning opponent."[47]

The Federalists argued that their opponents were being misled by
agents of foreign powers. Earlier in the decade, Paterson had chided
foreigners who came to America and meddled in political affairs. Now he
was more blunt, challenging them to return to Europe "and leave us in
quietude and peace."[48] But most of his animosity was reserved for "certain
writers" who were motivated by party passion, personal resentment, disappointed ambition, and foreign influence to mislead the people about
Washington and the Federalists.

> They represent our administration as being composed of designing,
> ambitious, and wicked men, hostile to republicanism, and leagued for
> its destruction. With matchless effrontery they assert, that the presi-
> dent and other officers of the executive department have intentionally
> violated the constitution, acted contrary to the law, usurped authority,
> and in short are peculators, tyrants, and perjured villains.

Rather, according to Paterson, it was the opposition that was hostile to
republicanism. It was certain, he believed, that the "torrent of invective"
against the administration "could not have proceeded from mere diversity
of sentiment with respect to political opinions," but must be the work of
"the virulent calumniator or insidious imposter" who always "merited
contempt."

We call ourselves Republicans, and glory in the name; let us then speak and act with decency, candor, and sacred regard to the truth, and thus verify the character. Persons who expect to gain popularity, or rise into office, or hunt others out, by misrepresentation, or falsity, slander or abuse, are unworthy members of society, and not fit for any appointment.[49]

As he suggested on another occasion, "party-men" were "violently opposed and desperately set against the very frame and constitution of the government, and of course against all men, and measures in its support."[50] The Alien and Sedition Acts were still many months away, but Paterson seemed already prepared to justify legal action against disruptive foreigners and opposition writers and publishers.

As the political crisis deepened, Paterson's duties on the circuit continued to be as laborious as ever. Although he escaped riding any circuit in the spring term of 1796, he was repaid by being assigned to the southern route in the fall. There were some compensations. The trip gave him the opportunity to look into business and real estate deals in Virginia and Georgia for some of his Jersey friends, but these could not have made up for the uncomfortable week's voyage from New York to Savannah and the almost constant danger of disease which, according to Paterson's letters home, had people in coastal Carolina cities dropping like flies. The unrelenting inconveniences of travel in the South were relieved somewhat by recommendations from friends about where along the road a decent inn could be found. Nothing, however, could make the long separation from his family any easier to bear.[51]

At home he was seeing to a new "plow and share" (probably for the tenant who still cultivated his Raritan farm), working ahead on the New Jersey laws, and remembering the saddlery repairs that were necessary before his next trip to Philadelphia. There was an unexpected windfall when Thomas Irwin, Paterson's brother-in-law who had not been heard of since he had fled to New Orleans seven years before, sent him some money on account. Irwin's letter reported that his son John had set himself up as a physician near New Orleans and was doing well, and there was the promise of more money to come. Irwin had a debt claim to 1,600 acres of land near Natchez that he was sure would soar in value now that the formalization of Pinkney's Treaty with Spain made the territory indisputably American. Soothing his conscience for having left Paterson to face his creditors before, he wrote: "You now have the best right to any advantage that fortune may turnup."[52]

It took a full two years for the climate to develop in which Paterson and the other Federalists would suspend their last ounce of bipartisan good judgment and threaten the political opposition with the intimidating power of the law. Washington's "Farewell Address," published in September 1796, and Jefferson's letter of the same year to Philip Mazzei testify to the heat of passion felt even then by American political leaders. Part of the increase in tension thereafter was due to the internal bickerings among the Federalists, which nearly cost John Adams the presidency in 1796 and left Thomas Jefferson as the vice president. But there was still cause for hope by those who envisioned an end to party strife. In March 1797, for example, Paterson wrote to Iredell with hopes that Adams's and Jefferson's choice of the same boarding house was a sign of "conciliation and healing."[53]

Although the tensions continued both inside and out of the Federalist ranks, the prime movers of American popular opinion were Talleyrand and the French Directory. Washington had recalled James Monroe as minister to France because of his overtly pro-French position, which threatened to undermine the neutral policy the government was trying to follow. When his successor, Charles Cotesworth Pinkney, was refused at Paris and ordered to leave the country, the French made it clear that they would not receive another American minister until amends had been made for the signing of the Jay Treaty with England. Faced with a situation similar to the one between America and Britain in 1794 which had prompted Jay's mission, President Adams now chose a delegation to go to Paris and negotiate a solution to the problems. The French, however, were less cooperative than the British had been during Jay's mission three years earlier. The American plenipotentiaries were shocked at the demand for a $250,000 bribe before Talleyrand would even speak to them. When they returned and accounts of their treatment were made public, the three Frenchmen who had delivered the insulting demands—Messieurs X, Y, and Z—did more to increase the popularity of the Federalists at the expense of the pro-French Jeffersonian Republicans than any other argument the Federalists had advanced.[54]

As the nation prepared for what seemed like inevitable war with France, the Federalists were riding high. In the patriotic frenzy that overtook the country in the summer of 1798, laws were easily passed that promised to quiet the opposition by threatening troublesome aliens (some of the least respectful Republican newspaper editors were recent emigrants from Europe) and specifying punishments for sedition, which up till that time had been indictable only under common law.[55] One unique aspect of the new law, which went into effect immediately on July 14, was that for the first time it permitted the truth of the supposedly seditious statement to stand as a defense.[56] Still, the Alien and Sedition Acts served as a rallying point for the movement to silence the opponents of the Federalist regime.

Amid all this political good fortune, however, some Federalists could see the seeds of their eventual fall. Richard Buel has recently suggested that the Federalists can best be understood as representatives of a threatened elite. Unlike the Jeffersonians, whom he describes as confident in their own elite status and therefore able to follow the tenets of their republican ideology to its logical democratic conclusions, many Federalists naturally tended to feel insecure about their socioeconomic position and to become overprotective of their political power.[57] Such feelings could only be intensified by the political situation in which their popularity depended completely on hostility toward the French. They were constantly reminded, moreover, that Adams had beaten Jefferson for the presidency by only three votes.

Men such as Paterson, who had not been born to status and power, were more likely than most to harbor such feelings of insecurity. Only a few years before Paterson had been complaining that his brothers' financial failures threatened to put him in the poorhouse, and at the beginning of 1798 he wrote philosophically to his daughter hoping that she would not have to suffer "the cares, anxieties, and misfortunes" that had befallen him. Even the bodily strength he had relied on to get him through the physical exertions of his office seemed to be less sure. Although his letters to his wife had always revealed him as something of a complainer and hypochondriac, the tone seemed more serious now. "I am fast declining into the veil [vale] of life," he told Cornelia. "Every new year warns me of my decay, and that time to me will soon be no more."[58]

As he thought of his personal energy ebbing away, Paterson was more worried than ever about the future of his country. In a speech on the Fourth of July, 1798, he warned of the incipient decline of the United States unless the state of things changed very quickly. His remarks began with the same phrases he had used to open his "Address on the Rise and Decline of Nations" some twenty-five years before, and he repeated many of the ideas on government and society he had expounded in newspaper essays and public addresses since, but his concentration now was on the threat posed by France. It was not the military threat that upset him so much as the moral and ideological challenges that Jacobin revolutionaries in France and America were posing to the continued existence of American society.[59] He represented opposition party leaders in the United States as opportunists, who deluded, misrepresented, and deceived the people and who, given the chance, would destroy free government and become "despot[s] of the first magnitude." The way in which devoted Jeffersonians

still seemed attached to the French cause alarmed Paterson all the more
and dashed all the hopes he had for a diminution of parties. France was
"a monster in ambition, in despotism, in crime," which aspired after

> universal dominion, and aims to subvert all institutions civil and
> religious. She outvandalizes the Vandals, and threatens to demoralize
> and ensavage the world. God of Heaven! Thou only knowest what
> atrocities and bloodshed, what licentiousness and anarchy will ensue,
> before order can be restored, and new governments erected on the
> ruins of the old. When wilt thou say to the destroying angel, cease;
> it is enough.

But still, some Americans continued to be loyal in support of the "terrible
republic." In the same terms he had used years before to criticize the
British aristocracy, he charged that now it was the Jeffersonians who were
corrupted by luxury and immorality.

> What rapid progress have luxury and illuminated philosophy made
> in America? We tread close upon the heels of our brethren in Eur-
> ope. We imitate them in dress, in manners, in equipage, in senti-
> ments, in morals, in principles. Paine's *Age of Reason* is the Bible of
> many; Rousseau and Voltaire their apostles; the French Directory
> their guide, France their adopted and better country. Infatuated
> Americans, why renounce your country, your religion, and your God.
> Oh shame, where is thy blush? Is this the way to continue inde-
> pendent, and to render the 4th of July immortal in memory and
> song?

France threatened to "beguile and destroy the United States," and the
opponents of the Federalists were playing right into their hands. There was
no question in Paterson's mind: The nation stood on the brink of disaster.
If America did not reassert her national dignity in domestic as well as
diplomatic affairs, she was doomed to lose her independence. If the
American people did not join together in defense of that self-government
and self-respect that were the "life blood of the body politic," then,
Paterson summed up his speech, "ye deserve, yes, ye deserve to be slaves."[60]
    Under different circumstances, Paterson's political opinions on the crisis
of 1798 might have been restricted to his Fourth of July oration and a
few newspaper essays, but fate threw him into the fray when he drew
the eastern circuit for the fall of 1798. One of his first stops was at
Albany, New York, where he spent several days visiting the local notables

before setting out on the three-day trip to Rutland, Vermont.[61] There, early in October, Justice Paterson came face to face with the Jacobin menace in the person of Congressman Matthew Lyon.

Since the previous year, when Lyon had appeared in Congress for the first time representing western Vermont, he had been the object of all the anti-Republican sentiment the Federalists could mount. Deprecating comments about his Irish birth and his indenture as a servant when he arrived in America almost forty years before were injury enough, but when Roger Griswold, the leading Federalist from Connecticut, belittled Lyon's revolutionary war record in the House chamber, the Vermonter spat in his face. A few days later, Griswold tried to even the score by attacking Lyon with a cane as he sat at his desk in the House; they wrestled each other to the floor and had to be pulled apart by their shocked colleagues. Thereafter, whatever chance there had been of Lyon's outliving the taunts of the Federalists was lost. "The spitting beast," as they called him, knew that his enemies in Congress were out to get him. When the Alien and Sedition Acts were passed over his objection and that of other outspoken Republicans, Lyon observed that they were intended to silence the opposition in Congress and predicted that he would probably be singled out first.[62] So it happened that, when he returned to Vermont to run for reelection in the fall of 1798, Lyon became the first of fourteen critics of the administration to be indicted for violating the Sedition Act.[63]

Paterson's charge to the Rutland grand jury directed its attention to the new sedition law, which he read in its entirety. As Paterson put it, "false scandalous and malicious writings" had become so "frequent, dangerous, and alarming" that Congress had been forced to take action. The very existence of the republic was at stake, he explained: "No government, indeed, can long subsist, where offenders of this kind are suffered to spread their poison with impunity." He concentrated on the encouragement that antigovernment publications gave to "the rude and ill-informed part of the community, who delight in irregularity, sedition, and licentiousness as symptoms of freedom." Licentiousness, he concluded, was the "bane of republics, and more to be dreaded than hosts of foreign foes." Paterson's evident implication was that spoken and printed expressions of opposition were just one step away from armed rebellion. "They tend to anarchy, and anarchy always terminates in despotism." He closed with a prayer that the jurors would discharge their duties "with diligence, fidelity, and honest zeal." Two days later, they indicted Lyon for sedition.[64]

At three different points in the indictment, Lyon was referred to as a depraved man with a "wicked and diabolical disposition." There can be no doubt that Paterson was convinced of this and his actions in the courtroom reflected his feelings. He granted Lyon a two-day delay to allow his attorneys to arrive, but when neither of them could come, the congressman decided to act as his own lawyer, and the trial began. It was over the same day. Accounts of the case are incomplete, but it does appear that Lyon had at least some justification for his later complaints that he had been treated unfairly. In the choice of the jury, for example, Paterson allowed Lyon and the prosecution each to displace one juror for cause, but, since the defendant could produce no definite proof of bias on the part of other jurors, they were allowed to remain. As Lyon explained it later, his ignorance of courtroom procedure put him at a serious disadvantage. When he tried to introduce a plea that the Sedition Act was unconstitutional, Paterson refused to accept it and turned the case over to the prosecutor who presented evidence to support the indictment. Then, according to Lyon's account, as soon as the prosecutor had finished, Paterson arose to begin his charge to the jury. The defendant had to interrupt him to ask why his side of the case could not be heard, at which point Paterson "politely sat down" and invited Lyon to proceed.[65]

Lyon's three-pronged defense was to no avail. He argued, first, that the Sedition Act was unconstitutional; second, that the publication involved, a letter of his that had been published in a Vermont newspaper, was innocent and had no criminal intent; and, third, that what he had said in his letter was true. To support the validity of his comments on the "ridiculous pomp, foolish adulation, and selfish avarice" of President Adams, Lyon turned to question Justice Paterson: Had he not "dined with the president and observed his ridiculous pomp and parade?" Paterson admitted dining at the president's house from time to time, but far from pomp and parade, he had observed "a great deal of plainness and simplicity there." Lyon asked if there were not more "pomp and servants" at the Adamses than at the tavern in Rutland where he was lodged, but to this Paterson made no reply. After the prosecutor and Lyon had each summed up their argu ments, Paterson instructed the jury in tones that Paterson's hometown paper reported as "cool, candid, and perspicuous," but that the defendant later called "studiedly and pointedly severe."[66]

Paterson's charge to the Lyon jury opened with the injunction that the question of constitutionality was not for them to decide. Accounts agree that he was careful to remind the jury that, "if they leaned any way, it ought to be in favor of the defendant." But there were other areas in which the instructions seem to have been lacking. In terms of criminal intent, the jurors would have to consider, as Paterson put it, "whether language such as here complained of could have been uttered with any other intent than that of making odious or contemptible the president and government." Clearly he thought it impossible for such statements to be anything but seditious. He enjoined them not to allow "the political rank of the defendant" to deter them from bringing in a verdict of guilty if the evidence warranted one, but he failed to remind them that, if they believed the allegedly seditious statement to be true, they were free to acquit the defendant.[67] In contrast, Justice Chase had been careful to make this point in the even more controversial Callendar trial.[68] The effect of Paterson's charge was to render Lyon's defense completely ineffective. Within an hour, the jury found him guilty.

In pronouncing sentence against the congressman, Paterson again seized the opportunity to make a political argument. He instructed Lyon that he had failed in the responsibilities of his station. As an elected representative of the people, he should have known better than to have so irresponsibly spoken out against the people's government. Before fixing the penalty, Paterson listened to Lyon's pleas of financial distress, but paid no real attention. The fine he demanded was $1,000, and to Lyon's surprise Paterson also sent him to jail for four months.[69]

Paterson never seemed able to shake the reputation that came with his decision in the Lyon case. Several years later, critics of his handling of the case were still writing to him to debate the legal technicalities,[70] and in 1800 he was forced to face a sequel in the Haswell case. In his Bennington (Vermont) newspaper, Anthony Haswell had published an advertisement for a lottery set up to help pay Lyon's fine. The advertisement contained disparaging comments about the character of the federal marshal who was supervising Lyon's imprisonment. The second count in the indictment against Haswell concerned a paragraph he had reprinted from the Philadelphia *Aurora*. It charged that the Adams administration offered federal appointments to former Tories "who had fought against our independence, who had shared in the desolation of our homes, and the abuse of our wives and daughters." The trial of the case had been delayed from the previous fall, and by late April 1800, when Justice Paterson arrived in Windsor to preside over the next circuit session, Haswell and his friends had been able to formulate a defense based on the truth of his supposedly seditious statements.[71]

Addressing the court, Haswell maintained that the intent of the advertisement had not been seditious. They had only sought to criticize the actions of the marshal, not the authority of the government he represented. Haswell also produced certified copies of correspondence between General William Darke of the Virginia militia and Secretary of War James McHenry as evidence that "prominent old tories" did have the confidence of the administration. But, in his charge to the jury, Paterson effectively undermined Haswell's defense as he had Lyon's two years before. As the defendant subsequently recalled, Paterson argued that it was the "bad tendency" of the words, rather than the bad intent of the author, that had to be considered, and for truth to be accepted as a defense, it would have had to be proved that the same former Tory who had been trusted by the Adams administration had personally taken part in specific acts of rape and pillage during the revolutionary war. Since Haswell had not even attempted to prove this, there was nothing for the jury to do but find him guilty, which they did. Then Paterson fined him $200 and sentenced him to two months in jail.[72] Unlike those found guilty of treason in his court, Lyon and Haswell were sentenced only to pay fines and serve short prison terms. But in his handling of these cases, Paterson had furthered his association with the worst examples of the politically biased Federalist judiciary.[73]

The experience of the Alien and Sedition Acts offers unique evidence that the Federalists regarded themselves as a threatened elite. The conviction of Luther Baldwin, a New Jersey Republican, for sedition is an obvious case of overreaction. Baldwin had wished out loud that President Adams had had the seat of his pants warmed by the honor guards' salute that had been fired for him as he passed through Newark in the fall of 1798. Historians have usually treated Baldwin's case as a comic footnote to the history of the era, but it does suggest that some of the Federalist supporters of the law must have felt an abnormal degree of hypersensitivity to criticism.[74] When an offhand joke can become the target for serious prosecution, it is easier to see the Federalists as insecure men trying desperately to preserve their threatened status. However, if the framers of the law hoped it would intimidate the opposition, they were soon disappointed. Baldwin's case provided a field day for Republican editors, who treated him as the hapless victim of a flagrant Federalist conspiracy to wrest the freedom of speech from every ordinary American.[75] All their efforts to enforce the act had, eventually, the same result. Especially after the war fever waned, the crisis measures of 1798 made the Federalists appear all the more elitist and undemocratic and provided a convenient rallying point for Republican opposition.

Paterson's conceptions of morality, society, and politics were the same as they had been almost thirty years before when he was defending his colleagues at the bar from the licentious multitude and criticizing the corrupt British party men whom he blamed for much of England's moral decline. He realized that American politics were by nature more open to differences of opinion, but Paterson was not alone in the belief that opposing parties were destructive to the public interest—even some of the leading Republicans held this view.[76] Paterson had not become more conservative; America had simply passed him by and was growing politically in a way that he could not. There were some compromises he could make—on the revision of New Jersey's laws, for example, where he had clearly mellowed toward the people's distrust of lawyers. But, on the larger political issues, he was too much a man of the old order to be completely converted into the new.

In an earlier day, Paterson's motives might have been influenced by personal ambitions. Now he was thinking of nothing but the nation's future. As in an earlier period of patriotic fervor, however, his judgment gave way to his passionate convictions about stable government and social institutions. His concern for the stability of the young republic led him to apply his deepest beliefs about the nature of men and of political systems to his judicial activities, and men such as Philip Vigol, John Mitchell, Matthew Lyon, and Anthony Haswell seem to have suffered unjustly because of it.

During the Federalist era, and particularly in times of perceived crisis such as 1798, the federal judiciary became politicized. Judges like Paterson, who had been appointed as much for their political opinions as their legal knowledge, were bound to reflect this tendency. His position in the trials of the Whiskey Rebels and the Vermont sedition cases was and is indefensible. It provides a clear example of the ways in which the federal judiciary in the 1790s was deeply compromised by political bias. This is surprising in Paterson's case when we remember the firm stand he took in defense of an independent judiciary for New Jersey. His bias can only be understood in the context of his long-held conservative political and social ideas. Unlike some others whom Carl Prince has identified as tainted "by relatively crass political concerns," Paterson's prejudices were the result of deep convictions and a tendency to lose control of his usually sound judgment when he saw these beliefs openly threatened.[77] Had something happened in 1799 to cut short Paterson's public career, these unfortunate episodes might have completely ruined his historical reputation. As it was, however, he still had a few years to redeem himself and enhance his overall contribution to the new nation.

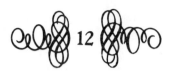

The Nation and the Court

At one time or another Paterson's judicial duties carried him to every one of the original states. His travels gave him a first-hand perspective on the great diversity in American life. When he wrote home from Portsmouth or Savannah, there was always something interesting to report, whether it concerned the late thaw that delayed the spring vegetation in New England or the November rain that was needed before Carolina farmers could plow and plant their winter grain. He was fascinated by the beautiful planned city of Savannah and compiled careful notes on the style of the buildings and the physical terrain. He liked Charleston more for its hospitality and polite society, which saw to it that political difference "never interrupts their intercourse, or disturbs their social happiness," and he also made observations about its commercial prospects, its recent smallpox epidemic, and the failure of the town fathers to require brick or stone construction as a protection against fire. But what impressed him most was the new capital city rising on the banks of the Potomac. He described for his wife the scene on populous Jersey Street, which, "for the elegance of its buildings and the beauty of its prospect is, by way of distinction, called the Avenue" and told her how he had commented to President Adams that the imposing White House ("built for perpetuity") symbolized the stability of the Constitution.[1]

Circuit riding took him to interesting places where he met interesting people, but it required tremendous energy and involved countless hours of legal study and paperwork. The Constitution was still young, and the powers of the new government were being tested everywhere. Legend has it that, while presiding over a circuit court at Richmond, Virginia, Paterson was confronted by a petty local bureaucrat who refused to allow the statehouse bell to be rung for the opening of court. Rather than complain to the official's superior, Justice Paterson ordered the federal marshal "to procure a tin horn and have it blown at the proper times." When the governor of Virginia heard of the incident, he immediately ordered that the marshal be given control of the bell, but it was too late. Paterson replied with thanks, explaining that he had "got along very well with his horn, and continued to have it blown as long as court sat."[2] Despite the obvious opportunity for political critics to turn a phrase, there is no record of anyone ever referring to Paterson as the "tin horn Justice."

Although the story does have humorous overtones, it also illustrates one of Paterson's most serious concerns. By acting independently and refusing to submit the problem to state authority, Paterson, as a federal judge, was maintaining the supremacy of his court and the Constitution it represented over any limitation by a subordinate power.

Paterson's defense of the Constitution as the supreme law of the land can be traced through his judicial career with respect to two basic principles: first, national supremacy over state governments (where federal matters were concerned), and, second, the right of the judiciary to review acts of Congress and be the final judge of their constitutionality. He participated in some of the most influential decisions of the time, each of which contributed in its own way to the stability of the Constitution and to the security of the basic elements of republicanism that Paterson had worked to preserve since the outbreak of the Revolution. During his later years on the Court, as Paterson's health and vigor waned, so did his steadfast Federalism. After the election of 1800, and especially during the arguments over the repeal of the Judiciary Act of 1801, Paterson proved himself a statesman, rather than a partisan, by leading his colleagues in accepting the Jeffersonians in power and avoiding an unnecessary constitutional confrontation.

Since the days of the Confederation, Paterson had favored a national government strong enough to place limits on irresponsible state legislatures. The supremacy clause included in the Constitution had originally been proposed as a part of Paterson's New Jersey Plan. When it came to establishing the federal judiciary and setting straight the nation's financial system, Senator Paterson viewed the Constitution with the same broad interpretation that was soon associated with the Federalists. By the time he took his seat on the bench, the Supreme Court had become the chief watchdog over the activities of the states. In its decisions regarding the actions of the various state governments, the judiciary emerged as the most consistent defender of national supremacy.

The most frequently cited example of the Federalist-controlled Supreme Court's restriction of a state's sovereignty came just a few weeks before Paterson's appointment. As mentioned in the previous chapter, the shock wave that accompanied the decision in the case of *Chisolm* v. *Georgia* created one of the Court's first real controversies. A constitutional amendment, the first since the Bill of Rights, had to be brought about to protect states from being sued by nonresidents in the federal courts.[3] Paterson's decisions from the bench were not so famous (or infamous) as this, but they do illustrate many of his ideas and chart the direction in which he was helping the Court to move. In the case of *Talbot* v. *Jansen,* for example, Paterson argued that a state law concerning expatriation or renunciation of state citizenship could not affect an individual's citizenship in the United States. As he put it, "allegiance to a particular state is one thing; allegiance to the United States is another. . . . The sovereignties are different." This formula for sharing the authority between state and federal governments was the most distinctive element in the American Constitution. "We have sovereignties moving within a sovereignty," he went on to explain, and such a new and untried system "requires a penetrating eye fully to explore, and steady and masterly hands to keep [it] in unison and order."[4] Paterson's most important decisions that helped to define the issues in which national authority had to prevail over that of the states were *Penhallow v. Doane's Administrators* and *Ware* v. *Hylton.*

In the first of these, Paterson expounded a nationalist interpretation of the revolutionary and Confederation periods. The question before the Court dated back to the revolutionary war, when a New Hampshire court had ordered the forfeiture of a vessel captured as a prize only to have the case appealed to the Continental Congress. The case was referred to a congressional committee and later to a court of appeals set up by the Congress (and authorized in Article 9 of the Articles of Confederation), which reversed the decision of the state court and ordered that the property be restored to its original owners. But the decree was never enforced. After 1789, when the new federal courts were set up, application was made to the district and the circuit courts (which upheld the preceding decision), and eventually to the Supreme Court of the United States, which heard the case in the February term of 1795.

In his long and detailed opinion, Paterson defended the jurisdiction of the Continental Congress as representing the "supreme will" of the American people.

> The powers of Congress were revolutionary in nature, arising out of events, adequate to every national emergency, and co-extensive with the object to be attained. Congress was the general, supreme, and controlling council of the nation, the centre of the union, the centre of force, and the sun of the political system.

To counter New Hampshire's contention that her state court could decide prize cases, Paterson pointed out that such questions were incidental to the "rights and powers of war and peace" that had been concentrated in the Continental Congress with the acquiescence and approval of the people: "The states individually, did not, and, with safety, could not exercise" such authority, for, "in such case, there would have been as many supreme wills as there were states, and as many wars as there were wills." Instead,

> the danger being imminent, and common, it became necessary for the people or colonies to coalesce and act in concert, in order to divert, or break, the violence of the gathering storm; they accordingly grew into union, and formed one great political body, of which Congress was the directing principle and soul. As to war and peace, and their necessary incidents, Congress by the unanimous voice of the people, exercised exclusive jurisdiction, and stood, like Jove, amidst the deities of old, paramount and supreme.

As Julius Goebel has observed, Paterson "was evidently transported by his own rhetoric."[5]

Getting back to the specifics of the case, Paterson pointed out that during the Revolution, despite the absence of a written constitution granting the central government sole power over foreign affairs, other nations dealt with Congress as the sovereign, and he reminded the representatives of New Hampshire that their state had accepted this arrangement all during the war.

> As long as she [New Hampshire] continued to be one of the federal states, it must have been on equal terms. If she would not submit

to the exercise of the act of sovereignty contended for by Congress, and the other states, she should have withdrawn herself from the confederacy.

Paterson's words were intentionally harsh, and they had a predictable effect. The Supreme Court's decision to uphold the circuit decision and overrule the court of New Hampshire met with fiery opposition. The state legislature remonstrated against "a violation of state independence and an unwarrantable encroachment in the courts of the United States."[6]

In the other major case, *Ware* v. *Hylton,* Paterson and his fellow justices reaffirmed the status of treaties as the "supreme law of the land," by deciding a case referred to them by the circuit court for the State of Virginia and requiring that the debt provisions of the Treaty of 1783 with Great Britain be enforced to the letter. The result was to declare invalid a Virginia law that had allowed debtors to pay monies owed to British creditors into the state's loan office during the war and to receive certificates that would absolve them from further responsibility for the debt. Virginia was prepared to settle accounts with the original creditors in the name of such certificate holders, but only under the provisions of a subsequent state law that allowed for payment of state obligations at the depreciated value of the currency originally exchanged or contracted for. The effect would have been to cause a serious loss to those Englishmen whose debtors had made payments into the loan office, while the other English creditors could still sue for the entire amount of their original debt. Paterson's opinion concentrated on interpreting the relevant article of the treaty, which he found to be unequivocal in its intent to "comprehend all creditors, and all debtors" equally. He thought it "incredible" to presume that "the creditors, whose debtors paid into the loan office, be in a worse situation than the creditors whose debtors did not thus pay." He went on, in terms that Hamilton and Federalist creditors would have approved of, to argue for the importance of financial integrity.

> The confidence, both of an individual and national nature, on which the contracts were founded, ought to be preserved inviolate. Is not this the language of honesty and honor? Does not the sentiment correspond with the principles of justice, and the dictates of the moral sense? In short, is it not the result of right reason and natural equity?[7]

The case had given Paterson the opportunity to wax eloquent on one of his oldest and most favorite themes—the moral responsibility of the borrower to hold his contract as a sacred trust—but this was secondary to the central issue. No matter what the treaty had provided, according to Paterson, its provisions by their very nature superseded the acts of a state legislature: In such matters the national government was supreme.

The second basic issue in Paterson's defense of the Constitution was the Supreme Court's right to declare acts of Congress unconstitutional. Here the questions were more complex. That the Court had such authority over state laws was clearly implied in the Constitution and specifically set down in Article 25 of the Judiciary Act of 1789. But the Court's authority over acts of Congress was less clear. The question had been debated in the Philadelphia convention, but no direct statement on such jurisdiction was included in the Constitution, and some argued that to give the judiciary such power was to give it legislative authority and to make it superior to the Congress, thereby upsetting the separation of powers. Recognition of judicial review of federal legislation as a regular and accepted process would wait until the Dred Scott decision of 1857, but the crucial foundations on which it was built were laid while Paterson sat on the Court.[8]

Paterson's single most memorable case, the one for which he was best known in his own lifetime, was directly related to the principle of judicial review and anticipated by eight years the famous case of *Marbury* v. *Madison*. The case was *Van Horne's Lessee* v. *Dorrance,* and it came up in the Pennsylvania circuit in the spring term of 1795—the same session during which the Whiskey Rebels were tried. Although the case involved Paterson's disallowance of a state law as unconstitutional and thus did not amount to a constitutional innovation, the language in which he couched his opinion (included in his charge to the jury) clearly enunciated the principle of judicial review of federal as well as state legislation. There were obvious political overtones to the case, which pitted the interests of land speculators against the claims of plain people who for decades had cultivated and improved their farms. But Paterson avoided making any political comments and phrased his opinion in very formal legal terms. It was thought to be such a significant argument in favor of the sanctity of the Constitution and the authority of the judiciary that it was printed as a pamphlet and widely circulated.[9]

At the heart of the matter were the long-contested claims of Connecticut settlers in Pennsylvania's Wyoming Valley and the validity of a Pennsylvania statute that bore upon their claims. The lawyers had argued the issues for fifteen days before Paterson addressed the jury, but he was quickly able to draw their attention to the pertinent point in question. The title of the plaintiff (the speculators or Van Horne's lessee) could be traced all the way back to a grant from the Penn family. It was "clearly deduced and legally correct," while the claim of the defendant (one of the Connecticut claimants named Dorrance) was most questionable. After summarily rejecting the defendant's claim to title from Connecticut and from the Indians, Paterson concentrated on the 1787 Pennsylvania statute that had been meant to confirm the Connecticut claimants on their lands; he found the law to be unconstitutional.

To illustrate the principle, Paterson contrasted the British system, in which there is no written constitution and the "power of parliament is absolute and transcendant," with America, where every state's constitution is "reduced to written exactitude and precision." Then he proceeded to deliver a lecture on the nature of constitutional government.

> What is a constitution? It is the form of government, delineated by the mighty hand of the people, in which certain first principles of [or?] fundamental laws are established. The constitution is certain and fixed; it contains the permanent will of the people, and is the supreme law of the land; it is paramount to the power of the legislature, and can be revoked or altered only by the authority that made it. . . .
>
> What are legislatures? Creatures of the constitution; they owe their existence to the constitution; they derive their powers from the constitution; It is their commission; and, therefore, all their acts must be conformable to it, or else they will be void. The constitution is the work or will of people themselves, in their original, sovereign, and unlimited capacity. Law is the work or will of the legislature in their derivative or subordinate capacity. The one is the work of the Creator and the other of the creature. The constitution fixes the limits of legislative activity and prescribes the orbit within which it must move. In short, gentlemen, the constitution is the sun of the political system, around which all legislative, executive, and judicial bodies must revolve. Whatever may be the case in other countries, yet in this, there can be no doubt, that every act of the legislature, repugnant to the constitution, is absolutely void.

For examples, Paterson went to the Pennsylvania constitution and pointed to its guarantees of religious liberty and election by ballot. If the state legislature passed an act contrary to one of these expressly stated constitutional provisions, Paterson claimed that it would be void.

> The constitution of a state is stable and permanent, not to be worked upon by the temper of the times, nor to rise and fall with

the tide of events: notwithstanding the competition of opposing interests, and the violence of contending parties, it remains firm and immovable, as a mountain amidst the strife of storms, or a rock in the ocean amidst the raging of waves. I take it to be a clear position; that if a legislative act oppugns a constitutional principle the former must give way, and be rejected on the score of repugnance. I hold it to be a position equally clear and sound, that, in such a case, it will be the duty of the court to adhere to the constitution, and to declare the act null and void. The constitution is the basis of legislative authority; it lies at the foundation of all law, and is a rule and commission by which both legislators and judges are to proceed. It is an important principle, which in the discussion of questions of the present kind, ought never to be lost sight of, that the judiciary in this country is not a subordinate, but co-ordinate branch of the government.

Unlike England, then, where Parliament is supreme, the fundamental nature of the Constitution allows the judiciary and the executive branches of the American government to be the equals of the legislature.[10]

Paterson's unequivocal justification of judicial authority was convincing, but the direct legal impact of his decision was not so significant. After all, it was only a state law being set aside, and this had been done before.[11] A few years later, the government of Pennsylvania arranged to indemnify the speculators and assured the settlers the continued possession of their lands that Paterson's decision had put into doubt. Pennsylvania Federalists had been pleased with the decision, but Connecticut men of every political stripe had been incensed.[12]

The 1796 case of *Hylton* v. *The United States* was a more direct precedent for judicial review of federal laws. In this first example of what can be called a test case, Daniel Hylton challenged the constitutionality of the federal tax on carriages before the Supreme Court. The Court did assume responsibility for determining the constitutionality of the tax, but Paterson and the other justices were unanimous in supporting the law.[13] It would be another seven years before Chief Justice Marshall formally established the authority of the Court by finding an act of Congress unconstitutional for the first time. In the meanwhile, however, Paterson's opinion in *Van Horne's Lessee* v. *Dorrance* stood as the fullest theoretical expression of the supremacy of the Constitution and the authority of the Court.

For Paterson, upholding the sanctity of the Constitution became the duty of the judiciary because legislators could not always be trusted to do so. He had complained of this problem in New Jersey politics for years, and he had spoken of it in his decision for Van Horne's lessee.

> Shame to American legislation! That in England, a limited monarchy, where there is no written constitution, where the parliament is omnipotent, and can mould the constitution at pleasure, a more sacred regard should have been paid to property, than in America, surrounded as we are with a blaze of political illumination; where the legislatures are limited; where we have republican governments, and written constitutions, by which the protection and enjoyment of property are rendered inviolable.[14]

But, as the Republicans saw it, the shame was less over property rights and more over laws like the Alien and Sedition Acts, and the responsibility was to be shared by the Federalist Congress and the Supreme Court justices who so vigorously enforced them. In their partisan charges to grand juries and in the sentences meted out to Republican editors, judges like Paterson had clearly allowed their political opinions to influence what should have been impartial judgments. Many Republicans opposed the Federalists' position that the Supreme Court enjoyed final authority to interpret the Constitution and were incensed by statements such as Paterson's (in his charge to the jury in the Lyon case) to the effect that questions of constitutionality were for the judges alone to decide. Federalist judges also upset Republicans by their incorporation of English common law into federal court procedure; to the opposition it appeared an arbitrary and gratuitous expansion of power over matters on which Congress had not even seen fit to legislate.[15]

All these issues came to a head in the election of 1800 and its aftermath. The political passions that had ignited in the crisis of 1798 and had grown to an inferno as the presidential election neared were blazing in Paterson's New Jersey. What had begun as a defense of Federalist measures such as the Alien and Sedition Acts against Jacobins "in the habit of venting their spleen against the government"[16] became a vicious mud-slinging campaign against Jefferson's candidacy. The *Newark Gazette* tried to dramatize the decision for the legislators who would choose New Jersey's presidential electors by stating "the Grand Question" as they saw it: "Shall I continue in allegiance to God—and a Religious President; or impiously declare for Jefferson—And No God?" The Trenton *Federalist* went so far as to suggest that, if elected, Jefferson would carry out a "division of property." The story was based on a barroom conversation in which a Salem, New Jersey, Republican was supposed to have argued for Jefferson's election to give himself a "chance at success." When asked whether this meant preventing a richer man from "enjoying the fruits" of his own "honest industry," the Republican answered "Yes" and explained that he was "laboring from day to day at hard work, while many a man is rolling in great wealth and splendor." Finally the "unwary Jacobin" was said to have let down his guard and admitted that he wanted to share in the property of his richer acquaintance because he had "got too much."[17]

No one could doubt where Paterson stood. The local papers had proudly trumpeted the news of his stand at the Lyon trial, and when the Masonic lodge was attacked by the Republicans in 1800 as a secret organization in league with the Federalists, Paterson's membership in the Masons was used as part of their defense.[18] In 1798 and again in 1800, a series of essays appeared (in the *Guardian* and *Federalist,* respectively) over the same pseudonym that Paterson had employed a few years before. Although Paterson's authorship cannot be definitely established, the pro-Federalist and anti-Jeffersonian sentiments expressed therein were identical with his own.[19]

The Federalist campaign, however, achieved only limited results. The October elections sent a Republican delegation to Congress, but the Federalists were still in control of the state legislature. This assured that all seven of the state's electoral votes would go to Adams, but New Jersey's support was not enough to stem the Republican tide. Thanks in part to Hamilton, who had publicly demeaned the president and accentuated the differences among the Federalists, Thomas Jefferson and Aaron Burr each received 73 electoral votes to defeat Adams with 65 and C. C. Pinkney with 64.[20]

The 1800 campaign had been marked by lies and vicious rumors on both sides, and afterwards some Federalist leaders were unwilling to accept the reality of their defeat. It seemed that their worst fears about Jacobinism rising in America were coming true. While some of the Federalists in Congress schemed to take advantage of the electoral deadlock and have Burr chosen over Jefferson, they all joined in an effort to strengthen the judiciary as a bulwark against the Republicans in power. As Paterson had looked about in the 1780s for a way to limit the powers of the popular legislature, the Federalists now sought to build a powerful stronghold against the expected arbitrary decisions of a Republican president and Congress. The judiciary suited them perfectly because of their previous pronouncements on the Court as the final arbiter of constitutionality and also because the life tenure of judges made its Federalist appointees safe from removal by the opposition. Although the election of

Jefferson over Burr was accomplished in March 1801, through the efforts of James A. Bayard, a staunch Federalist from Delaware who had decided that the stability of the government took precedence over the partisan intrigues of some of his colleagues, the struggle that the Federalists conducted by means of the federal court was to continue for another two years. The overriding question during this critical time was whether most Federalists could—like Bayard—set aside their vehement opposition and accept the transition of authority from Adams to Jefferson with the magnanimity that the best interests of the republic required.[21] For the following twenty-four months, the answer seemed to be a resounding *no,* as the Supreme Court provided the fuel for continuing confrontation.

The lame duck Federalists first had to decide on the appointment of a new chief justice. Adams's choosing Oliver Ellsworth as his trusted personal envoy to France in 1799 had served as final proof to Republicans that the federal bench had become "simply an annex to the Federalist Party."[22] In October 1800, Ellsworth wrote from Europe that he was too ill to make the crossing before winter and submitted his resignation as chief justice. Most of the Federalists in Congress thought of William Paterson as the logical successor because of his knowledge and experience, his seniority on the bench, and his steadfast application of the Federalist philosophy in his judicial decisions. But by this time the results of the election were clear, and the dissension caused by the Hamiltonian wing of the party had brought Adams's relations with the rest of the Federalists to an absolute low point. Apparently without consulting with any of them, the president first offered the office to John Jay. After procrastinating for a time, Jay refused the appointment and Adams turned instead to his loyal secretary of state, John Marshall. Congress was incensed that Paterson had been passed over. Expressing the feelings of his Federalist colleagues, Congressman Jonathan Dayton wrote to Paterson "with grief, astonishment, and almost indignation" to tell him the news. "The eyes of all parties had been turned upon you whose pretensions [Adams] knew were, in every respect the best," Dayton continued, and he suggested a plan whereby the Senate might insist that Paterson be given the chief justiceship, and Marshall offered a seat as an associate justice.[23] Paterson's supporters managed to stall the confirmation for a full week while negotiations were carried out on his behalf, but finally they gave in and approved Marshall's appointment. As Dayton explained to Paterson,

> we thought it adviseable to confirm Mr. Marshall, lest another not
> so well qualified, and most disgusting to the Bench, should be sub-
> stituted, and because it appeared that this gentleman was not privy

to his own nomination, but had previously exerted his influence with the President on your behalf.[24]

Although few Federalists in Congress agreed with it at first, there was reason for Marshall's preferment. Besides his loyal service as secretary of state at a time when the president could have had little faith in the rest of his cabinet, Marshall was skilled in the law and had previously been offered a seat on the bench.[25] In case Jay refused, Adams had first intended to follow the line of seniority in the Supreme Court and offer the post to Justice William Cushing, and then to Paterson. But the issue became complicated because of a provision in the judiciary reform bill (then in its last stages of debate in the House), which was to reduce the authorized number of judges on the court from six to five. The most convenient way for Adams to assure that six Federalist judges remained on the Court when he left office (thereby requiring that two either die or retire before Jefferson would be able to make any appointment) was to choose a chief justice from outside the present ranks, which had been already reduced to five by Ellsworth's resignation.[26] Besides, Cushing was aging and infirm, and, although Adams seems never to have voiced them, there may have been some objections to Paterson. After all, he had earlier been associated with Hamilton, now Adams's detested enemy, and, according to one newspaper account, Connecticut Federalists were still upset about Paterson's 1795 decision in the case of *Van Horne's Lessee* v. *Dorrance*.[27] The only reason Adams actually gave for not turning directly to Paterson after Jay declined was his desire not to hurt Cushing's feelings, but he may have been thinking in the long term, too. Paterson was fifty-six and, although basically healthy, had always been slight in appearance and somewhat frail. Marshall was a robust figure ten years younger than Paterson and, according to the actuarial charts, a far better risk. As it turned out, Marshall outlived Paterson by almost thirty years and was able to extend the Federalists' influence over Supreme Court decisions into the second third of the nineteenth century. Finally, Adams's stubborn streak probably had something to do with it. During the week that the Senate stalled before confirming Marshall, a group of Federalists tried to persuade the president to change his mind in favor of Paterson. As Dayton reported,

> it must be gratifying to you to learn that all voices with the exception of one only were united in favor of the conferring of this appointment upon you. The President alone was inflexible, and declared that he would never nominate you.[28]

Adams's choice of a chief justice had hardened some Federalists still further in their opposition to the president, but Paterson was not one of them. When Dayton had first heard of Marshall's nomination, he had written that Adams "manifested such a debility or derangement of intellect" that he and many of his colleagues were convinced "that another four years of administration in his hands would have exposed us to destruction." A week later, after the president had stood firm against a compromise, Dayton referred to the president as "a wild freak of a man whose administration, happily for this country, is soon to terminate."[29] Paterson, however, tried to calm his young champion. He wrote to Dayton on January 25 that he had never expected the appointment in the first place, and that had it been offered he would have considered it "a complimental thing, a mere feather, which might tickle a vain mind, but which I neither wished nor wanted." He described Marshall as "a man of genius," whose "talents have at once the lustre and solidity of gold." Then Paterson closed the letter with an interesting comment on his own political state of mind, which was apparently a good deal calmer than that of most of his Federalist friends on the eve of Jefferson's rise to power.

> Many things strange . . . have turned up in the world of politics in the course of a few months. But you lay matters too seriously to heart. Why grieve and lament? Give me the easy chair of the jolly, laughing philosopher, Democritus, and anybody for me shall be welcome to the gloomy tale of weeping Heraclitus. "Laugh where we can" is one of the best maxims to pass through life with ease and comfort.[30]

Dayton was pleased to report to fellow Federalists that Paterson was not insulted at being passed over and would not resign in a huff as some had feared. Later he apologized to Paterson.

> I wrote in a temper more than unusually warm. You have however reproved, or rather corrected me, in that gay, playful style and manner, which you understand so well how to employ, in order to bring back your friends to a good humor with themselves and the world.[31]

Meanwhile, unhurt by Adams and unruffled by Jefferson, Paterson hurried to congratulate his new superior.

Within a week of his confirmation, the new chief justice was thanking

Justice Paterson for his "kind sentiments" and bringing him up to date on the judiciary reform bill being rushed through Congress. The idea of reorganizing and strengthening the courts was not new. Proposals to relieve the Supreme Court justices of circuit duty could be traced all the way back to 1790, and the Federalists' bill to expand the federal courts and widen their jurisdiction had been discussed in committee, debated, amended, and postponed since early 1799. But pressure for passage mounted as the lame duck Congress entered its final weeks. The bill, which the House passed on the same day that Marshall was confirmed, would have the effect of overruling the compromise provisions of the original judiciary system. In the 1789 Senate debate, Paterson had fought to have the authority of the federal courts brought to the doors of the people and stressed that the national government should not rely on the state courts to enforce its laws, but as the 1789 act passed (allowing state courts wide concurrent jurisdiction over federal laws), it did exactly that. The Judiciary Act of 1801 opened up the federal courts to many more cases by reducing the minimum amount of suits that could be brought there (from $2,000 to $400) and eliminating such restrictions entirely when land titles were involved. This increased the volume of federal court business, and more personnel were required to handle it. By increasing the number of circuits from three to six and allowing for the appointment of additional judges specifically to preside over them, the new system brought the federal courts much closer to the people. The "most essential feature[s]," as Marshall described them to Paterson, were "the separation of Judge of the Supreme Court from those of the circuit courts, and the establishment of the latter on a system capable of extension commensurate with the necessities of the nation." Marshall's hopes for the bill's passage were gratified when it was enacted into law on February 13, 1801.[32]

Paterson and his overworked colleagues could at last breathe a sigh of relief. In the past, they had tried various ways to lighten the load by exchanging assignments and sitting in for each other from time to time.[33] Now their sole responsibility would be to the Supreme Court, which was to meet twice each year in Washington. Young William B. Paterson, then a student at Princeton, wrote to his stepmother that "it will ease Papa of a great part of his burden."[34] No longer would the justices have to face the distractions encountered in their annual tours around the nation, and the grueling exertions required of eighteenth-century travelers could now be expended on more important business.

The philosophy of the new law was in tune with the Federalists' (and Paterson's) ideas on the scope of national authority and the powers of the courts. It did away with some unfortunate aspects of the earlier system (the possibility, for example, of a judge's hearing the appeal in the Supreme Court of a case he had decided on the circuit), but it was also politically practical. Federalist creditors and land speculators would benefit from the widened jurisdiction of the courts, particularly since the new judges would be chosen by the Federalist administration in the few remaining weeks before Jefferson took over. Moreover, freed from burdensome circuit duty, the Supreme Court judges could concentrate on keeping the Republican executive and legislative branches within the bounds of the Constitution. In Republican minds, on the other hand, the Judiciary Act of 1801 was a bold-faced and diabolical scheme to defeat the will of the people as expressed in the presidential election, and Adams's so-called midnight appointments rubbed salt in the wound. As they stepped into power, radical leaders of the Republican opposition vowed to strike down the continuing symbol of Federalist power and influence.[35]

The history of the repeal of the judiciary act had all the elements of high political drama: conflict, suspense, and—at least for some—a surprising conclusion. The endeavor of radical Republicans to repeal the judiciary act and purge the courts of Federalist control was opposed not only by a well-organized Federalist minority in Congress, but by more moderate voices in the Republican party as well. Jefferson did not hesitate to remove Adams's midnight appointments. The new federal judges were an exception though, because they were protected by the Constitution. In addition, Jefferson withdrew those commissions that had not been delivered before he took office. Along with hundreds of other Federalist appointees, he swept from office most Federalist court clerks and marshals and replaced them with his own appointees.[36] But he was not quite ready to call for outright repeal of the judiciary act—a move that might be seen as a challenge to the constitutional principle of an independent judiciary and to the life tenure of judges. What apparently convinced him and other Republican moderates to mount the campaign for repeal was the Supreme Court's December 18, 1801, decision to hear arguments in the case of William Marbury and three other of the midnight appointments— justices of the peace for Washington, D.C., who sought a writ of mandamus to force Secretary of State Madison to deliver their commissions, which had been signed by President Adams almost nine months before. All eyes in the government looked to see what would emerge from this confrontation between the Federalist-dominated Supreme Court and a Republican president. The hearing was not scheduled until the next court term, but, when Jeffersonians considered it in conjunction with renewed Federalist attempts to bring sedition indictments against Republican editors, the decision stiffened their resolve to defeat the new judicial system.[37] There were still questions about the constitutionality of depriving judges of their positions on the bench by repealing the law that authorized their appointment, and some Republicans recognized the inexpediency of resurrecting the old inefficient system, but Republican party leaders worked to keep the moderates in line, and the repeal was finally passed.[38]

Then came the suspense. In their long debate against repeal, the Federalist minority in Congress had argued again that, since the Supreme Court held the ultimate right to decide on the constitutionality of legislative acts, the Court should not be diminished by the same Congress it was meant to check; otherwise the balance of the Constitution would be destroyed. At least one protagonist had openly threatened that, if the repeal went through, the Supreme Court would simply declare it unconstitutional, and some Republicans apparently feared such an eventuality.[39] The repeal act was not slated to go into effect until July 1802, and, in order to deny the Court an opportunity to act on it before that date, another bill was rushed through that shifted the times for the Court's regular terms in such a way that it would not meet again until February 1803.[40] Besides creating an open challenge to judicial independence, the schedule change presented the judges with a real dilemma. They could not decide on the constitutionality of the repeal until the February term, but in the meanwhile the law required them to ride the old circuits as before. If they obeyed the law, they would make themselves accomplices in the unseating of the midnight judges. If they disobeyed, the Republicans would have a field day with public opinion and could build up compelling evidence for possible impeachment charges in the future. What would the judges do?

Judge Samuel Chase tried to encourage his colleagues to resist the repeal. "The object of postponing the Meeting of the Judges of the Supreme Court till Feb. is obvious," he wrote Paterson, "we are to be made the instruments to destroy the independence of the judiciary." Realizing that the only way he could persuade the others to stand against Congress and refuse to resume the circuits was to bring them together, Chase suggested such a meeting to Marshall. Until such a conference could be arranged, Chase hesitated to commit his full opinion to paper for fear "some accident" would put them into unfriendly hands. In the meantime, he contented himself with warning Paterson: "I believe a Day of severe trial is fast approaching for friends of the Constitution, and we, I fear, must be the principle actors and maybe sufferers therein."[41]

Chief Justice Marshall was no less displeased with the actions of the Republican Congress, but he viewed them with more detachment and moderation. Marshall believed that the repeal act was improper because

it put the judges back in the position where they had to act on appeals
from their own decisions in the circuit courts. "I confess I have some
strong constitutional scruples," he wrote to Paterson. "I cannot well perceive how performance of circuit duty by the judges of the supreme court
can be supported." But the issue was complicated, he said, by the fact that
the law only reinstituted a system that had been followed from 1789 to
1801. Marshall explained that if the question were new he would have
been uncomfortable acting without a consultation of all the judges. But,
as it was, he wrote, "I consider it decided and whatever my own scruples
may be I am bound by the decision." Moreover, legal precedents notwithstanding, the physical inconveniences occasioned by the judges traveling so
far and wide were being ameliorated. The same act that delayed the next
meeting of the Supreme Court until 1803 also reduced the two annual
Supreme Court sessions to one and sought to lighten the labors of circuit
riding by increasing the original three circuits to six, thereby making each
one easier to cover and allowing one Supreme Court justice to be regularly
assigned to each. The chief justice confided to Paterson that he was surprised at the arrangement for their duties in the future—"they are less
burdensome than heretofore or than I expected."[42]

Marshall was willing to poll the other judges about the questions raised
by Chase (who argued that they should refuse to meet the circuits because
they had not received specific commissions authorizing them to preside
again in the circuit courts) and his suggestion for a conference. Personally
he did not think Chase's objection to be valid, but Marshall presented it
as his duty and inclination to "be bound by the opinion of the majority of
the judges," and he asked Paterson to write to William Cushing for his
opinion.[43]

Unmoved by a second communique from Chase,[44] Paterson thought
they should abide by the law. He wrote to Cushing with an explanation
of the situation and a delineation of his own position on the matter.

> It appears to me that we must perform the duties of circuit judges
> under the existing law as we formerly did under the first law, or, in
> other words, that distinct commissions are not necessary. Practice in
> this particular has fixed the construction; which it is now too late to
> controvert.

His reply to Marshall was identical. If it were "open for discussion," the
question would "merit serious consideration," he explained, "but the practical exposition is too old, and strong, and obstinate to be shaken." If the

same opinion prevailed with the others, he thought there would be no use for an August meeting.[45]

Cushing agreed with Marshall, Paterson, and Bushrod Washington,[46] Chase was overruled, and the circuits were met. Although several cases arose there that questioned the authority of the reconstructed circuit tribunals and challenged the constitutionality of the federal law, they all failed. The most significant was the case of *Stuart* v. *Laird* in which it was not only argued that Congress lacked the power to authorize the transfer of cases from one inferior court to another (from the now-defunct circuit courts set up in 1801 back to the ones that had existed before), but also that Congress had no right to require circuit duty of Supreme Court justices. Presiding over the Fifth Federal Circuit Court in Virginia, Chief Justice Marshall declined to overrule an act of Congress and rejected both arguments, but the case was immediately appealed to the Supreme Court and was placed on the docket for the long-awaited 1803 term. Despite the arguments of the Federalists and their lobbying among the justices, the Court's response, led by the judgment of Marshall and Paterson, was measured and moderate.[47]

When the justices congregated in Washington the following February for the first time in thirteen months, the conciliatory spirit that still prevailed would be evident in the two most important decisions to be offered that term. One of them was the appeal of Marshall's circuit court decision in the case of *Stuart* v. *Laird.* Since he had already heard the case, the chief justice stepped aside and allowed Paterson to prepare the Court's formal decision.[48] But on February 24, a week before Paterson's ruling was read, the case of *Marbury* v. *Madison* was decided, and the opinion was announced by Marshall. The matters at stake in this case were equally controversial in terms of Republican and Federalist politics, but no one expected the issue of judiciary review to be involved.

Although the chief justice adhered to his usual practice and prepared the formal opinion himself, it clearly represented the considered judgment of Paterson and his colleagues as well.[49] The first two-thirds of the opinion amounted to a political attack on Jefferson and the Republicans for denying the rightful commissions to Marbury and the other midnight appointees who had applied for redress. But the final and most significant point explained why the Supreme Court lacked the authority to do anything about it. The provision of the Judiciary Act of 1789 that authorized the Court to issue a writ of mandamus was declared unconstitutional.[50]

Six days later, Paterson read the decision in *Stuart* v. *Laird,* to the effect that the Judiciary Repeal Act could stand. He made the point as

plainly as possible: The Congressional assignment of Supreme Court justices to circuit courts was within the bounds of the Constitution. To stress
the point, he returned to some of the same words he had used in his correspondence with the other justices—years of practice had "fixed the
construction." The "practical exposition" was "too strong and obstinate to
be shaken or controlled." He closed by declaring that "the question is at
rest and ought not now to be disturbed."[51]

The timing of these two decisions seems too neat to be purely coinci-
dental. The justices knew that within a week they would officially decline
to take issue with Congress on judiciary repeal. As noted, Marshall's correspondence with Paterson proves that, as early as eight months before
the decision was announced, they and the other justices (except Chase)
had agreed that the repeal act was constitutionally correct. In all likelihood, observers would interpret this as an admission by the Court that
their claims to judicial review had been mistaken. What could be more
natural than to first establish the principle with as little fanfare as possible
in a decision that practically guaranteed that the opposition would accept?
While seizing the opportunity to criticize Jefferson politically, the Court
had avoided a direct constitutional confrontation with the executive
branch. The proscription of legislative power was tempered by the fact
that the Court was at the same time acknowledging constitutional limits
to its own authority and that the law set aside was one passed long before
the Republicans came into office. While Republican editorials complained
about Federalist polemics in the introductory comments, they could not
really oppose the Court's decision because, on the surface at least, Jefferson
had won. Marbury, the Federalist, had been denied his job.[52]

Any or all of the justices may have been hunting for an issue on which
to exercise judicial review before they were forced to proclaim on *Stuart
v. Laird*. We can do no more than speculate about what credit Paterson
may deserve, but the speculations are intriguing. Paterson did have an
uncanny knack for digging up a legal technicality when it would serve his
political purpose. His challenge to hold the 1787 convention to its restrictive formal authorization is perhaps the best example. Now his position was absolutely unique. Associate Justice Paterson was helping to
decide that a section of the Judiciary Act of 1789, which, as a member of
the first Senate, he had helped to write, was in violation of the Constitution, which he had also helped to write. As a member of the Senate
assigned to the committee that prepared the judiciary act and as one of
its leading supporters, Paterson had spent weeks grappling with the intricacies of the federal judicial system when it was first proposed. We know
from his own notes that he took special interest in the problem of jurisdic-

tion, the most controversial question in the lengthy congressional debate and the central issue in *Marbury* v. *Madison*. It is easy to picture him closeted in his rooming house in New York carefully going over each section of the law again and again looking for discrepancies that the opposition might raise. Who would be more likely to come up with a troublesome technicality; who could be better qualified to discover a litigious detail?[53] Besides, the pertinent paragraphs in Marshall's opinion did little more than paraphrase what Paterson had written eight years before in *Van Horne's Lessee* v. *Dorrance*. "Certainly," Marshall wrote, "all those who have framed written constitutions contemplate them as forming the fundamental and paramount law of the nation, and, consequently, the theory of every such government must be, that an act of the legislature, repugnant to the constitution is void."[54]

If *Marbury* v. *Madison* offered the Republicans a mixed victory in their struggle with those Federalists who were still in power, then Paterson's decision in *Stuart* v. *Laird* was even more significant as an expression of a spirit of conciliation between the opposing parties. Here was the Federalist Supreme Court finally acquiescing to the "revolution of 1800." As firm as the individual justices remained in their political beliefs, Paterson and his colleagues had admitted that the Republicans had not set aside the Constitution, at least not yet. Moreover, the justices had chosen to preserve judicial integrity at the expense of personal scruples, physical inconvenience, and significant political considerations. It might have been good politics to deny the right of the Congress to repeal the Judiciary Act of 1801 and to obstruct Republican plans by refusing to take up the circuits again. Paterson certainly believed they had the power to do so, and, at another time, under different circumstances, he might have joined with Chase in seeking a technicality with which to foil the opposition. But now he seemed to be coming to grips with the reality of the Republicans in power. His belief in the Court's unique authority over questions of constitutionality had not faltered. Just a week before he had joined the unanimous decision on *Marbury* v. *Madison* and had heard Marshall go out of his way to emphasize the principle of judicial review that he had voiced himself years before. But, as indicated in *Stuart* v. *Laird,* Paterson was not prepared to exercise that authority where sound legal judgment would not support it.

Perhaps it was the willingness of the Republican Congress to compromise on the structure of the circuits and make them more workable that softened his partisanship. From the first, Paterson had accepted the Republican ascendancy with more calm than many of his overwrought Federalist friends. Perhaps he simply came to realize that Jefferson did not after all intend to import the most radical tenets of French Jacobinism into America.[55] But whatever the reason, Paterson seemed to be making the same personal commitment that James A. Bayard had made two years before in ending the electoral challenge to Jefferson—to preserve the public interest above all else by maintaining the stability of governmental institutions. That Justice Paterson should follow such a course should not have been surprising. He had argued all along for the sanctity of the Constitution and the importance of law and order. The specter of mass uprising in the Whiskey Rebellion and the emotional crisis of 1798 had led him to stray from the path of honor he had set for himself as a young man, but his political volatility was being calmed, and hereafter he would stray no more. Responsible leaders at the time praised the *Stuart* v. *Laird* decision, and scholars have since set it apart for its "striking non-partisanship."[56] It was the last significant judicial decision of Paterson's career and the one that best illustrated Paterson's continuing attitude toward maintaining republican institutions.

At the same time that Paterson was so intimately involved in such critical national affairs, he was also preoccupied with family matters, especially with his children's future. His son had been a student at the College of New Jersey since 1797, and the summer of 1801 found him "in the woods preparing for his last collegiate examination." He graduated that September and took up the study of law while also pursuing a Master of Arts degree at the college. Finally Paterson helped him to set up a law office in New York City where he studied and waited patiently for business much as his father had done thirty years before.[57]

Paterson took pride in his son's advancement, but his daughter Cornelia's rise was far more spectacular. In 1802 she married Stephen Van Rensselaer, the owner of an estate near Albany, New York, where his ancestors had settled as feudal lords almost two hundred years before. The bridegroom, a Harvard graduate, a veteran of both houses of the New York legislature, and a former lieutenant governor, had run unsuccessfully in 1801 for governor against George Clinton. It was the second marriage for Van Rensselaer, who was sixteen years older than Cornelia. But the status and prestige that went with such a family connection could only have delighted the father of the bride who in his youth had pretended to come from better stock than he had. Cornelia became stepmother to three children from her husband's first marriage to Margaret Schuyler (daughter of General Philip Schuyler), and, when the eldest of them, a problem child, was sent to Princeton, Paterson volunteered to supervise his studies and keep him away from bad company. Within a few years, Cornelia had children of her own (eventually there were nine), and proud grandparents were making regular visits from New Brunswick. As General Van Rensselaer, Paterson's son-in-law would command the troops on the northern frontier during the War of 1812, represent New York in Congress (casting the decisive vote for John Quincy Adams in the disputed election of 1824), and found a school in Troy, New York, which was later incorporated as Rensselaer Polytechnic Institute.[58] Paterson had seen both of his children off to a good start.

Besides family affairs, Paterson had interests in education and business enterprise. He stayed active as a trustee of the College of New Jersey, participating in meetings whenever his schedule allowed, attending commencements, and maintaining contacts with his Cliosophic brothers. When problems arose, such as the fire in March 1802 that destroyed much of the campus, Paterson could be relied on to appeal to his many friends and acquaintances for assistance in rebuilding the school.[59]

Despite (or perhaps because of) the training received in his father's country store and his own experience at shopkeeping, Paterson eschewed business and mercantile involvements as a young man to concentrate on politics and the law. His brothers' unfortunate experiences also left Paterson with a bad taste for business, but after 1790 his associations with business leaders increased. When Philadelphia entrepreneur John Bayard married Euphemia Paterson's sister and moved to New Brunswick in 1788, he soon came to influence his new brother-in-law's outlook on business affairs. Paterson's position as governor between 1790 and 1793 required him to be aware of business matters and involved him with Bayard in the Society for Establishing Useful Manufactures. Thereafter he took part in several other enterprises, each meant to earn a profit while improving commerce and travel throughout New Jersey and around New Brunswick in particular.

For example, the New Jersey legislature had authorized the building of a toll bridge over the Raritan River in New Brunswick in November 1790, but it took over two years to get the project going. Paterson and his brother-in-law Bayard were among the six men who subscribed shares at the organizational meeting in February 1793. Although they agreed to take only five and eight shares, respectively, it ended up as a considerable investment (only two investors committed themselves to more than ten shares). All six subscribers agreed to pay £5 (about $13) per share to start, another £45 (about $120) in three installments over the next year, and whatever additional money the company required "each share paying its own proportion and no more." At the next meeting a week later, Paterson was chosen president. Responsibilities on the Supreme Court and circuit riding forced him to miss some meetings, but he was reelected to

the presidency year after year for the next decade. By the time the bridge
was completed in 1796, each share had cost its owner $866.95. The assess-
ments must have taken a sizeable bite out of Paterson's $875 quarterly
salary as a judge, but by this time his five shares were worth a total of
almost $4,500.[60] The bridge itself, lighted, guarded, and tended for tolls
twenty-four hours a day, was more than a business venture. In a day of
terrible roads and dangerous river crossings, it was a real asset to the
community.

Riding for twenty years from one New Jersey county court to another
and then traveling the federal circuits from New Hampshire to Georgia
made Paterson peculiarly sensitive to the state of America's roads, and
late in life he became involved in the movement to improve them with
privately built toll roads and turnpikes. He had been stuck in the mud,
bumped over holes, and jostled through frozen ruts until it seemed foolish
merely to continue complaining about it. In 1795, he devoted one of his
Horatius essays in the *Genius of Liberty* to the problem. Explaining that
it was foolhardy to let out contracts for bridge or road building to the
lowest bidder who might do an inferior job, Paterson argued that if a
road were built well in the first place it would provide far better service
and require much less repair. Part of the problem had to do with design.
It appeared that some highway builders had also intended the road to serve
as a sewer.

> To make a good road, it is necessary to raise it highest in the mid-
> dle, with a gradual descent or slope on each side, and a gutter to
> carry off the water. . . . Look at most of our high ways and the
> reverse is the rule.

Another difficulty was that the public officials entrusted to oversee the
condition of the roads had been shirking their duties, and Paterson hoped
that grand juries would soon take them to task. He stressed that good
roads would open the lucrative trade of New York and Philadelphia for
more New Jersey agricultural products and pointed to farmers who had
"made fortunes" with a garden of three acres which yielded "more clear
profit than a farm of 300 acres" because of the proximity of the market.[61]

By 1804, Paterson had become convinced that "the cheapest and only
feasible" way to improve the condition of the highways was to form
"companies, which, for a proper consideration or toll, may be induced to
turnpike our principle roads." He had studied the way turnpikes were
built in Europe and in neighboring states, and now he shared his recommendations with the legislature, which still looked to the former governor

for legal advice. Fearing that local interests would insist on diverting the new roads through every little hamlet, Paterson argued that the authorizing legislation should do no more than fix the beginning and ending points, leaving the specific path to be followed up to the company formed to do the job. The entrepreneurs themselves, he thought, could be relied on to choose the most efficient and most traveled route (usually a straight line between two major towns), thereby decreasing the construction costs, increasing the likely traffic of toll payers, and encouraging wary investors to risk their capital. Paterson feared that, if the laws placed too many restrictions on potential turnpike builders, few projects would ever get beyond the planning stage.[62]

Although his arguments were directed at the general benefits to be derived from better roads, Paterson's advice to the legislators was not without a more specific purpose. He drew their special attention to the road between Trenton and New Brunswick ("at the head of the navigable waters of the Delaware and Raritan," respectively) and recommended that a bill for its improvement be separated from any similar legislation "for turnpiking eastward of this place," where "interfering interests" were likely to defeat any project. It is clear that Paterson was intimately involved in plans for what soon became the Trenton and New Brunswick Turnpike Company, for only weeks after his supposedly candid comments to the assembly, John Rutherfurd and others were trying to persuade him to accept the company's presidency. He turned down the offer, encouraging the younger Rutherfurd to take it instead, but he retained his interest in the improvement of highways and the turnpike companies that promised to combine the blessings of private enterprise with public utility.[63]

If the roads had been better, Paterson might have avoided the violent accident he suffered on October 26, 1803, when his coach went off the road and overturned down a ten-foot embankment. His son escaped unhurt, and his wife was shaken up, but Paterson sustained injuries to his right side and shoulder that kept him house-ridden for weeks.[64]

While recuperating from the accident, he placed an advertisement in the *Guardian* offering to sell the house he lived in and all the real estate he owned in the New Brunswick area (one parcel of one hundred acres and another of seventy-five acres). Perhaps with the children on their own, he was thinking of moving Euphemia and himself to Washington or closer to the growing Van Rensselaer family in New York. Such a move may have been on his mind a few months before when he declined reelection to the presidency of the New Brunswick Bridge Company, a post he had held for over ten years. But whatever the plan, he failed to find a buyer, and, after running for eight consecutive weeks, the advertisement was withdrawn from the newspaper.[65]

Paterson was still not well enough to journey to Washington for the February 1804 session of the Supreme Court, but the period of convalescence forced on him by the carriage accident had allowed time for him to reevaluate his situation in life. During that winter, thoughts of retirement must have crossed his mind. He was nearly sixty years of age, and the exertions of office were a terrible drain. Lately, he seemed always to have a cold, sore throat, or some other complaint. Eventually, however, he set aside any thought of moving from New Brunswick, and the winter of 1805 found him on his way to the capital once more—this time by sled to Philadelphia, then by wagon to Baltimore (crossing the Susquehanna on the ice), and finally by stage to Washington.[66]

The docket for the 1805 session of the Supreme Court was full to the point of overflowing, but, in contrast to momentous cases such as *Marbury* v. *Madison* and *Stuart* v. *Laird,* most of the business was rather ordinary. The justices considered the application of laws against usury, interpretations of marine insurance policies, and technicalities in various suits for debt. In one interesting case, *U.S.* v. *Benjamin More,* the Court decided that it had no jurisdiction over appeals in criminal cases from the District of Columbia, a strict interpretation of the Constitution and the Judiciary Act of 1789.[67] However, little of this session's work was of lasting significance.

The real excitement to be found in Washington in the early months of 1805 concerned the impeachment trial of Paterson's colleague, Samuel Chase. He was accused of having committed improprieties in the trials of John Fries (for insurrection) and James Callendar (for sedition), attempting to intimidate a Delaware grand jury into enforcing the Sedition Act in 1799 and of presenting a brazenly anti-Republican charge to a Baltimore grand jury in 1803. Joseph H. Nicholson, a Republican congressman who had just distinguished himself by managing the impeachment of Federal District Court Judge John Pickering, had considered bringing charges against Chase in 1803 and had discussed the matter with the House leadership, but it was John Randolph, perhaps the most outspoken of Federalist critics, who demanded that Chase be investigated in January 1804, and proceeded to draw up the articles of impeachment.[68]

Although Randolph's crusade against Chase owed its origins as much to factional in-fighting among the Republicans as it did to the Chase's outbursts of partisan rhetoric, hard-line Federalists interpreted the prosecution as simply another phase of a carefully orchestrated Republican conspiracy to purge the judiciary and make it submissive to their will. Chase had begun preparing his defense early, and in a letter to Paterson he expressed confidence. If the most serious "charges had any foundation in truth," he wrote, then "I would be very uneasy." Others, however, were less sanguine. Judge Jeremiah Smith of New Hampshire thought it was only a matter of time until the prosecutions were widened. "They hate Marshall, Paterson, etc. more than they hate Chase," he explained to William Plumer in Congress, "because they are men of better character." Plumer agreed that all the justices were in danger of being removed: "They are *denounced* and must fall, but not all at one time, that would occasion too much alarm."[69] Smith and Plumer were especially sensitive because of the recent fate of their poor friend Pickering, who had not only been publicly belittled, impeached, and removed from office but now faced criminal charges, despite his evident insanity. But it was clear that, if the Republicans were successful in forcing Chase out of office on such flimsy charges,[70] other prosecutions would follow. Paterson's name would no doubt be high on the list. Though he never believed that he had acted improperly, he was aware that Republican troublemakers might voice objections to his treatment of the Whiskey Rebels or Matthew Lyon. A few years earlier, Joseph H. Nicholson, who was now one of the chief prosecutors in Congress, had written Paterson a series of letters badgering him for alleged technical improprieties in the Lyon case.[71] Thoughts of his own future must have passed through Paterson's mind as he watched the team of top-notch Federalist attorneys ready themselves for the trial of Chase in the Senate.

It took almost four weeks for the trial to run its course, but almost from the beginning it was an anticlimax. Writing home to Euphemia, Paterson described Chase's opening statements as "long and argumentative," but although he closely followed the proceedings, he discreetly stayed away from the crowded Senate sessions.[72] Chase was ably defended by an imposing group of lawyers who argued, among more technical points, that other judges had concurred with his actions and that it had long been a practice for judges to exhort grand juries in addresses that combined both moral and political rhetoric.[73] As the trial entered its second and then its third week, it became more and more evident that the radicals would fall short of the two-thirds vote necessary to convict. As Paterson put it to his son-in-law, "My sentiments in favor of his acquittal are strengthened every day. The infusion made on the public mind here in his behalf is very deep; and this will operate much to his advantage."[74]

Chase did escape removal from office, but he was not completely exonerated, and the motives behind the moderate Republican votes that helped to acquit him were more closely related to party politics than they were to popular opinion. Seen in its most positive light, the radicals' failure to convict Chase is evidence for the fair judgment of some Jeffersonians who, as much as they disapproved of Chase's politics and his style on the bench, could not find it consistent "with their ideas of justice [to] find him guilty of high crimes and misdemeanors." Like Paterson's opinion in *Stuart* v. *Laird,* their decision could not be taken as a reconciliation of Federalist and Jeffersonian philosophies, but the moderates in the Senate had allowed the spirit of the law to rise above political partisanship.[75]

After returning home from the Washington Court session in March, Paterson devoted the remaining months of 1805 to riding the circuits. Despite the persistent pains in his side and breast that he admitted alarmed him from time to time, he made two complete circuits (New York, Connecticut, and Vermont) between April and November. After some weeks' rest he was feeling strong again and set off from New Brunswick on January 24. He made the trip to Washington in five days, foregoing a rest stop in Baltimore to take advantage of the favorable conditions of the weather and the roads.[76]

As it had the year before, the 1806 session of the Supreme Court concerned mostly mundane matters. In the case of *Hopkirk* v. *Bell,* the Court found provisions of a Virginia law unconstitutional and again upheld the debt provisions of the Treaty of 1783. Paterson himself prepared the decision in *Randolph* v. *Ware,* which concerned a thirty-year-old incident involving a shipload of tobacco lost at sea. The Virginia owners were now attempting to sue their former British factors for failing to secure insurance before the boat sailed, but the justices were unsympathetic.[77]

While in Washington, Paterson seemed in good health and paid more interest than usual to the issues facing Congress, especially the continuing British interference with American ships on the high seas. But he fell sick soon after returning home to New Brunswick in the spring. Stricken with an ailment he described as an "inflammatory fever," he was confined for more than eight weeks. "I am so feeble," he wrote explaining why he could not go to meet the Connecticut circuit courts in April, "that a few turns in my room bring on lassitude." He observed that his "naturally delicate and slender" constitution seemed "to be almost worn out."[78] Yet from somewhere he drew the energy to travel to New York in June to preside over the circuit court with district judge Matthias Tallmadge. Had he foreseen the trouble awaiting him there, he might have stayed home.

The last judicial decision of Paterson's career, and his last public act of any kind, involved two adventurers, Samuel G. Ogden and William S. Smith, who had been charged with making war against a friendly nation by giving aid to the South American revolutionary Francisco Miranda in his attack on Caracas, Venezuela, the year before. The preliminaries to the trial were more interesting than the case itself. The defendants insisted that their defense, which was based on the claim that President Jefferson had approved their participation in Miranda's scheme, required the testimony of three members of the cabinet: Secretary of State James Madison, Secretary of War Henry Dearborn, and Secretary of the Navy Robert Smith. These officials responded to the court's subpoenas with a letter explaining that, in the president's opinion, their official duties prevented them from leaving Washington to appear at the trial. For three days, the defense attorneys argued that the court should either delay the trial or issue an attachment to the witnesses for contempt of court, and, as Paterson required, they tried to prove that the testimony of the three administration officials was material to the case.[79]

Paterson's long and carefully reasoned decision assured that, though his body might be failing, his mind was as sharp as ever. To begin with, he established that the simple declaration of the president that his cabinet members were needed in Washington was not sufficient justification to ignore the summons of the court. He had not, however, been convinced that the witnesses' testimony was pertinent to the defense. Even if the president had approved Miranda's scheme (and the only evidence presented in court was Miranda's claim that he had), the defendants would not be absolved. The president's power to defend the nation against invasion, Paterson argued, could not be extended to mounting invasions against nations at peace with the United States. The statute in question left no room for interpretation. It enjoined all "military enterprises against nations with which the United States are at peace" and did not give the president authority to grant a dispensation from the law. At one point in his opinion, Paterson succinctly proclaimed once more the concept on which he had based his entire career—the supremacy of the law, and especially the Constitution.

The law, like the beneficent author of our existence, is no respecter of persons; it is inflexible and even-handed, and should not be subservient to any improper considerations or views. This ought to be the case particularly in the United States, which we have been always led to consider as a government not of men, but of laws, of which the constitution is the basis.

Both Paterson and Tallmadge agreed that the testimony of the witnesses was not directly material to the case and ordered that the trial begin immediately. They differed, however, on the matter of executing the subpoenas. Paterson would have insisted that Madison and the others show cause why they should not be held in contempt, but Tallmadge disagreed, and so no official action could be taken unless the matter were appealed to the Supreme Court.[80]

The trip to New York, the long hours of argument, and the preparation of his detailed decision had broken Paterson's frail health for the last time. Smith and Ogden had requested a few more days before beginning the trial, and at first Paterson had thought such a delay might enable him to recover strength enough to continue. But finally he decided against any postponement on his own account and ordered that the trial proceed, leaving Tallmadge to hear the case on his own. A few days later, the jury acquitted the defendants, even without the testimony of the experts from Washington. The case had involved some interesting issues. In the famous treason trial of Aaron Burr the following year, Luther Martin would refer to Paterson's argument in support of his attempt to force the president himself to testify.[81] But Paterson would not live to see that confrontation.

A few months earlier, convinced that his end was near, Paterson had put his affairs in order. As he explained to a friend, "a wise man ought to endeavor to arrange all his concerns, both for time and eternity, in such a manner, that, when his last hour approaches, he may have nothing to do but die." Leaving New York City, Paterson traveled to his daughter's home near Albany, where after several weeks of continuing illness, he died and was buried on the grounds of the Van Rensselaer manor.[82] He was sixty-one years old.

Many of the founding fathers had outlived Paterson, but only a few had been able to play as influential a role in filling out the framework of government prescribed by the Constitution. For thirteen years he had sat on the federal bench and helped build a judicial system commensurate with the tasks of a national government. From the outset a man of integrity, Paterson had been a strong voice for moderation in the critical period following the election of 1800. Had he encouraged Dayton in his crusade to overturn Marshall's appointment as chief justice or joined Chase in his attempt to force a constitutional confrontation over the Judiciary Act of 1801, the transition from a Federalist to Republican administration might have left permanent scars on the national consciousness. But Paterson's Federalism gave way to less partisan concerns.

He helped to smooth the transition, moderate the opposition, and convince Americans that the verities of the Constitution were more important than transient political differences. His final years on the Supreme Court had proved Paterson to be a true statesman.

Conclusion

"Every young man must be the maker of his own fortune," Paterson wrote to his son in November 1805. He was trying to buoy up the novice attorney who was depressed about the lack of business in his New York office and to encourage him to continue studying the law. "It is your profession," the stern father explained, "and [it] must be the means of your rising in life."[1]

No one was better qualified to give such advice than William Paterson, who had built his own career as lawyer, jurist, and statesman through an astute combination of working hard, biding his time, and cultivating influential friends. Had he not made the law the means of his own "rising in life," Paterson might never have outgrown his evident self-consciousness about the mediocre social position into which he had been born. But Paterson was talented as well as ambitious, and he proved himself able to fill each role that was offered to him. In the end he had won fame, considerable fortune, and a social position akin to the Van Rensselaers'. He had come a long way from his father's general store.

The education he had received at the College of New Jersey was an enduring influence in his life. Even after taking his two degrees, Paterson retained his association with the school as a loyal member of the Cliosophic Society and later as a trustee. He was honored with degrees from Dartmouth (1805) and Harvard (1806). No one knew better that the outward marks of education brought social status, but the impact of his college training was even more evident in Paterson's innermost thoughts on society and government.

His personality was shaped by his aspirations to the extent that he consciously labored to adopt the air of a gentleman. Yet feelings of insecurity and a lack of self-confidence seemed, at least at the start, to have discouraged him from setting his goals very high. As fame followed success, he became less timid and maintained social ties with the nation's most powerful men (including two presidents). But he always claimed to be more comfortable at home in his study than abroad in the company of more outgoing men. Perhaps this retiring style helped keep him from land speculations and other daring schemes and deprived him of chances for greater financial success. As a family man, he was heartbroken by the death of his young wife Cornelia and their little daughter, but he was hurt almost as much by his brothers' irresponsibility with money. When he heard from his brothers again in 1805, after fifteen years of separation, they were still asking for funds.[2] Paying off their debts had temporarily upset his plans for the financial security of his second wife and his two children, but in the last dozen years or so Paterson did manage to amass an estate that included four parcels of land in addition to his Raritan farm and the house in New Brunswick, as well as stock in several corporations.[3] Euphemia and the children were well provided for.

If we accept the testimony of his New Brunswick minister, Paterson made his peace with God before he died. Until then, he had not sought full membership in the Calvinist church, but his close associations with evangelical protestantism begun during his college years had left an indelible mark on his ideas and values. When he pressed the point with regard to the language issue in the Dutch Reformed Church in Raritan, for example, Paterson wrote that "our eternal peace is at stake, and therefore we cannot forbear." He never set aside the moralistic rhetoric shared by many evangelical brethren who also condemned licentious living and speculation. During the 1790s, he even tried to incorporate some of these values into his proposals for reforming those laws of New Jersey that restricted activities on the sabbath, regulated taverns, and would have banned the playing of billiards. There is evidence, however, that, as his life progressed, he became more tolerant of men with different ideas—such as some of his fellows in the Freemasons and the American Philosophical Society must have been—and less successful in adhering to his own rigorous ideals. For example, he never seems to have spoken out against the aristocratic lifestyle practiced by his friend and brother-in-law John Bayard, who at one time or another entertained in his fine home all the nation's luminaries as they passed through New Brunswick on their way to Philadelphia or New York, and Paterson himself collected a well-stocked wine cellar, which was bequeathed to his son. Still, Paterson never allowed himself to be swept away in a passion for material luxuries. His sins were those of omission rather than of commission, and he was never far from the fold.

Paterson's public life had been more uniformly successful. Catapulted from a poor rural practice to the office of state attorney general during the revolutionary war, he had earned tremendous popularity as delegate to the federal convention and as United States senator. By the time he became governor in 1791, the people of New Jersey treated him as a true favorite son.

If one were to erect a typology for the evolving political parties in this period, it might seem that Paterson exhibited several typically Republican traits along with some characteristic of the Federalists. His background (from a family of Scotch-Irish Presbyterians) marks him as a likely Jeffersonian according to some, and Jackson Turner Main might be so impressed with how little Paterson traveled before 1787 to brand him a "localist" and expect to find him opposed to the Constitution.[4] We know, of course, that, even though he stayed close to home, Paterson had a broad perspective, but there were other factors, too. Paterson was a self-made man with no English friends or business contacts. Had he come from Massachusetts, Paul Goodman might have found him a likely candidate for the opposition, but in New Jersey such matters were less important, and no one seemed to mind that Paterson had equally sharp words for scheming British agents and diplomats as he had for their enemies, the French.[5] More unusual was Paterson's outspoken concern over the possible social and moral consequences of an unequal distribution of wealth, expressed before the Revolution in his "Address on the Rise and Decline of Nations" and afterward in his newspaper essays of the 1790s. This, and his continuing criticism of luxury-loving aristocracy, can best be understood in the light of the evangelical Calvinist values that persisted in his personality. He was a member of the Freemasons, a group that was criticized as a secret engine of aristocracy, but he maintained for himself a modest lifestyle, which set him apart from many of the Federalist elite.[6] Finally, his denunciation of speculators during the panic of 1793 was so inflamed with moral outrage that it might have been written by any Republican opponent of the Federalists' financial philosophy.

If one studies Paterson's positions on the most significant issues of the day, however, one can have no doubt of his enduring commitment to Federalism. Paterson was an outspoken defender of the Constitution and the need for vigorous national government, a life-long believer in hard money and the sanctity of contracts, a supporter of Hamilton in the first Senate and spokesman for his financial program, George Washington's appointee to the Supreme Court, and, when the situation became really desperate, his candidate for secretary of state as well. Anyone who, like Paterson, was a defender of the Jay Treaty and publicist for other administration causes, an early (though not immediate) opponent of the French Revolution, effective enforcer of the Sedition Act against Matthew Lyon and others, and consistent critic of Jeffersonian efforts to "dupe" an uneducated electorate with "shameless demagoguery" into replacing "devoted public servants" (the Federalists) with factious Republicans seeking to advance their "petty and local" self-interests could be nothing but a Federalist.

His early association with the just-emerging Federalist frame of mind in the mid-1780s was brought about by his opposition to paper money and other expedients sought by debtors in New Jersey. An understanding of this position with all of its political and social ramifications is basic for a full comprehension of Paterson's involvement in the movement for the new Constitution and his later activities in public life. However, the points where his background and experience depart from the typical Federalist profile are instructive, too. This is true especially of his early association with evangelical protestantism, which helps to explain his moral contempt for the adventurous speculator and the ostentatious luxury of the wealthy elite.

Paterson was an independent spirit who, rather than simply following in the paths of others, developed his own rationale to guide him through the political storms of the young republic, just as he had come to his own personal justification for supporting the Revolution. He lived in a period when profound changes opened new opportunities for talented people, and his own steps to prominence can be traced through the struggle for independence. Yet he saw the war not as a social revolution, but as a way to preserve the traditional structure of colonial life. He developed a multifaceted and complex philosophy of society and politics, but at different times one concern might strike him as more important than another. For example, he disliked both luxury-loving aristocrats and debtors who sought to avoid living up to their obligations, but conditions seemed to make the former problem more of an issue before the Revolution and the latter one more significant in the 1780s. He believed in the right to overthrow a tyrannical ruler, but in the 1790s he saw the threat of tyranny coming from the Francophile Republicans. He was firmly committed to the even-handed administration of justice and a judiciary independent of political influence, but he forgot these principles on several occasions and used his own judicial powers to support a political philosophy, without regard for the rights of defendants before the bar.

He attacked the Jeffersonian Republicans as demagogues who threatened to tear down everything that the founding fathers had built into the Constitution and the laws, but after 1800 he realized that his personal feelings about Jefferson and his supporters were less important than the preservation of the republic and the smooth transition from one regime to the other.

I referred earlier to the conclusions reached by Richard Hofstadter in his analysis of the origins of American political parties: The first regime in power considered itself "not as a party that had taken the reins of government but as the government itself" and saw the opposition as a "wholly unconstructive faction, an anti-government."[7] William Paterson seems the embodiment of Hofstadter's observation. His ideas and actions were founded on a system of ideological beliefs imbibed at Princeton in the 1760s, adapted to Republicanism in the 1770s, and vigorously upheld throughout the 1790s. They did not seem to him like elements open to partisan debate.

What did distinguish his personality, however, and what allowed him to refurbish his reputation for posterity after several unfortunate excesses on the Supreme Court in 1795 and 1798, was his basic moderation and open-mindedness. Unlike Jonathan Dayton and other hard-line Federalists who came to see John Adams as a wild man and a fool because of his unwillingness to follow the logic of Federalist party interest into a war with France, Paterson remained calm. After 1800, when it became clear that Jefferson's presidency was not the disaster that had been predicted, Paterson moderated his stance even further and led his colleagues to accept the realities of the situation for the well-being of the nation. In his political essays and his pointed grand jury addresses of the 1790s, Paterson had sounded quite smug and self-satisfied, convinced of the correctness of his position. Yet, a few years later he proved willing to compromise. Changes of mind did not come easily to William Paterson, especially when they involved the framework of political and social beliefs he had carried with him for almost forty years. But part of his greatness was his ability to grow and to learn.

In the same way, he helped to evolve a new theory of sovereignty during and after the Philadelphia convention (moving from "Sovereignty is an Integral thing," to the concept of shared sovereignty that was unique to America in the eighteenth century). And, by eventually accepting the fact that the opposition was not out to destroy the republic and leave it in ruins, Paterson helped edge the nation toward recognition of the two-party system.

On the Supreme Court, as before, Paterson assumed a low profile, whenever possible leaving the public attention to others, but in historical perspective his contributions to the new nation emerge clearly. Whether he was preserving law and order in revolutionary New Jersey, holding firm for equal representation at the Philadelphia convention, helping to frame the Judiciary Act of 1789, reforming the laws of New Jersey, or encouraging the Supreme Court to assume its full role in governing the new nation, Paterson worked consistently for social and political stability. In striving to secure and preserve, he was often working against the more democratic forces unleashed in the movement for independence, but his was none the less a constructive statesmanship. It was men such as Paterson, men who knew when to stand firm and when to compromise, who enabled the young republic to grow more democratic gradually, without a social upheaval, and without completely losing touch with its Whiggish origins.

Abbreviations

AHR	*American Historical Review*
AJLH	*American Journal of Legal History*
HSP	Historical Society of Pennsylvania
JAH	*Journal of American History*
JLC	*Journal of the Legislative Council of the State of New Jersey*
LC	Library of Congress
MCS	*Minutes of the Council of Safety of the State of New Jersey*
MHS	Massachusetts Historical Society
NEQ	*New England Quarterly*
NJA	*New Jersey Archives*
NJH	*New Jersey History*
NJHS	New Jersey Historical Society
NJSL	New Jersey State Library
NYHS	New York Historical Society
NYPL	New York Public Library
PCCS	*Minutes of the Provincial Congress and Council of Safety*
PNJHS	*Proceedings of the New Jersey Historical Society*
PSQ	*Political Science Quarterly*
PUL	Princeton University Library
RUL	Rutgers University Library
RULJ	*Rutgers University Library Journal*
SCHQ	*Somerset County Historical Quarterly*
WMQ	*William and Mary Quarterly*
YUL	Yale University Library

Notes

CHAPTER 1

1. See *New York Genealogical and Biographical Record,* Vol. 23 (New York, 1892), p. 82.
2. Ibid., p. 81.
3. Writing in 1912 with access to the last Paterson descendants, A. Van Doren Honeyman pinpointed Paterson's birthplace as Antrim, Ireland, and the date as December 24, 1745. Paterson's father's family were Protestants who had come to Northern Ireland from Scotland some years before, but nothing was known about his mother except her name, Mary, and the year of her death (1772). According to Honeyman, they had five children (three sons and two daughters), but he was able to confirm the existence of only one girl. A. Van Doren Honeyman, "The Early Career of Governor William Paterson," *SCHQ,* 1 (July 1912): 161–163, 172n.
4. *NJA,* first series, 31: 47.
5. Ibid. An account book giving details of the store's prosperity between 1765 and 1768 can be found among the William Paterson Papers at William Paterson College in Wayne, New Jersey.
6. See Henry L. Savage, *Nassau Hall: 1756–1956* (Princeton, 1956).
7. See receipts to and from Richard Paterson, Paterson Papers, PUL.
8. Part of this interest in nontheological subjects was due to the necessity of winning a charter from the royal governor of New Jersey, but the combination of religious studies with secular literature and other disciplines was common in dissenting academies that had grown up in England and Scotland in the previous decades. See Thomas Jefferson Wertenbaker, *Princeton, 1746–1898* (Princeton, 1946), pp. 18–22, 81–86. See also Douglas Sloan, *The Scottish Enlightenment and the American College Ideal* (New York, 1971), Chapters 1 and 2.
9. Sloan, *Scottish Enlightenment and the American College Ideal,* p. 51.
10. Ibid., p. 52. See also Alan Heimert, *Religion and the American Mind from the Great Awakening to the Revolution* (Cambridge, Mass., 1966), pp. 187–194.
11. See Francis Broderick, "Pulpit, Physics & Politics: The Curriculum of the College of New Jersey 1746–1794," *WMQ,* third series, 6 (1949): 42–48; Sloan, *Scot-*

tish Enlightenment and the American College Ideal; and Lyman H. Butterfield, ed., *John Witherspoon Comes to America* (Princeton, 1953). For general information on the college, see John MacLean, *History of the College of New Jersey from Its Origin in 1746 to the Commencement of 1854* (2 vols.; Philadelphia, 1877).

12. [Samuel Blair], *An Account of the College* (Woodbridge, N.J., by order of the Trustees of the College of New Jersey, 1764), p. 28.

13. John Witherspoon, "Address to the Inhabitants of Jamaica and Other West India Islands in Behalf of the College of New Jersey," in Richard Hofstadter, ed., *Documentary History of American Education,* (2 vols.; Chicago, 1961), Vol. 1, pp. 137–138. One interesting account of the daily regimen of the students can be found in J. R. Williams, ed., *Philip Vickers Fithian, Journal and Letters, 1767–1774* (2 vols.; Princeton, 1930 and 1934), Vol. 1, pp. 6–10.

14. [Blair], *Account of the College,* p. 35.

15. Most of this manuscript material is preserved in the Paterson Collection at the Princeton University Library, but some of the college essays are to be found among the Paterson Papers at the Library of Congress and at the Rutgers University Library.

16. Commonplace book, box 1, Paterson Collection, PUL. Although it cannot be established, of course, that Paterson shared every opinion that he noted in his commonplace book, it is safe to assume that he wrote down those ideas and opinions that he thought worth remembering.

17. "On Simplicity of Language" n.d., college composition folder, box 1, Paterson Collection, PUL.

18. Essay fragment, n.d., college composition folder, box 1, Paterson Collection, PUL.

19. "On Personal Appearance," n.d., college composition folder, box 1, Paterson Collection, PUL.

20. "On the Need for Recreation in Academic Life," n.d., college composition folder, box 1, Paterson Collection, PUL.

21. "On Conduct," n.d., college composition folder, box 1, Paterson Collection, PUL.

22. Commonplace book, box 1, Paterson Collection, PUL.

23. H. Trevor Colbourn, *The Lamp of Experience: Whig History and the Intellectual Origins of the American Revolution* (Chapel Hill, 1965), pp. 4, 20, and passim.

24. See Richard Gummere, *The American Colonial Mind and the Classical Tradition* (Cambridge, Mass., 1963), passim.

25. Carl Becker, *The Heavenly City of the Eighteenth Century Philosophers* (New Haven, 1932), p. 17 and passim. Also see Lawrence Cremin, *American Education: The Colonial Experience* (New York, 1970), p. 470.

26. Gordon Wood, *The Creation of the American Republic: 1776–1787* (Chapel Hill, 1969), pp. 7–8.

27. Commonplace book, box 1, Paterson Collection, PUL.

28. Ibid.

29. Commonplace book, box 1, Paterson Collection, PUL. On the translations of ancient historians, see Wood, *Creation of the American Republic,* p. 50; Gummere, *American Colonial Mind and the Classical Tradition,* passim; and William Gribbin, "Rollin's Histories and American Republicanism," *WMQ,* third series, 24 (1972): 611–622.

30. Commonplace book, box 1, Paterson Collection, PUL.

31. Ibid.

32. His political essays of the 1790s concentrated on the factionalism of the day and the threat it presented to the maintenance of the public interest. See Paterson Papers, RUL.

33. Wood, *Creation of the American Republic*, p. 29. See also the analysis of Paterson's "Address on the Rise and Decline of Nations" in Chapter 3.

34. On the general decline of rigorous Calvinism in the eighteenth century see Joseph Haroutunian, *Piety Versus Moralism: The Passing of the New England Theology* (New York, 1932).

35. Paterson did not pay much attention to natural science. The real growth of interest in that field came only after Witherspoon's arrival in 1768.

36. Commonplace book, box 1, Paterson Collection, PUL.

37. Ibid.

38. "On the Passions," n.d., Paterson Papers, LC. Perhaps this is the same essay that Paterson later lent to John Davenport, a friend at the college. See William Paterson to John Davenport, July 10, 1769, original letterbook, box 1, Paterson Collection, PUL.

39. Commonplace book, box 1, Paterson Collection, PUL.

40. "Oration on the Degeneracy of the Times," n.d., college compositions folder, box 1, Paterson Collection, PUL.

41. [Samuel Davis], *The Military Glory of Great Britain* (Philadelphia, 1762).

42. Cremin, *American Education*, pp. 465–468; Wertenbaker, *Princeton*, pp. 56–57.

43. *New York Gazette or Weekly Post Boy*, October 2, 1766, quoted in *NJA*, first series, 25, p. 219. The newspaper credited Paterson with a speech in which "Elegance in Composition and Grace and Force of Action were equally conspicuous."

44. "On the Effeminacy and Dissoluteness of Modern Manners," n.d., Paterson Papers, LC.

45. Ibid. See also "On Conduct," n.d., college compositions folder, box 1, Paterson Collection, PUL.

46. Oration on the Degeneracy of the Times, n.d., political essays folder, box 1, Paterson Collection, PUL.

47. See Chapter 3.

48. David Ramsay, *History of the American Revolution* (2 vols.; Philadelphia, 1789), Vol. 2, p. 321, quoted in Cremin, *American Education*, p. 468.

49. Cremin, *American Education*, pp. 467–471. Bernard Bailyn, *Education and the Forming of American Society* (Chapel Hill, 1960), p. 89, stresses the possible importance of college studies in the evolution of revolutionary thought and calls for further research in the area. See also Sloan, *Scottish Enlightenment and the American College Ideal*, p. 268.

50. For the importance of deference in early American politics, see J. R. Pole, "Historians and the Problem of Early American Democracy," *AHR*, 67 (1962): 626–646; and Richard Buel, "Democracy and the American Revolution: A Frame of Reference," *WMQ*, third series, 21 (1964): 165–190.

51. See, for example, Sheldon S. Cohen and Larry R. Gerlach, "Princeton and the Coming of the American Revolution," *NJH*, 92, 2 (Summer 1974): 69–92; and an unpublished paper by Cohen, "Harvard College on the Eve of the American Revolution," presented at annual meeting of the Organization of American Historians in April 1975.

52. The literalness with which he accepted the lessons of his teachers and the social patterns of his classmates is evident from many of the letters he wrote to his

college friends (see Chapter 2). For Paterson's comments on tutor Samuel Stanhope Smith, also see Chapter 2.

53. By the time of the Revolution, he was phrasing some of his public utterances in the form of Puritan jeremiads (see Chapter 3).

54. According to Sloan, *Scottish Enlightenment and the American College Ideal,* between 1766 and 1775 a total of 75 graduates (41 percent) became ministers, but between 1777 and 1794 only 30 (13 percent) followed that path. Sloan concludes that "the decline in graduates headed for the ministry was somewhat greater at the College of New Jersey than at Harvard and Yale, although it was a general phenomenon" (p. 131).

55. Heimert, *Religion and the American Mind,* pp. 98–101 and passim. See also Richard Hofstadter, *America at 1750* (New York, 1971), pp. 278–279, 286–287, and Chapters 7 and 8. For a revision of Heimert's interpretation and a reminder of the broader background of millenarian thought in early America see Nathan O. Hatch, *The Sacred Cause of Liberty: Republican Thought and the Millenium in Revolutionary New England* (New Haven, 1977).

56. John Witherspoon, the president of Princeton after 1768, was the epitome of this revolutionary ministry. His *Lectures on Moral Philosophy* have been credited with helping to shape the minds of some of America's foremost revolutionary leaders. See James Smiley, "Madison and Witherspoon: Theological Roots of American Political Thought," *Princeton University Library Chronicle,* 22 (1961): 118–132.

57. Paterson's 1763 commencement oration (composed and spoken in Latin) was entitled "A Cliosophic Oration," misc. mms., PUL.

58. John MacPherson, who went to Philadelphia after graduation to study law under John Dickinson, provides the clearest contrast (see Chapter 2).

59. As late as the 1790s Paterson was writing newspaper essays on the virtues of unselfish public service. See newspaper essays, oversize collection, Paterson Papers, RUL.

60. "On Honor," n.d., college composition folder, box 1, Paterson Collection, PUL.

CHAPTER 2

1. James Madison to Richard Paterson, April 3, 1770, James Madison Collection, PUL.

2. After graduating, Paterson had correspondence with most of these men.

3. "On Friendship," n.d., college composition folder, box 1, Paterson Collection, PUL.

4. William Paterson to Josiah Stoddard, October 26, 1767; to Theodore Romeyn, August 14, 1770; to Luther Martin, June 2, 1769; to John Woodhull, August 1, 1769; to Samuel Tucker, April 30, 1770; to Robert Ogden, Jr., May 18, 1769, original letterbook, box 1, Paterson Collection PUL.

5. William Paterson to Hosea Hulbert, October 5, 1772, Gratz Collection, HSP. This letter describes some of Paterson's attempts to keep in touch with his college friends.

6. William Paterson to John MacPherson, January 26, 1767; May 11, 1767; November 16, 1768; January 27, 1769; May 23, 1767; and July 20, 1767, original letterbook, box 1, Paterson Collection, PUL.

7. William Paterson to John MacPherson, January 17, 1767, original letterbook, box 1, Paterson Collection, PUL.

8. John MacPherson to William Paterson, November 16, 1767, William Hornar Collection, HSP.

9. William Paterson to John MacPherson, July 1, 1767, original letterbook, box 1, Paterson Collection, PUL.

10. Ibid.

11. William Paterson to John MacPherson, July 31, 1768; and May 21, 1767, original letterbook, box 1, Paterson Collection, PUL.

12. William Paterson to John MacPherson, July 31, 1768, original letterbook, box 1, Paterson Collection, PUL.

13. John MacPherson to William Paterson, January 17, 1768; May 23, 1770; August 4, 1768; and April 9, 1769, William Hornar Collection, HSP.

14. William Paterson to John MacPherson, May 7, 1768, original letterbook, box 1, Paterson Collection, PUL.

15. Merrill Jensen, *The Founding of a Nation: A History of the American Revolution, 1763–1776* (New York, 1968), pp. 363–364.

16. John MacPherson to William Paterson, May 23, 1770, William Hornar Collection, HSP.

17. John MacPherson to William Paterson, July 24, 1770, William Hornar Collection, HSP. William Paterson to John MacPherson, July 27, 1770, and July 30, 1770, original letterbook, box 1, Paterson Collection, PUL. See also Jensen, *Founding of a Nation*, p. 366.

18. William Paterson to John MacPherson, September 4, 1772, original letterbook, box 1, Paterson Collection, PUL.

19. William Paterson to John MacPherson, June 26, 1772, original letterbook, box 1, Paterson Collection, PUL.

20. William Paterson to John MacPherson, July 27, 1770, original letterbook, box 1, Paterson Collection, PUL.

21. William Paterson to John MacPherson, November 12, 1771, original letterbook, box 1, Paterson Collection, PUL.

22. C. R. Williams, *The Cliosophic Society* (New York, 1919), pp. 1–3; James Beam, *The American Whig Society* (Princeton, 1933), pp. 7–12.

23. Williams, *Cliosophic Society*, pp. 3–6 and passim. The term "cliosophic" is thought to be a composite word from a Greek root spelled in English as it sounded in Greek; see Beam, *American Whig Society*, pp. 39–41.

24. See *Catalogue of the Cliosophic Society* (Princeton, 1845) and *Catalogue of the American Whig Society* (Princeton, 1845). There were, of course, American Whigs who later became Federalists such as John Beatty, president of the Medical Society of New Jersey and Federalist congressman in the 1790s; Gunning Bedford, appointed by Washington to the federal judiciary; and James A. Bayard, Federalist senator from Delaware. A few sons of Clio also rose to prominence as Republicans, for example, the mercurial Aaron Burr and Henry Brockholst Livingston, who was appointed by Jefferson to fill the seat on the U.S. Supreme Court left vacant by Paterson's death. However, Burr had belonged to the Whig Society before switching over to Clio, and Livingston was listed as a member of both clubs for 1774. See also Beam, *American Whig Society*, p. 24.

25. Lowell Simpson, *The Little Republics: Undergraduate Literary Societies at Columbia, Dartmouth, Princeton, and Yale, 1753–1865* (unpublished Ph.D. dissertation, Teachers College, Columbia University, 1976).

26. "Skit on Literary Composition," n.d., college composition folder, box 1, Paterson Collection, PUL.

27. W. Jay Mills, ed., *Glimpses of Colonial Society and the Life at Princeton College, 1766–1773* (New York, 1903), pp. 109–126. Mills is usually unreliable for quotation, but in this case the manuscript document cannot be located.

28. "Oration on the Degeneracy of the Times," n.d., political essays folder, box 1, Paterson Collection, PUL.

29. "On Musick," dated January 1773, college composition folder, box 1, Paterson Collection, PUL.

30. "Address before the Cliosophic Society on the Anniversary of Its Founding," n.d., college composition folder, box 1, Paterson Collection, PUL.

31. Quoted in Charles F. Mullet, *Fundamental Law and the American Revolution, 1760–1776* (New York, 1939), p. 8.

32. Richard B. Morris, "Legalism *versus* Revolutionary Doctrine in New England," *NEQ*, 4 (1931): 195–215. See also E. S. Corwin, *The "Higher Law" Background of American Constitutional Law* (Ithaca, N.Y., 1955).

33. The most important among the many new studies that have traced these intellectual trends are Caroline Robbins, *The Eighteenth Century Commonwealthman: Studies in the Transition, Development and Circumstance of English Liberal Thought from the Restoration of Charles II until the War with the Thirteen Colonies* (Cambridge, Mass., 1959); Bernard Bailyn, *The Ideological Origins of the American Revolution* (Cambridge, Mass., 1967); and Gordon S. Wood, *The Creation of the American Republic* (Chapel Hill, 1969). See also George Athan Billias, ed., *Law and Authority in Colonial America* (Boston, 1965), and Mullet, *Fundamental Law and the American Revolution*, passim.

34. "Is It Legal to Kill a Tyrant?" n.d., Paterson Papers, LC. Paterson also made note of the same principle in his college commonplace book, box 1, Paterson Collection, PUL.

35. Stockton's house, in which he also kept his office, is now the governor's mansion of the State of New Jersey.

36. "On Study," n.d., college composition folder, box 1, Paterson Collection, PUL. Although he had passed his examination in November, Paterson's official scroll was not received until the following February because Governor William Franklin was not available to sign it.

37. William Paterson to John MacPherson, November 16, 1768, and July 26, 1769, original letterbook, box 1, Paterson Collection, PUL. [*King v. Lord Stirling*], legal brief in Paterson's hand dated November 1768, general mss., misc., PUL.

38. Honeyman was able to locate the village known as New Bromley as one of two crossroads in Somerset County in an area populated by wealthy farmers. The exact location of Paterson's second office in the area referred to as Raritan is not clear, but Honeyman placed it near the present South Branch. "The Early Career of Governor William Paterson," *SCHQ*, 1 (July 1912): 169, 172. In matters relating to Paterson's legal training and career as a lawyer, I have relied heavily on Richard Haskett, *William Paterson, Counsellor at Law* (unpublished Ph.D. dissertation, Princeton University, 1952). His careful analysis of the county court records in the area where Paterson did most of his legal work in these early years is the basis for his conclusion that Paterson's early career was not very successful. According to Haskett, Paterson's cases in Hunterdon and Somerset counties and his cases before the supreme court of the province totaled up to

1769   2 cases
1770   4 cases
1771   9 cases
1772   4 cases
1773   5 cases
1774   6 cases
1775   15 cases (nine of which were representing his father).

See also Haskett, "William Paterson, Attorney General of New Jersey: Public Office and Private Profit in the American Revolution," *WMQ*, third series, 7 (1950): 33–34.

39. William Paterson to John MacPherson, July 27, 1770, and July 30, 1770, original letterbook, box 1, Paterson Collection, PUL.

40. William Paterson to Edward Paterson, January 2, 1770, original letterbook, box 1, Paterson Collection, PUL.

41. Certificate of Appointment as Surrogate of the Province of New Jersey, August 1, 1769, general mss., misc., oversize file, PUL.

42. William Paterson account book, box 1, Paterson Collection, PUL. See also Richard Haskett, "Village Clerk and Country Lawyer: William Paterson's Legal Experience, 1763–1772," *PNJHS*, 66 (1948): 164–168.

43. See Haskett, "Village Clerk and Country Lawyer," and Chapter 4.

44. *Dunlap's Pennsylvania Packet*, January 30, 1775, quoted in *NJA*, first series, 231: 46–47.

45. For a detailed description of this affair, see Haskett, "William Paterson, Counsellor at Law," p. 78–83. Haskett concludes of Paterson's legal maneuver: "If not precisely fraudulent, this affair does have an unpleasant air about it" (p. 82n). See also Middlesex mortgages, book 2, p. 53; and Somerset Mortgages, book D, p. 11, cited in Honeyman, "Early Career of Governor William Paterson," p. 165.

46. Richard Stockton to Robert Ogden, September 13, 1765, in *PNJHS*, first series, 2 (1846–1847): 149.

47. For a discussion of the protest against the Stamp Act in New Jersey, see Donald L. Kemmerer, *Path to Freedom: The Struggle for Self-Government in New Jersey, 1703–1776* (Princeton, 1940), pp. 285–291. A more detailed account can be found in Larry R. Gerlach, *Prologue to Independence* (New Brunswick, 1976), pp. 115–142.

48. Kemmerer, *Path to Freedom*, pp. 278–282.

49. William Paterson to Luther Martin, June 2, 1769, original letterbook, box 1, Paterson Collection, PUL.

50. Leonard Lundin, *Cockpit of the Revolution: The War for Independence in New Jersey* (Princeton, 1940), pp. 57–58.

51. Gerlach, *Prologue to Independence*, p. 45.

52. Larry R. Gerlach, *Revolution or Independence? New Jersey 1760–1776* (unpublished Ph.D. dissertation, Rutgers University, 1968), pp. 85–86.

53. Lundin, *Cockpit of the Revolution*, p. 65.

54. Greene, *Revolutionary Generation*, p. 86.

55. "On the Clamor against Lawyers," n.d., political essays folder, box 1, Paterson Collection, PUL.

56. Ibid.

57. Ibid.

58. Gerlach, *Revolution or Independence*, p. 86.
59. Alan Heimert, *Religion and the American Mind from the Great Awakening to the Revolution* (Cambridge, Mass., 1966), p. 180.
60. In the Dutch Reformed Church, the revival was complicated by the issue of independence from the church hierarchy in Holland. The two groups were the Conferentie, which sought to adhere to the old forms, and the Coetus, which insisted on a purely American church. Hardenburg was one of the first Dutch Reformed clergymen to be licensed and ordained in America and was a leader of the Coetus faction. See *Tercentenary Studies, 1928, Reformed Church in America, a Record of Beginnings* (New York, 1928), pp. 209–234.
61. See William H. S. Demerest, *A History of Rutgers College,* (New Brunswick, 1924), pp. 1–74, and Richard P. McCormick, *Rutgers: A Bicentennial History* (New Brunswick, 1966), pp. 1–12.
62. [Petition of the English Speaking members of the Dutch Reformed Church of Raritan], n.d., box 1, Paterson Collection, PUL.
63. Ibid. See also Heimert, *Religion and the American Mind,* Chapter 4.
64. See *Records of the First Presbyterian Church of New Brunswick,* microfilm collection, RUL. For evidence of his regular church attendance and constant participation in church affairs, see Joseph Clark, *Sermon on the Death of the Honorable William Paterson,* (New Brunswick, 1806).
65. Lester King, *The Medical World of the Eighteenth Century* (Chicago, 1958), p. 3, Chapters 1 and 2 passim.
66. Commonplace book, box 1, Paterson Collection, PUL.
67. Fred B. Rogers and A. Reasoner Sayre, *The Healing Art: A History of the Medical Society of New Jersey* (Trenton, 1966), pp. 1–27.
68. William Paterson to Aaron Burr, October 26, 1772, original letterbook, box 1, Paterson Collection, PUL.
69. King, *Medical World of the Eighteenth Century,* pp. 320–325. For a contemporary account that is more detailed in its description, see Larry R. Gerlach, "Smallpox Inoculation in Colonial New Jersey: A Contemporary Account," *RULJ,* 31 (1967): 21–28. See also Richard Shryock, *Medicine and Society in America: 1660–1860* (New York, 1960) and John Duffy, *Epidemics in Colonial America* (Baton Rouge, 1953).
70. "On Musick," January 1773, college composition folder, box 1, Paterson Collection, PUL.
71. "Beware of Doctors," n.d., college composition folder, box 1, Paterson Collection, PUL.
72. Ibid.
73. [On Doctors], n.d., Paterson Papers, LC.
74. Ibid.
75. Ibid.
76. Petition to Regulate the Practitioners of Medicine (addressed to William Franklin, Governor), dated 1771, signed by William Paterson, Richard Paterson, and fourteen others, 1939 Calendar No. 47, NJSL.
77. Rogers and Sayre, *The Healing Art,* pp. 32–34.
78. William Paterson to John MacPherson, September 15, 1773, original letterbook, box 1, Paterson Collection, PUL.

CHAPTER 3

1. Richard Haskett, *William Paterson, Counsellor at Law* (unpublished Ph.D. dissertation, Princeton University, 1952), p. 99, and Haskett's "William Paterson, Attorney General of New Jersey: Public Office and Private Profit in the American Revolution," *WMQ*, third series, 7 (1950): 26–39.

2. Richard Stockton to Robert Ogden, September 13, 1765, in *PNJHS*, first series, 2 (1846–1847): 149. See also Donald L. Kemmerer, *Path to Freedom: The Struggle for Self-Government in New Jersey, 1703–1776* (Princeton, 1940), pp. 283–286.

3. William Paterson to John MacPherson, July 30, 1770, original letterbook, box 1, Paterson Collection, PUL.

4. William Paterson to John MacPherson, June 26, 1772, original letterbook, box 1, Paterson Collection, PUL. That Paterson shared the widespread concern over aristocracy and social pretension in the English Church in America is indicated by his use of the term "high fliers." See Carl Bridenbaugh, *Mitre and Sceptre: Transatlantic Faiths, Ideas, Personalities and Politics, 1689–1775* (New York, 1962), pp. 182, 183, and 213–214.

5. This was an opinion Paterson had voiced while defending his colleagues in the legal profession against popular opposition in 1769. See discussion in Chapter 2.

6. James K. Martin has recently placed Paterson among the lower echelon of the colonial elite, whom he sees as motivated to revolution by a desire to attain higher level offices. Although his analysis of the Revolution's effect on careers such as Paterson's is convincing, his implication that personal ambition was the major factor in such men's decision to revolt is not. *Men in Rebellion* (New Brunswick, 1973). For a cogent comment on Martin's study see Richard D. Brown's review in *NJH*, 94 (Spring 1976): 38–40.

7. See H. Trevor Colbourn, *The Lamp of Experience: Whig History and the Intellectual Origins of the American Revolution* (Chapel Hill, 1965). Such ideas were common to those thinkers whom Caroline Robbins has called the *Eighteenth Century Commonwealthman* (Cambridge, Mass., 1959). See also Bernard Bailyn, *Ideological Origins of the American Revolution* (Cambridge, Mass., 1967), pp. 70–77 and passim; Lawrence Leder, *Liberty and Authority: Early American Political Ideology, 1689–1769* (Chicago, 1968), pp. 79–94; and Pauline Maier, "The Beginnings of American Republicanism," in *The Development of a Revolutionary Mentality*, Papers Presented at the First Library of Congress Symposium on the American Revolution (Washington, D.C., 1972).

8. See Richard Gummere, *The American Colonial Mind and the Classical Tradition* (Cambridge, Mass., 1963); Gordon Wood, *The Creation of the American Republic, 1776–1787* (Chapel Hill, 1969), passim; and Howard Mumford Jones, *O Strange New World, American Culture: The Formative Years* (New York, 1964), pp. 248–250, Chapters 7 and 9 passim. Paterson's college commonplace book contains numerous examples of his interest in history and the classics, box 1, Paterson Collection, PUL. In later years Paterson himself adopted three different classical pseudonyms for newspaper essays he wrote in the 1790s. Newspaper essays, oversize file, Paterson Papers, RUL.

9. For the impact of Enlightenment rationalism on the Revolution, see Henry Steele Commager, "America and the Enlightenment," in *Development of a Revolu-*

tionary Mentality (Washington, D.C., 1972), pp. 7–29; Peter Gay, "The Enlightenment," in C. Van Woodward, ed., *The Comparative Approach to American History* (New York, 1968), pp. 34–46; and Bernard Bailyn, "Political Experience and Enlightenment Ideas in Eighteenth Century America," *AHR*, 67 (1962): 339–351.

10. It has been suggested that American lawyers in the decades before the Revolution came to associate the English common law with a fundamental law that superseded both legislative statute and royal command. See, for example, George Athan Billias, ed., *Law and Authority in Early America* (Barre, Mass., 1965), pp. xi–xiv. See also Charles F. Mullet, *Fundamental Law and the American Revolution, 1760–1776* (New York, 1939), passim.

11. Perry Miller, *The New England Mind: From Colony to Province* (Cambridge, Mass., 1953), pp. 27–28 and passim.

12. See Alan Heimert, *Religion and the American Mind from the Great Awakening to the Revolution* (Cambridge, Mass., 1966), passim. The clearest example of this revolutionary ministry in New Jersey was John Witherspoon's "Pastoral Letter" dated June 29, 1775, and read to all Presbyterian congregations in the Synod of New York and Philadelphia. Witherspoon advised the faithful to support the Continental Congress and urged them to purify their lives "if possible to prevent God's vengeance by unfeigned repentance." Witherspoon went on: "If it is undeniable, that universal profligacy makes a nation ripe for divine judgements, and it is the natural means to bring them to ruin, reformation of manners is of the utmost necessity in our present distress." John Rodgers, ed. *The Works of John Witherspoon* (4 vols.; Philadelphia, 1800), Vol. 2, pp. 599–603. See also Nathan O. Hatch, *The Sacred Cause of Liberty: Republican Thought and the Millenium in Revolutionary New England* (New Haven, 1977).

13. *New York Gazeteer*, October 12, 1775, in *NJA*, first series, 31:205–206.

14. "Address on the Rise and Decline of Nations," n.d., political essays folder, box 1, Paterson Collection, PUL. The remainder of this chapter consists primarily of an analysis of this address. Unless otherwise noted, all subsequent quotations have been drawn from it.

15. Donald L. Kemmerer, *Path to Freedom: The Struggle for Self-Government in New Jersey, 1703–1776* (Princeton, 1940), pp. 304–306; Larry R. Gerlach, *Revolution or Independence? New Jersey 1760–1776* (unpublished Ph.D. dissertation, Rutgers University 1968), pp. 403–409; William Franklin to Lord Hillsborough, September 29, 1770, in *NJA*, first series, 10:200–201.

16. Leonard Lundin, *Cockpit of the Revolution: The War for Independence in New Jersey* (Princeton, 1940), p. 59; also see account in *NJA*, first series, 10:549–552.

17. On George III and the British political scene, see Louis Namier, *The Structure of English Politics at the Accession of George III*, 2nd ed. (London, 1957); and *England in the Age of the American Revolution*, 2nd ed. (London, 1961); also see Richard Pares, *King George III and the Politicians* (Oxford, 1953).

18. This episode took place in 1770–1771. See Paterson's "Beware of Doctors," n.d., college composition folder, box 1, Paterson Collection, PUL.

19. Bailyn, *Ideological Origins*, pp. 144–159 and passim.

20. Petitions of Princeton inhabitants, quoted in Gerlach, *Revolution or Independence*, p. 140.

21. Gerlach, *Revolution or Independence*, p. 159.

22. Ibid., pp. 151–163. See also John Shy, *Towards Lexington: The Role of the*

British Army in the Coming of the American Revolution (Princeton, 1965), pp. 389-391.

23. Quoted in Helmert, *Religion and the American Mind,* p. 498; see also pp. 93, 250-251, 423, 494-497.

24. Wood, *Creation of the American Republic,* pp. 73-74. Most of the scholarship concerning this factor of increasing stratification has concerned New England: James A. Henretta, "Economic Development and Social Structure in Colonial Boston," *WMQ,* third series, 22 (1965): 75-92. See also Charles S. Grant, *Democracy in the Connecticut Frontier Town of Kent* (New York, 1961); and Kenneth Lockridge, *A New England Town, the First Hnudred Years; Dedham, Massachusetts, 1636-1736* (New York, 1970).

25. Commonplace book, box 1, Patterson Collection, PUL.

26. William Paterson, *Laws of the State of New Jersey,* revised and published under the authority of the legislature (Newark, 1800).

27. Shy, *Towards Lexington,* pp. 379-380, 387, 393.

28. John Witherspoon, "Address to the Inhabitants of Jamaica and Other West India Islands in Behalf of the College of New Jersey," in Richard Hofstadter, ed., *Documentary History of American Education* (2 vols.; Chicago, 1961), Vol. 1, p. 140.

29. January 1773, college composition folder, box 1, Paterson Collection, PUL.

30. Quoted in Wood, *Creation of the Republic,* p. 110.

31. Edmund S. Morgan and Helen M. Morgan, *The Stamp Act Crisis: Prologue to Revolution* (Chapel Hill, 1953), Chapter 2 passim; Bailyn, *Ideological Origins,* pp. 277-281.

32. Quoted in Lundin, *Cockpit of Revolution,* p. 94n.

33. Quoted in Wood, *Creation of American Republic,* p. 212.

34. Colbourn, *Lamp of Experience,* p. 181.

35. Wood, *Creation of the American Republic,* pp. 107-108.

36. This new interpretation is fully developed in Gerlach, *Revolution or Independence.* A summary explanation of this point of view can be found in the same author's "New Jersey and the Coming of the American Revolution," in *New Jersey in the American Revolution: Political and Social Conflict,* Papers Presented at the First New Jersey History Symposium (Trenton, 1970).

37. Gerlach, *Revolution or Independence,* pp. xxii-xxiii, and Gerlach, "New Jersey in the Coming of the American Revolution," p. 14.

38. See Gordon S. Wood, "Rhetoric and Reality in the American Revolution," *WMQ,* third series, 23 (1966): 3-32.

39. According to Gordon Wood, "enlightened rationalism and evangelical Calvinism were not at odds in 1776; both when interpreted by Whigs placed revolutionary emphasis on the general will of the community and on the responsibility of the collective people to define it." *Creation of the American Republic,* p. 60. See also pp. 53-70 on the "public good" and the "need for virtue."

40. See Bailyn, *Ideological Origins,* pp. 301-319.

CHAPTER 4

1. Clinton Rossiter used these words to describe Richard Bland of Virginia; see *Six Characters in Search of a Republic* (New York, 1964), p. 151.

2. Merrill Jensen, *The Founding of a Nation: A History of the American Revolution, 1763–1776* (New York, 1968), pp. 464–470, 474–477.

3. Donald Kemmerer, *Path to Freedom: The Struggle for Self-Government in New Jersey, 1703–1776* (Princeton, 1940), p. 320; Larry R. Gerlach, *Prologue to Independence* (New Brunswick, 1976), pp. 209–214.

4. The activities in New Jersey for the relief of Boston are described in Gerlach, *Prologue to Independence,* pp. 216–218.

5. On the county committees and the enforcement of the Continental association, see Gerlach, *Prologue to Independence,* pp. 232–236. At first, Governor Franklin thought the decisions of the Congress would have little support in New Jersey, but within weeks he was forced to report differently. See William Franklin to Lord Dartmouth, October 29 and December 6, 1774, in *NJA,* first series, 10:500, 503.

6. On the little resistance that came from royal officials, Tory publicists, Anglican ministers, and Quakers, see Gerlach, *Prologue to Independence,* pp. 236–243.

7. Elmer's speech is quoted in Gerlach, *Prologue to Independence,* p. 258.

8. Ibid., p. 552.

9. "Essay on the Clamor against Lawyers," n.d., political essays folder, box 1, Paterson Collection, PUL. William Livingston, Paterson's friend and later wartime governor of New Jersey, showed the same hesitation to throw in his lot with the rabble of the sons of liberty. See David Bernstein, *New Jersey in the American Revolution: The Establishment of a Government amid Civil and Military Disorder, 1770–81,* (unpublished Ph.D. dissertation, Rutgers University, 1970), p. 232.

10. Kemmerer, *Path to Freedom,* pp. 327–328; Gerlach, *Prologue to Independence,* pp. 259–261.

11. Edmund S. Morgan, *The Birth of the Republic* (Chicago, 1956), p. 70.

12. On the mobilization of the New Jersey militia, see Gerlach, *Prologue to Independence,* pp. 259–260.

13. Historians dispute which gathering of New Jersey patriots should be called the First Provincial Congress. Bernstein, *New Jersey in the American Revolution,* calls the meeting of July 1774, the First Provincial Congress and the Trenton gathering of 1775 the Second. Charles Erdman, *New Jersey Constitution of 1776* (Princeton, 1929), also singles out the 1774 meeting, but allows that some might prefer "to apply that name to the extra-legal meeting of the assembly in 1765 when delegates to the Stamp Act Congress were chosen" (p. 10). Kemmerer, *Path to Freedom,* and Gerlach, *Prologue to Independence,* however, reserve that title for the May 23, 1775, meeting in Trenton. I have chosen to follow this latter view. It appears that, as significant as the earlier meetings may have been, they were singular instances in the protest struggle. The congress that came together in May 1775 continued to reconvene (albeit with some changes in membership) until 1776 when the constitution it wrote went into effect. Besides, this was the first meeting at which all thirteen counties were represented.

14. "Address on the Rise and Decline of Nations," n.d., college composition folder, box 1, Paterson Collection, PUL.

15. *PCCS* (Trenton, 1879), p. 114.

16. Ibid., pp. 114–115.

17. Only Essex, Middlesex, and Hunterdon had sent more delegates. For a complete analysis of the delegates, see Gerlach, *Prologue to Independence,* pp. 267–268.

18. *PCCS*, p. 170. Sergeant had graduated in 1762 while Paterson was still a student, but Frelinghuysen had only received his degree in 1770. Samuel Tucker from Hunterdon County was chosen vice president.
19. The date was May 30, 1775; *PCCS*, p. 175.
20. Ibid., pp. 171–172.
21. Ibid., p. 176.
22. Ibid., pp. 176–177.
23. Ibid., pp. 180–183.
24. John R. Alden, *The American Revolution* (New York, 1954), pp. 34–39.
25. Jensen, *Founding of a Nation*, Chapters 22 and 23 passim.
26. John Rodgers, II, ed., *Works of John Witherspoon*, (4 vols.; Philadelphia, 1800), Vol. 2, pp. 599–600. See also Chapter 3.
27. *PCCS*, pp. 184–185.
28. Ibid., pp. 185–186.
29. Ibid., pp. 187–194.
30. See Chapter 2.
31. *PCCS*, p. 197.
32. Ibid., pp. 200, 203. The Congress had resolved to reappoint him to the post before it was known whether or not he would be able to attend.
33. See Chapter 2 on his father's bankruptcy. See also Petition, dated January 25, 1776, signed by Paterson and others, seeking the appointment of a militia officer, mss. MG 42, NJHS.
34. *PCCS*, pp. 203, 341. When Carey did not attend the sitting, two other delegates (Clark and Stewart) were offered the job and declined on the grounds that it would interfere "with the duty of their stations as delegates." Only then was Paterson reappointed. Mss. minutes, February 2, 1776, NJHS. Paterson resumed the secretarial chores, but until May 1775 he carried on as a nondelegate. It is unclear whether or not he was paid a salary for this period.
35. Jensen, *Founding of a Nation*, pp. 641–643.
36. Kemmerer, *Path to Freedom*, pp. 337–338; Gerlach, *Prologue to Independence*, pp. 294–295.
37. Leonard Lundin, *Cockpit of the Revolution: The War for Independence in New Jersey* (Princeton, 1940), p. 74; Kemmerer, *Path to Freedom*, p. 340.
38. See Jensen, *Founding of a Nation*, Chapters 23 and 24 passim.
39. W. Jay Mills, ed., *Glimpses of Colonial Society* (New York, 1903), p. 23.
40. Most of the minutes of the second session of the Second Provincial Congress as well as the minutes of the Third (elected in May 1776) and the convention which it later became have survived in manuscript form and are in Paterson's hand. They are preserved in the collections of the New Jersey Historical Society. With a few significant exceptions, the discrepancies between the published *PCCS* and the manuscript minutes are inconsequential, but wherever possible I have noted references to the manuscript minutes (hereafter referred to as Mss. minutes).
41. Mss. minutes, February 3 and February 5, 1776, NJHS; *PCCS*, pp. 370–373. On the requirements for voting in New Jersey, see Richard P. McCormick, *History of Voting in New Jersey* (New Brunswick, 1953), pp. 67–68 and passim.
42. *PCCS*, p. 379. Even though the new election was called for before the completed suffrage legislation was formally passed into law by the Congress, it is clear that the intent of the new election was to accommodate the newly enfranchised

voters. The Congress had already agreed on the principle of the wider suffrage and was delayed in the final passage because of the working out of some of the details. *PCCS*, pp. 373–374.

43. Mss. minutes, March 1, 1776, NJHS.
44. Jensen, *Articles of Confederation* (Madison, Wis., 1940), pp. 10n and 55–103 passim.
45. Commonplace book, box 1, Paterson Collection, PUL.
46. "Is It Lawful to Kill a Tyrant?" n.d., Paterson Collection, LC.
47. Ibid.
48. Jensen, *Founding of a Nation*, pp. 670–699 passim.
49. Larry R. Gerlach, "New Jersey and the Coming of the American Revolution," in *New Jersey in the American Revolution: Political and Social Conflict*, Papers Presented at the First New Jersey History Symposium (Trenton, 1970), passim.
50. Quoted in Jensen, *Founding of a Nation*, p. 684.
51. Quoted in Erdman, *New Jersey Constitution of 1776*, p. 25.
52. The only poll list that survives indicates that only 699 Morris County voters cast ballots. "Morris County Poll List, May 1776," *PNJHS*, 66 (1948): 114–121. The white male population of the county came close to 2,500, according to Gerlach, *Prologue to Independence*, p. 330. Only a very few of the newly chosen delegates openly opposed independence. In all they represented no more than "a scant dozen in a total of 65." Erdman, *New Jersey Constitution of 1776*, p. 26.
53. Bernstein, *New Jersey in the American Revolution*, p. 163.
54. *PCCS*, pp. 449–450.
55. Attorney General Cortlandt Skinner fled to New York in December 1775; see Lundin, *Cockpit of Revolution*, p. 74.
56. See Gerlach, *Prologue to Independence*, pp. 328–329.
57. *PCCS*, pp. 454–457.
58. Ibid., pp. 457, 461, 462, 467, 470; and mss. minutes, June 21, 1776, NJHS.
59. *PCCS*, p. 460; Gerlach, *Prologue to Independence*, pp. 335–336.
60. Mss. minutes, June 21, 1776, NJHS; Jensen, *Articles of Confederation*, pp. 111–116.
61. Mss. minutes, June 22, 1776, NJHS.
62. Mss. minutes, June 23, 1776, NJHS.
63. For analysis of the 1776 Constitution, see Erdman, *New Jersey Constitution of 1776*, pp. 43–69.
64. Mss. minutes, July 18, 1776, NJHS.
65. Mss. minutes, June 23–July 2, 1776, passim, NJHS.
66. The allegation was made by Cortland Parker in a speech at Princeton in 1899; see Erdman, *New Jersey Constitution of 1776*, pp. 34–35.
67. Mss. minutes, July 2, 1776, NJHS.
68. Erdman, *New Jersey Constitution of 1776*, p. 33n; Richard Haskett, *William Paterson, Counsellor at Law* (unpublished Ph.D. dissertation, Princeton University, 1952), p. 99. Certainly Haskett goes too far by describing Paterson as "more of a thoroughgoing radical than many of his fellows."
69. Erdman, *New Jersey Constitution of 1776*, p. 151.
70. Mss. minutes, July 3, 1776, NJHS.
71. See Chapter 5.
72. See Chapter 6.
73. *PCCS*, pp. 373–379. Paterson was not officially a member of the delegation at the

time, but he was present as the secretary of the Congress and must have been aware of why his Somerset fellows voted the way they did.

74. "The Constitution was framed in a very critical juncture, and, as it were, on the spur of the occasion. It was at the time considered as a temporary thing resulting from the exigency of the moment, and expected, it would undergo a dispassionate and thorough revision." Newspaper essay on the Office of Governor and Chancellor of New Jersey, oversize file, Paterson Papers, RUL; see also *Guardian*, March 20, 1973.

75. I can find no analysis of the 1776 constitution that makes mention of this crucial fact.

76. Mss. minutes, July 2, 1776, NJHS.

77. The British landed without difficulty on Staten Island so that they could avoid an immediate confrontation with the Americans on Manhattan and Long Island. Staten Island became a staging area for the Battle of Long Island later that summer. See Henry P. Johnson, *The Campaign of 1776 around New York and Brooklyn*, Memoirs of the Long Island Historical Society, Vol. 3 (Brooklyn, N.Y., 1878), p. 94.

78. Mss. minutes, July 2, 1776, NJHS.

79. "Popular approbation" was thought to be of particular importance because there was no provision for popular ratification. Erdman, *New Jersey Constitution of 1776*, p. 38.

80. The 1776 constitution of New Jersey is displayed in the State Museum at Trenton.

81. *JLC* (Burlington, 1777), p. 14.

CHAPTER 5

1. William Paterson to Cornelia Bell, August 29, 1777; February 9, 1778; February 27, 1778; and April 20, 1778; Paterson Papers, LC.

2. Paterson kept a record of family marriages, births, and deaths in his own hand. See notebook, n.d., misc. mss., Paterson Papers, NJHS.

3. Massachusetts Historical Society *Collections*, sixth series, 4, p. 104, quoted in Elisha P. Douglas, *Rebels and Democrats* (Chapel Hill, 1955), p. 156. See also Chapter 1.

4. *JLC*, first session, passim.

5. William Paterson to William Livingston, October 21, 1776, Livingston Papers, MHS. The militia unit in question was probably the "Flying Camp" that had been established the previous June. William Paterson to William Livingston, October 21, 1776, Livingston Papers, MHS.

6. For a complete analysis of the ineffectiveness of the revolutionary legislature and the vacuum filled by Livingston's and Paterson's leadership of the Council of Safety and the Privy Council, see David Bernstein's, *New Jersey in the American Revolution: The Establishment of a Government amid Civil and Military Disorder, 1770–81* (unpublished Ph.D. dissertation, Rutgers University, 1970). Some of his conclusions were summarized in a paper entitled, "William Livingston: The Role of the Executive in New Jersey's Revolutionary War," in *New Jersey in the American Revolution II* (Trenton, 1973), pp. 12–30.

7. Bernstein, *New Jersey in the American Revolution*, Chapter 9 passim.

8. Philemon Dickinson to William Paterson, March 13, 1777, folder 1, Paterson Papers, RUL.

9. Amicus to William Paterson, n.d., folder 1, Paterson Papers, RUL.

10. The charge, which was made by "A Jersey Farmer," in the October 8, 1778, *New Jersey Gazette,* was incorrect, because the constitution, which specified that members of the assembly not hold multiple offices, did not mention legislative councillors in this regard.

11. Mss. minutes, July 2, 1776, NJHS.

12. *PCCS,* for 1776 passim.

13. Leonard Lundin, *Cockpit of the Revolution: The War for Independence in New Jersey* (Princeton, 1940), pp. 141ff and passim.

14. Newspaper essay, [c. 1793–1796], oversize file, Paterson Papers, RUL.

15. Lundin, *Cockpit of the Revolution,* Chapter 7 passim.

16. *Votes and Proceedings of the General Assembly of New Jersey* (Burlington, 1777), pp. 99–100 (hereafter referred to as *Votes and Proceedings*).

17. See *PCCS,* passim.

18. *JLC,* p. 65 (March 12, 1777).

19. This document, which Paterson called "Address to a Conference," is clearly the speech he offered in March 1777. A cover sheet bears the date 1776, but, since the address discusses the events of the winter of 1776–1777, we can only assume that Paterson added the erroneous date later on. Folder 1, Paterson Papers, RUL.

20. "Address to a Conference" [March 15, 1777], folder 1, Paterson Papers, RUL.

21. Ibid.

22. Ibid.

23. See Chapter 4.

24. Mss. minutes, July 4, 1776, NJHS.

25. On the side of stability, see Clarence VerSteeg, *The Formative Years* (New York, 1964), p. 276; Michael Zuckerman, *Peaceable Kingdoms: New England Towns in the Eighteenth Century* (New York, 1970), pp. 22, 227; Charles Sydnor, *Gentlemen Freeholders: Political Practices in Washington's Virginia* (Chapel Hill, 1952), pp. 75–85; and Robert A. Gross, *The Minutemen and Their World* (New York, 1976), passim. For evidence of upheaval in local institutions, see, for example, Edward Countryman, "Consolidating Power in Revolutionary America: The Case of New York," *Journal of Interdisciplinary History,* 6, 4 (Spring 1976): 645–679.

26. Dennis P. Ryan, *Six Towns: Continuity and Change in Revolutionary New Jersey, 1772–1792,* (unpublished Ph.D. dissertation, New York University, 1974), pp. 194–241.

27. On New Jersey's counties, see Edward Q. Keasby, *Courts and Lawyers in New Jersey 1661–1912* (3 vols.; New York, 1912), Vol. 2, pp. 813–822.

28. The *New Jersey Gazette* was set up with the aid of the legislature in 1776. For discussion of a similar sort of "courthouse culture" that existed in Virginia in the years just before independence see Rhys Isaac's "Dramatizing the Ideology of Revolution: Popular Mobilization in Virginia, 1774–1776," *WMQ,* third series, 33, 3 (July 1976): 357–385.

29. *PCCS,* passim.

30. For further examples of the temporary vacuum that existed in local government in the winter of 1776–1777, see Bernstein, *New Jersey in the American Revolution,* p. 277.

31. *JLC,* March 15, 1777.
32. The most complete analysis of the Council of Safety is in Bernstein, *New Jersey in the American Revolution,* Chapter 8.
33. Ibid., passim. See also *MCS* (Jersey City, N.J., 1872).
34. *MCS,* passim.
35. "Address on Loyalism," n.d., folder 1, Paterson Papers, RUL. Paterson began to write these comments on the same page where he completed his address before the legislative conference of March 15. There can be no doubt, however, that these later pages were written after that date, because they include reference to the imprisonment of John Fell, justice of the state supreme court and Paterson's fellow legislative councillor, who was captured by the British on April 22, 1777, and taken by them to New York. The tone of Paterson's remarks suggests that he may have been encouraging the legislature to widen the power of the Council of Safety, as they did on several occasions.
36. Ibid. It is possible that this speech was made in support of a clause in the June 1777 treason law that provided the death penalty for those apprehended on their way to the enemy lines.
37. *MCS,* passim; and Bernstein, *New Jersey and the American Revolution,* Chapter 8 passim. As Richard Haskett points out, there were very few sittings of the Supreme Court during this period, leaving most of the business to the county courts; see *William Paterson, Counsellor at Law* (unpublished Ph.D. dissertation, Princeton University, 1952), pp. 127, 139, 141. See also Haskett, "Prosecuting the Revolution," *AHR,* 59 (1954): 583.
38. *MCS,* passim.
39. See Paterson's notes in the *State* v. *Moses Beivers,* Sussex Sessions, November 1779, William Paterson Papers, William Paterson College, Wayne, N.J.
40. See Paterson's notes on the trial of Joseph and Catherine Brown, et. al., William Paterson Papers, William Paterson College, Wayne, N.J. Unfortunately, Paterson's notes provide neither the county, date, nor outcome of the trial.
41. Ibid.
42. Lundin, *Cockpit of the Revolution,* p. 408.
43. See Austin Scott, "*Holmes* v. *Walton:* The New Jersey Precedent," *AHR,* 4 (1899): 456–469.
44. Wallace Brown, *The King's Friends: The Composition and Motives of the American Loyalist Claimants* (Providence, 1966), p. 111.
45. Ibid.
46. See Adrian C. Leiby, *The Revolutionary War in the Hackensack Valley: The Jersey Dutch in the Neutral Ground* (New Brunswick, 1962); and Ruth M. Keesey, "Loyalism in Bergen County, New Jersey," *WMQ,* third series, 18 (October 1961): 558–576.
47. Cornelia Bell to Andrew Bell, January 30, 1777, Andrew Bell Papers, LC. See also Paul Smith, *Loyalists and Redcoats* (Chapel Hill, 1964), passim.
48. Abraham V. D. Honeyman, "Concerning the New Jersey Loyalists in the American Revolution," *PNJHS,* Vol. 51 (1933): 117–133. Cornelius Vermule, "Active Loyalists of New Jersey," *PNJHS,* Vol. 52 (1934): 87–95. Vermule suggested that there were as few as five hundred.
49. Paul Smith, "New Jersey Loyalists and the British Provincial Corps in the War for Independence," *NJH,* 87 (1969): 69–78.
50. [Bridgeton] *Plain Dealer,* January 1, 1776, mss. copy, RUL.

51. "Address on Loyalism," n.d., folder 1, Paterson Papers, RUL.

52. Lundin, *Cockpit of the Revolution,* pp. 160–161.

53. See Andrew Bell Papers, LC.

54. Bell Papers, NJHS.

55. These letters are in the Andrew Bell Papers, LC.

56. Cornelia Bell to Andrew Bell, January 30, 1777, Andrew Bell Papers, LC.

57. Cornelia Bell to Andrew Bell, April 2, 1777, Andrew Bell Papers, LC.

58. Cornelia Bell Paterson to Andrew Bell, April 5, 1779, Andrew Bell Papers, LC.

59. Cornelia Bell Paterson to Andrew Bell, September 12, 1779, and August 26, 1780, Andrew Bell Papers, LC.

60. William Paterson to Cornelia Bell Paterson, March 17, 1779, Paterson Papers, LC.

61. William Paterson to Cornelia Bell Paterson, September 12, 1779, and August 26, 1780, Paterson Papers, LC.

62. William Paterson to Cornelia Bell, June 27, 1778, Paterson Papers, LC.

63. William Paterson to Cornelia Bell Paterson, June 2, 1782, Paterson Papers, LC.

64. William Paterson to Cornelia Bell Paterson, February 27, 1779, Paterson Papers, LC.

65. William Paterson to Cornelia Bell Paterson, March 17, 1779, Paterson Papers, LC.

66. William Paterson to Cornelia Bell Paterson, March 29, 1779, Paterson Papers, LC.

67. Newspaper essay, n.d., Paterson Papers, LC.

68. Wallace Brown, *The Good Americans: The Loyalists in the American Revolution* (New York, 1969), Chapter 5, passim.

69. Ruth M. Keesey, "New Jersey Legislation Concerning Loyalists," *NJH,* 79, 2 (1961): 82–83.

70. Ibid., pp. 87–90 and passim. See also Lundin, *Cockpit of the Revolution,* pp. 286–293.

71. Charge of William Stout, July 27, 1779, Nelson Papers, NJHS.

72. "Address on Loyalism," n.d., folder 1, Paterson Papers, RUL.

73. Jurors of Monmouth County Report to William Paterson of Charge against Edward Price, July 1779, misc. mss., Paterson Papers, NJHS.

74. Ibid.

75. Bill of Particulars against Edward Price and William Harbert, under indictment for treason, signed by William Paterson, May 1782, misc. mss., Paterson Papers, NJHS.

76. Form of Judgement in Sentence of Death against Robert Whitaker, n.d., mss no. W. J. 28, NJHS.

77. The only complete study of New Jersey's colonial courts is Keasby, *Courts and Lawyers,* passim.

78. Form of Judgement in Sentence of Death against Robert Whitaker, n.d., mss. no. W. J. 28, NJHS.

79. William Paterson to Aaron Burr, June 1, 1779, misc. mss., Paterson Papers, NJHS. The story is related in Haskett, *William Paterson: Counsellor at Law,* pp. 147–148; and in Matthew L. Davis, *Memoris of Aaron Burr* (2 vols.; New York, 1836), passim.

80. Certificate of Sale, April 14, 1779, folder 1, Paterson Papers, RUL; Cornelia Bell Paterson to Andrew Bell, September 12, 1779, Andrew Bell Papers, LC.

81. Michael P. Riccards, "Patriots and Plunderers: Confiscation of Loyalist Lands in New Jersey, 1776–1786," *NJH,* 86, 1 (1968): 25.

82. Cornelia Bell Paterson to Andrew Bell, September 12, 1779, Andrew Bell Papers, LC.
83. Ibid.
84. Cornelia Bell to Andrew Bell, March 11, 1778, and April 7, [1779], Andrew Bell Papers, LC. She also acknowledged the safe receipt of at least some of the articles. Cornelia Bell Paterson to Andrew Bell, September 12, 1779, Andrew Bell Papers, LC.
85. Richard Haskett, "William Paterson, Attorney General of New Jersey: Public Office and Private Profit in the American Revolution," *WMQ*, third series, 7 (1950): 29.
86. Ibid.
87. Ibid.
88. Ibid., passim.
89. See Davis, *Memoirs of Aaron Burr*, Vol. 1, pp. 217–222.
90. Haskett, "William Paterson, Attorney General of New Jersey," pp. 32–33.
91. Ibid., p. 31.
92. Lundin, *Cockpit of the Revolution*, pp. 86–87.
93. William Paterson to Henry Laurens, March 6, 1778, misc. mss., Paterson Papers, NYHS.
94. William Paterson to Alexander Stevens, December 4, 1780, misc. mss., Paterson Papers, NYHS.
95. Haskett, "William Paterson, Attorney General of New Jersey," p. 36.
96. Bill of Particulars against Edward Price and William Harbert under indictment for treason, signed by William Paterson, May 1782, misc. mss., Paterson Papers, NJHS.
97. Richard P. McCormick, *Experiment in Independence: New Jersey in the Critical Period, 1781–1789* (New Brunswick, 1950), p. 36.
98. Paterson to Speaker of Assembly, March 17, 1783, folder 2, Paterson Papers, RUL.
99. Cornelia Bell Paterson to Andrew Bell, September 12, 1779, Andrew Bell Papers, LC.
100. James K. Martin, *Men in Rebellion* (New Brunswick, 1973), pp. 80–81.
101. Haskett, "William Paterson, Attorney General of New Jersey," p. 26.

CHAPTER 6

1. See Richard P. McCormick, *Experiment in Independence: New Jersey in the Critical Period, 1781–1789* (New Brunswick, 1950), Chapter 1 passim.
2. William Peartree Smith to Elias Boudinot, April 1783, in *PNJHS*, first series, 4 (1849): 122.
3. Ibid. Smith's idolization of Washington was typical in revolutionary America. "Washington the patriot of patriots," he wrote to Boudinot on another occasion. "Talk of yr. Catos, yr. Brutus, & your Cassius—they are all mere Fools to him. In short, he is too good for an ingrate, base, degenerate world." April 22, 1783, in *PNJHS*, first series, 4 (1849): 123.
4. William Paterson to Thomas Paterson, May 12, 1783, Bancroft Transcripts, NYPL. William Paterson to Andrew Bell, February 27, 1784, Andrew Bell Papers, LC.
5. Notice of death of Richard Paterson in *New Jersey Gazette*, August 8, 1781. William Paterson to Thomas Paterson, July 1783, Bancroft Transcripts, NYPL.

6. Cornelia Bell Paterson to Andrew Bell, October 23, 1779, Andrew Bell Papers, LC.

7. Mss. notebook, n.d., misc. mss., Paterson Papers, NJHS.

8. Ibid.

9. Cornelia Bell Paterson to Andrew Bell, July 31, 1783, and Andrew Bell to Cornelia Bell Paterson, Andrew Bell Papers, LC.

10. Mss. notebook, n.d., misc. mss., Paterson Papers, NJHS.

11. Mss. poem, n.d., Paterson Papers, LC.

12. William Paterson to Andrew Bell, March 2, 1784, Andrew Bell Papers, LC.

13. Cornelia Bell Paterson to Andrew Bell, April 5, 1779, Andrew Bell Papers, LC. Mss. notebook, n.d., misc. mss., Paterson Papers, NJHS.

14. Richard Haskett, *William Paterson, Counsellor at Law*, (unpublished Ph.D. dissertation, Princeton University, 1952), pp. 189–191.

15. Ibid.

16. Ibid., pp. 223–224. See also Mss. account book, Paterson Papers, RUL.

17. McCormick notes that the boundary dispute occupied so much of the proprietors' attention, that they missed their opportunity to play an influential role in other important issues of the period and seriously weakened the conservative cause. He goes on to suggest that some lawyers deeply involved in the boundary dispute (such as John Stevens, Sr., James Parker, and Robert Morris) were so busy with it that they showed no particular interest in other matters such as paper money and debtor laws. Paterson was apparently one of the few who played a role in the boundary question and was still active in other affairs. *Experiment in Independence*, pp. 147–157. The description in this chapter is based on McCormick's detailed account.

18. "Notes for a Legislative Hearing," November 2, 1784, Pyne Henry mss., PUL.

19. William Paterson to Robert Morris, December 12, 1785, general mss. misc., PUL.

20. McCormick, *Experiment in Independence*, p. 145. Haskett, *William Paterson, Counsellor at Law*, pp. 205–206.

21. For a general discussion of the case and its repercussions, see Richard P. McCormick, "The East Jersey Estate of Sir Robert Barker," *PNJHS*, 64, 3 (1946): 119–155. On Parker's mixed loyalties, see Leonard Lundin, *Cockpit of the Revolution: The War for Independence in New Jersey* (Princeton, 1940), pp. 78–80.

22. James Parker to Robert Barker, August 16, 1783, quoted in McCormick, "East Jersey Estate of Sir Robert Barker," p. 128. Parker closed the letter offering his services by listing as references former royal governor William Franklin, Cortlandt Skinner (his brother-in-law), "or any Gentlemen of note in England" who had fled from New Jersey out of loyalty to the king.

23. Ibid., pp. 131–132.

24. Haskett, *William Paterson, Counsellor at Law*, pp. 206–208.

25. Ibid., p. 26.

26. William Paterson to Robert Morris, December 12, 1785, general mss. misc., PUL.

27. William Paterson to the President of Congress, March 26, 1785, general mss. misc., PUL. The dispute had to do with Massachusetts's claim to lands within the reserved boundary of New York, and, in accordance with the Articles of Confederation, a court was set up by Congress to consider the dispute. Edmund C. Burnett, *The Continental Congress* (New York, 1941), p. 601.

28. William Paterson to Thomas Paterson, May 12, 1783, Bancroft Transcripts, NYPL.

29. The return of the Loyalists to New Jersey is discussed by McCormick in *Experiment in Independence*, pp. 28–39 passim. R. R. Palmer notes that the percentage of returning Loyalists was far less in America than it was in France after their revolution, and he considers it significant evidence for the contention that the American Revolution was a "real revolution," *Age of Democratic Revolutions* (Princeton, 1956), vol. I, pp. 188–189.

30. William Paterson to Thomas Paterson, May 12, 1783, Bancroft Transcripts, NYPL.

31. William Paterson to Andrew Bell, March 2, 1784, Andrew Bell Papers, LC. On Bell's later life, see Alfred Jones, "The Loyalists of New Jersey in the Revolution," *PNJHS*, 11, 2 (1926): 219–221.

32. The Humble Petition of Merchants and Other Citizens of the State of New Jersey, December 12, 1783, NJSL.

33. William Paterson to John Lawrence, February 9, 1785, Paterson Papers, LC.

34. "Notes on a Contested Election before the House of Assembly," 1788, legal opinions folder, box 1, Paterson Collection, PUL. See also McCormick, *Experiment in Independence*, pp. 93–94.

35. Haskett, *William Paterson, Counsellor at Law*, pp. 191–192.

36. For the complete and detailed description on which my comments are based, see McCormick, *Experiment in Independence*, Chapters 7 and 8.

37. Ibid., p. 205n.

38. "Essay on Principles of Legislation," n.d., Paterson Papers, RUL.

39. Newspaper essay on the financial expedients of the 1780s; Horatius no. 15, [c. 1793–1796], oversize file, Paperson Papers, RUL.

40. Ibid.

41. "Notes of a Legislative Hearing," November 2, 1784, Pyne Henry mss., PUL.

42. McCormick, *Experiment in Independence*, p. 163.

43. Ibid., pp. 159–164.

44. Newspaper essay on the financial expedients of the 1780s; Horatius no. 15 [c. 1793–1796], oversize file, Paterson Papers, RUL. Although internal evidence clearly identifies them as having been written in the 1780s, so few New Jersey newspapers from the period have survived that it is impossible to specify when and where the earlier essays cited in notes 46 and 49 were published.

45. "Essay on Principles of Legislation," n.d., Paterson Papers, RUL.

46. "Essay on a New Emission of Paper Money," n.d., Paterson Papers, RUL.

47. McCormick, *Experiment in Independence*, p. 169.

48. Ibid. Also see McCormick for a discussion of New Jersey paper money before the war, pp. 190–192.

49. "Value of Gold No. 2," n.d., Paterson Papers, RUL.

50. Ibid.

51. Ibid.

52. Ibid.

53. Ibid.

54. "Essay on a New Emission of Paper Money," n.d., Paterson Papers, RUL.

55. Ibid.

56. Ibid.

57. McCormick, *Experiment in Independence*, pp. 191, 195, 206, 217. Also see Curtis Nettles, *Emergence of a National Economy, 1775–1815* (New York, 1962), pp. 80–81.

58. "Essay on Principles of Legislation," n.d., Paterson Papers, RUL.
59. Ibid.
60. McCormick, *Experiment in Independence*, p. 193.
61. "Value of Gold No. 2," n.d., Paterson Papers, RUL.
62. E. James Ferguson, *Power of the Purse: A History of American Public Finance, 1776–1790* (Chapel Hill, 1961), p. 166 and passim. The plan again proposed the impost that had been turned down by the states in 1781 and also called for a pattern of supplementary taxes to be collected by the states for Congress.
63. Ibid., p. 222; McCormick, *Experiment in Independence*, pp. 173–176.
64. E. James Ferguson, "The Nationalists of 1781–1783 and the Economic Interpretation of the Constitution," *JAH*, 16, 2 (1969): 246; Ferguson, *Power of the Purse*, Chapter 11 passim.
65. Ferguson, *Power of the Purse*, p. 225.
66. McCormick, *Experiment in Independence*, pp. 238–240.
67. Ibid., p. 240.
68. Quoted in McCormick, *Experiment in Independence*, p. 242.
69. Ibid., pp. 242–243.
70. Draft of Petition, [May 1786], Bancroft Transcripts, NYPL.
71. Ibid. See also McCormick, *Experiment in Independence*, p. 239.
72. Draft of Petition, [May 1786], Bancroft Transcripts, NYPL.
73. McCormick, *Experiment in Independence*, pp. 80–81.
74. Jackson Turner Main, "Government by the People: The American Revolution and the Democratization of the Legislatures," *WMQ*, third series, 23, 3 (1966): 391–407 passim.
75. See Bernard Bailyn, *Ideological Origins of the American Revolution* (Cambridge, Mass., 1967), pp. 302ff.
76. McCormick, *Experiment in Independence*, pp. 201–202. On the upper house, see Jackson Turner Main, *The Upper House in Revolutionary America* (Madison, Wis., 1967).
77. North Brunswick Tax Records, 1788, NJSL. Haskett, *William Paterson, Counsellor at Law*, did find ten cases where Paterson was suing for a debt due to himself, but it is likely that most of these were for fees due from his clients (p. 198).
78. R. R. Livingston to Elias Boudinot, June 25, 1789, Elias Boudinot Papers from the American Bible Society, PUL.
79. "Value of Gold No. 2," Paterson Papers, RUL.
80. North Brunswick Tax Records, 1788, NJSL.
81. "Essay on Principles of Legislation," n.d., Paterson Papers, RUL.
82. See Gordon Wood, *Creation of the American Republic, 1776–1787* (Chapel Hill, 1969), p. 273.
83. Paterson was not a man who had always concerned himself with economic and financial affairs. He showed no interest in such matters before the Revolution, and after 1790 his attention would turn to matters of foreign affairs and political partisanship. Perhaps the reason he became so involved in financial arguments during the 1780s was simply that these were the major issues of the day—the issues in which the constitutional and political questions that interested him were most clearly reflected.
84. Palmer, *Age of Democratic Revolutions*, Vol. 1, pp. 214–217.
85. Ibid. On the developing idea of a constitution, see also Wood, *Creation of the American Republic*, pp. 273–282.

86. "Essay on Principles of Legislation," n.d., Paterson Papers, RUL.
87. See Chapter 3.

CHAPTER 7

1. See Merrill Jensen, *The New Nation: A History of the United States during the Confederation* (New York, 1950), and Richard P. McCormick, *Experiment in Independence: New Jersey in the Critical Period, 1781–1789* (New Brunswick, 1950), passim.
2. McCormick, *Experiment in Independence*, pp. 233–244.
3. Newspaper essay on the benefits of the Constitution, [c. 1793–1796], oversize file, Paterson Papers, RUL.
4. McCormick, *Experiment in Independence*, pp. 219–220.
5. Ibid., p. 240; see also Chapter 6.
6. Newspaper essay on the benefits of the Constitution, [c. 1793–1796], oversize file, Paterson Papers, RUL.
7. E. James Ferguson, "The Nationalists of 1781–1783 and the Economic Interpretation of the Constitution," *JAH*, 16, 2 (1969): passim.
8. According to John C. Miller, "success in the policy of gradual change would have merely blunted the wedge which Hamilton hoped to drive into the heart of the Articles." *Alexander Hamilton: Portrait in Paradox* (New York, 1959), p. 140.
9. McCormick, *Experiment in Independence*, p. 253.
10. Miller, *Alexander Hamilton*, p. 138.
11. McCormick, *Experiment in Independence*, pp. 255–256.
12. Ibid., pp. 256n, 276–277.
13. Ibid., p. 256.
14. For Paterson's political and moral outlook on Confederation finance, see Chapter 6. For the specific interests of some of the other delegates, see Charles Beard, *Economic Interpretation of the Constitution of the United States* (New York, 1913); and Forrest McDonald, *We the People: The Economic Origins of the Constitution* (Chicago, 1958).
15. One of the very fortunate circumstances of the convention was the fact that very few of those who were opposed to a new stronger government were in attendance in Philadelphia. See Stanley M. Elkins and Eric McKitrick, "The Founding Fathers, Young Men of the Revolution," *PSQ*, 76, 2 (1961): 212 and passim.
16. Max Farrand, *The Records of the Federal Convention of 1787* (4 vols.; New York, 1937, and New Haven, 1966), Vol. 3, p. 90.
17. Ibid.
18. Clinton Rossiter, *1787: The Grand Convention* (New York, 1966), pp. 160–161; Irving Brant, *James Madison: The Nationalist* (New York, 1948), Chapters 25 and 26; and Brant, *James Madison: Father of the Constitution* (New York, 1950), Chapter 1. See also Farrand, *Records*, Vol. 3, pp. 23, 409.
19. Farrand, *Records*, Vol. 1, pp. 20–22.
20. Madison had proposed a sweeping interpretation of the implied powers of the Confederation Congress in 1781, and in a committee report to the Congress he had suggested an amendment to the Articles that would have granted Congress the authority to use force against the states that did not conform. The proposal was never submitted to the states. Jensen, *New Nation*, p. 59.

21. According to Gordon Wood, "the Federalists of the late eighties wanted and believed they needed much more than the nationalists of the early eighties had sought." *Creation of the American Republic, 1776–1787* (Chapel Hill, 1969), p. 475.

22. Hamilton now wondered how he could have previously sought to increase the powers of so democratic a body. See Miller, *Alexander Hamilton*, pp. 131–150 passim. Of course, Hamilton did not think the Virginia Plan went far enough either.

23. McCormick, *Experiment in Independence*, p. 259.

24. Forrest McDonald, *E. Pluribus Unum* (Boston, 1965), pp. 164–165.

25. Farrand, *Records*, Vol. 1, pp. 10–11n.

26. The manuscript copy of Paterson's notes is preserved at the Library of Congress. With a very few minor exceptions, Farrand, *Records*, represents a correct transcription.

27. Farrand, *Records*, Vol. 1, p. 27. For Hamilton's comment, see McHenry's notes, ibid.

28. Read's nationalism would be obvious throughout the convention. He had had the foresight to request that Delaware instruct their delegation specifically not to assent to unequal representation. This way he would not be forced to participate in any "disagreeable argumentation: over the question." Rossiter, *1787*, p. 151.

29. On June 5, Paterson had formally requested that Randolph's resolution for guaranteeing the territory and republican government of the individual states be considered only after "the point of representation could be decided." Farrand, *Records*, Vol. 1, p. 121.

30. Wilson suggested setting up special districts from which the people could directly choose senators. Presumably Delaware and New Jersey would each be a part of a district larger than themselves. Ibid., Vol. 1, pp. 151–153.

31. Ibid., Vol. 1, pp. 152–156.

32. Ibid., Vol. 1, p. 167.

33. Ibid., Vol. 1, p. 168.

34. Ibid., Vol. 1, p. 185; Vol. 3, p. 584.

35. Ibid., Vol. 1, pp. 178, 185–186.

36. Ibid., Vol. 1, pp. 132, 168, 179. Partly because of these populistic-sounding statements, David Hacket Fischer has described Paterson's attitude as somewhat of "a puzzle." *Revolution of American Conservatism* (New York, 1965), p. 325.

37. Farrand, *Records*, Vol. 1, pp. 178–186. Irving Brant suggests that the "proposal of a hotchpot and redivision was about as practicable as a motion to carve up the moon." *James Madison: Father of the Constitution* (New York, 1950), p. 51.

38. By this time, the Virginians and Pennsylvanians had skillfully twisted the phrases around so that for them "equality of representation" meant an equal representation for every person rather than for every state. See Farrand, *Records*, Vol. 1, pp. 180, 187–188.

39. Ibid., Vol. 1, p. 179.

40. Ibid., Vol. 1, p. 22.

41. Ibid., Vol. 1, p. 121. See also William Wiecek, *The Guarantee Clause of the United States Constitution* (Ithaca, N.Y., 1972), p. 53.

42. See notes for his speech in Farrand, *Records*, Vol. 1, p. 188.

43. Farrand, *Records*, Vol. 2, p. 664. It is interesting to note that New Jersey's instructions to its delegates did not restrict them to only "revising." Vol. 3, p. 588.

44. The New Hampshire representatives did not show up until July 23, the day Paterson left for home. Ibid., Vol. 3, p. 588.

45. See Chapter 6.

46. McCormick, *Experiment in Independence*, pp. 233–244; Farrand, *Records*, Vol. 3, p. 563; Brant, *James Madison: Father of the Constitution*, p. 65.

47. McCormick, *Experiment in Independence*, pp. 220–233.

48. Luther Martin and Jonathan Dayton were probably the most intimately involved in land speculation.

49. Farrand, *Records*, Vol. 2, pp. 464–466.

50. When Madison later reported Paterson's speech to Jefferson, the "hotchpot" idea was all that he thought was important enough to mention. Brant, *James Madison: Father of the Constitution*, p. 52.

51. Elkins and McKitrick, "The Founding Fathers," p. 203.

52. He had suggested in his "Address on the Rise and Decline of Nations" before the war that in a declining state "men of unbounded ambition frequently break in upon the principles of the constitution, &, if joined to an innovating spirit, seldom fail to model the government anew," and, in a 1798 Fourth of July speech, he suggested that any sudden increase in the power of government might prove fatal: "A great and sudden enlargement of dominion and power, generally indicate a great and sudden declension and ruin." Political essay folder, box 1, Paterson Collection, PUL.

53. See Chapter 5.

54. Farrand, *Records*, Vol. 1, p. 274.

55. See Christopher Collier, *Roger Sherman's Connecticut: Yankee Politics and the American Revolution* (Middletown, Conn., 1971), p. 263.

56. Farrand, *Records*, Vol. 1, p. 16.

57. The idea of a "hotchpot," for example, was mentioned in Brearly's seconding speech before Paterson had a chance to develop the idea. Ibid., Vol. 1, pp. 177–178.

58. Ibid., Vol. 1, p. 174.

59. Ibid., Vol. 1, p. 240.

60. According to Rossiter, it "showed the strains of its multiple paternity." *1787*, p. 175.

61. Farrand, *Records*, Vol. 1, pp. 242–245.

62. That he wrote this article is clear from his later letters that acknowledged the fact and carefully pointed out the precise phrasing of his proposal that would have benefitted his friends at home in Maryland. Ibid., Vol. 3, pp. 286–287.

63. Until 1786, there were legislative roadblocks to court settlement of such debt cases, but after that year debts could be collected through the courts with no restriction other than the requirement that payment be accepted in state paper money. Jensen, *New Nation*, pp. 278–279.

64. Maryland and New Jersey had been the most obstreperous members of Congress when it came to settling questions of the western lands. They were also the home states of some of the most active speculators. Jensen, *New Nation*, pp. 350–359.

65. Farrand, *Records*, Vol. 1, p. 245. Surprised to find such apparently nationalistic feeling in the small states, Rossiter uses the word "astonishing" to describe the clause, but he seems not to have appreciated just how extraordinary Martin's devious reasoning actually was. Rossiter, *1787*, p. 176.

66. Martin himself later described these intentional loopholes in the proposal. Farrand, *Records,* Vol. 3, pp. 286–287. See also Jensen, *New Nation,* pp. 278–279; Brant, *James Madison: Father of the Constitution,* p. 66.
67. Farrand, *Records,* Vol. 1, p. 316.
68. It must be noted here that Article 14 of Madison's proposals as they lay on the table read

> that provision ought to be made for the admission of states; lawfully arising within the limits of the United States, whether from the voluntary junction of government and territory, or otherwise, with the consent of a number of voices in the national legislature less than the whole.
>
> Farrand, *Records,* Vol. 1, p. 231.

The wording suggested that—contrary to the final wording adopted for Article 4, Section 3 of the Constitution as signed—a junction of territory might be involuntary, and that it would not require a vote of any state legislature. The final wording was not proposed in the convention until the Committee of Detail suggested it on August 6, and it was not approved until August 30, after two days of heated debate with Martin in the opposition. Ibid. Vol. 2, pp. 188, 464.
69. Ibid., Vol. 3, pp. 286–287; Brant, *James Madison: Father of the Constitution,* pp. 67–68. In their recent biography of Martin, Paul S. Clarkson and R. Samuel Jett are more generous to him. They suggest that his concern was primarily with the protection of personal liberty and was especially tied to the fact that the new federal Constitution would have no bill of rights. *Luther Martin of Maryland* (Baltimore, 1970), pp. 114–118.
70. Brant suggests that Yates and Lansing were willing to support the movement for equal representation because they hoped it would torpedo the entire convention. *James Madison: Father of the Constitution,* p. 65. See also Farrand, *Records,* Vol. 3, pp. 612–613.
71. In one of the early drafts of the plan, Paterson indicated that he would bring up the "hotchpot" idea again. Perhaps because he figured that the loophole left by Martin for the dividing up of the rest of the states was explicit enough a reminder of the land issue, he dropped the "hotchpot" proposal from the final document. Ibid., Vol. 3, p. 613.
72. Ibid., Vol. 3, pp. 615–616.
73. Ibid., Vol. 3, p. 613.
74. He had made this point in 1777 when arguing for the establishment of a council of safety and had referred to it as well on June 9, and again on June 16. Ibid., Vol. 1, pp. 186, 274. See also Chapter 5.
75. Charles Warren, *The Making of the Constitution* (Boston, 1928), p. 225.
76. Farrand, *Records,* Vol. 1, p. 242.
77. He even used the fact that voting in the convention was done on an equal basis to strengthen his point. Ibid., Vol. 1, pp. 249–250.
78. His own notes for the speech identified Maryland and New Jersey as the states most interested in the western lands issue. Ibid., Vol. 1, p. 274.
79. The notes of Madison, Yates, King, and Hamilton each mention Paterson's consideration of the Confederation as a solemn contract, but to find a note of his fear that too much innovation would undermine the stability of the new system one must look at his own notes. Ibid., Vol. 1, pp. 250, 258, 264, 268, 274.
80. Ibid., Vol. 1, pp. 251–252.
81. See notes for June 16, 18, and 19. Ibid., Vol. 1, pp. 260–322.

82. There were two attempts to prolong the debate and have the resolutions presented one at a time on the floor (one by Ellsworth and another by Dickinson), but each failed. Ibid., Vol. 1, pp. 255, 282.
83. Historians have as a rule been rather generous to the New Jersey Plan, treating it as a serious attempt to offer an alternative to each of Randolph's original proposals. In 1913 Max Farrand wrote, "it is altogether possible, if the New Jersey Plan had been presented to the convention at the same time as the Virginia Plan, that is, on May 29, and if without discussion a choice had been made between the two, that the former would have been selected. It would seem," he continued, "as if the New Jersey plan more nearly represented what most of the delegates supposed that they were sent to do. But in the course of the two weeks' discussions, many of the delegates had become accustomed to what might well have appeared to them at the outset as quite radical ideas." *The Framing of the Constitution of the United States* (New Haven, 1913), p. 89. These "might have beens" can sometimes raise interesting historical theories, but in this case it is impossible to guess what might have happened two weeks earlier. The particulars of the New Jersey Plan were shaped primarily by the situation in the convention after Paterson's arguments failed on June 9 and by the very diverse (at times even contradictory) interests of the particular men who drew it up. If conceived two weeks earlier, before things seemed to get out of hand for the small states, the document probably would have looked very different.
84. See Brant, *James Madison: Father of the Constitution*, p. 54.
85. Farrand, *Records*, Vol. 1, p. 261.
86. According to Farrand, Dickinson went on to explain that "some members from the small states wish for two branches in the General Legislature, and are friends to a good National Government; but we would sooner submit to a foreign power, than submit to be deprived of an equality of suffrage, in both branches of the legislature, and thereby be thrown under the domination of the large States." Ibid., Vol. 1, p. 242n.
87. Ibid., Vol. 1, p. 321. Later in life, Madison remembered in a letter that "the main object of [the Paterson Plan] being to secure to the smaller States an equality with the larger in the structure of the Govt.," it was impossible to presume that the other elements of the plan were sincerely agreed upon by all the plan's supporters. On the question of the powers to be granted to Congress, for example, Madison said that no "abstract" opinions could be perceived until the matter of representation was finally settled. Ibid., Vol. 3, p. 496.
88. Roger S. Boardman, *Roger Sherman, Signer and Statesman* (Philadelphia, 1938), p. 245. Within two days of the vote, Sherman, Ellsworth, and Johnson were each on the floor calling for compromise. Farrand, *Records*, Vol. 1, pp. 334, 341, 354. Connecticut, on the basis at least of the western lands issue, could afford to compromise more than Delaware, Maryland, and New Jersey could. They had won a reserve of western territory for themselves in their confrontation with Pennsylvania during the Confederation. Jensen, *New Nation*, p. 336; see also Brant, *James Madison: Father of the Constitution*, p. 65.
89. Farrand, *Records*, Vol 1, pp. 322–323, 324.
90. As it appeared in Randolph's first resolution. Ibid., Vol. 1, pp. 134–135.
91. See Rossiter, *1787*, pp. 180–181.
92. Yates stopped keeping his notes on July 5. Farrand, *Records*, Vol. 3, p. 588, 590.

93. Ibid., Vol. 1, pp. 437–445; Vol. 3, p. 272.
94. Ibid., Vol. 1, pp. 445–451.
95. Ibid., Vol. 1, p. 464.
96. Ibid., Vol. 1, p. 468.
97. Ibid., Vol. 1, pp. 481–482.
98. A few days later, Bedford backed down from his previous position, explaining that speaking in such an animated fashion was one of the weaknesses of his profession—he was a lawyer. Ibid., Vol. 1, pp. 492, 531–532.
99. Ibid., Vol. 1, p. 510.
100. Ibid., Vol. 1, p. 511.
101. The convention had already agreed that representation in the first house should be proportional. Now they were suggesting that apportionment should be one representative for every 40,000 individuals. Ibid., Vol. 1, p. 526.
102. Ibid., Vol. 1, p. 529.
103. Ibid., Vol. 1, p. 530.
104. Ibid., Vol. 1, p. 536.
105. Ibid., Vol. 1, p. 551.
106. Ibid., Vol. 1, p. 554.
107. Ibid., Vol. 1, p. 573.
108. Ibid., Vol. 1, p. 561. A few years later, Paterson was criticizing those who had worked against the Constitution. He called the three-fifths question a fuss over nothing. "Slaves are men and also a species of property, and therefore of double value in a land of liberty." Newspaper essay on parties and the Constitution, *Guardian*, March 20, 1793; see also oversize file, Paterson Papers, RUL.
109. Farrand, *Records*, Vol. 1, p. 561.
110. Ibid., Vol. 1, p. 604. See also Caleb Strong, Ibid., Vol. 1, p. 7.
111. Ibid., Vol. 2, p. 16.
112. Ibid., Vol. 2, pp. 17–18.
113. Ibid.
114. Ibid., Vol. 2, p. 18.
115. Ibid., Vol. 2, p. 5.
116. Ibid., Vol. 2, p. 18.
117. Ibid., Vol. 2, p. 19.
118. Ibid.
119. Madison recorded that there were even some small-state men at the meeting, but he did not mention any names. Ibid., Vol. 2, p. 20.
120. Rossiter, *1787*, p. 183.
121. Leonard Boyne Rosenberg, *The Political Thought of William Paterson* (unpublished Ph.D. dissertation, New School for Social Research, 1967), pp. 98–109.
122. Rossiter, *1787*, pp. 193–194.
123. Farrand, *Records*, Vol. 4, p. 70.
124. Ibid., Vol. 2, p. 84.
125. Ibid., Vol. 4, p. 73.
126. Ibid., Vol. 3, p. 73.
127. Ibid., Vol. 4, p. 73.
128. Ibid.
129. Ibid., Vol. 2, p. 664.
130. Paterson had seconded a motion by Ellsworth on July 23 to send the completed Constitution to the state legislatures rather than special conventions, but he had

left for home before the vote on the question was taken later in the day. Ibid., Vol. 2, pp. 88, 91, 93. If Paterson had been motivated by his scrupulous legalistic mind when he opposed going beyond the instructions of the Congress, he certainly should not have now signed the Constitution that called for ratification by only nine states and in those states by conventions especially called for the purpose. On both points, the Constitution ignored the established procedures of the Articles of Confederation.

131. For some unknown reason, Paterson did not sign the official report submitted to the state legislature by the delegation he had led. McCormick, *Experiment in Independence*, p. 264n.

132. Ibid., p. 272; McDonald, *We the People*, p. 126.

133. McCormick, *Experiment in Independence*, p. 272. Paterson realized the importance of the assumption of state debts, and he included in his notes for the last day he attended the convention a reference to a speech by Oliver Ellsworth: "The debt will go with the Govt.—this is a prevailing idea." Farrand, *Records*, Vol. 2, p. 96.

134. Abraham Clark was one of the few who even questioned the Constitution publicly. McCormick, *Experiment in Independence*, pp. 276–277.

135. Newspaper essay on the benefits of the Constitution, [c. 1793–1796], oversize file, Paterson Papers, RUL.

136. Fourth of July Oration [July 4, 1798], political essays folder, box 1, Paterson Collection, PUL.

CHAPTER 8

1. *Brunswick Gazette*, July 10, July 17, July 26, July 31, August 7, 1787.

2. See Richard P. McCormick, *Experiment in Independence: New Jersey in the Critical Period, 1781–1789* (New Brunswick, 1950), p. 272; and Forrest McDonald, *We the People: The Economic Origins of the Constitution* (Chicago, 1958), pp. 123–129.

3. Lambert Cadwallader to George Mitchell, October 8, 1787, quoted in McCormick, *Experiment in Independence*, p. 264.

4. The date of the vote was December 18. Only Pennsylvania and Delaware ratified earlier.

5. *Brunswick Gazette*, September 11, 1787.

6. See misc. legal correspondence in folder 4, Paterson Papers, RUL.

7. William Bell to William Paterson, July 6, 1786, folder 3, Paterson Papers, RUL. A man named Stacy Hepburn also claimed that Edward had drawn a £20 note on Paterson's account "before they went off." Stacy Hepburn to William Paterson, July 6, 1786, folder 3, Paterson Papers, RUL.

8. John Donaldson to William Paterson, May 25, 1789, folder 4, Paterson Papers, RUL.

9. Thomas Irwin to William Paterson, June 30, 1788, Paterson Papers, LC.

10. Mss. copy of William Paterson's letter to Edward Paterson, December 11, 1788, folder 4, Paterson Papers, RUL.

11. Ibid.

12. Ibid.

13. Mss. copy of William Paterson's letter to Thomas Paterson, December 18, 1788, folder 4, Paterson Papers, RUL.

14. Ibid.
15. John Donaldson to William Paterson, May 25, 1789, and September 29, 1790, folders 4 and 5, Paterson Papers, RUL. A little over half of the debt was assumed by James Hunter of Philadelphia and was repaid to him by Paterson before the end of 1790. James Hunter to William Paterson, November 10, 1789, and October 18, 1790, folders 4 and 5, Paterson Papers, RUL.
16. Thomas Irwin to William Paterson, April 26, 1796, folder 6, Paterson Papers, RUL.
17. In 1798 and again in 1801, Tom asked his brother to help him find a position more suited to his apparently serious rheumatic condition, but there is no evidence that Paterson replied. Thomas Paterson to William Paterson, July 3, 1798, and December 6, 1801, Paterson Papers, LC.
18. "The New Roof," reprinted from the *Pennsylvania Packet,* in the *Trenton Weekly Mercury,* January 22, 1788.
19. McCormick, *Experiment in Independence,* p. 289n.
20. William Paterson to Euphemia Paterson [1788?], folder 12, Paterson Papers, RUL.
21. See John Chetwood to William Paterson, October 7, 1788, folder 4, Paterson Papers, RUL. In his letter to his wife noted above, Paterson wrote that "I regret my promise and wish I could resume it, but this cannot be done with any tolerable grace. I have made advances of this nature, and in the present state and ferment of parties I was not without hopes of it being accepted, but in this I have been disappointed."
22. John Chetwood to William Paterson, October 7, 1788, folder 4, Paterson Papers, RUL.
23. See McCormick, *Experiment in Independence,* pp. 290–301.
24. William Paterson to Euphemia Paterson, March 24, 1789, folder 12, Paterson Papers, RUL.
25. William Paterson to Euphemia Paterson, March 27, 1789, Paterson Papers, RUL.
26. *Documentary History of the First Congress, Senate Legislative Journal,* pp. 7–11. Later Charles Carroll of Maryland and Ralph Izard of South Carolina were added to the committee.
27. See *Elliot's Debates,* cited in Warren, "New Light on the Judiciary Act of 1789," pp. 55n. See also Warren, pp. 55–56, 65, and William Crosskey, *Politics and the Constitution* (Chicago, 1953), p. 755. Note that Crosskey stresses inaccessibility of the federal courts as another factor in his analysis of the 1789 act (pp. 754–756).
28. Eighteen months before, Ellsworth had confronted Lee in the press for his "implacable hatred of General Washington, his well known intrigues against him in the late war," and his scurrilous attacks against the new constitution. "Letters of a Landholder," No. 6, *New York Journal,* December 10, 1787. Quoted in Warren, "New Light on the Judiciary Act of 1789," p. 58.
29. On Paterson's role in the committee work, see Warren, "New Light on the Judiciary Act of 1789," pp. 50, 60. According to Warren, "Paterson played a more considerable part in drafting the bill than he has hitherto been given credit for, as the Senate files show that the first nine sections, with alterations and interlineations, are in his handwriting" (p. 60).
30. Quoted in Warren, "New Light on the Judiciary Act of 1789," p. 73.
31. By this wording, criminal cases under the common law would have been put beyond the realm of the district courts. According to Warren, the omission of the final phrase ("and defined by the laws of the same") from the final draft

indicated an intention of the Senate to open jurisdiction to common law criminal cases. But subsequent Supreme Court cases interpreted the meaning differently. "New Light on the Judiciary Act of 1789," pp. 73, 77.

32. For fear that this would lead to too many cases being referred to the circuit courts, this wording was later changed to read: when "the suit is between a citizen of the state where the suit is brought and the citizen of another state." Ibid., pp. 77–78.

33. The scope of appeals of state court decisions to the Supreme Court was so restricted until the Fourteenth Amendment required that "all state laws affecting life, liberty and property were subject to the review of the Federal Judiciary." John C. Miller, *The Federalist Era, 1789–1801* (New York, 1960), p. 30.

34. William Maclay, *Journal, 1789–1791* (New York, 1927), p. 83. Warren, "New Light on the Judiciary Act of 1789," p. 67.

35. Mss. notes for a speech, n.d., folder 4, Paterson Papers, RUL.

36. Ibid.

37. This point was later made by Ellsworth as well; see Warren, "New Light on the Judiciary Act of 1789," p. 66.

38. Mss. notes for a speech, n.d., folder 4, Paterson Papers, RUL.

39. Ibid.

40. Ibid.

41. For a detailed description of the entire debate and its significance, see Warren, "New Light on the Judiciary Act of 1789," passim. For the text of the law as it was finally written into law on September 24, 1789, see Richard Peters, *Statutes at Large of the United States* (8 vols.; Boston, 1845), Vol. 1, pp. 72–93.

42. It is interesting to note that one of the distinguishing features of Paterson's 1787 New Jersey Plan was that it called for no federal courts other than the Supreme Court. On Paterson's support of defendants' rights, see Maclay, *Journal*, p. 90, and Warren, "New Light on the Judiciary Act of 1789," p. 96. On his opposition to extending equity jurisdiction see Maclay, *Journal*, p. 93; and Warren, "New Light on the Judiciary Act of 1789," pp. 96–98. See also Paterson's notes on the debates over the judiciary bill, folder 4, Paterson Papers, RUL; and mss. folder on Judiciary Act of 1789, Sen 1A–B1, Security Section SE–4, National Archives, Washington, D.C.

43. E. James Ferguson, *Power of the Purse: A History of American Public Finance, 1776–1790* (Chapel Hill, 1961), p. 291.

44. *Documentary History of the First Federal Congress*, Vol. 1, pp. 28, 51, 148; and Paterson's mss. notes on the debate over customs house oaths, Paterson Papers, PUL.

45. Maclay, *Journal*, p. 112; and Paterson's mss. notes on the debate over the power of removal from office, folder 4, Paterson Papers, RUL.

46. Comment by Charles Beard in introduction to 1927 edition of Maclay's *Journal*, p. vi.

47. Maclay, *Journal*, p. 114.

48. *Documentary History of the First Federal Congress*, Vol. 1, pp. 227, 242, 302.

49. Ibid., p. 229.

50. See Paterson's notes on the debate on the naturalization bill, n.d., Bancroft Transcripts, NYPL.

51. *Documentary History of the First Federal Congress*, Vol. 2, pp. 62, 93.

52. William Paterson to Euphemia Paterson, February 6, 1790, folder 13, Paterson

Papers, RUL. Staying at the boarding house did not guarantee a place for solitary retreat. Paterson's boarding bills for the second session, which totalled up to almost £100, included his portion of what the housekeeper called "the club account for wine and spirits." Presumably the distinguished members did not drink alone. Receipts for boarding expenses, August 12 and 13, 1790, folder 5, Paterson Papers, RUL.

53. William Paterson to John Irwin, March 5, 1791, folder 6, Paterson Papers, RUL.

54. William Paterson to Euphemia Paterson, January 30, 1790, folder 13, Paterson Papers, RUL.

55. Ferguson, *Power of the Purse*, pp. 289–305. Hamilton offered this appraisal as he was leaving the Treasury Department several years later; see his "Defence of the Funding System," July 1795, in Harold Syrett, ed. *Papers of Alexander Hamilton* (25 vols.; New York, 1973), Vol. 19, pp. 72–73.

56. Ferguson, *Power of the Purse*, pp. 293–295.

57. Ibid., pp. 297–299. Senator Maclay was one of those who wanted to pay only 3 percent interest on the whole debt and tried unsuccessfully to convince Madison to support that formula. Maclay, *Journal*, p. 194.

58. *Documentary History of the First Federal Congress*, Vol. 1, p. 347; Maclay, *Journal*, pp. 282–283.

59. Ibid., p. 289. Committee Report on "An Act Making Provision for the Debt of the United States," n.d., Record Group 46, Sen. 1A–D1, National Archives, Washington, D.C.

60. *Documentary History of the First Federal Congress*, Vol. 1, pp. 289–290; William Paterson's mss. notes on the debate on the debt bill, folder 4, Paterson Papers, RUL.

61. Peters, *Statutes at Large of the U.S.*, Vol. 1, August 20, 1790, pp. 138–144.

62. On assumption, see Ferguson, *Power of the Purse*, pp. 306–325.

63. Ibid.

64. William Paterson's mss. notes on the debate over the location of the national capital, n.d., box 1, Paterson Papers, PUL. The most recent analysis of these events suggests that the deal on assumption was based more on compromised financial questions than on the site for the permanent seat of government. Jacob E. Cooke, "The Compromise of 1790," *WMQ*, third series, 27, 4 (October 1970): 523–545.

65. Maclay, *Journal*, pp. 206, 228, 274.

66. See Richard Hofstadter, *Idea of a Party System* (Berkeley, 1969), passim.

67. See Charles Beard, *Economic Origins of Jeffersonian Democracy* (New York, 1915). Beard's critics on this issue include Joseph Charles, *The Origins of the American Party System* (Williamsburg, Va., 1956), and Noble E. Cunningham, *The Jeffersonian Republicans, The Formation of Party Organization* (Chapel Hill, 1957).

68. For recent indications of the continuity of political alignments before and after the Constitution, see Jackson Turner Main, *Political Parties before the Constitution* (Chapel Hill, 1973); and Norman K. Risjord and Gordon DenBoer, "The Evolution of Political Parties in Virginia, 1782–1800," *JAH*, 60, 4 (March 1974): 961–1002.

69. Richard Buel, Jr., *Securing the Revolution: Ideology in American Politics, 1789–1851* (Ithaca, N.Y., 1972), pp. 8–17.

70. Ibid., pp. 72–90.

CHAPTER 9

1. William Paterson to Nathaniel Hazard, June 27, 1791, mss. copy, mss. laws volume, pp. 832–833, Paterson Papers, RUL.
2. *Burlington Advertizer*, August 31, 1790.
3. Michael Lewis Levine, *The Transformation of a Radical Whig under Republican Government: William Livingston, Governor of New Jersey, 1776–1790*, (unpublished Ph.D. dissertation, Rutgers University, 1975), passim.
4. William Paterson to Euphemia Paterson, August 1, 1790, folder 13, Paterson Papers, RUL. James S. Young, *The Washington Community, 1800–1828* (New York, 1966), Chapter 3.
5. "A Governor for New Jersey," *Brunswick Gazette*, August 17, 1790, and *Burlington Advertizer*, August 24, 1790; Jonathan Dayton to William Paterson, August 17, 1790, folder 5, Paterson Papers, RUL.
6. Copies of many of these addresses and Paterson's replies are bound in mss. laws volume, Paterson Papers, RUL.
7. *Brunswick Gazette*, July 12, 1791.
8. Further appeal to the federal Supreme Court became possible after 1789.
9. See Levine, *Transformation of a Radical Whig*.
10. William Paterson, political essays, oversize file, Paterson Papers, RUL.
11. William Paterson to Euphemia Paterson, n.d., folder 12, Paterson Papers, RUL. This letter, probably written sometime in 1788, reports the legislature's plans to withdraw the loan office notes. See also McCormick, *Experiment in Independence: New Jersey in the Critical Period, 1781–1789* (New Brunswick, 1950), pp. 285–286.
12. N.J. Session Laws, 12th Session, 1st Sitting, November 3, 1787; 16th Session, 1st Sitting, November 24, 1791; and 17th Session, 1st Sitting, November 28, 1792.
13. Of the total amount (principal plus interest) four-ninths was to be exchanged for 6 percent federal notes, two-ninths for 4 percent notes, and one-third for 3 percent notes. E. James Ferguson, *Power of the Purse: A History of American Finance, 1776–1790* (Chapel Hill, 1961), pp. 321, 330.
14. William Paterson to "The Honorable Senators of New Jersey in Congress," November 26, 1791, mss. laws volume, p. 836, Paterson Papers, RUL. Ferguson, *Power of the Purse*, p. 333.
15. William Paterson, political essays, oversize file, Paterson Papers, RUL.
16. See Jacob E. Cooke, "Tench Coxe, Alexander Hamilton, and the Encouragement of American Manufactures," *WMQ*, third series, 32, 3 (June 1975): 369–392.
17. Tench Coxe to William Paterson, January 11, 1790, folder 5, Paterson Papers, RUL. Most issues of the *Brunswick Gazette* for this period have not survived, and Coxe's article has not been located among the few that still exist.
18. See *Votes and Proceedings*, 15th Session, 1st Sitting, p. 97, and *Legislative Council Proceedings*, 15th Session, 1st Sitting, p. 34. The council vote was taken November 25, 1790.
19. Quoted in Joseph Stancliffe Davis, *Essays in the Earlier History of American Corporations*, Vol. 1 (Cambridge, Mass., 1917), pp. 350-351.
20. Ibid., pp. 351–354.
21. Theophilus Cazenove to Stadnitski, August 23, 1791, quoted in Thomas Jefferson, *Papers*, Julian Boyd, ed. (19 vols.; Princeton, 1950–1974), Vol. 19, p. 453. The

320

two quotations may be translated, "all these arrangements require secrecy" and "this important matter could not be entrusted to anyone with more prudence than Mr. Hamilton."

22. Ibid. Translated, "accord the favors that are identified in the prospectus as necessary preliminaries."
23. Mss. records of stock sales, SUM Papers, Passaic County Historical Society, Paterson, New Jersey.
24. See Chapter 6.
25. *Brunswick Gazette*, November 22, 1791.
26. N.J. Session Laws, 16th Session, 1st Sitting, pp. 104–115, 116.
27. Davis, *Essays*, Vol. 1, pp. 395–398.
28. Cooke, "Tench Coxe," p. 388.
29. See Davis, *Essays;* and Broadus Mitchell, *Alexander Hamilton: The National Adventure, 1788–1804* (New York, 1962).
30. Cooke, "Tench Coxe," pp. 386–389.
31. Robert F. Jones, "William Duer and the Business of Government in the Era of the American Revolution," *WMQ*, third series, 32, 3 (June 1975): 412.
32. Ibid., pp. 412–413.
33. John Bayard to Elisha Boudinot, September 1, 1792, Dreer Collection, HSP, referred to in Davis, *Essays*, Vol. 1, p. 452.
34. Mitchell, *Alexander Hamilton*, Vol. 2, p. 191.
35. "Essay on Speculation," n.d., political essay folder, box 1, Paterson Collection, PUL.
36. Cooke, "Tench Coxe," p. 390.
37. Davis, *Essays*, Vol. 1, pp. 414–415, 418–419.
38. Ibid., pp. 437–451. The charter scroll, dated December 17, 1792, and signed by Paterson, is in the public library at Paterson, New Jersey.
39. See Mitchell, *Alexander Hamilton*, Vol. 2, pp. 190–191. For an interesting mss. record of the attempts to make the factories operable, see the Nicholas Low Papers, RUL.
40. John C. Miller, *Alexander Hamilton and the Growth of the New Nation* (New York, 1959), p. 310.
41. N.J. Session Laws, 15th Session, 1st Sitting, November 25, 1796.
42. Numerous examples of each of these activities are to be found recorded in the manuscript copies Paterson kept of many of his official papers, mss. law volume, Paterson Papers, RUL. For the proclamation on the uniform for the militia, see New Brunswick *Guardian*, January 30, 1793.
43. See chart in note 49.
44. Richard Hildreth, *History of the United States of America*, rev. ed. (6 vols.; New York, 1877), Vol. 4, p. 302.
45. Ibid.
46. William Paterson to Elias Boudinot, January 4, 1792, mss. law volume, Paterson Papers, RUL.
47. Ibid.; see also William Paterson to Philemon Dickinson, January 29, 1792, mss. copy, mss. law volume, Paterson Papers, RUL. For a full exposition of the argument Paterson espoused, see the notes on Jonathan Dayton's speech before the House of Representatives on November 21, 1791, *Annals of Congress*, 2nd Congress, pp. 201–202.

48. Hildreth, *History*, Vol. 4, p. 303.

49. *Apportionment of Seats in the House of Representatives:*

	As provided in the Constitution and as maintained in the second Congress	As provided in the unsuccessful House bill of November 1791	As eventually agreed to in 1792 and maintained thereafter until the census of 1800
New Hampshire	3	4	4
Massachusetts	8	15	14
Rhode Island	1	2	2
Connecticut	5	7	7
New York	6	11	10
New Jersey	4	5	5
Pennsylvania	8	14	13
Delaware	1	1	1
Maryland	6	9	8
Virginia	10	21	19
North Carolina	5	11	10
South Carolina	5	6	6
Georgia	3	2	2
Vermont		2	2
Kentucky		2	2
Total membership of the House of Representatives	65	112	105

50. Aurelius was the first of three pseudonyms he used. The others were Horatius and Hortensius.

51. William Paterson, "Essay on Candid and Liberal Sentiments," n.d., political essays, oversize file, Paterson Papers, RUL. See also *Guardian*, February 13, 1793.

52. William Paterson, "Essay on a Well Regulated Militia," n.d., political essays, oversize file, Paterson Papers, RUL. See also *Guardian*, February 20, 1793.

53. William Paterson, "Essay on the Office of the Governor and Chancellor of New Jersey," n.d., political essays, oversize file, Paterson Papers, RUL.

54. William Paterson, "Essay on the Independence of the Judiciary," n.d., political essays, oversize file, Paterson Papers, RUL. See also *Guardian*, April 24, 1793.

55. George Washington, *Writings*, John C. Fitzpatrick, ed. (39 vols.; Washington, D.C., 1931–1944), Vol. 32, pp. 352, 353.

56. Paterson's own observations on the office stressed the judicial responsibilities of the governor in the Court of Chancery. While Paterson was certainly well qualified to fulfill the role of chancellor, a full appreciation of his contributions in that area will have to await the detailed analysis of chancery court records recently discovered in the state archives. As of this writing, the chancery court papers consist of hundreds of parchment scrolls completely uncatalogued and too brittle to handle. The New Jersey Historical Commission is seeking a grant to have them studied and made accessible to scholars.

57. *Guardian*, April 3, 1793.

CHAPTER 10

1. See William Crosskey, *Politics and the Constitution* (2 vols.; Chicago, 1953), Vol. 1, p. 595.
2. Samuel Allinson, *Acts of the General Assembly of the Province of New Jersey* (Trenton, 1776), hereafter referred to as Allinson, *Laws.*
3. Peter Wilson, *Acts of the General Assembly of the State of New Jersey* (Trenton, 1784), hereafter referred to as Wilson, *Laws.*
4. N.J. Session Laws, 17th Session, 1st Sitting, pp. 794–795.
5. The only overall treatment of this topic is to be found in Elizabeth G. Brown, *British Statutes in American Law, 1776–1836* (Ann Arbor, 1964). For an account of Jefferson's Virginia revision see Dumas Malone, *Jefferson The Virginian* (Boston, 1948). For an interesting perspective on one aspect of the revision in New York see Mark DeWolfe Howe, "The Process of Outlawry in New York: A Study in the Selective Reception of English Law," *Cornell Law Quarterly,* 23 (1937–38): 559.
6. Paterson's observations, prepared by him to accompany the draft bills sent to the legislature, are found in his manuscript notebook on the revision, mss. law volume, Paterson Papers, RUL.
7. Mss. law volume, Paterson Papers, RUL, pp. 1, 5, 6, 57, 293.
8. Ibid., pp. 211–214, 248–251.
9. Ibid., pp. 443, 446, 564.
10. William Paterson to Speaker of the Assembly, March 30, 1793, misc. papers, non-military folder, NJSL.
11. N.J. *Session Laws,* 17th Session, 1st Sitting, 1973, p. 734. For the Pennsylvania penal reform, see Allan Nevins, *The American States during and after the Revolution, 1776–1789* (New York, 1924), pp. 454–455.
12. William Paterson to Speaker of the Assembly, March 30, 1793, misc. papers, non-military folder, NJSL.
13. Even so, execution for second offenses was rare as well. See Henry Clay Reed, *Chapters in a History of Crime and Punishment in New Jersey* (unpublished Ph.D. dissertation, Princeton, 1939), p. 394. Reed provides an interesting summary of criminal justice in colonial New Jersey. For the most recent general treatment of colonial criminal codes and punishments, see David Rothman, *The Discovery of the Asylum: Social Order and Disorder in the Young Republic* (Boston, 1971), pp. 48–52. For evidence of Paterson's protracted discussion with the assembly leaders, see James Kinsey to William Paterson, July 16, 1793, and December 12, 1794, Paterson Papers, RUL.
14. Richard P. McCormick, *Experiment in Independence: New Jersey in the Critical Period, 1781–1789* (New Brunswick, 1950), pp. 63–68. For a comparison with other colonies, see Merrill Jensen, *The New Nation* (New York, 1950), Chapter 6, passim.
15. Nevins, *The American States during and after the Revolution,* pp. 459–462. The humanization of punishments begun in 1790 was reaffirmed and extended in other laws of 1791 and 1794. See also two pamphlets: William Bradford, *An Enquiry How Far the Punishment of Death Is Necessary in Pennsylvania* (Philadelphia, 1793), and Robert James Turnbull, *A Visit to the Philadelphia Prison* (Philadelphia, 1796).
16. *New Jersey State Gazette,* March 8, 1796.

17. William Paterson, *Laws of the State of New Jersey* (Newark, 1800), pp. 208–222. See also mss. law volume, Paterson Papers, RUL, pp. 11–53.

18. The relevant statutes were those of June 28, 1766 (Allinson, *Laws*, p. 287), and June 12, 1780 (Wilson, *Laws*, pp. 136–137).

19. See Reed, *Crime and Punishment*, pp. 389–394.

20. Act of November 15, 1791, N.J. Session Laws, 16th Session, 1st Sitting, p. 725.

21. Act of December 6, 1769, Allinson, *Laws*, pp. 332–333.

22. Wilson, *Laws*, p. 136. The 1780 act also proved ineffective and was repealed in November 1786. N.J. Session Laws, 11th Session, 1st Sitting, p. 340.

23. Paterson, *Laws*, p. 213.

24. Act of November 4, 1741, Allinson, *Laws*, pp. 122–123. See also Reed, *Crime and Punishment*, pp. 571–586.

25. Paterson was particularly touched by the plight of the mother. In another draft bill, he provided for any woman to be exempt from questioning about her "pregnancy, or supposed pregnancy, until one month after she shall be delivered." Mss. law volume, Paterson Papers, RUL, p. 255. This provision was deleted by the legislature.

26. N.J. Session Laws, 16th Session, 2nd Sitting, p. 725.

27. *Newark Gazette and New Jersey Advertiser*, February 19, 1799.

28. Act of March 18, 1796, Paterson, *Laws*, pp. 208–222.

29. Rothman, *Discovery of the Asylum*, pp. 59–62.

30. *Newark Gazette and New Jersey Advertiser*, February 19, 1799.

31. Ibid.

32. Ibid. For the final act, see "An Act for the Establishment of Workhouses in the Several Counties of this State," passed February 20, 1799, Paterson, *Laws*, pp. 378–380. For treatment of the workhouses that were finally established in the last third of the nineteenth century, see Harry Elmer Barnes, *A History of the Penal, Reformatory and Correctional Institutions of the State of New Jersey* (Trenton, 1918), p. 334.

33. *Guardian*, February 21, 28, and March 7, 14, 21, and 28, 1797. See also William Paterson, political essays, oversize file, Paterson Papers, RUL.

34. Paterson, *Laws*, p. 334.

35. For Paterson's observations, see mss. law volume, Paterson Papers, RUL, pp. 551–552, 564. See also Paterson, *Laws*, p. 328.

36. Mss. law volume, Paterson Papers, RUL, pp. 530–532.

37. Ibid., p. 564.

38. *Guardian*, March 13, 1793. See also William Paterson, political essays, oversize file, Paterson Papers, RUL. Paterson, *Laws*, pp. 44, 53–54 (the date was October 6, 1780). See also Act of August 26, 1784, N.J. Session Laws, 8th Session, 2nd Sitting, pp. 97–98.

39. Articles of Agreement between William Paterson and Moses Coombs, n.d., Ely Collection, NJHS.

40. Act of March 2, 1786, N.J. Session Laws, 13th Session, 1st Sitting, pp. 486–488.

41. Arthur Zilversmit, *The First Emancipation: The Abolition of Slavery in the North* (Chicago, 1967), p. 161.

42. Ibid., pp. 185–187.

43. William Paterson to Speaker of the Assembly, October 2, 1797, mss. copy in mss. law volume, Paterson Papers, RUL, pp. 868–870.

44. Zilversmit, *First Emancipation*, p. 188.

45. The basic fine had been set at £20 in 1786. As near as New Jersey conversion rates for this period can be ascertained, £1 was worth about $2.66. As late as 1796, Paterson purchased a slave for £85 (about $226). William Paterson folder, New Brunswick Historical Club Papers, RUL.

46. Paterson, *Laws*, p. 307–313.

47. William Paterson, political essays, oversize file, Paterson Papers, RUL. In another essay, he called for the creation of associations to see to the education of the poor. Ibid.

48. *Newark Gazette and New Jersey Advertizer*, February 19, 1799. See also the "Act for the Establishment of Workhouses," Paterson, *Laws*, pp. 378–380; and Rothman, *Discovery of the Asylum*, pp. 20–29.

49. William Nelson, *Americanization of the Common Law: The Impact of Legal Change on Massachusetts Society, 1760–1830* (Cambridge, Mass., 1975). See also David H. Flaherty, "Law and the Enforcement of Morals in Early America," in *Perspectives in American History*. Vol. 5, 1971, pp. 203–256, who differs with Nelson in his belief that the tendency away from legislating morality began before the Revolution.

50. Paterson, *Laws*, pp. 208–210.

51. "An Act against Billiards," mss. law volume, Paterson Papers, RUL, p. 686.

52. William Paterson, "Essay in Defense of the Christian Sabbath," n.d., political essays, oversize file, Paterson Papers, RUL. The issue of the newspaper in which this essay appeared has not been found.

53. Mss. law volume, Paterson Papers, RUL, pp. 1–10, 419–429; Paterson, *Laws*, pp. 235–240, 329–333; *Guardian*, June 20, 1797. Another of Paterson's essays on taverns appeared in the same paper on June 27, 1797.

54. One of the few corporal punishments provided for in the revised laws was for another moral offense, cursing within the hearing of a justice of the peace. Such an offense could bring up to four hours in the public stocks. "Act for Suppressing Vice and Immorality," passed March 16, 1798, Paterson, *Laws*, p. 331.

55. William Paterson to Speaker of the Assembly, October 2, 1797, mss. copy in mss. law volume, Paterson Papers, RUL, pp. 868–870.

56. William Paterson to Speaker of the Assembly, October 2, 1796, mss. copy in mss. law volume, Paterson Papers, RUL, pp. 863–867.

57. William Paterson to Speaker of the Assembly, January 25, 1798, mss. copy in mss. law volume, Paterson Papers, RUL, pp. 871–877.

58. William Paterson to Speaker of the Assembly, January 22, 1799, mss. copy in mss. law volume, Paterson Papers, RUL, p. 881.

59. Stanley N. Katz, "The Politics of Law in Colonial America: Controversies over Chancery Courts and Equity Law in the Eighteenth Century," in *Perspectives in American History*, Vol. 5, 1971, pp. 259–260.

60. Edward Q. Keasby, *Courts and Lawyers in New Jersey 1661–1912* (3 vols.; New York, 1912), Vol. 2, pp. 506–509.

61. William Paterson, political essays, Paterson Papers, oversize file, RUL.

62. "Essay on the Office of the Governor and Chancellor of New Jersey," n.d., political essays, oversize file, Paterson Papers, RUL. Paterson, *Laws*, 428–436.

63. McCormick, *Experiment in Independence*, p. 181.

64. "An Act for the Regulating and Shortening of Proceedings in the Courts of Law," August 30, 1784, N.J. Session Laws, 8th Session, 1st Sitting, pp. 75–84.

65. Ibid.

66. William Paterson to John Lawrence, February 1785, Paterson Collection, LC.

67. Charles Warren, *History of the American Bar* (Boston, 1911), Chapter 10; Maxwell Bloomfield, *American Lawyers in a Changing Society, 1776–1876* (Cambridge, Mass., 1976), Chapter 2; and especially Richard E. Ellis, *The Jeffersonian Crisis: Courts and Politics in the Young Republic* (New York, 1971), Chapter 8, pp. 114–116.

68. Ellis, *The Jeffersonian Crisis*, p. 115.

69. William Paterson to Speaker of Assembly, January 25, 1798, mss. copy in mss. law volume, Paterson Papers, RUL, pp. 871–877.

70. McCormick's description of this 1788 law as a "thorough revision" cannot be substantiated. *Experiment in Independence*, p. 287. "An Act to Amend and Act Entitled 'An Act for the Regulating and Shortening of the Proceedings in the Courts of Law,'" November 26, 1788, N.J. Session Laws, 13th Session, 1st Sitting, pp. 488–489.

71. "An Act to Regulate Practice in the Courts of Law," February 4, 1799, Paterson, *Laws*, pp. 354–366.

72. Paterson's observations in mss. law volume, Paterson Papers, RUL, pp. 635–640.

73. William Paterson to Speaker of Assembly, January 25, 1798, mss. copy in mss. law volume, Paterson Papers, RUL, pp. 871–877.

74. Matthias Williamson et al. to William Paterson, March 5, 1799, folder 7, Paterson Papers, RUL.

75. William Paterson to Matthias Williamson et al., March 16, 1799, folder 7, Paterson Papers, RUL. "Act Respecting Fees," passed June 13, 1799, Paterson, *Laws*, pp. 418ff.

76. William Paterson to Speaker of the Assembly, January 25, 1798, mss. copy in mss. law volume, pp. 871–877, Paterson Papers, RUL.

77. William Paterson to Matthias Williamson et al., March 16, 1799, folder 7, Paterson Papers, RUL.

78. "Act Relative to Statutes," Paterson, *Laws*, pp. 435–436.

79. Warren, *History of the American Bar*, p. 232.

80. Nelson, *Americanization of the Common Law*, passim; Morton J. Horwitz, *The Transformation of American Law, 1780–1860* (Cambridge, Mass., 1977), passim.

81. Ellis, *Jeffersonian Crisis*, passim.

82. Paterson's observations in mss. law volume, pp. 635–640, Paterson Papers, RUL.

83. William Paterson to Speaker of Assembly, October 31, 1804, mss. copy in mss. law volume, p. 695, Paterson Papers, RUL; William Paterson to Gershom Dunn, November 8, 1804, Paterson Papers, RUL.

CHAPTER 11

1. *Wood's Newark Gazette and Paterson Advertiser*, July 10, 1793. The occasion was a Fourth of July celebration in Orange, New Jersey.

2. For the general history of the early Supreme Court including the period before Paterson's appointment, see Julius R. Goebel, Jr., *History of the Supreme Court of the United States: Antecedents and Beginnings to 1801* (New York, 1971); Charles Warren, *The Supreme Court in United States History* (2 vols.; Boston, 1928); Charles Grove Haines, *The Role of the Supreme Court in American Government and Politics, 1789–1835* (2 vols.; Berkeley, 1944); and Dwight F. Henderson, *Courts For a New Nation* (Washington, D.C., 1971).

3. George Washington to James Madison, September 25 [?], 1789, quoted in Leonard D. White, *The Federalists: A Study in Administrative History, 1789–1801* (New York, 1948), p. 259; for general information on Washington's appointments policy, pp. 253–266.

4. Quoted in White, *Federalists*, p. 259. For the most recent evaluation of Federalist appointees to the federal bench see Carl Prince, *The Federalists and the Origins of the Civil Service* (New York, 1977), Chapter 10.

5. George Washington to Charles Pickering, September 27, 1795, quoted in White, *Federalists*, p. 46.

6. George Washington to William Paterson, February 20, 1793, in George Washington, *Writings*, John C. Fitzgerald, ed. (39 vols.; New York, 1931–1944), Vol. 32, pp. 352, 353, 362–363.

7. Richard Hofstadter, *The Idea of a Party System* (Berkeley, 1969), pp. 4, 12, and passim.

8. *Guardian*, February 13, 1793. Like most of Paterson's newspaper essays that have been identified, the original manuscript copies of his Aurelius essays are preserved in the oversize file of the Paterson Papers at RUL.

9. *Guardian*, February 27, 1793.

10. According to the latest work on the New Jersey Federalists, they were, as a group, slow to follow the lead of other Federalists with respect to support for England; they opposed the French Revolution only after the execution of the king, they only became pro-British as a result of their partisan support of the Jay Treaty, and even then their ardor for the British cause was less than warm. Rudolph Pasler and Margeret C. Pasler, *The New Jersey Federalists* (Rutherford, N.J., 1975), pp. 64–66. For Dayton's proposal, see John C. Miller, *The Federalist Era, 1789–1801* (New York, 1960), p. 151.

11. On the American Philosophical Society, see Louis B. Wright, *The Cultural Life of the American Colonies, 1607–1763* (New York, 1957), pp. 231, 236; and Russel B. Nye, *The Cultural Life of the New Nation, 1776–1830* (New York, 1960), pp. 51, 71–72, 156. On the significance of Freemasonry as a social meeting-ground for community leaders in eighteenth-century Europe and America and for some interesting observations on the influence of Masonic doctrines on the free-thinking ways of such influential American members of the order as Benjamin Franklin and George Washington, see Bernard Fay, *Revolution and Freemasonry, 1680–1800* (Boston, 1935), pp. 150–167, 307–317, and passim. An interesting analysis of Freemasonry as an influence in the politics and society of another state is to be found in Dorothy Ann Lipson, *Freemasonry in Federalist Connecticut* (Princeton, 1977). It should be pointed out again that evangelical leaders such as Edwards and Whitfield, as well as many of their followers, did not carry their religious orthodoxy to the point of closing their minds to intellectual inquiry, but many New Side Calvinists must have had trouble distinguishing the intellectuals from the skeptics.

12. The only evidence of Paterson's participation in religious affairs and the source for the passages quoted in this paragraph is Joseph Clark, *A Sermon on the Death of the Hon. William Paterson* (New Brunswick, 1806), 24 pp.

13. See the final chapters of Alan Heimert, *Religion and the American Mind from the Great Awakening to the Revolution* (Cambridge, Mass., 1966). For Boudinot, see David Hackett Fischer, *The Revolution of American Conservatism* (New York, 1965), p. 322. See also, Clifford S. Griffin, *Their Brothers' Keepers* (New

Brunswick, 1960), pp. 9–22. Griffin refers to the Federalists as the first political expression in the United States of a sense of moral stewardship, which he traces from 1800 through until the Civil War.

14. *Guardian,* March 20, 1793. See also Richard P. McCormick's "Political Essays of William Paterson," *RULJ,* 18 (June 1955), p. 48.

15. Justice William Cushing wrote in March 1793 to tell Paterson that he had been assigned to the southern circuit. Mss. draft of letter, March 5, 1973, Cushing Papers, MHS.

16. See Letters of Paterson to Euphemia in Paterson Papers, RUL.

17. Manuscript copies of eleven of Paterson's addresses to grand juries can be found in the Paterson Papers, RUL. These addresses must not be confused with the charge or instructions given to the petit jury after the presentation of evidence in a particular case and before the deliberation of the verdict. Several examples of these will be considered later. For a general discussion of the grand jury charge used as a form of political indoctrination during this period, see Ralph Kerner, "The Supreme Court as Republican Schoolmaster" in Philip B. Kurland, ed., *The Supreme Court Review,* (1967), pp. 127–180.

18. The repetition of such a situation was later made impossible by the passage of the eleventh amendment to the Constitution.

19. *New Jersey State Gazette,* June 19, 1793.

20. See grand jury addresses folder, Paterson Papers, RUL.

21. For a more complete summary of these events, see Miller, *Federalist Era,* pp. 126–139.

22. Warren, *Supreme Court,* pp. 108–111; Miller, *Federalist Era,* p. 136; Thomas Jefferson to William Paterson, July 12, 1793, Jefferson Papers, LC.

23. Warren, *Supreme Court,* pp. 114–118. Paterson's participation in the decision was noted in *New Jersey State Gazette,* March 5, 1794. The case was of additional importance because of its relevance to the development of admiralty jurisdiction in the federal courts. For a detailed analysis see Goebel, *History of the Supreme Court of the United States: Antecedents and Beginnings,* pp. 760–765.

24. In the first of these, the Court refused to compel U.S. District Judge Lawrence to reverse his decision not to grant a warrant for the arrest of the captain of a French frigate who had abandoned ship. The administration had brought the case to the Supreme Court at the request of the French vice-consul, but was apparently pleased with the decision not to involve America deeper in French affairs.

In the second case, U.S. District Judge Peters of Pennsylvania was ordered not to interfere in the case of the French privateer, *Cassius,* since the ship was French-owned and, although outfitted illegally in the United States, was exempt from judicial seizure as the property of a French citizen. Out of fear of British reaction, the administration's objections had been primarily to prizes that had been captured by American owned and/or manned ships working in the service of France. Washington had decided to allow prizes captured by bona-fide French ships to be sold in American ports, not because the 1778 treaty required it, but because there was no law against it.

In the third case, the Court finally proclaimed that there was no legal right for a foreign power to commission privateers in this country. On a related question involving the right of national expatriation, Paterson presented a long and eloquent opinion on the nature of the new federal system. This will be fully discussed in Chapter 12. Alexander Dallas, *Reports of Cases in the Courts of the United States and Pennsylvania, 1790–1800*, 2nd ed. (4 vols.; New York, 1882), Vol. 3, pp. 42, 121, 133; Warren, *Supreme Court*, pp. 121–122, 133–134; Miller, *Federalist Era*, p. 136.

25. *Guardian*, January 9 and 16, 1973. The diplomatic situation would not become complicated for America until later in the year when France declared war on England.
26. "Essay in Defense of the Christian Sabbath," n.d., newspaper essays, oversize file, Paterson Papers, RUL.
27. "Essay on the Threat of Foreign Influence in Domestic Politics," n.d., newspaper essays, oversize file, Paterson Papers, RUL. See also Miller, *Federalist Era*, p. 137.
28. Miller, *Federalist Era*, pp. 151–152.
29. "Essay on the Manners and Morals of Foreigners," n.d., newspaper essays, oversize file, Paterson Papers, RUL.
30. "Essay on the Threat of Foreign Influence in Domestic Politics," n.d., newspaper essays, oversize file, Paterson Papers, RUL. Paterson later crossed out the word "again."
31. See Leland D. Baldwin, *The Whiskey Rebels: The Story of a Frontier Uprising* (Pittsburgh, 1939).
32. Grand jury address no. 3, addresses to grand juries folder, Paterson Papers, RUL. Although the address is undated, internal evidence identifies it with the Whiskey Rebellion.
33. Baldwin, *Whiskey Rebels*, pp. 259–272. The manuscript court records are fragmentary but illuminating. See record group 21, records of the U.S. Circuit Court for the Eastern District of Pennsylvania, Criminal Case Files and Minute Book, 1793–1795, Federal Archives and Records Center, Philadelphia. Paterson's handwritten notes on the testimony presented before the court can be found in the William Paterson Papers, William Paterson College, Wayne, New Jersey.
34. A model for the proper form of such instructions can be found in Paterson's presentation to the jury in the trial of *John Etienne Guinet et al., for Fitting out and Arming a French Armed Vessel*, in the very same term of the circuit court in Philadelphia. He told them in objective terms to "consider the indictment; and give such verdict as shall comport with evidence and law." The opinion of the jurors themselves was to prevail. Francis Wharton, *State Trials of the United States* (Philadelphia, 1849), pp. 100–101.
35. Dallas, *Reports*, Vol. 2, p. 347. In a similar case several years later (The Northampton County Pennsylvania insurrection of Jacob Fries against the federal direct tax), Judge Iredell made the same point about the possible spreading of the spirit of rebellion. But, unlike Paterson, he also stressed the jurors' duty to divest themselves of "all manner of prejudice and partiality one way or the other. . . . You ought not, and I hope you will not, take into your consideration at all whether the safety of the United States requires that the prisoner should suffer, on the one hand, or whether, on the other, it may be more agreeable to your feelings that he should be acquitted. It is solely your duty to say whether he is guilty of the crime charged to him or not." Wharton, *State Trials*, pp. 587–597.
36. Dallas, *Reports*, Vol. 2, p. 355.
37. Richard Hofstadter has argued that Washington's intention was not to descend into the partisan arena himself, but to point out the danger of all political

parties to peaceful republican government. Still, whether the president realized it or not, the effects of his remarks were to stir up even more partisan opposition. *Idea of a Party System*, pp. 92–95. For a complete treatment of the societies, see Eugene Perry Link, *The Democratic-Republican Societies, 1790–1800* (New York, 1942).

38. Hofstadter, *Idea of a Party System*, pp. 86–87.
39. Miller, *Federalist Era*, p. 159. Baldwin, *Whiskey Rebels*, p. 264, goes on to argue that Mitchell was poorly defended by his lawyer and notes that the sympathies of Philadelphia's philanthropists were touched by what Baldwin calls the "obvious" insanity of Vigol and the fact that Mitchell was a "simpleton." They therefore petitioned President Washington for the pardon. Paterson felt less sympathetic. When Washington asked him for a summary of the case, Paterson described the offenses and the defendants' abortive attempts at defense in tones that implied his firm belief in the justice of the sentence. See William Paterson to Edmund Randolph, June 6, 1795, Jefferson Papers, LC.
40. Samuel Flagg Bemis, *Jay's Treaty* (New Haven, 1962), pp. 337–343 and passim. Miller, *Federalist Era*, p. 165, feels that Hamilton's conversations with the British had no effect on Jay's negotiations. Whether they had an effect or not, though, the people knew nothing of Hamilton's machinations. For the fullest account of Hamilton's leaks to the British, see Julian Boyd's *Number Seven* (Princeton, 1964).
41. Warren, *Supreme Court*, pp. 129–131; Miller, *Federalist Era*, p. 171; and Richard Buel, *Securing the Revolution: Ideology in American Politics, 1789–1815* (Ithaca, N.Y., 1972), pp. 107–108.
42. Buel, *Securing the Revolution*, pp. 108–112.
43. Washington, *Writings*, Washington to Paterson, Vol. 34, pp. 331, 348. Paterson's name had been recommended to Washington by Tench Coxe; see Tench Coxe to William Paterson, August 27, 1795, manuscript collections, YUL.
44. Horatius No. 1, *Genius of Liberty*, October 5, 1795.
45. Horatius No. 2, "Essay on the Influence of the Summer Heat upon the Opposition to the Jay Treaty," n.d., newspaper essays, oversize file, Paterson Papers, RUL. Although the issue is no longer extant, it is evident that this essay was published in the *Genius of Liberty* for October 12, 1795.
46. Horatius No. 3, "Essay on the Opposition to the Jay Treaty," n.d., newspaper essays, oversize file, Paterson Papers, RUL. Although the issue is no longer extant, it is evident that this essay was published in the *Genius of Liberty* for October 19, 1795. See also Miller, *Federalist Era*, p. 168.
47. Horatius No. 4, *Genius of Liberty*, October 26, 1795.
48. Horatius No. 8, "Essay on European Emigrants to America," n.d., newspaper essays, oversize file, Paterson Papers, RUL.
49. Horatius No. 9, "Essay on Critics of the President and Other Public Officers," n.d., newspaper essays, oversize file, Paterson Papers, RUL.
50. "Essay on Opposition and Party," n.d., newspaper essays, oversize file, Paterson Papers, RUL.
51. William Paterson to Euphemia Paterson, October 10, November 5, and November 28, 1796, folder 13. Henry Wm. De Saussure to William Paterson, October 30, 1796, folder 6, Paterson Papers, RUL.
52. Receipts signed by Paterson dated May 2, 1796, and July 19, 1796, and Thomas

Irwin to William Paterson, April 29, 1796, folder 6, Paterson Papers, RUL. The Pinkney Treaty with Spain was unanimously ratified by the Senate, and the ratification was exchanged officially with the Spanish on April 25, 1796. Samuel Flagg Bemis, *Pinkney's Treaty* (New Haven, 1960), pp. 302 and passim.

53. William Paterson to James Iredell, March 7, 1797, Griffin J. McRee, *Life and Correspondence of James Iredell* (2 vols.; New York, 1857–1858), Vol. 2, p. 495.

54. Miller, *Federalist Era*, pp. 196–209; see also Stephen Kurtz, *The Presidency of John Adams: The Collapse of Federalism, 1795–1800* (Philadelphia, 1957); and Manning J. Dauer, *The Adams Federalists* (Baltimore, 1953).

55. Common law jurisdiction in federal courts was another matter of hot debate between Republicans and Federalists. The former believed that common law had no place there. Indeed, many of the Jeffersonians had been trying to have their states reject the common law system completely and replace it with a simple and specific code. Richard E. Ellis, *The Jeffersonian Crisis: Courts and Politics in the Young Republic* (New York, 1971), passim. Paterson took no part in the several cases during the first decade of the Court that involved common law indictments, and there are no direct statements of opinion on the issue to be found in his papers. I have found no concrete evidence to prove the contention of Leonard W. Levy that while on the federal bench Paterson "accepted jurisdiction of common law crimes." *Legacy of Suppression* (Cambridge, Mass., 1960), p. 241. The one common law indictment that was scheduled to be brought before him was one that charged John Daly Burk, editor of the New York *Time Piece*, with the common law crime of sedition, but the charge was dropped when Burk, a recent immigrant, agreed to leave the country. Ibid., p. 140; James Morton Smith, *Freedom's Fetters: The Alien and Sedition Acts and American Civil Liberties* (Ithaca, N.Y., 1956), pp. 204–220. Although we have no incontrovertible proof of his action on a common law indictment in a federal jurisdiction, we do have Paterson's broad interpretation of federal authority as spelled out in his grand jury addresses. In addition, we can cite his defence of the common law in New Jersey. Such evidence gives us every reason to believe that Paterson went along with his Federalist colleagues and would have admitted common law indictments had they been presented to him

56. Richard Peters, *Statutes at Large of the United States* (8 vols.; Boston, 1845), Vol. 1, July 14, 1798, pp. 596–597.

57. Buel bases his conclusions on various patterns of trade and land ownership that resulted in the old elite of the southern states being more secure in their social and economic positions than their New England counterparts. *Securing the Revolution*, pp. 81–83.

58. William Paterson to Cornelia Paterson, January 20, 1798, folder 13, Paterson Papers, RUL.

59. Paterson had always held that war would be destructive of the nation. He was one of the few Federalists who opposed the extension of the navy to meet the current crisis. He wrote that the building of the ships would take so long that they would not be worth the expenditure. "Essay on the Navy," n.d., Paterson Papers, RUL. Part of his fear of war in 1798 may have been influenced by southern friends. One of these, who wrote to Paterson in July 1798, expressed all the proper commitment to national honor in the face of French provocation, but was also very fearful of a war in which southern slaves might be used by

the French as they had been in the case of Toussaint L'Ouverture. Even after such a French-sponsored slave insurrection was crushed, as the correspondent was sure it would be, life in the slave South would never be the same. J. Y. Noel to William Paterson, July 20, 1798, folder 6, Paterson Papers, RUL.

60. Fourth of July Address, n.d., Paterson Collection, PUL. Clear internal evidence dates the address as 1798.

61. William Paterson to Euphemia Paterson, September 25, 1798, folder 13, Paterson Papers, RUL.

62. Smith, *Freedom's Fetters*, pp. 221–231; Wharton, *State Trials*, p. 339.

63. There had been several common law prosecutions for sedition begun even before the act had been passed through Congress. Smith, *Freedom's Fetters*, pp. 188–220.

64. Grand Jury Address No. 7, addresses to grand juries folder, Paterson Papers, RUL. Although undated, the address can clearly be identified through internal evidence.

65. Wharton, *State Trials*, pp. 334–335. The original manuscript indictment and other papers relating to the Lyon case can be found in record group 21, records of the U.S. Circuit Court for the District of Vermont, Criminal Case Files and Docket Book, 1798, Federal Archives and Records Center, Waltham, Mass.

66. Wharton, *State Trials*, pp. 331–340; Smith, *Freedom's Fetters*, pp. 231–235. The complete indictment can be found reprinted in the *Annals of Congress* for the 16th Congress, 2nd Session, pp. 478–485. The date was December 4, 1820, and the occasion was a plea by Lyon to have the decision overturned and the fine refunded. For the local reaction in New Jersey, see *Guardian*, October 30, 1798.

67. There is no doubt that Paterson was aware of this fact, since, in later arguments in favor of the law, Paterson argued precisely this point. Had he stressed it here, the jurors might have decided differently. "On Freedom of the Press," n.d., Paterson Papers, PUL. Lyon later accused Paterson of falsely claiming the "seditious" letter he had read in public was a forgery, but there is no other source to verify Lyon's unsubstantiated charge. Wharton, *State Trials*, p. 340.

68. Wharton, *State Trials*, pp. 712–713.

69. Ibid., pp. 336–337; Smith, *Freedom's Fetters*, p. 235.

70. See Joseph H. Nicholson to William Paterson, March 2, 1801, and June 23, 1801, and Paterson's replies, February 23, 1801, and June 29, 1801, NYHS.

71. Wharton, *State Trials*, pp. 484–485; Smith, *Freedom's Fetters*, pp. 359–367.

72. Wharton, *State Trials*, pp. 485–487; Smith, *Freedom's Fetters*, pp. 367–373.

73. See especially Stephen Presser, "A Tale of Two Judges: Richard Peters, Samuel Chase, and the Broken Promise of Federalist Jurisprudence," *Northwestern University Law Review*, 73 (1978): 26–111.

74. Smith, *Freedom's Fetters*, pp. 270–274.

75. Ibid.

76. Jefferson himself had been firm in his dislike of party and faction. Neither Republicans nor Federalists accepted the idea of contending parties becoming institutionalized within a permanent two-party system. Each believed that they represented the true public interest, and each intended to destroy the other and return in the end to a no-party system. See Hofstadter, *Idea of a Party System*, pp. 1, 2, and passim.

77. Prince, *The Federalist Origins of the U.S. Civil Service*, p. 241.

CHAPTER 12

1. William Paterson to Euphemia Paterson, November 5, 1796; May 19 and November 17, 1800, folder 14, Paterson Papers, RUL. See also his "Notes on Savannah," n.d., Paterson Papers, PUL.
2. L. Q. C. Elmer, *The Constitution and Government of the Province and State of New Jersey* (Newark, 1872), p. 95.
3. The Eleventh Amendment to the Constitution was proposed in 1794 and declared ratified on September 25, 1798.
4. Alexander Dallas, *Reports of Cases in the Courts of the United States and Pennsylvania, 1790–1800,* 2nd ed. (4 vols.; New York, 1882), Vol. 3, pp. 152–154.
5. Ibid. pp. 79–82. Julius R. Goebel, Jr., *History of the Supreme Court of the United States: Antecedents and Beginnings to 1801* (New York, 1971), p. 768.
6. Dallas, *Reports,* Vol. 3, pp. 78–82. Quoted in Charles Grove Haines, *The Role of the Supreme Court in American Government and Politics, 1789–1835* (2 vols.; Berkeley, 1944), Vol. 1, p. 141.
7. Dallas, *Reports,* Vol. 3, pp. 249–256.
8. Charles Grove Haines, *The American Doctrine of Judicial Supremacy,* 2nd ed. (New York, 1958) pp. 122–147. One of the early precedents on the state level was *Holmes* v. *Walton,* a New Jersey case of 1780 when Paterson was attorney general. Ibid., pp. 92–95.
9. There were two editions of the pamphlet, both printed in Philadelphia. The first was printed by Samuel Smith in 1796, and the second in 1801 by Z. Paulson.
10. Dallas, *Reports,* Vol 2, pp. 304–320.
11. Charles Warren cites the case of a Rhode Island statute declared unconstitutional by the federal district court in 1792. *The Supreme Court in United States History* (2 vols.; Boston, 1928), Vol. 1, pp. 67–69. It is also interesting to note that the main element of Paterson's decision in *Van Horne's Lessee* v. *Dorrance* was the law's being inconsistent with the Pennsylvania state constitution. In a postscript to the decision, Paterson did go on to establish that a related act was also in contravention of the federal Constitution, but this does not alter the weakness of the case as a legal (as opposed to a philosophical) precedent for declaring the acts of Congress unconstitutional. Dallas, *Reports,* Vol. 2, pp. 319–320. Louis Boudin is most insistent on this point, referring to Paterson's decision as a discussion of the issue of judicial review, but in no way a precedent. *Government by Judiciary* (2 vols.; New York, 1932), Vol. 1, pp. 183–185.
12. Julian P. Boyd, "William Paterson, Forerunner of John Marshall," in Willard Thorpe, ed., *Lives of Eighteen from Princeton* (Princeton, 1947), pp. 16–18.
13. In this case, the court and Mr. Hylton had to agree on the fiction that he owned 125 carriages strictly for his personal use, for otherwise the money involved would not have amounted to the minimum required for the circuit court to have jurisdiction (the carriage tax was only $16 for each). Dallas, *Reports,* Vol. 3, pp. 178-181. See also Haines, *Role of the Supreme Court,* Vol. 1, p. 147.
14. Dallas, *Reports,* Vol. 2, p. 413.
15. For the clearest analysis of the Republicans' criticisms of the Federalist judiciary, see Haines, *Role of the Supreme Court,* Vol. 1, pp. 159–177.
16. "Numa," in the *Trenton Federalist; or New Jersey State Gazette,* January 7, 1799.
17. Both the *Newark Gazette* and the Trenton *Federalist* pieces appeared on September 30, 1800.

18. New Brunswick *Guardian,* June 3, 1800.
19. New Brunswick *Guardian,* May 8, 15, 22, and 29, 1798. Trenton *Federalist & New Jersey State Gazette,* July 2 and September 16, 1800.
20. For an analysis of the election and the fragmentation of the Federalist party, see Manning Dauer, *The Adams Federalists* (Baltimore, 1953). The contest in New Jersey is covered in Rudolph J. Pasler and Margaret C. Pasler, *The New Jersey Federalists* (Rutherford, N.J., 1975), pp. 45–46, 99–101; and Carl Prince, *New Jersey's Jeffersonian Republicans* (Chapel Hill, 1964), pp. 41–68.
21. On Bayard, see Morton Borden, *The Federalism of James A. Bayard* (New York, 1955).
22. Warren, *Supreme Court,* Vol. 1, p. 167.
23. Jonathan Dayton to William Paterson, January 20, 1801, folder 7, Paterson Papers, RUL.
24. Jonathan Dayton to William Paterson, January 28, 1801, folder 7, Paterson Papers, RUL. Marshall's previous support for Paterson's nomination is supported by his famous biographer Albert Beveridge, *John Marshall* (4 vols.; Boston, 1919), Vol. 2, p. 553.
25. There was some debate, however, about how far this skill went. See Warren, *Supreme Court,* Vol. 1, pp. 180–182.
26. Kathryn Turner, "The Appointment of Chief Justice Marshall," *WMQ,* third series, 17, 2 (April 1960): 143–163. Adams was thinking of appointing Jared Ingersoll as an associate justice, but the prospective appointee made matters difficult by expressing his desire not to be appointed unless the circuit duties were reduced by the bill currently before Congress, and Adams could not wait. Ibid., pp. 147–148.
27. *Aurora,* January 24, 1801; January 22, September 20 and 28, 1803.
28. Jonathan Dayton to William Paterson, January 28, 1801, folder 7, Paterson Papers, RUL.
29. Jonathan Dayton to William Paterson, January 20 and 28, 1801, folder 7, Paterson Papers, RUL.
30. William Paterson to Jonathan Dayton, January 25, 1801, Gratz Collection, HSP.
31. Jonathan Dayton to William Paterson, February 1, 1801, folder 7, Paterson Papers, RUL.
32. John Marshall to William Paterson, February 2, 1801, folder 7, Paterson Papers, RUL. For the best analysis of the Judiciary Act of 1801 and its precedents, see Kathryn Turner, "Federalist Policy and the Judiciary Act of 1801," *WMQ,* third series, 22 (January 1965): 3–32. See also Richard Peters, *Statutes at Large of the United States,* (8 vols.; Boston, 1845), Vol. 2, p. 89.
33. See, for example, William Cushing to William Paterson, March 5, 1793, and July 20, 1794; and William Paterson to William Cushing, August 9, 1794. Robert Treat Paine Papers, MHS.
34. William B. Paterson to Euphemia Paterson, February 5, 1801, folder 13, Paterson Papers, RUL.
35. Kathryn Turner, "Federalist Policy and the Judiciary Act of 1801," is most enlightening on the new law as it would apply to land title cases. For the Jeffersonians' plans to destroy the judiciary, see Richard E. Ellis, *The Jeffersonian Crisis* (New York, 1971). Ellis stresses the factional differences among the Republicans in explaining their outlook on the Court.
36. The New Brunswick *Guardian* reported on July 9, 1801, that Andrew Bell,

Paterson's brother-in-law, who had returned from Loyalist exile to become an active Federalist, had been removed from the office of customs collector at Perth Amboy. According to Leonard D. White, Bell was only one of the twenty-six collectors removed by Jefferson, but at the same time White points out that Jefferson used the removal power with considerable moderation. *The Jeffersonians: A Study in Administrative History, 1801–1829* (New York, 1951), p. 379. Carl Prince, "The Passing of the Aristocracy, Jefferson's Removal of the Federalists, 1801–1805," *JAH*, 57, 3 (December 1970): 563–575, sees Jefferson's removals as "sweeping" and suggests that they had "a shattering impact on the American elite" (p. 575).

37. The general discussion of the Jeffersonians' treatment of the judiciary has been based on the most complete and balanced analysis available, that of Ellis, *Jeffersonian Crisis*, pp. 41–45.

38. Ibid., pp. 45–51.

39. The outspoken Federalist was Samuel Dana of Connecticut. Ibid., p. 58.

40. An Act to Amend the Judicial System of the United States was passed into law on April 29, 1802. *U.S. Statutes at Large*, Vol. 2, pp. 156–167.

41. Samuel Chase to William Paterson, April 6, 1802, NYHS.

42. John Marshall to William Paterson, April 6, 1802, folder 7, Paterson Papers, RUL.

43. John Marshall to William Paterson, April 19, 1802, folder 7, Paterson Papers, RUL.

44. Samuel Chase to William Paterson, April 24, 1802, NYHS.

45. William Paterson to William Cushing, May 6, 1802; and William Paterson to John Marshall, quoted in letter of William Paterson to William Cushing, May 26, 1802. Misc. mss., NYHS.

46. There is no information available on the opinion of Justice Alfred Moore.

47. Ellis, *Jeffersonian Crisis*, pp. 62–64.

48. The record suggests that Marshall might have offered the honor to William Cushing if that judge had not been ill at the time. In a letter to Euphemia, Paterson described the unusual conditions where, because several of the justices were unwell, they were holding court in the rooming house in which they stayed. William Paterson to Euphemia Paterson, February 17, 1803, Paterson Papers, folder 14, RUL.

49. Previous to Marshall's appointment, most Supreme Court decisions had been made *seriatim*, with each justice pronouncing his own opinion and explaining the legal principles on which he based it. Marshall changed this by preparing most of the formal opinions himself after the judges reached a consensus in conference on each case. Clearly this gave Marshall a dominant position, yet he always insisted that he was willing to follow the will of the majority on a specific issue. See, for example, the case of *Little et al. v. Barreme et al.*, February 27, 1804, (William Cranch, *Reports of Cases in the Supreme Court of the U.S.*, 3rd ed. [New York, 1882], pp. 170–79) in which he "conceded that his brethren on the court had changed his mind."

50. Cranch, *Reports of Cases*, Vol. 1, pp. 175–180.

51. Cranch, *Reports of Cases*, Vol. 1, p. 308. Even Beveridge confirmed this conclusion: "Justice Paterson of the Supreme Court said all that Marshall repeated in *Marbury* v. *Madison* upon the power of the judiciary to declare legislation void." *John Marshall*, Vol. 3, p. 612.

52. See Ellis, *Jeffersonian Crisis*, pp. 66–68.

53. Paterson's personal notes on these Senate debates are to be found in Paterson Papers, RUL. See also Chapter 8.
54. Cranch, *Reports of Cases*, Vol. 1, p. 77.
55. In his *Idea of a Party System*, pp. 161–165, Richard Hofstadter does note the propriety of Federalist concern over the repeal of the Judiciary Act, but he stresses the Jeffersonians' moderation in refraining from packing the court.
56. Warren, *Supreme Court*, Vol. 1, p. 272. Louis Boudin, after criticizing Marshall for the decision in *Marbury* v. *Madison*, presumed that the repeal act should have been declared unconstitutional and described *Stuart* v. *Laird* as a cowardly and dishonest attempt of the justices to escape impeachment. *Government by Judiciary*, Vol. 1, pp. 244–247. No evidence has been found to support this conclusion.
57. William Paterson to Euphemia Paterson, August 26, 1801, folder 14, Paterson Papers, RUL; William B. Paterson to William Paterson, July 20, 1804, and March 27, 1806, folder 8, Paterson Papers, RUL.
58. For Paterson's supervision of young Stephen Van Rensselaer at Princeton, see William Paterson to Kolloch, December 8, 1804, and December 31, 1804; and Stephen Van Rensselaer to William Paterson, January 7, 1805, folder 8, Paterson Papers, RUL.
59. See manuscript minutes of Princeton trustees, Princeton University Archives, and John Marshall to William Paterson, April 6, 1802, folder 7, Paterson Papers, RUL.
60. Records of the New Brunswick Bridge Company, RUL. Although the extent of his investment is unknown, there is also reason to believe that he held stock in two early canal companies, the Raritan Navigation Company, established in 1802, and the New Jersey Navigation Company, set up in 1804, which was authorized to build a canal from the Raritan to the Delaware. According to Robert T. Thompson, "both of these abortive companies were significant chiefly as the first steps in the direction of a goal which remained tantalizingly elusive for another quarter of a century." *Colonel James Neilson: A Businessman of the Early Machine Age in New Jersey, 1784–1862* (New Brunswick, 1940), p. 158n.
61. *Genius of Liberty*, December 1, 1795.
62. William Paterson to Gershom Dunn, November 8, 1804, folder 8, Paterson Papers, RUL.
63. John Rutherfurd to William Paterson, January 18, 1805, and transcript of Paterson's reply dated January 21, 1805, folder 8, Paterson Papers, RUL.
64. He wrote to Chase that "it was several weeks before I could change my position in bed and rise out of my chair without help." William Paterson to Samuel Chase, February 1, 1804, NYHS. See also William Paterson to John Marshall, December 31, 1803, folder 7, Paterson Papers, RUL.
65. The advertisement appeared in the *Guardian* from December 22, 1803, until February 9, 1804. On his decision regarding the leadership of the bridge company, see Records of the New Brunswick Bridge Company, RUL.
66. William Paterson to Euphemia Paterson, January 31, 1805, folder 14, Paterson Papers, RUL.
67. Cranch, *Reports of Cases*, Vol. 3, pp. 159–174 and passim.
68. This discussion on the Chase impeachment has been based primarily on Ellis, *Jeffersonian Crisis*, pp. 69–107. See also Lynn Turner, "The Impeachment of John Pickering," *AHR*, 54 (1949): 485–507; Richard B. Lillich, "The Chase Impeachment," *AJLH*, 4 (1960): pp. 49–72.

69. Jeremiah Smith to William Plumer, William Plumer to Bradbury Cilley, January 15, 1805, mss. copy, New Hampshire State Library.

70. Several of the charges were purely political, and the leaders of the impeachment movement were attempting to interpret the meaning of the Constitution in a particularly broad way. Plumer reported to Smith on January 16, 1805, that Randolph had proposed in the committee of investigation that the rule that judges hold their offices during good behavior "was designed only as a bar against executive removals, & not to prevent him from removing [them] from office when requested by a majority of the representatives of the people." Mss. copy, New Hampshire State Library. In short, he was defining an impeachable offense as whatever a simple majority of the Congress thought it to be at any particular time, clearly a political threat against an independent judiciary.

71. See Joseph H. Nicholson to William Paterson, March 2, 1801, and June 23, 1801; and Paterson's replies of February 23 and June 29, 1801, NYHS.

72. William Paterson to Euphemia Paterson, February 6, 1805, folder 14, Paterson Papers, RUL.

73. See Samuel E. Smith, *Trial of Judge Samuel Chase* (2 vols.; Washington, D.C., 1806), Vol. 1, pp. 187–188.

74. William Paterson to Steven Van Rensselaer, February 23, 1805, Gratz Collection, HSP.

75. See Ellis, *Jeffersonian Crisis*, pp. 102–107. The quotation is from a letter written by George Clinton to Pierre Van Cortlandt, March 3, 1805, quoted in ibid., p. 102.

76. William Paterson to Euphemia Paterson, April 1, May 2, and September 2 and 17, 1805; January 26 and 30, 1806, folder 14, Paterson Papers, RUL.

77. Cranch, *Reports of Cases* Vol. 3, pp. 454–458, 503–515.

78. William Paterson to Euphemia Paterson, February 3, 8, and 26, 1806, folder 14, Paterson Papers, RUL; note dated April 16, 1806; and mss. copy of William Paterson to William Gibbons, May 21, 1806, folder 8, Paterson Papers, RUL.

79. See *The Trial of William S. Smith and Samuel G. Ogden* (New York, 1807), passim.

80. Ibid. See also *Federal Cases* #16, 342.

81. Ibid. See also Beveridge, *John Marshall*, Vol. 3, p. 436.

82. Mss. copy, William Paterson to William Gibbon, May 21, 1806, folder 8, Paterson Papers, RUL. *Guardian*, September 28, 1806.

CONCLUSION

1. William Paterson to William B. Paterson, November 19, 1805, folder 16, Paterson Papers, RUL.

2. Edward Paterson to William Paterson, December 12, 1805, folder 8, Paterson Papers, RUL.

3. William Paterson, Will, September 7, 1806, NJSL.

4. Alan Heimert, *Religion and the American Mind from the Great Awakening to the Revolution*, especially final chapters; and Jackson Turner Main, *Political Parties before the Constitution* (Chapel Hill, 1973), pp. 32–33 and passim.

5. See Paul Goodman, *The Democratic Republicans of Massachusetts* (Cambridge, Mass., 1964), pp. 116–118; also see James M. Banner, *To the Hartford Convention: The Federalists and the Origins of Party Politics in Massachusetts 1789–1815*

(New York, 1970), pp. 49–51, 90–91, and 191–192. On New Jersey's Federalists, see Rudolph J. Pasler and Margaret C. Pasler, *The New Jersey Federalists* (Rutherford, N.J., 1975), passim.

6. This aristocratic lifestyle was common to some influential New Jersey Federalists, including some close to Paterson, such as John Bayard, the husband of his sister-in-law and fellow luminary of New Brunswick. See Pasler and Pasler, *New Jersey's Federalists*, p. 204. For an interesting discussion of the social life of Philadelphia's Federalists, see Ethel Rasmussen, "Democratic Environment—Aristocratic Aspiration," *Pennsylvania Magazine of History and Biography*, 90 (1966): 155–182.

7. Richard Hofstadter, *The Idea of a Party System* (Berkeley, 1969), pp. 86–87.

Bibliographical Note

MANUSCRIPT SOURCES

The most significant manuscript sources are designated by an asterisk.

Boston Public Library
  Autograph Collection
Federal Archives and Records Center, Philadelphia, Pennsylvania
  Records of the U.S. Circuit Court for the Eastern District of Pennsylvania
Federal Archives and Records Center, Waltham, Massachusetts
  Records of the U.S. Circuit Court for the District of Vermont
Free Public Library of Philadelphia.
  Hampton Lawrence Carson Collection
Historical Society of Pennsylvania
  Gratz Collection
  William Hornar Collection
Houghton Library, Harvard University
  Dearborn Collection
*Library of Congress
  Andrew Bell Papers
  Thomas Jefferson Papers
  William Paterson Papers
  George Washington Papers
Massachusetts Historical Society
  William Livingston Papers
  Robert Treat Paine Papers
  Timothy Pickering Papers
National Archives
  Records of the Supreme Court of the United States
  Records of the United States Senate
New Hampshire State Library
  William Plumer Papers
*New Jersey Historical Society
  Andrew Bell Papers

　　Eastburn Collection
　　Holmes Papers
　　Miscellaneous Papers
　　William Nelson Papers
　　New Jersey Papers
　　William Paterson Papers
New Jersey State Library
　　Miscellaneous Manuscripts
　　North Brunswick Tax Records
New York Historical Society
　　William Alexander Papers
　　Miscellaneous Manuscripts
　　Slavery Manuscripts
New York Public Library
　　Bancroft Collection
　　Emmet Collection
Princeton University Archives
　　Trustees' Minute Books
*Princeton University Library
　　Elias Boudinot Papers
　　Bound Collection
　　General Manuscripts—Miscellaneous
　　General Manuscripts—Oversize
　　Pyne Henry Papers
　　William Paterson Collection
*Rutgers University Library
　　New Brunswick Bridge Company Papers
　　New Brunswick Historical Club
　　William Paterson Papers
　　John Reynell Papers
*William Paterson College
　　William Paterson Papers
Yale University Library
　　Historical Manuscripts—Miscellaneous
　　Knollenberg Collection

NEWSPAPERS

[Bridgeton] *Plain Dealer*
Burlington Advertiser, or Agricultural and Political Intelligencer
[Elizabethtown] *New Jersey Journal*
[Elizabethtown] *Political Intelligencer. And New Jersey Advertiser*
[Morristown] *Genius of Liberty*
[Newark] *Centinel of Freedom*
Newark Gazette
[Newark] *Woods's Newark Gazette*
[New Brunswick] *Brunswick Gazette*
[New Brunswick] *Guardian*
[New Brunswick] *Political Intelligencer. And New Jersey Advertiser*

[Trenton] *Federalist*
[Trenton] *New Jersey Gazette*
[Trenton] *New Jersey State Gazette*

PUBLISHED SOURCES

Paterson's life and career involved him in so many matters of historical concern that a complete bibliography of relevant published sources would be impractical here. The reader will find many more works cited in the notes, which also include some suggestions for further reading on specific subjects. I have restricted myself in this section to singling out those secondary materials and published primary sources that have proven most useful.

Until now, the most comprehensive analyses of Paterson's career were four Ph.D. dissertations: my "William Paterson and the American Revolution, 1763–1789" (CUNY, 1974), which closely parallels the first seven chapters of this book; Leonard B. Rosenberg's "The Political Thought of William Paterson" (New School for Social Research, 1967); Richard Haskett's "William Paterson, Counsellor at Law" (Princeton, 1952); and Gertrude S. Wood's "William Paterson of New Jersey, 1745–1806" (Columbia, 1933), which was privately published in Fairlawn, New Jersey. Haskett's study of Paterson's legal career led to several articles of note: "Village Clerk and Country Lawyer: William Paterson's Legal Experience, 1763–1772," *PNJHS*, new series, 66 (1948): 155–171; "Prosecuting the Revolution," *AHR*, 59 (1954): 578–587; and, especially, his "William Paterson, Attorney General of New Jersey: Public Office and Private Profit in the American Revolution," *WMQ*, third series, 7 (1950): 26–38. In addition, there are Julian P. Boyd's article, "William Paterson, Forerunner of John Marshall," in Willard Thorpe, ed., *Lives of Eighteen From Princeton* (Princeton, 1947), and Michael Kraus's treatment of Paterson in Leon Friedman and Fred L. Israel, eds., *Justices of the United States Supreme Court, 1789–1969: Their Lives and Major Opinions* (6 vols., New York, 1969).

For further background on Paterson's education at Princeton, see John MacLean's *History of the College of New Jersey from Its Origin in 1746 to the Commencement of 1854* (2 vols., Philadelphia, 1877), Thomas Jefferson Wertenbaker's *Princeton, 1746–1898* (Princeton, 1946), Douglas Sloan's *The Scottish Enlightenment and the American College Ideal* (New York, 1971), and Francis Broderick's "Pulpit, Physics & Politics: The Curriculum of the College of New Jersey, 1746–1794," *WMQ*, third series, 6 (1949): 42–68. On the development of political ideas at Princeton and the College's inclination toward the American Revolution, see James Smiley, "Madison and Witherspoon: Theological Roots of American Political Thought," *Princeton University Library Chronicle*, 22 (1961): 118–132. Numerous errors in transcription make W. Jay Mills, ed., *Glimpses of Colonial Society and the Life of Princeton College, 1766–1773* (Philadelphia, 1903), totally unreliable for quotation, but the book remains a convenient, if imperfect, survey of many of Paterson's college writings.

For material related to the influence of history and moral philosophy on Paterson's character, see Richard Gumere's *The American Colonial Mind and the Classical Tradition* (Cambridge, Mass., 1963), and H. Trevor Colburn's *The Lamp of Experience: Whig History and the Intellectual Origins of the American Revolution* (Chapel Hill, 1965). Two especially valuable aids to an understanding of the religious issues disturbing Americans in the revolutionary era and before are Alan Heimert, *Religion and the American Mind from the Great Awakening to the Revolution* (Cambridge, Mass.,

1966), and Nathan O. Hatch, *The Sacred Cause of Liberty: Republican Thought and the Millenium in Revolutionary New England* (New Haven, 1977).

The literature on the American Revolution's ideological background has expanded exponentially in the past decade, but the most important works remain Bernard Bailyn's *The Ideological Origins of the American Revolution* (Cambridge, Mass., 1967), and Gordon S. Wood's *The Creation of the American Republic, 1776–1787* (Chapel Hill, 1969). For one of the most cogent and readable surveys of the events leading to the Revolution, see Merrill Jensen, *The Founding of a Nation: A History of the American Revolution, 1763–1776* (New York, 1968). The most essential source for understanding the coming of the Revolution in New Jersey is Larry R. Gerlach, *Prologue to Independence* (New Brunswick, 1976). On the revolutionary war and its effects in New Jersey, Leonard Lundin, *Cockpit of the Revolution: The War for Independence in New Jersey* (Princeton, 1940), is still useful, but it should be supplemented with more recent sources such as Adrian C. Leiby, *The Revolutionary War in the Hackensack Valley: The Jersey Dutch in the Neutral Ground* (New Brunswick, 1962), and with unpublished dissertations such as David Berstein's "New Jersey in the American Revolution: The Establishment of a Government Amid Civil and Military Disorder, 1770–81" (Rutgers, 1970), and Dennis P. Ryan's "Six Towns: Continuity and Change in Revolutionary New Jersey, 1772–1792" (New York University, 1974). On New Jersey in the decade after independence, Richard P. McCormick's *Experiment in Independence: New Jersey in the Critical Period, 1781–1789* (New Brunswick, 1950), is unsurpassed.

For analysis of the motives behind the men at the Philadelphia convention, especially those motives shaping Paterson's responses, see Merrill Jensen, *The New Nation: A History of the United States during the Confederation* (New York, 1950); E. James Ferguson, *The Power of the Purse: A History of American Public Finance, 1776–1790;* and Ferguson's "The Nationalists of 1781–1783 and the Economic Interpretation of the Constitution," *JAH*, 16 (1969): 241–261. See also Forrest McDonald's *We The People: The Economic Origins of the Constitution* (Chicago, 1958), and his *E Pluribus Unum* (Boston, 1965). The most indispensable source for reconstructing events at the Philadelphia convention is Max Farrand, ed., *The Records of the Federal Convention of 1787* (4 vols., New Haven, 1937). Two especially useful analyses of the convention are Irving Brant's *James Madison: Father of the Constitution* (New York, 1950), and Clinton Rossiter's *1787: The Grand Convention* (New York, 1966). On the first Senate and the role it played in filling out the Constitution and putting it to work, we must still rely primarily on original sources such as William Maclay's *Journal, 1789–1791* (New York, 1927), and Linda Grant De Pauw, ed., *Documentary History of the First Federal Congress of the United States of America*, Vol. 1, *Senate Legislative Journal* (Baltimore, 1972).

Paterson's revising and reforming of the *Laws of New Jersey* (Trenton and Newark, 1800) should be understood in the context of recent scholarship in early American legal history. Among the most important recent contributions to that literature are Elizabeth G. Brown, *British Statutes in American Law, 1776–1836* (Ann Arbor, 1964); William E. Nelson, *Americanization of the Common Law: The Impact of Legal Change on Massachusetts Society, 1760–1830* (Cambridge, Mass., 1975); Morton J. Horwitz, *The Transformation of American Law, 1780–1860* (Cambridge, Mass., 1977); and Maxwell Bloomfield, *American Lawyers in a Changing Society, 1776–1876* (Cambridge, Mass., 1976).

Finally, for the Federalist Supreme Court see Julius R. Goebel, Jr., *History of the*

Supreme Court of the United States: Antecedents and Beginnings to 1801 (New York, 1971); Charles Grove Haines, *The Role of the Supreme Court in American Government and Politics, 1789–1835* (2 vols., Berkeley, 1944); and Dwight F. Henderson, *Courts for a New Nation* (Washington, D.C., 1971); but do not neglect the older standard study by Charles Warren, *The Supreme Court in United States History* (2 vols., Boston, 1928). For an especially cogent analysis of the Federalist and Jeffersonian opinions on the federal judiciary, see Richard E. Ellis, *The Jeffersonian Crisis* (New York, 1971).

Index

A

Adams, John, 17, 163, 169, 238, 242, 243, 247, 248, 250, 259, 260, 261, 262, 284
Adams, John Quincy, 271
Adams, Samuel, 69
Address of the People of England to the Inhabitants of America (Dalrymple), 62
Age of Reason (Paine), 244
Age of Revelation (Boudinot), 228
Alexander, William (Lord Stirling), 32, 108
Alien and Sedition Acts, 241, 242–243, 258; Federalist party and, 248; Matthew Lyon and, 245–247; *see also* Sedition Act
Allinson, Samuel, 203
American Philosophical Society, 227, 228
American Revolution, administration of justice during, 88–111; decision for independence and, 68–87; education and, 5, 17–18; extremists in, 89; ideological origins of, 48–67; moral decline theme and, 17; religion and, 19; social, feared, 45, 66, 78
Anglicans, 64; *see also* Church of England
Annapolis convention (1786), 133–136
armies (standing), fear of, 55, 56, 65, 71
Articles of Confederation, 132, 144, 149
assumption issue, 180; Congress and, 178–179; Hamilton and, 175, 176, 177
Aurelius [pseud. William Paterson], 197–198, 225, 229
Austin, Benjamin, 221

B

Baldwin, Luther, 152, 248
Barker, Sir Robert, 119
Bassett, Richard, 169
Bayard, James A., 260, 270
Bayard, John, 190, 271, 281
Bayard, Nicholas, 184
Beccaria, Cesare, 209
Bedford, Gunning, 138, 152, 154
Beivers, Moses, 99
Bell, Andrew (brother-in-law), 102–103, 107, 116, 120
Bell, Cornelia, *see* Paterson, Cornelia Bell
Bell, John (father-in-law), 88, 107
Bell, William, 165, 167
Bernard, Francis, 62
Bill of Rights, 252
Bloomfield, Joseph, 227
Boston massacre, troops, 56
Boston Port Bill, 69
Boudinot, Elias, 115, 119, 128, 168, 190, 191–192, 196, 228
Boudinot, Elisha, 100
Brackenridge, Hugh Henry, 28
Brandine, Thomas, 99
Brearly, David, 133, 138, 139, 152, 160
British constitution, *see* constitution (British)
Brown, Catherine, 99, 100
Brown, Joseph, 99, 100
Bull Law (1786), 121
Burke, Edmund, 30

Burr, Aaron (1716–1757), 9
Burr, Aaron (1756–1836), 9, 22, 41, 107, 108, 259, 260, 278

C

Cadwallader, Lambert, 164
Callendar, James, 247
Calvinism, 14, 38, 227; wealth and, 57
canals, 192
Carey, John, 75
Carleton, Sir Guy, 102
Cato's Letters (Trenchard and Gordon), 224
Cazenove, Theophile, 190
Chancery Act (1799), 217
Charles I (King of England), 79, 82
Charleston (S.C.), 250
Chase, Samuel, 247, 265, 269, 274, 275–276
Chetwood, John, 168, 184
Chisolm v. *Georgia*, 230, 252
Church of England, 49, 65
Clark, Abraham, 126, 127, 133, 134, 168, 218
classics, education in, 9, 11, 17, 50, 64
Clinton, George, 270
Clinton, Henry, 102
Cliosophic Society, 27–30, 51, 271
Coke, Sir Edward, 23, 31
College of New Jersey, *see* Princeton University
colleges (colonial), *see* education
Commentaries (Blackstone), 31, 204
commerce, Annapolis convention, 142; Paterson supports during Confederation, 120; *see also* trade
Committee of Safety, formation of, 74
common law, 31–32; indictments in U.S. Supreme Court, 242, 330; in law reform, 204; reception of, 221–222
Common Sense (Paine), 76
Congress (Confederation period), 119, 122, 126, 127, 132, 133
Congress (Continental), *see* Continental Congress
Congress (federal), 199–200, 233, 245, 251, 258, 261, 262–263, 264, 265, 268, 269, 274–276; powers of, 174; reapportionment of, 195–197; Virginia Plan,

Congress (federal) (*continued*)
146; *see also* House of Representatives (U.S.); New Jersey Plan; Senate (U.S.); Virginia Plan
conspiracy, fear of, 41–42, 55, 66
constitution (British), 50; contrasted with U.S. Constitution, 256–257; encroachments on, 54, 55, 63; moral decline theme, 52; politics, 129
constitution (New Jersey state) (1776), confusion in, 203; framing of, 83–86; governor's powers, 186; law enforcement, 93; revision of, urged, 198–199
Constitution (U.S.): framing of, 134–160; judiciary, 172; New Jersey and, 163–164; opposition to, 170; Paterson and, 229, 251; powers of, 257; ratification process, 164, 167–168; reported out, 161; supremacy clause of, 147, 251; *see also* representation
Continental Congress, 69, 70, 75, 77, 78, 81, 82, 168; currency, 122; debt, 127; independence movement, 76, 79, 80, 83; New Jersey and, 72, 126; Paterson and, 48, 109; Paterson on authority of, 252–253
Continental currency: withdrawal of, 122; *see also* currency
contracts, Paterson on sanctity of, 114, 121–122, 125, 126, 161, 219–220, 254–255
Convention of the State of New Jersey, 84
conversion experience, 18
corruption, *see* moral decline
Council of Safety: creation of, 91–92; executive power, 96; Loyalists and, 98
court system (county): failures of, 93–94; Loyalists, 98; Paterson's career, 34; restored, 95
court system (federal): Constitution, 252; formulation of, 169–173; judge selection, 172; New Jersey Plan, 147; politics and, 248, 249 (*see also* Federalists); powers of, 263–264; state courts and, 172–173, 253–254
court system (New Jersey state): Paterson on, 199; reform of, 216–220; Revolution, 89–90, 93–96, 106–107

court system (state), federal courts and, 172–173, 253–254

Coxe, Tench, 188, 189, 192

Cromwell, Oliver, 79, 115–116

currency: colonial paper money, 35, 49, 64, 123; Continental, 122; devaluation, 113; inflation, 134; New Jersey paper money, 122–126, 187

Cushing, William, 261, 266, 267

D

Dalrymple, Sir John, 62

Darke, William, 247

Davie, William R., 155

Davies, Samuel, 8–9

Davis, Mary, 99

Dayton, Elias, 227

Dayton, Jonathan, 134, 152, 155, 157, 160, 184, 226, 227 233, 260, 261, 262, 278

Dearborn, Henry, 277

death penalty, 104, 205, 206, 207, 236

debt (government): assumption of states', 178–179, 187; funding proposals, 175–179; states' repayment during Confederation, 126–127, 187

debtors: law reform and, 219–220; New Jersey, 34, 35–36; 49–50; 118–126, 187; Paterson's family as, 34, 165–167; relief of, 113, 134

Declaration of Independence, 32, 64, 79

Defense of American Constitutions (Adams), 163

deference: colonial politics, 49; erosion of after Revolution, 86

degeneracy, *see* moral decline

democracy: fears of, 135; Paterson and, 182; restraint of, 140

Democratic-Republican societies, 231, 236

Dewhurst, John, 192

Dickinson, John, 9, 23, 25, 76, 78, 137, 148

Dickinson, Philemon, 90, 102

Donaldson, John, 167

Dred Scott decision, 255

Duer, William, 192, 193, 194

Dunmore, Lord, 81

Dutch Reformed Church, 6, 38, 39–40, 228

E

education: college curriculum, 11–15; influence on Revolution, 5, 17–18; and social stability, 230–231; *see also* Princeton University; Rutgers University

Edwards, Jonathan (1703–1758), 9, 18, 37, 41

Edwards, Jonathan (1745–1801), 28

elections: of 1789, 168–169; of 1796, 243; of 1800, 251, 258–259; of 1824, 271; fraud allegations in New Jersey, 120; to Provincial Congress, 71, 74, 75, 79–80; *see also* voting

Elements of Criticism (Kames), 10

Ellsworth, Oliver, 22, 152, 154, 155, 157, 161, 169, 171, 174, 177, 178, 260, 261

Elmer, Jonathan, 70, 168

embargo: Boston Port Bill, 69; *see also* nonimportation

English Civil War, 78, 79, 224

executive power: during Revolution, 86, 91, 93, 96; Paterson as governor, 186

F

factions, *see* parties (political)

Farmers Letters, The (Dickinson), 25

Federalists, 223, 237, 261–262, 278, 282–283, 284; and Chase impeachment, 275–276; divisions among, 242, 243, 259–260, 282–284; and election of 1800, 228–229; and French Revolution, 242, 244; involvement with Society for Establishing Useful Manufactures, 194; and Jay Treaty, 237–240; and Judiciary Act of 1801, 264; in New Jersey, 226–228; Paterson as supporter of, 182, 226, 229, 243; Paterson on, 229, 231, 240–241; and repeal of Judiciary Act of 1801, 265–267; as threatened elite, 243; and U.S. Supreme Court, 224, 249, 252, 258

Few, William, 169

First Continental Congress, *see* Continental Congress

Fisher, Hendrick, 71

franchise, *see* voting

Franklin, Benjamin, 152

Franklin, William (Governor), 54, 76, 80, 81–82
Frelinghuysen, Frederick (1753–1804), 28, 71, 107, 119
Frelinghuysen, John (1727–1754), 38
Frelinghuysen, Theodorus Jacobus, 38
French Revolution, 231; moral decline perceived in, 243–244; parties (U.S.) and, 233; Supreme Court and, 232
Freneau, Philip, 28
Fries, John, 274
funding proposals, Hamilton, 175, 176, 177

G

Genêt, Edmond, 231, 232, 233
George III (King of England), 53, 55, 72
Gerry, Elbridge, 153, 155, 158
Glass v. *Sloop Betsy*, 232
Gordon, Thomas, 31, 224
government (local): post-Revolution, 116; source of stability during Revolution, 94–95; as training ground for republicanism, 210–211
Great Awakening, 8, 14, 18, 37, 51
Great Compromise, 114, 141, 144, 171; formulation of, 151–159; New Jersey and, 161, 164
Griswold, Roger, 245

H

Hamilton, Alexander, 114, 132, 133, 150, 175, 176, 178, 180, 182, 188, 190, 191, 192, 193, 194, 223, 225, 231, 234, 238, 259, 261
Hardenburg, Jacobus Rutsen. 38
Haswell, Anthony, 247–248
Heard, Nathaniel, 81
Henry, Patrick, 17
History of the American Bar (Warren), 219
History of the American Revolution (Ramsay), 17
Hopkins, George, 239
Hopkirk v. *Bell*, 276
Horatius [pseud. William Paterson], 272
House of Representatives (U.S.), funding proposals discussed, 176; New Jersey

House of Representatives (*continued*)
election (1789), 168; reapportionment, 195–197; Rep. Matthew Lyon in, 245
Houston, William Churchill, 118, 133, 134
Howe, Lord Richard, 85, 89
Howell, Richard, 227
Hylton v. *The United States*, 257

I

imposts, 126, 133, 148, 164, 173
indents, 127
independence: Continental Congress, 83; movement toward, 77; New Jersey and, 77–78, 79, 80, 82; opposition to, 76; talk of, 70
industrialization, 181, 188, 211–212
interstate rivalry: abatement in, 131; New England, 133; western lands, 139, 146
Intolerable Acts (1774), 69
Iredell, James, 242
Irwin, John (nephew), 166, 175, 241
Irwin, Thomas (brother-in-law), 107, 165, 167, 241

J

Jay, John, 230, 237, 238, 239–240, 260, 261
Jay Treaty (1795), 180, 237–238, 239
Jefferson, Thomas, 17, 182, 189, 192, 203, 205, 238, 242, 243, 259, 260, 261, 264, 268, 269–270, 277
Jeffersonians, 243–244, 276; *see also* Republicans
Johnson, Thomas, 199
Jones, Samuel, 203
judicial review: of acts of Congress, 251, 255, 267–270; of state acts, 255–257
judiciary, independence of, 199–200
Judiciary Act (1789), 114, 169, 173, 255, 267–268, 274, 285
Judiciary Act (1801), 182, 251, 263, 264, 269, 278; repeal of, 264–265

K

Keletas, Abraham, 57
Kent, James (1753–1847), 222

King, Rufus, 154, 160, 177
Kinsey, James, 119
Kirkpatrick, Andrew, 28

L

LaGrange, Bernardus, 36, 107, 109
Lansing, John, 145, 148, 149, 150, 152
Laurens, Henry, 109
law(s): American Revolution, 31; British/ American compared, 31–32; problem of enforcement, 92–93; morality and, 14–15; proliferation of in colonial period, 55, 58, 65; revision and reform of, 202–222
Lee, Henry, 22
Lee, Richard Henry, 169, 170, 171, 173
legal profession: creditors and debtors, 34, 35–36, 118–126; law reform, 218–220; Paterson's defense of, 36–37, 70; popular attitudes toward, 36; regulation of, 37, 120; training for, 23–24
Legislative Council (New Jersey state), 186; Paterson member of, 89–90, 94
legislature (New Jersey state): composition and powers of, 83, 84, 90, 128; Council of Safety and, 96, 98; debtors and, 121–126; Governor Paterson and, 186, 188; inefficiency of, 90–91; paper money measures, 122–123, 125; private property and, 126, 129–130; revision of laws and, 203, 204, 205, 210, 212, 214, 216, 218, 220; and Society for Establishing Useful Manufactures, 191
legislatures (colonial): representation in, 128; supplanted, 74; upper houses of, 62
L'Enfant, Pierre, 192
Light, Elizabeth, 99
Light, John, 99, 100
Livingston, Robert R., 128, 238
Livingston, William (Governor), 28, 86–87, 90, 91, 96, 108, 114, 134, 143, 160, 183–184, 186
London, 26
Low, Nicholas, 192
Loyalists: Council of Safety and, 96; Paterson and, 88, 104; Paterson's family and, 102–103, 107; personal inter-

Loyalists (continued)
ests, 109; problem of, 91, 92, 97–98; punishments for, 90, 104–105; return of, 120; threat of, 89, 109
luxury: Paterson on, 59–62; see also moral decline
Lyon, Matthew, 245–247, 248, 258, 259, 275, 283

M

McCasland, Alex, 23
McHenry, James, 247
Maclay, William, 169, 174, 177, 178
MacPherson, John, 23, 24, 25, 26, 27, 29, 32, 43, 49, 73, 76
Madison, James, 22, 28, 132, 133–136, 138, 140, 146–147, 148, 150, 151, 152, 153, 154, 155, 156, 158, 159, 160, 177, 178, 180, 225, 264, 277, 278
Marbury, William, 264, 268
Marbury v. Madison, 255, 267, 269, 274
Marshall, John, 257, 260, 261, 262, 263, 265, 266, 267, 268, 269, 278
Martin, Luther, 22, 35, 145, 148, 149, 150, 151, 152, 153, 155
Masons, 227, 228, 259
Mather, Cotton, 41
Mather, Increase, 41
Mazzei, Philip, 242
medical profession: Paterson on, 40–42, 55; regulation of, 37
militia, 83; organization of, 70; Paterson on, 197, 198; Provincial Congress and, 74, 77
millinarianism, 18
Miranda, Francisco, 277
Mitchell, John, 234, 236
mobility (social), 26, 27; American Revolution and, 110–111; decline in, 57
Monroe, James, 242
Montesquieu, 10, 12
moral decline, 15, 16–17, 30, 51, 87; Britain and, 29, 45, 46, 52, 53, 55; debtors and, 37, 123–124; French Revolution and, 243–244; law reform, 214–216; Paterson on, 59–60, 64, 248–249, 281
morality, law, 14–15, 214–216

Morris, Gouverneur (1752–1816), 153, 154, 155, 156
Morris, Lewis (1671–1746), 217
Morris, Robert (1745–1815), 108, 118, 119, 132

N

national imposts, 126, 133, 148, 164, 173
Neilson, John, 108, 134
Newburgh conspiracy, 115
Newburyport (Mass.), 28
New Jersey: and Annapolis convention, 133–134; Boston Port Bill, 69; boundary conflict in, 118–119; British markets, 226; commercial situation of, 120, 126, 188; Constitution (federal) and, 161, 163–164; decision for independence, 76, 77–78, 79, 80, 82; law revision and reform, 202–222; manufacturing in, 188–189 (see also Society for Establishing Useful Manufactures); penal code reform, 205–208; senator selection in, 168; see also constitution (New Jersey state); court system (New Jersey state); legislature (New Jersey state); Provincial Congress (New Jersey)
New Jersey Plan, 114, 251; presentation of, 145–151
New Side beliefs, 14, 38, 65, 227; education, 13; Paterson, 18; Princeton University, 19; Revolution, 51; wealth distribution, 57
New York City, 120, 270; British invasion of, 79, 85; British occupation of, 100, 101; federal government in, 168–169; merchants of, 25; New Jersey dependence on, 64; social life in, 174–175; Stamp Act Congress meets in, 35
Nicholson, Joseph H., 274
nonimportation, 25, 53, 69

O

Ogden, Aaron, 28, 220
Ogden, Abraham, 119
Ogden, David M., 220
Ogden, Robert, Jr., 22, 28
Ogden, Samuel G., 277, 278

On Crimes and Punishments (Beccaria), 209
Order of Freemasons, 227, 228, 259
Otis, James, 89

P

Paine, Thomas, 76, 102, 228, 244
Parker, James (1725–1797), 119
Parliament (British), 77, 129; Crown and, 55; currency act (1764), 35; mercantilist legislation, 25; Stamp Act, 34; supremacy of, 31, 257
parties (political): development of, 223–224, 284; French Revolution and, 233; growth in, 181; Paterson on, 53, 163, 210, 228, 229; see also Federalists, Republicans
Paterson, Cornelia (daughter), 102, 116, 243, 270
Paterson, Cornelia Bell (wife), 88–89, 101, 107; death of, 113, 117, 183; war years, 116
Paterson, Edward (brother), 7, 165, 166
Paterson, Euphemia White (wife), 117, 190, 271, 275
Paterson, Frances (sister), 7, 116, 117
Paterson, Richard (father), 7–8, 34, 50, 116
Paterson, Thomas (brother), 7, 165, 166
Paterson, William: birth of, 7; career and offices, 1–2, 3, 33, 46–47, 71–75, 108–109, 110, 114, 160, 163, 168, 181, 223, 238; courtship of, 104; death of, 281; education of, 5–6, 9–20, 22–24, 34; finances of, 34, 118, 128–129, 165–167; marriage of, 88–89, 103, 117; religion and, 39–40, 227–228; reputation, 284
Paterson, William B. (son), 117, 270
Paterson Plan, see New Jersey Plan
Penhallow v. Doane's Administrators, 252, 253–254
Persian Letters (Montesquieu), 10
Philadelphia, 21, 23, 24, 25, 227; British occupation of, 101; convention in, 22, 134–160; New Jersey dependence on, 64; U.S. circuit court in, 233–236
Pickering, John, 274, 275
Pierce, William, 134

Pinkney, C. C., 150, 155, 242
Pinkney's Treaty, 241
Plumer, William, 275
political parties, *see* parties (political)
Presbyterianism, *see* New Side beliefs
Price, Edward, 105–106, 109
Princeton (N.J.): Princeton University moves to, 8; settlement in, 7
Princeton University (College of New Jersey), 270; attraction of, 28; curriculum at, 9, 18; Dutch Reformed Church and, 38; founding of, 8; New Side beliefs, 19; Paterson trustee of, 195, 271; social respectability, 5–6
prison reform, 206, 208–209; *see also* workhouses
private property, *see* property rights
Privy Council (British), currency acts, 54, 76
profiteering, legal problem of, 100
Prohibitory Act (1775), 76
property rights, 123, 132; debtor relief and, 134; New Jersey, 85, 129–130; popular government and, 126; protection of, 187; *see also* contracts
Provincial Assembly (N.J.): boundary conflict, 118; on independence, 76
Provincial Congress (N.J.), 71, 75, 76, 80–81; authority of, 84; decision for independence, 68–87; franchise, 77; Governor Franklin and, 81–82; local government and, 95; structure of, 74
Puritan Revolution, 78, 79, 224

Q

Quakers: anti-slavery, 212; Crown support, 101; military service, 74
quartering of troops: New Jersey, 64, 65; petitions against, 55–56
Quebec (Canada), attacked, 76
Queen's College, *see* Rutgers University

R

Ramsay, David, 17, 61
Randolph, Edmund, 134, 137, 140, 143, 145, 146, 150, 156–157, 158, 159, 238

Randolph, John, 274
Randolph v. Ware, 276
Rawle, William, 234
Read, George, 137
Reeve, Tapping, 22
Rensselaer Polytechnic Institute, 271
representation: Congress (federal), 139–140, 141, 151, 154, 164; land policy and, 143; Madison and, 150–151; New Jersey Plan, 114, 148, 149; slavery, 155; small-state position, 142, 144; Virginia Plan, 136
Republicans, 2, 182, 223, 240–241, 248, 249, 251, 258, 283–284; background of supporters, 28, 282; in election of 1800, 259; and judicial review, 268; in power, 264–265, 267, 269, 270, 274–276; *see also* Jeffersonians
Revolution, *see* American Revolution; French Revolution; Puritan Revolution
Rollin, Charles, 12
Romeyn, Theodore, 22
Rousseau, Jean Jacques, 244
Rush, Benjamin, 22
Rush, Jacob, 22, 24–25
Rutgers University (Queens College), 38
Rutherfurd, John (1760–1840), 118, 273

S

Savannah (Ga.), 250
Schureman, James, 133
Schuyler, Margaret, 270
Schuyler, Philip, 270
Scudder, Nathaniel, 85, 92
Second Continental Congress, *see* Continental Congress
Sedition Act (1798), 182, 274; *see also* Alien and Sedition Acts
Self Knowledge (Mason), 14
Senate (U.S.), 160; Paterson in, 168–180; representation in, 1, 164; selection of, 138, 168
Sergeant, Jonathan Dickinson, 22, 71, 74, 75
Shays, Daniel, 147, 180; rebellion, 133
Sherman, Roger, 144, 145, 148, 154, 155, 157
Skinner, Cortlandt, 76, 101, 102, 103, 109

slaves and slavery: legal reform regarding, 206, 212–213; Paterson and, 129, 212; Paterson family and, 8; representation discussed, 155

Smith, Jeremiah, 275

Smith, Robert, 277, 278

Smith, Samuel Stanhope, 29

Smith, William Peartree, 115

Smith, William S., 277

Society for Establishing Useful Manufactures (SUM), 181, 188–194, 271; criticism of, 191, 194

speculation, Paterson on, 128, 228

Spring, Samuel, 28

Stamp Act (1765), 34–35, 49, 53

Stamp Act Congress (1765), 35

Stamp Act crisis, 16

Stirling, Lord, see William Alexander

Stockton, Richard (1730–1781), 15, 20, 32, 34, 35, 49, 71, 83, 101–102

Stockton, Richard (1764–1828), 119

Stoddard, Josiah, 22

Story, Joseph, 222

Stout, William, 105

Strong, Caleb, 155, 169

Stuart v. Laird, 267, 274, 276

suffrage, see voting

SUM, see Society for Establishing Useful Manufactures

Supreme Court (N.J.), 28, 120, 200

Supreme Court (U.S.): Federalists and, 224, 249, 252, 258, 260–261, 263; issues relating to French Revolution, 231–232; judicial review, 265–269; Paterson and, 1, 171, 182, 223, 228, 229–230, 232, 278–279, 285; powers of, 255, 265–266

Symmes, John Cleves, 92, 227

T

Talbot v. Jansen, 232

Tallmadge, Matthias, 276, 278

taxation: Congress (federal), 132; Constitution (federal), 161, 164; federal government, 172, 173, 176; Provincial Congress (N.J.), 74

Tories, see Loyalists

town meetings, 95, 210

Townshend duties (1767), 25, 49, 53

trade: illegal, 100; regulation of, 132; see also commerce

Treaty of Paris (1783), 146, 254, 276

Trenchard, John, 31, 224

Trenton (N.J.), capital city, 193

Trenton and New Brunswick Turnpike Company, 273

Troup, Robert, 108

Tucker, Samuel, 36, 81

U

United States: see Congress (federal); Constitution (U.S.); court system (federal)

United States v. Benjamin More, 274

United States v. Judge Lawrence, 232

United States v. Richard Peters, 232

Universal History (Voltaire), 13

utopianism, Paterson, 63

V

Van Horne's Lessee v. Dorrance, 255–256, 257, 261, 269

Van Rensselaer, Stephen (son-in-law), 270–271

Varick, Richard, 203

Vigol (Weigel), Philip, 234, 235

Virginia Plan, 152, 156; Paterson on, 138–139, 140–142; preface to, 146; presentation of, 134–136

virtue (public), 66; in government, 19; patriotism as, 16, 17, 46; public service as, 163

voting: election laws, 210; for Provincial Congress (N.J.), 77, 80, 81; qualifications for, 74, 128; Paterson on, 198

W

Walnut Street jail (Philadelphia), 209

Ware v. Hylton, 252, 254–255

War of 1812, 271

Washington, Bushrod, 267

Washington, George, 91, 152, 169, 197, 199, 224, 228, 231, 233, 237, 238, 242

wealth: distribution of, 55, 56–57, 58, 65;
  legislature (N.J.) and, 128; Paterson on,
  57–58, 211–212
Weigel, Philip, *see* Vigol, Philip
western lands: Annapolis convention, 142–
  143; disposition of, 132, 157–158; interstate jealousy, 139, 146
Whig party, 68, 80, 82
Whippo, Isaac, 193
Whiskey Rebellion, 233–236, 255, 270, 275
Whitaker, Robert, 106
White, Anthony (father-in-law), 88, 102,
  108, 117
White, David, 107
White, Euphemia, *see* Paterson, Euphemia
  White
White, Johanna, 190
Whitfield, George, 25, 37

Williamson, Hugh, 144, 155
Williamson, Matthias, 220
Wilson, James, 137, 138, 139, 144, 150,
  151, 152, 153, 154, 155, 156, 158, 160
Wilson, Peter, 203
Wingate, Paine, 169
Witherspoon, John, 9, 60, 71, 80, 83
Woodhull, John, 22
workhouses, 209, 214

X

XYZ affair, 242

Y

Yates, Robert, 135, 148, 152